Lecture Notes in Artificial Intelligence   8256

Subseries of Lecture Notes in Computer Science

Lecture Notes in Artificial Intelligence 8296

Subseries of Lecture Notes in Computer Science

LNAI Series Editors

Randy Goebel
University of Alberta, Edmonton, Canada
Yuzuru Tanaka
Hokkaido University, Sapporo, Japan
Wolfgang Wahlster
DFKI and Saarland University, Saarbrücken, Germany

LNAI Founding Series Editor

Joerg Siekmann
DFKI and Saarland University, Saarbrücken, Germany

Francesco Masulli   Gabriella Pasi
Ronald Yager (Eds.)

Fuzzy Logic and Applications

10th International Workshop, WILF 2013
Genoa, Italy, November 19-22, 2013
Proceedings

 Springer

Volume Editors

Francesco Masulli
University of Genoa
DIBRIS
Via Dodecaneso 35, 16146 Genoa, Italy
E-mail: francesco.masulli@unige.it

Gabriella Pasi
University of Milano Bicocca
Dept. of Informatics, Systems, and Communication
Viale Sarca 336, 20126 Milan, Italy
E-mail: pasi@disco.unimib.it

Ronald Yager
Iona College
Dept. of Information Systems
710 North Ave, New Rochelle, NY 10801, USA
E-mail: yager@panix.com

ISSN 0302-9743   e-ISSN 1611-3349
ISBN 978-3-319-03199-6   e-ISBN 978-3-319-03200-9
DOI 10.1007/978-3-319-03200-9
Springer Cham Heidelberg New York Dordrecht London

CR Subject Classification (1998): I.2.3, I.2, F.4.1, F.1-2, I.4-5, H.3, G.2

LNCS Sublibrary: SL 7 – Artificial Intelligence

Typesetting: Camera-ready by author, data conversion by Scientific Publishing Services, Chennai, India

Printed on acid-free paper

Springer is part of Springer Science+Business Media (www.springer.com)

Preface

The 10th International Workshop on Fuzzy Logic and Applications, WILF 2013, held in Genoa (Italy) during November 19–22, 2013, covered topics related to theoretical, experimental, and applied fuzzy techniques and systems with emphasis on their applications in the analysis of high-dimensional data.

This event represents the pursuance of an established tradition of biannual interdisciplinary meetings. The previous editions of WILF have been held, with an increasing number of participants, in Naples (1995), Bari (1997), Genoa (1999), Milan (2001), Naples (2003), Crema (2005), Camogli (2007), Palermo (2009), and Trani (2011). Each event has focused on distinct main thematic areas of fuzzy logic and related applications. From this perspective, one of the main goals of the WILF workshops series is to bring together researchers and developers from both academia and high-tech companies and foster multidisciplinary research.

After a rigorous peer-review selection process, we selected 19 high-quality manuscripts from the submissions received from all over the world. These were accepted for presentation at the conference and are published in this volume. In addition to regular papers, the present volume comprises the contributions of the three keynote speakers:

- Isabelle Bloch (Telecom ParisTech and CNRS LTCI Paris, France) "Model-Based Image Interpretation Under Uncertainty and Fuzziness"
- Frank Klawonn (Ostfalia University of Applied Sciences, Wolfenbüttel, Germany) "What Can Fuzzy Cluster Analysis Contribute to Clustering of High-Dimensional Data?"
- Paulo Lisboa (Liverpool John Moores University, Liverpool, UK) "Interpretability in Machine Learning — Principles and Practice"

The contributions of the two tutorial presenters are also included:

- Nahla Ben Amor (University of Tunis, Tunisia) "Possibilistic Graphical Models: From Reasoning to Decision Making"
- Corrado Mencar (University of Bari, Italy) "Interpretable Fuzzy Systems"

The success of this workshop is to be credited to the contribution of many people, in particular to the Program Committee members for their commitment to provide high-quality, contructive reviews, to the keynote speakers and the tutorial presenters, and to the local Organizing Committee for the support in the organization of the workshop events.

September 2013

Francesco Masulli
Gabriella Pasi
Ronald Yager

Organization

WILF 2013 was jointly organized by the DIBRIS, University of Genoa, Italy, the EUSFLAT, European Society for Fuzzy Logic and Technology, the IEEE, Computational Intelligence Society, Italian Chapter, the INNS, International Neural Network Society, SIG Italy, and the SIREN, Italian Neural Networks Society.

Conference Chairs

Francesco Masulli   University of Genoa, Italy
Gabriella Pasi   University of Milano-Bicocca, Italy
Ronald Yager   Iona College, New York, USA

Program Committee

Plamen Angelov   Lancaster University, UK
Valentina Emilia Balas   Aurel Vlaicu University of Arad, Romania
Sanghamitra Bandyopadhyay   Indian Statistical Institute, Kolkata, India
Andrzej Bargiela   University of Nottingham, UK
Eric Benoit   LISTIC Université de Savoie, France
Gloria Bordogna   CNR, Italy
Humberto Bustince   UPNA, Spain
Christer Carlsson   Åbo Akademi University, Finland
Giovanna Castellano   University of Bari, Italy
Oscar Castillo   Tijuana Institute of Technology, Mexico
Gianpiero Cattaneo   University of Milano-Bicocca, Italy
Giulianella Coletti   University of Perugia, Italy
Celia Da Costa Pereira   Université de Nice Sophia Antipolis, France
Mario Fedrizzi   University of Trento, Italy
Anna Maria Fanelli   University of Bari, Italy
Brunella Gerla   University of Insubria, Varese, Italy
Ashish Ghosh   Indian Statistical Institute, Kolkata, India
Fernando Gomide   University of Campinas, Sao Paulo, Brazil
Ugur Halici   METU, Ankara, Turkey
Katsuhiro Honda   Osaka Prefecture University, Japan
Janusz Kacprzyk   Polish Academy of Sciences, Warsaw, Poland
Nik Kasabov   Auckland University of Technology,
                              New Zealand
László Koczy   Budapest University of Technology and
                              Economics, Hungary
Etienne Kerre   Ghent University, Belgium

Frank Klawonn	Ostfalia University of Applied Sciences, Wolfenbüttel, Germany
Donald Kraft	Colorado Technical University, USA
Vladik Kreinovich	University of Texas at El Paso, USA
Malay Kumar Kundu	Indian Statistical Institute, Kolkata, India
Luis Magdalena	European Centre for Soft Computing, Mieres, Asturias, Spain
Francesco Marcelloni	University of Pisa, Italy
Corrado Mencar	University of Bari, Italy
Javier Montero	Universidad Complutense de Madrid, Spain
Anca Ralescu	University of Cincinnati, USA
Alexander Shostak	University of Latvia, Latvia
Eulalia Szmidt	Systems Research Institute Polish Academy of Sciences, Poland
Domenico Tegolo	University of Palermo, Italy
Slawomir Zadrozny	Polish Academy of Sciences, Warsaw, Poland

Scientific Secretariat

Stefano Rovetta	University of Genoa, Italy
Mahdi Amina	University of Genoa, Italy
Angela Locoro	University of Genoa, Italy
Hassan Mahmoud	University of Genoa, Italy
Raffaella Rosasco	University of Genoa, Italy

WILF Steering Committee

Antonio Di Nola	University of Salerno, Italy
Francesco Masulli	University of Genoa, Italy
Gabriella Pasi	University of Milano-Bicocca, Italy
Alfredo Petrosino	University of Naples Parthenope, Italy

Congress Management

Rosa D'Eventi, Genoa (Italy)

Financing Institutions

DIBRIS, University of Genoa, Italy
EUSFLAT, European Society for Fuzzy Logic and Technology

Table of Contents

Applications

What Can Fuzzy Cluster Analysis Contribute to Clustering of High-Dimensional Data?

Frank Klawonn[1,2]

[1] Bioinformatics & Statistics
Helmholtz-Centre for Infection Research
Inhoffenstr. 7, D-38124 Braunschweig, Germany
frank.klawonn@helmholtz-hzi.de
[2] Department of Computer Science
Ostfalia University of Applied Sciences
Salzdahlumer Str. 46/48, D-38302 Wolfenbuettel, Germany
f.klawonn@ostfalia.de

Abstract. Cluster analysis of high-dimensional data has become of special interest in recent years. The term high-dimensional data can refer to a larger number of attributes – 20 or more – as they often occur in database tables. But high-dimensional data can also mean that we have to deal with thousands of attributes as in the context of genomics or proteomics data where thousands of genes or proteins are measured and are considered in some analysis tasks as attributes.

A main reason, why cluster analysis of high-dimensional data is different from clustering low-dimensional data, is the concentration of norm phenomenon, which states more or less that the relative differences between distances between randomly distributed points tend to be more and more similar in higher dimensions.

On the one hand, fuzzy cluster analysis has been shown to be less sensitive to initialisation than, for instance, the classical k-means algorithm. On the other, standard fuzzy clustering is stronger affected by the concentration of norm phenomenon and tends to fail easily in high dimensions. Here we present a review of why fuzzy clustering has special problems with high-dimensional data and how this can be amended by modifying the fuzzifier concept. We also describe a recently introduced approach based on correlation and an attribute selection fuzzy clustering technique that can be applied when clusters can only be found in lower dimensions.

1 Introduction

Cluster analysis is an exploratory data analysis technique which aims at partitioning data into groups (clusters). Instances in the same cluster should be similar, instances from different clusters should be dissimilar. This might sound like a very well defined task, but there are actually various open questions involved whose answers are not unique at all.

Although the original intension of cluster analysis is a grouping of the data in terms of a partition, clustering is often applied to identify one or a few single

F. Masulli, G. Pasi, and R. Yager (Eds.): WILF 2013, LNAI 8256, pp. 1–14, 2013.

clusters containing only a fraction of the whole data set. We will not discuss this question in more detail in this paper.

Cluster analysis is based on the concept of similarity or – the dual notion – distance. Some clustering techniques like hierarchical clustering require only the pairwise distances between the instances in the data set to form the clusters. Whether these distances are based on the Euclidean distance, on some correlation measure or other notions, is not important for this type of clustering algorithm. Most clustering algorithms are designed to handle real-valued data, i.e. the data set is assumed to be a subset of $\mathbb{R}^m$. In this paper, we will also restrict our considerations to such data. It should be noted that it is common to carry out a normalisation of the single dimensions – see for instance [1] – before cluster analysis is applied. Normalisation is not the topic of this paper. So we assume that the data set to be clustered is already normalised if a normalisation is recommended.

For such data, clustering is then often based on the Euclidean distance or – more generally – on a metric derived from an L^p-norm. There are still different notions of what a cluster is. In most cases, clusters are assumed to be "compact clouds" of data. Sometimes, a more general notion of a cluster as a "dense and connected region" is considered. Especially for high-dimensional spaces, it can be difficult to define what a densely populated region is, since the high-dimensional space is more or less always sparsely populated with data and the density can vary significantly.

Figure 1 illustrates the notion of ideal clusters in three dimensions. There are three clusters that are well-separated from each other. Unfortunately, clusters in higher dimensions cannot be visualised in such a simple way and, even worse, high-dimensional data have peculiar properties making it more difficult to define what clusters are and to identify clusters in high-dimensional data.

In the following section, we will shortly recall problems caused by high-dimensional data in the context of cluster analysis. Section 3 provides a brief review on ideas of fuzzy cluster analysis, especially of those concepts that are relevant for clustering high-dimensional data. Specific advantages and disadvantages of applying fuzzy clustering to high-dimensional data are discussed in Section 4.

2   What Are Clusters in High-Dimensional Data?

Data of dimensionality 30 or more can easily be found in many applications like industrial production where measurements from a larger number of sensors are recorded simultaneously and constantly. Patient data in medicine including laboratory results can also have a large number of attributes. But there are also data with 10,000 or more dimensions, especially in the field of biology and medicine. High throughput technologies like microarrays can measure the expression of far more than 10,000 genes easily. It might then be interesting to cluster expression profiles of patients for better treatment and offer personalised medicine (see for instance [2]). In [3] growth curves of more than 4000 mutants of bateria

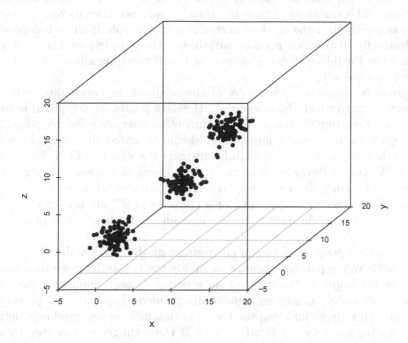

Fig. 1. Ideal clusters

under more than 100 conditions, i.e. dimensions, were measured by the VITEK®2 technology and clustered.

High-dimensional data exhibit properties that differ from low-dimensional data and these properties seem sometimes counterintuitive. One of the main causes for the differing properties of high-dimensional data is the concentration of norm phenomenon (CoN). It can formally be described in the following way[1] [5,6]. Let X_m be an m-dimensional random vector and let $d_m(x)$ denote the distance of $x \in \mathbb{R}^m$ to the origin of the coordinate system based on a suitable distance measure, for instance the Euclidean distance. Let $n \in \mathbb{N}$ be the size of the sample that is taken from the random vector X_m. Let $d_m^{(\max)}$ and $d_m^{(\min)}$ denote the largest and the smallest distance of a point in the sample to the origin of the coordinate system. Then

$$\lim_{m \to \infty} \mathrm{Var}\left(\frac{d_m(X_m)}{\mathrm{E}(d_m(X_m))}\right) = 0 \Rightarrow \frac{d_m^{(\max)} - d_m^{(\min)}}{d_m^{(\min)}} \to_p 0 \qquad (1)$$

holds, where $\to_p$ denotes convergence in probability. In other words, when the relative variance – relative with respect to the mean distance – of the distances

---

[1] This description is taken from [4].

to the origin converges to zero for higher dimensions, then the relative difference of the closest and farthest point in the data set goes to zero with increasing dimensions. The requirement that the relative variance goes to zero is, for instance, satisfied when the random vector X_m is a sample from m independent and identically distributed random variables with finite expectation and variance and the Euclidean distance is used as the distance measure. The converse theorem also holds [6].

It should be noted that the choice of the origin of the coordinate system as the query point to which the distances of the data points are computed is not of importance. Equation (1) is also valid for any other query or reference point. The same applies to the distance measure. It should be noted that other L^p-norms than the Euclidean norms can slightly mitigate the effect of CoN, but cannot avoid it. Without a deviation from the strict axioms of a norm, it is impossible to avoid CoN. Other distances, like fractional distances are investigated in [7]. Unbounded distance measures on compact subsets of $\mathbb{R}^m$ are proposed in [8]. A discussion on various distance measures in connection with CoN is provided in [9,10].

Why can CoN pose a problem for clustering high-dimensional data? If we have to deal with well-separated clusters as in Figure 1, just in more dimensions, CoN does not apply to the data set as a whole. It only applies to the single clusters. CoN mainly causes an algorithmic problem. Especially for prototype-based clustering algorithms that start with initial, more or less randomly defined cluster centres and then try to adjust and fit these cluster centres step by step to the data. Such a randomly defined cluster centre will have roughly the same distance to all data clusters and therefore to all data due to CoN. This means that it is extremely difficult for the algorithm to adjust such cluster centres, since more or less all data points fit equally bad to all clusters. This algorithmic problem will be discussed in more detail in Section 4.

But there are more difficulties with high-dimensional data than just this algorithmic problem. Even for low-dimensional data, there might be dimensions or attributes that do not contribute to the clustering which is usually not a series problem since one or a few irrelevant attributes will have little effects. But if the large majority of attributes in high-dimensional data is irrelevant for the clusters and the distances are computed using all attributes, this simply means the largest part of the distance is noise. Indeed, for high-dimensional data it cannot be expected that all attributes contribute to the clusters. Therefore, for high-dimensional data it is very common to apply subspace clustering (see for instance [11,12,13]). Figure 2 illustrates by a three-dimensional example what subspace clustering aims at. The attribute z is irrelevant for the clusters. A projection of the data set to the x/y-plane would already reveal the clusters. So the suitable subspace in this case would be the x/y-plane. Of course, the projection plane in which clusters are detected does not need to be axes-parallel. If only axes-parallel projections are considered, subspace clustering can be seen as a feature selection technique.

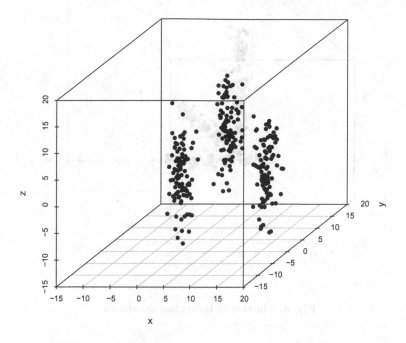

Fig. 2. Clusters in a subspace

Challenges for subspace clustering are the search for the right projection in which the clusters can be found and the possibility of spurious clusters in very high-dimensional data [4].

If subspace clustering is restricted to axes-parallel projections, it assumes that all clusters are characterised by the corresponding subset of attributes. This idea can be generalised in the sense that each cluster has its individual subset of attributes that are relevant for it. This situation is illustrated for a low-dimensional data set in Figure 3. For each of the three clusters one of the three dimensions is irrelevant. The values of the irrelevant attribute spread over the whole range of values and the attribute does not provide any information for the cluster. This concept of clusters was discussed in [14], but not in the context of high-dimensional data. This idea is related to biclustering [15,16] or two-mode clustering [17] where records and attributes are clustered simultaneously. Correlation clustering is an even more general concept of clustering for high-dimensional data. It is assumed that each cluster is located in its own subspace which can be a simple hyperplane or a more complex structure (see for instance [13]).

After a brief review of fuzzy clustering concepts, we will discuss how fuzzy techniques can contribute to clusters in high-dimensional data in the sense of Figures 1 and 3. Subspace clustering will not be discussed in detail here.

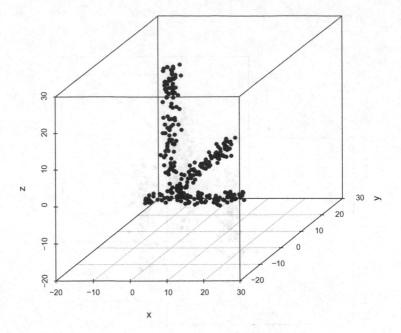

Fig. 3. Clusters in individual subspaces

3   Fuzzy Cluster Analysis

Fuzzy c-means clustering (FCM) [18,19] can be viewed as a generalisation of the classical k-means clustering algorithm [20]. In both cases the number of clusters must be fixed in advance. There are additional techniques to determine the number of clusters. But determining the number of cluster is another issue and will not be discussed in the context of this paper. FCM uses cluster centres or prototypes. These prototypes should be positioned in such a way that the sum of the (squared Euclidean) distances d_{ij} between data point x_j in cluster i and cluster centre v_i are minimised. Each data point x_j is assigned to the clusters i in terms of degrees u_{ij}. FCM is therefore based on the objective function

$$f = \sum_{i=1}^{k} \sum_{j=1}^{n} u_{ij}^{w} d_{ij} \tag{2}$$

to be minimised under the constraints

$$\sum_{i=1}^{k} u_{ij} = 1 \quad \text{for all } j = 1, \ldots, n. \tag{3}$$

It is assumed that c clusters should be found in the data set. If the so-called fuzzifier w is chosen as $w = 1$, FCM reduces to the classical k-means algorithm.

The larger the fuzzifier w is chosen, the more fuzzy or overlapping the clusters tend to be. An alternating optimisation scheme is applied to minimise the objective function (2). Cluster centres are initialised randomly. Assuming these cluster centres to be fixed, there is a closed-form solution for the minimum of (2) as a function of the membership degrees u_{ij}.

$$u_{ij} = \frac{1}{\sum_{k=1}^{c} \left(\frac{d_{ij}}{d_{kj}}\right)^{\frac{1}{w-1}}}, \tag{4}$$

Then these membership degrees are considered to be fixed and a closed-form solution for the minimum of (2) as a function of the cluster centres v_i can be calculated.

$$v_i = \frac{\sum_{j=1}^{n} u_{ij}^{w} x_j}{\sum_{j=1}^{n} u_{ij}^{w}}, \tag{5}$$

This alternating update scheme of the membership degrees and the cluster centres is repeated until convergence, i.e. until the changes are below a chosen threshold. Of course, this alternating optimisation scheme cannot guarantee convergence to the global mimimum of the objective function (2). It will usually only converge in a local optimum that might not reflect a good or desired clustering result.

One advantage of FCM is that it is less sensitive to the initialisation. This is not only an empirical observation. It can be demonstrated that the introduction of the fuzzifier can reduce the number of undesired local minima in the objective function [21]. Nevertheless, FCM has other disadvantages and can lead to undesired results, especially when clusters tend to vary in density. Therefore, in [22], the concept of polynomial fuzzifier (PFCM) was introduced. The objective function (2) is changed to

$$f = \sum_{i=1}^{k} \sum_{j=1}^{n} \left(\alpha u_{ij}^2 + (1-\alpha)u_{ij}\right) d_{ij} \tag{6}$$

where $\alpha \in [0,1]$ is a fixed parameter. This is nothing else, but a convex combination of the FCM objective function with fuzzifier $w = 2$ and the k-means objective function. For $\alpha = 1$, one obtains FCM with fuzzifier $w = 2$ and for $\alpha = 0$ it results in standard k-means clustering. In this way, PFCM combines the advantages of FCM and k-means clustering.

k-means and its fuzzified versions can also be extended to fit more flexible cluster shapes [23] or clusters of different sizes [24]. For a more detailed overview on fuzzy cluster analysis we refer to [25,26]. To be able to adapt to more flexible cluster shapes means also that more parameters are introduced, leading to more local minima of the objective function. Even worse, for high-dimensional data, basic assumptions of such more complex clustering approaches migt be violated. The Gustafson-Kessel algorithm [23] suffers from this problem in a similar way as EM clustering based on Gaussian mixture models. Both approaches estimate the cluster shape based on a covariance matrix. For very high-dimensional data the covariance matrices are often degenerated. For 10,000-dimensional data the covariance matrices of the clusters are automatically degenerated when the number of data points is less than 10,000.

Nevertheless, we will consider one specific extension of (fuzzy) clustering which reflects the idea of clusters as shown in Figure 3. A weighting of attributes is introduced into the objective function (2) by modifying the distance.

$$d_{ij} = \sum_{s=1}^{m} \beta_{i,s}^{t} \left(x_j^{(s)} - v_i^{(s)} \right)^2 \tag{7}$$

where $x_j^{(s)}$ and $v_i^{(s)}$ are the values of the s-th attribute of the data point x_j and the cluster centre v_i, respectively. $\beta_{i,s}$ is the weight that attribute s obtains for cluster i. The weights must satisfy the constraint

$$\sum_{s=1}^{m} \beta_{i,s} = 1. \tag{8}$$

$t > 1$ is a fixed parameter which controls how much the clusters are forced to focus on attributes. For $t \to 1$, each cluster will put its full weight on only one attribute. For $t \to \infty$ all attributes will obtain the same weight as in the usual clustering algorithms. The algorithm is described in detail in [14].

4   Fuzzy Cluster Analysis for High-Dimensional Data

Let us first consider the case of high-dimensional data where clusters are well-separated as illustrated in Figure 1 for the low-dimensional case. As mentioned above, this mainly turns out to be an algorithmic problem. If we knew the location of the cluster centres, we could easily verify that we have well-separated clusters. Standard k-means has a high chance to get lost in a local minimum where some prototypes cover more than one data cluster and other protoytpes split a data cluster into smaller artificial clusters. As mentioned above, FCM can reduce the number of local minima in the objective function and one would expect that FCM could therefore better cope with high-dimensional data. Unfortunately, FCM performs even worse for high-dimensional data than k-means clustering. It happens very often that all or most of the prototypes – the computed cluster centres – gather closely around the centre of gravity of the whole data set. Taking a closer look at the update equation (4) of FCM and taking CoN into account, this is no surprise. The membership degrees are computed based on the relative distances of the data points to the prototypes. At the start of FCM, the prototypes will usually not be close to the centres of the data clusters. In this case, CoN shows its effects and all data points will have roughly the same relative distance to a prototype, so that the membership degrees also become roughly the same for all data points. When the prototypes are updated by Equation (5), all data points obtain roughly the same weight and the prototypes end up close the centre of gravity of the whole data set.

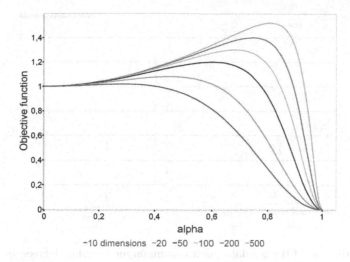

Fig. 4. The objective function of fuzzy clustering has a local minimum in the centre of all data points for high-dimensional data

Figure 4 from [27] explains this effect. It shows the objective function (2) of fuzzy clustering reduced to one parameter for a specific data set. The data set consists of a fixed number of well-separated clusters – each of them concentrated in a single point – distributed uniformly on the surface of an $(m-1)$-dimensional unit hypersphere. The cluster prototypes are first all placed into the origin, i.e. the centre of gravity of all the data points. Then the cluster prototypes are moved along the lines connecting each cluster prototype with one of the true cluster centres. So at 0 on the x-axis in Figure 4 all prototypes are at the origin (radius=0), at 0.5 they are halfway between the origin and the true cluster centres and at 1 each of the prototypes is placed exactly in one of the cluster centres. As can be seen from the figure, the clear global minimum of the objective function is at 1, i.e. when all prototypes are placed in the true cluster centres. But there is a local minimum at the origin, separated by a local maximum from the global minimum. The local maximum is shifted more to the right for higher dimensions. Since the algorithm to minimise the objective function of fuzzy clustering can be viewed as a gradient descent technique [28], the cluster prototypes will end up in the local minimum at the origin when the initialisation is not close enough to the true cluster centres.

According to [27], one possible solution to this problem is an adjustment of the fuzzifier. The higher the dimension of the data, the smaller the fuzzifier should be chosen. This is, however, a tedious parameter adjustment task and it is difficult to define rules of thumb for the choice of the fuzzifier based on the dimensionality of the data set. But it was demonstrated in [27] that PFCM does not suffer from the problems of FCM. In contrast to FCM, PFCM assigns zero membership degrees to data points that are very far away from a prototype. But it also avoids the problems of k-means clustering. Since k-means clustering

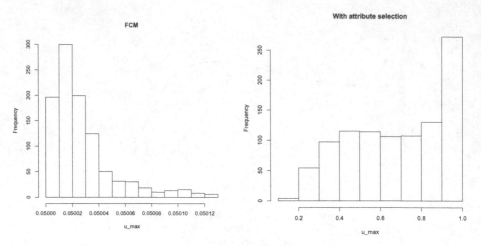

Fig. 5. Distribution of the per data point maximum membership degrees for standard FCM (left) and FCM with attribute selection (right)

assigns each data point to a unique cluster, a prototype has no information about data points that are close, but a little bit closer to another cluster. The objective function of PFCM will also have the undesired local minimum shown for FCM in Figure 4. However, the local maximum will be very close to zero and PFCM will only get lost in the undesired local minimum when all prototypes are initialised very close to the centre of gravity of the whole data set. It was also demonstrated in [27] with various benchmark data sets that PFCM performs much better than k-means clustering and FCM.

Another interesting clustering approach for high-dimensional data borrowing from fuzzy concepts was recently introduced in [29]. The underlying principle of the clustering algorithm is based on the following obvious observation. For each point in the data set consider its distances to all other data points. For any two points in the data set, the correlation between their distance lists can be computed. One would expect a higher correlation for points from the same cluster than for points from different clusters. The algorithm puts points with a high correlation in their distance lists together in one cluster. The correlation measure plays a crucial role in this algorithm. The most popular Pearson correlation is very sensitive to outliers which are very common in the distance lists. The points in the same cluster will yield small distance values, all others large ones, so that the Pearson correlation will not be a proper choice. Rank correlation coefficients like Kendall's tau do not have these problems. However, rank correlation coefficients are not well suited for real-valued data with noise. They only consider whether one value is greater than another. But for similar values, i.e. distances of points far away from the considered cluster, it is more or less a random event which distance is larger. A more suitable correlation coefficient for this clustering concept is the robust gamma introduced in [30,31]. This robust gamma correlation coefficient is based on fuzzy orderings and fuzzy equivalence relations and gives little weight to the ordering of almost identical values, i.e.

similar distance values in the clustering context. The same benchmark data sets as in [27] were used in [29] to evaluate the performance of this clustering approach with respect to high-dimensional data. The results were again far better than the ones obtained by k-means clustering and FCM.

Finally, we investigate whether it is possible to detect clusters as illustrated in Figure 3 in high-dimensional data on the basis of the distance function in Equation (7) with a weighting of attributes. We consider an artificial data set of 20 dimensions. There are 20 clusters and each of them contains 50 data points. For each cluster, all but one attribute follow a standard normal distribution with mean 0 and variance 1. For each dimension, there is one cluster in which the corresponding attribute follows a normal distribution with mean 8, so that only in this specific dimension, the cluster is very well separated from the other clusters.

We first apply standard FCM. For each of the 1000 data points, we choose the highest membership degree to the 20 clusters and plot a histogram over these membership degrees. This histogram is shown on the left-hand side of Figure 5. The maximum membership degrees are all very close to 0.05. For 20 clusters, the average membership degree will be 0.05. This means no data point has a significantly high membership degree to any cluster. Incorporating the attribute selection technique as described in [14], we obtain the histogram on the right-hand side of Figure 5 which indicates that clusters have been better identified. But how well were the clusters identified?

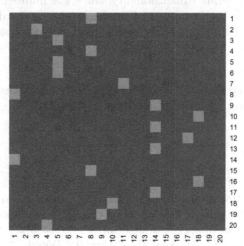

Fig. 6. Heatmap for the weights $\beta_{i,s}$

In order to see this we take a look at the weights $\beta_{i,s}$, i.e. how much influence attribute s has on cluster i. Figure 6 visualises these weights in the form of a heatmap. The rows correspond to the clusters, the columns to the attributes. The positive result is that each cluster more or less focuses on a single attribute, i.e. in each cluster all except one attribute have a weight close to zero. The negative result is that some clusters have chosen to focus on the same attribute which means that these clusters share the same data cluster. And therefore, some clusters have not been discovered. This problem actually comes along with the problem of determining the number of clusters. We have assumed the number of clusters to be known in advance, which is not a realistic assumption. One way to determine the number of clusters, is to start the clustering algorithm with a sufficiently large number of clusters and then merge similar clusters together in a similar way as described in the compatible cluster merging strategy in [32]. In this way, one would discover the 20 clusters correctly.

5   Conclusions

Fuzzy cluster analysis can contribute to clustering high-dimensional data. One must, however, be very careful with the choice of the methods. Standard FCM has even more difficulties with high-dimensional data than k-means clustering unless the fuzzifier is carefully adapted to the number of dimensions. PFCM as a mixture of crisp and fuzzy clustering can better cope with high-dimensional data. The underlying assumption is in any case that (almost) all attributes are actually relevant for the clusters. If clusters should be found in subspaces, subspace clustering techniques are a better choice. If it is assumed that each cluster has its own specific set of characteristic attributes, FCM or PFCM in combination with weighting of attributes can be applied. This approach is, however, limited to data of moderate dimensionality, since the number of additional parameters is $c \cdot m$ where c is the number of clusters and m is the dimensionality of the data set. For $m = 10,000$, this approach is not really feasible from the computational point of view.

Acknowledgments. The author gratefully acknowledges partial support from the EU Project OPTIRAIL (Reference FP7-314031).

References

1. Berthold, M., Borgelt, C., Höppner, F., Klawonn, F.: Guide to Intelligent Data Analysis: How to Intelligently Make Sense of Real Data. Springer, London (2010)
2. Kerr, G., Ruskin, H., Crane, M.: Techniques for clustering gene expression data. Computers in Biology and Medicine 38(3), 383–393 (2008)
3. Pommerenke, C., Müsken, M., Becker, T., Dötsch, A., Klawonn, F., Häussler, S.: Global genotype-phenotype correlations in pseudomonas aeruginosa. PLoS Pathogenes 6(8) (2010), doi:10.1371/journal.ppat.1001074

4. Klawonn, F., Höppner, F., Jayaram, B.: What are clusters in high dimensions and are they difficult to find? In: Proc. CHDD 2013, Springer, Berlin (to appear, 2013)
5. Beyer, K., Goldstein, J., Ramakrishnan, R., Shaft, U.: When is "nearest neighbor" meaningful? In: Beeri, C., Bruneman, P. (eds.) ICDT 1999. LNCS, vol. 1540, pp. 217–235. Springer, Heidelberg (1998)
6. Durrant, R.J., Kabán, A.: When is 'nearest neighbour' meaningful: A converse theorem and implications. J. Complexity 25(4), 385–397 (2009)
7. François, D., Wertz, V., Verleysen, M.: The concentration of fractional distances. IEEE Trans. Knowl. Data Eng. 19(7), 873–886 (2007)
8. Jayaram, B., Klawonn, F.: Can unbounded distance measures mitigate the curse of dimensionality? Int. Journ. Data Mining, Modelling and Management 4, 361–383 (2012)
9. Aggarwal, C.C.: Re-designing distance functions and distance-based applications for high dimensional data. SIGMOD Record 30(1), 13–18 (2001)
10. Hsu, C.M., Chen, M.S.: On the design and applicability of distance functions in high-dimensional data space. IEEE Trans. Knowl. Data Eng. 21(4), 523–536 (2009)
11. Domeniconi, C., Papadopoulos, D., Gunopulos, D.: Subspace clustering of high dimensional data. In: Proceedings of SIAM Conference on Data Mining 2004, pp. 517–521 (2004)
12. Parsons, L., Haque, E., Liu, H.: Subspace clustering for high dimensional data: A review. ACM SIGKDD Explorations Newsletter 6(1), 90–105 (2004)
13. Kriegel, H.P., Kröger, P., Zimek, A.: Clustering high-dimensional data: A survey on subspace clustering, pattern-based clustering, and correlation clustering. ACM Trans. Knowl. Discov. Data 3(1), 1–58 (2009)
14. Keller, A., Klawonn, F.: Fuzzy clustering with weighting of data variables. International Journal of Uncertainty, Fuzziness and Knowledge-Based Systems 8, 735–746 (2000)
15. Madeira, S., Oliveira, A.: Biclustering algorithms for biological data analysis: A survey. IEEE Trans. Comput. Biol. Bioinf. 1(1), 24–45 (2004)
16. Tanay, A., Sharan, R., Shamir, R.: Biclustering algorithms: A survey. In: Aluru, S. (ed.) Handbook of Computational Molecular Biology. Chapman and Hall, Boca Raton (2006)
17. Van Mechelen, I., Bock, H.H., De Boeck, P.: Two-mode clustering methods: a structured overview. Statistical Methods in Medical Research 13, 363–394 (2004)
18. Dunn, J.: A fuzzy relative of the isodata process and its use in detecting compact well-separated clusters. Cybernetics and Systems 3(3), 32–57 (1973)
19. Bezdek, J.: Pattern Recognition with Fuzzy Objective Function Algorithms. Plenum Press, New York (1981)
20. Duda, R., Hart, P.: Pattern Classification and Scene Analysis. Wiley, New York (1973)
21. Jayaram, B., Klawonn, F.: Can fuzzy clustering avoid local minima and undesired partitions? In: Moewes, C., Nürnberger, A. (eds.) Computational Intelligence in Intelligent Data Analysis. SCI, vol. 445, pp. 31–44. Springer, Heidelberg (2013)
22. Klawonn, F., Höppner, F.: What is fuzzy about fuzzy clustering? Understanding and improving the concept of the fuzzifier. In: Berthold, M.R., Lenz, H.J., Bradley, E., Kruse, R., Borgelt, C. (eds.) IDA 2003. LNCS, vol. 2810, pp. 254–264. Springer, Heidelberg (2003)
23. Gustafson, D., Kessel, W.: Fuzzy clustering with a fuzzy covariance matrix. In: IEEE CDC, San Diego, pp. 761–766 (1979)

24. Keller, A., Klawonn, F.: Adaptation of cluster sizes in objective function based fuzzy clustering. In: Leondes, C. (ed.) Intelligent Systems: Technology and Applications. Database and Learning Systems, vol. IV, pp. 181–199. CRC Press, Boca Raton (2003)
25. Bezdek, J., Keller, J., Krishnapuram, R., Pal, N.: Fuzzy Models and Algorithms for Pattern Recognition and Image Processing. Kluwer, Boston (1999)
26. Höppner, F., Klawonn, F., Kruse, R., Runkler, T.: Fuzzy Cluster Analysis. Wiley, Chichester (1999)
27. Winkler, R., Klawonn, F., Kruse, R.: Fuzzy c-means in high dimensional spaces. Fuzzy System Applications 1, 1–17 (2011)
28. Höppner, F., Klawonn, F.: A contribution to convergence theory of fuzzy c-means and its derivatives. IEEE Transactions on Fuzzy Systems 11, 682–694 (2003)
29. Krone, M., Klawonn, F., Jayaram, B.: RaCoCl: Robust rank correlation based clustering – an exploratory study for high-dimensional data. In: FuzzIEEE 2013, Hyderabad (2013)
30. Bodenhofer, U., Klawonn, F.: Robust rank correlation coefficients on the basis of fuzzy orderings: Initial steps. Mathware and Soft Computing 15, 5–20 (2008)
31. Bodenhofer, U., Krone, M., Klawonn, F.: Testing noisy numerical data for monotonic association. Information Sciences 245, 21–37 (2013)
32. Krishnapuram, R., Freg, C.: Fitting an unknown number of lines and planes to image data through compatible cluster merging. Pattern Recognition 25, 385–400 (1992)

Interpretability in Machine Learning
– Principles and Practice

P.J.G. Lisboa

School of Computing and Mathematical Sciences, Liverpool John Moores University,
Liverpool L3 3AF, UK

Abstract. Theoretical advances in machine learning have been reflected in many research implementations including in safety-critical domains such as medicine. However this has not been reflected in a large number of practical applications used by domain experts. This bottleneck is in a significant part due to lack of interpretability of the non-linear models derived from data. This lecture will review five broad categories of interpretability in machine learning - nomograms, rule induction, fuzzy logic, graphical models & topographic mapping. Links between the different approaches will be made around the common theme of designing interpretability into the structure of machine learning models, then using the armoury of advanced analytical methods to achieve generic non-linear approximation capabilities.

1   Introduction

The practical application of decision support systems of various types is the eventual outlet for machine learning research. While commercial products has existed for some time including in safety-related applications [1] and much research is published in medical decision support [2-3], there are still very few routinely used products, given the huge volume of the available literature and the fast pace of theoretical developments in computational intelligence. This is especially the case outside of signal processing where pragmatic applications of fuzzy logic and neural networks have been commercially exploited [4]. This observation raises important issues about the practical utility of machine learning methods more generally, hence the societal value of the research investment in this area.

In many application domains, the key limitation of generic non-linear methods is lack of interpretation. This is key especially in safety-related applications but also more widely, since learning systems are generally one of several components in an integrated software application, for instance for decision support, where central aspects of acceptance testing are verification and validation (v&v). Verification tests that the system is correctly matching the initial specification and design ('doing things right') and validation tests that the software system as a whole meets its intended operational purpose ('doing the right things').

F. Masulli, G. Pasi, and R. Yager (Eds.): WILF 2013, LNAI 8256, pp. 15–21, 2013.

In the context of machine learning applications, the requirement of verifiability includes not just computational integrity but also a sound match with the domain user expertise. This includes checking that a predictive model is not exploiting data artifacts instead of the correct data structure, and also controlling any risks arising from model operation in response to novel data i.e. unexpected outliers [5].

Validation of predictive models is a test of the generality of the model i.e. its validity in generalising to out-of-sample data. This aspect has been the subject of much theoretical research.

In summary, the requirements for v&v are met in part if machine learning models are designed to be interpretable, in the sense that they meet the following requirements [6]:

- Mapping to domain knowledge.
- Ensure safe operation across the full range of operational inputs.
- Accurate modelling of non-linear effects.

The latter aspect is the default condition for machine learning models beyond generalised statistical models. The other two requirements are the reality checks that are needed before a system can be put to practical use. The last two bullet points capture two complementary aspects of the model: reliability, in other words knowing when the model output can be trusted, and uncertainty of model predictions, which measures the precision of predictions when the model is reliable.

This position paper relates specifically to the importance of mapping learning models to expert knowledge.

The first thing to note is that predictive accuracy is not enough for predictive systems. This is because few data bases are artefact free by design, therefore the more powerful a non-linear predictive model is, so the better it becomes at exploiting structural noise, in the form of artifacts of the data acquisition process, so that improvements in predictive accuracy can be achieved which in no way represent generalisations to future data. An example of this would be if image acquisition for predictive modelling contains central figures to be detected against a mixed background, but the camera setting is not controlled to ensure that depth of focus is maintained across the full data set, with the consequence that the images containing the features of interest have the background out-of-focus while the images omitting the central figures are totally in focus. Any blur detector will consistently separate images into the correct sets, while capturing no information at all about the structure of the features of interest. In more generally data-based applications artifacts are easily introduced unknowingly, potentially resulting in fictional generalisation accuracy unless the operation of the classifier is explained.

How do these basic principles of interpretability apply in practice to machine learning models? To start answering this question we need to look into the range of information processing methods, shown in fig. 1.

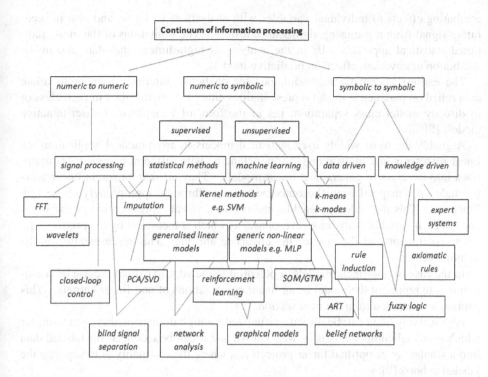

Fig. 1. Information processing has in practice significant overlaps between different high level requirements. This diagram is intended as a pragmatic landscape of modelling methodologies, noting their different aims and the overlaps in the approaches to implementation.

Broadly speaking machine learning approaches are alone in the spectrum in their lack of interpretability. At either end, both signal processing and knowledge-based methods are accessible to direct interpretation and that is a major part both in theory and in practice. Statistical methods are in part restricted by modelling assumptions, but this parametric requirement in return opens a route to interpretation. In fact classes of models such as logistic regression were originally designed to explain variation in the data, as an extension of ANOVA for many covariates. The prediction would result naturally from the model insights generated in explaining the variation in the data.

In recent decades, the focus on predictive accuracy [7] has lost sight of the value of interpretation in data analysis. The rest of the paper presents a very brief overview of current analytical methods with interpretation capabilities, together with emerging directions that provide alternative approaches to traceability of data-driven models.

2   Competing Methodologies, or Complementary?

Traceability is a central pillar of data analysis. It comes in the form of modeling from first principles e.g. in probability theory, in breaking down random variation and attributing effects to individual variables with analysis of variance, and also in separating signal from noise using significance testing. The limitations of the more traditional statistical approaches lie in the analysis of high-dimensional data and in the attribution of covariate effects in predictive models.

The earliest systematic methodologies for predictive inference with multivariate data relied on parametric model representations either to generate data in each class or to directly model class separation, i.e. in the form of generative or discriminative models [8].

Arguably the most widely used statistical models in any practical application are linear regression and logistic regression, extending with different parametric assumptions into the class of generalized linear models. They all share a single linear scoring index $\beta.x$ mapped onto the outcome variable through appropriately chose link functions. This methodology enables the use of a visual representation of the influence of each variable in the model response, as which is measured by the produce of a linear coefficient and the size of the covariate attribute. This representation is the nomogram.

In the case of non-linear models, a potential framework to extend the use of nomograms is to represent the model using linear combinations of non-linear kernels. This approach is returned to in the next section.

Alternatively, data can be directly visualized through dimensionality reduction, for which principal components is as well-known and it can be extended for labeled data into a similar set of optimal linear projections, where the optimality is to separate the labeled cohorts [9].

When the data set is no linearly separable, visualization can be achieved with latent variable models [10]. This is a powerful class of models for mapping high-dimensional data into relevant low-dimensional manifolds. However, the interpretation of latent variable representations is not straightforward since the attribution of influence for particular outcome responses applies to a composite variable and not to each individual covariate. Similar issues arise with related methods for direct non-linear visualization in the form of manifold learning methods, typically SOM and GTM, but also principal manifolds for static data and invariant manifolds for dynamical systems [11].

To many users understanding is best represented by deduction. For data-driven models, this typically involves the use of rule induction methods, which may have mutually exclusive tree structures but can alternatively apply non-orthogonal search methods to detect overlapping but low-order rules [12, 13]. Interestingly, these methods show that successful prediction does not equate with the correct decision boundaries for the Boolean logic generating the data [14].

Fuzzy logic is an established methodology of particular power to model reasoning with linguistic information. This can be driven by data, generating the necessary rules for predictive inference.

Nevertheless, when analytical classifiers are replaced with rules extracted to explain their operation, it is found that very little accuracy is lost and the rules apply typically to all but a small percentage of the data which are correctly identified as outliers [15].

In the case of rich data sets, the mapping of multivariate associations requires efficient structure finding algorithms that are scalable for many variables [16]. In the case where non-linear associations are captured with discrete data, fuzzy logic systems may be used to provide multiple interpolation from quantized variables back to the real-valued domain [17].

A final generic approach to reasoning to promote traceablity is to convert predictive inference into efficient retrieval of relevant reference cases. This is the methodology of case based reasoning [18]. It also has potential for combining with fuzzy predicates to model possibilistic reasoning [19].

3   New Directions

The methodologies to-date largely fit into separate silos with little interaction between them. In other cases, there is still too high a reliance on heuristic approaches.

A current interest is to represent generic non-linear models using nomograms. This requires a parametric representation capable of representing non-linear decision boundaries, but using linear combinations of discriminant functions. To do this effectively further requires the integration of these guiding principles into a parsimonious framework such as the SVM. An interpretation of SVM classifiers in terms of univariate effects and bivariate interactions is an emerging direction that is already showing promise [20].

Turning to case based reasoning, the need to principled approaches requires a rigorous definition of a central and ubiquitous concept in pattern recognition – the similarity between two sets of observations. This has been discussed within linear methods with the definition, for instance of the Mahalanobis distance, and also in terms of information content with the definition of Fisher information. The latter is a bona fide metric and so can be used to define a local, Riemannian metric, that defines the similarity locally between a pair of data points infinitesimally close to each other. This, in turn, can be efficiently mapped onto geodesic distances [21].

A final emerging direction is to use principled similarity metrics to define similarity matrices which define networks of observations, from which prototypes can be derived using spectral methods [22].

4   Conclusions

The wide range of reviewed methodologies clearly shows that interpretability is a many faceted. There are different approaches that may be regarded as complementary, but no general agreement on what makes a predictive inference model interpretable. To some extent, this value judgment depends heavily on both the nature of a particular application and the subjective interests of the domain user. Many of these approaches seem to be treated separately and could potentially gain from combining into integrated approaches to data modeling.

More generally, machine learning has generated particularly powerful paradigms that are especially difficult to render interpretable. In this respect, new research directions are emerging that provide principled and efficient approaches to replicate current models using rules, graphs, networks and even nomograms.

Given that non-linear modeling capability has long been established for widely different algorithms among them the broad class of artificial neural networks, it seems that the really important question for making machine learning more relevant to practice is not whether we can model regression and classification data, but how can this be best done with parametric or semi-parametric models that are interpretable by design. In other words, it is now possible to construct a restricted class of non-linear models, with defined interpretation capabilities, that form the basis for data modeling. It is only then that we can remove the risk of developing effective artifact detectors and be sure that the right predictions are being achieved by the right reasons.

Acknowledgements. The author is grateful to V. van Belle, I.H.Jarman, T.A. Etchells and H. Ruìz for helpful discussions and production of figures for this paper.

References

1. Lisboa, P.J.G.: Industrial use of safety-related artificial neural networks. HSE CR 237/2001, HMSO (2001), `http://www.hse.gov.uk/research/crr_pdf/2001/crr01327.pdf`
2. Lisboa, P.J.G.: A review of evidence of health benefit from artificial neural networks in medical intervention. Neural Networks 15(1), 9–37 (2002)
3. Lisboa, P.J.G., Taktak, A.F.G.: The use of artificial neural networks in decision support in cancer: A systematic review. Neural Networks 19(4), 408–415 (2006)
4. Chiu, S.: Developing commercial applications of intelligent control. IEEE Control Syst. Mag. 17(2), 94–100 (1997)
5. Vellido, A., Lisboa, P.J.G.: Handling outliers in brain tumour MRS data analysis through robust topographic mapping. Computers in Biology and Medicine 36(10), 1049–1063 (2006)
6. Van Belle, V., Lisboa, P.J.G.: Research Directions in Interpretable Machine Learning. In: European Symposium on Artificial Neural Networks, Computational Intelligence and Machine Learning (ESANN), Bruges, April 24-26, pp. 191–196 (2013)
7. Breiman, L.: Statistical Modeling: The Two Cultures. Statistical Science 16(3), 199–231 (2001)
8. Bacciu, D., Lisboa, P.J.G., Sperdutti, A., Villmann, T.: Probabilistic Modelling in Machine Learning. In: Alippi, C., et al. (eds.) Handbook on Computational Intelligence. Springer (accepted, 2013)
9. Lisboa, P.J.G., Ellis, I.O., Green, A.R., Ambrogi, F., Dias, M.B.: Cluster-based visualisation with scatter matrices. Pattern Recognition Letters 29(13), 1814–1823 (2008)
10. Bartholomew, Knott, Moustaki: Latent Variable Models and Factor Analysis: A Unified Approach, 3rd edn. (2011)
11. Gorban, A.N., Zinovyev, A.: Principal manifolds and graphs in practice: from molecular biology to dynamical systems. International Journal of Neural Systems 20(3), 219–232 (2010)

12. Etchells, T.A., Lisboa, P.J.G.: Orthogonal search-based rule extraction (OSRE) from trained neural networks: A practical and efficient approach. IEEE Transactions on Neural Networks 17(2), 374–384 (2006)
13. Rögnvaldsson, T., Etchells, T.A., You, L., Garwicz, D., Jarman, I.H., Lisboa, P.J.G.: How to find simple and accurate rules for viral protease cleavage specificities. BMC Bioinformatics 10, 149 (2009)
14. Lisboa, P.J.G., Etchells, T.A., Pountney, D.C.: Minimal MLPs do not model the XOR logic. Neurocomputing, Rapid Communication 48(1-4), 1033–1037 (2002)
15. Jarman, I.H., Etchells, T.A., Martín, J.D., Lisboa, P.J.G.: An integrated framework for risk profiling of breast cancer patients following surgery. Artificial Intelligence in Medicine 42, 165–188 (2008)
16. Bacciu, D., Etchells, T.A., Lisboa, P.J.G., Whittaker, J.: Efficient identification of independence networks using mutual information. Computational Statistics 28(2), 621–646 (2013)
17. Fernandez, F., Duarte, A., Sanchez, A.: Optimization of the Fuzzy Partition of a Zero-order Takagi-Sugeno Model. In: Proc. Eleventh International Conference on Information Processing and Management of Uncertainty in Knowledge-based Systems (IPMU 2006), vol. I, pp. 898–905. Editions EDK (2006)
18. López de Mántaras, R., McSherry, D., Bridge, D., Leake, D., Smyth, B., Craw, S., Faltings, B., Maher, M.-L., Cox, M., Forbus, K., Keane, M., Aamodt, A., Watson, I.: Retrieval, reuse, revision, and retention in case-based reasoning. Knowledge Engineering Review 20(3), 215–240 (2005)
19. Dutta, S., Bonissone, P.: Integrating Case Based And Rule Based Reasoning: The Possibilistic Connection. In: Proc. 6th Conference on Uncertainty in AI, Cambridge, MA, July 27-29, pp. 290–300 (1990)
20. Van Belle, V., Lisboa, P.J.G.: Automated Selection of Interaction Effects in Sparse Kernel Methods to Predict Pregnancy Viability. In: IEEE Symposium Series on Computational Intelligence, Singapore, April 16-19 (2013)
21. Ruiz, H., Etchells, T.A., Jarman, I.H., Martín, J.D., Lisboa, P.J.G.: A principled approach to network-based classification and data representation. Neurocomputing 112, 79–91 (2013)
22. Newman, M.E.J.: Modularity and community structure in networks. Proc. Natl. Acad. Sci. USA 103(23), 8577–8582 (2006)

Interpretability of Fuzzy Systems

Corrado Mencar

University of Bari "A. Moro", Italy

Abstract. Fuzzy systems are convenient tools for modelling complex phenomena because they are capable of conjugating a non-linear behaviour with a transparent description of knowledge in terms of linguistic rules. In many real-world applications, fuzzy systems are designed through data-driven design techniques which, however, often carry out precise systems that are not endowed with knowledge that is *interpretable*, i.e. easy to read and understand. In a nutshell, interpretability is not granted by the mere adoption of fuzzy logic, this representing a necessary yet not a sufficient requirement for modelling and processing linguistic knowledge. Furthermore, interpretability is a quality that is not easy to define and quantify. Therefore, several open and challenging questions arise while considering interpretability in the design of fuzzy systems, which are briefly considered in this paper along with some answers on the basis of the current state of research.

1 Introduction

Fuzzy systems are endowed with the capability of conjugating a complex behavior with a simple description, in terms of linguistic knowledge, that is *interpretable*, i.e. easy to read and understand by human users. In the simplest cases, the design of fuzzy systems is accomplished manually, with human knowledge purposely injected into fuzzy rules in order to model the desired behavior. (The rules could be eventually tuned to improve the system accuracy.) But the great success of fuzzy logic led to the development of many data-driven design techniques that made feasible the automatic design of fuzzy systems; however, these automatic techniques are often aimed at maximizing the accuracy of the fuzzy systems, which result almost unintelligible. Therefore, the fundamental plus of fuzzy logic is lost and the derived models are comparable to other black-box models (like neural networks) in terms of knowledge interpretability.

Roughly speaking, interpretability is not granted *a priori* by the mere adoption of fuzzy logic for knowledge representation, yet it is a highly requested quality, especially in some applicative domains (like Medicine) where fuzzy systems can be used to support critical decisions upon which users (e.g. physicians) must rely. Additionally, interpretability is a quality that is not easy to define and quantify; therefore, several open and challenging questions arise while considering interpretability in fuzzy systems: *What* is interpretability? *Why* interpretability is worth considering? How to *ensure* interpretability? How to *assess* interpretability? How to *design* interpretable fuzzy models? These questions are briefly considered in this paper along with some tentative answers on the basis of the current state of research.

F. Masulli, G. Pasi, and R. Yager (Eds.): WILF 2013, LNAI 8256, pp. 22–35, 2013.
© Springer International Publishing Switzerland 2013

2 What Is Interpretability and Why It Is Important?

Defining interpretability is challenging because it deals with the the relation occurring between two heterogeneous entities: a fuzzy system and a human user acting as an interpreter of the system's knowledge base and working engine. To pave the way for defining such a relation, some fundamental properties need to be incorporated into a fuzzy system, so that its formal description becomes compatible with the user's knowledge representation. The definition of interpretability, therefore, calls for the identification of several features; among them, the adoption of a fuzzy inference engine based on fuzzy rules is straightforward to approach the linguistic-based formulation of concepts which is typical of human abstract thought.

A distinguishing feature of a fuzzy rule-based system is the double level of knowledge representation: (i) the *semantic* level made by the fuzzy sets defined in terms of their membership functions, as well as the aggregation functions used for inference, and (ii) the *syntactic* level of representation, in which knowledge is represented in a formal structure where linguistic variables are involved and reciprocally connected by some formal operators (e.g. "AND", "THEN", etc.). A mapping is defined to provide the interpretative transition that is quite common in the mathematical context: semantics is assigned to a formal structure by mapping symbols (linguistic terms and operators) to objects (fuzzy sets and aggregation functions).

In principle, the mapping of linguistic terms to fuzzy sets could be arbitrary. Nevertheless, the mere use of symbols in the high level of knowledge representation implies the establishment of a number of semiotic relations that are fundamental for the preservation of interpretability of a fuzzy system. In particular, linguistic terms — as usually picked from natural language — must be fully meaningful for the expected reader since they denote concepts, i.e. mental representations that allow the reader to draw appropriate inferences about the entities she encounters. As a consequence, concepts and fuzzy sets are implicitly connected by means of the common linguistic terms they are related to; the key essence of interpretability is therefore the property of *cointension* [1] between fuzzy sets and concepts, consisting in the capability of referring to similar classes of objects: such a possibility is assured by the use of common linguistic terms.

The notion of semantic cointension is further strengthened by the Comprehensibility Postulate [2], which asserts that «*The results of computer induction should be symbolic descriptions of given entities, semantically and structurally similar to those a human expert might produce observing the same entities.* [...] ». The key-point of the postulate, which has been conceived in the general context of Machine Learning but can be directly applied to fuzzy systems, is the human centrality of the results of a computer induction process; the importance of the human component implicitly suggests this aspect to be taken into account in the quest for interpretability.

Actually, the semantic cointension is related to one facet of the interpretability process, which can be referred to as *comprehensibility* of the content and behavior of a fuzzy system. On the other hand, when we turn to consider the cognitive capabilities of human brains and their intrinsic limitations, then a different facet of the interpretability process can be defined in terms of *readability* of the bulk of information conveyed by a fuzzy model. In that case, simplicity is required to perform the interpretation process because of the limited ability to store information in the human brain's short term memory [3]. Comprehensibility and readability represent two facets of a common quality and both of them are to be considered for the design of interpretable fuzzy systems.

Interpretability is a complex requirement that has an impact on the design process. Therefore, it must be justified by strong arguments, like those briefly otlined in the following:

1. In an interpretable fuzzy system the acquired knowledge can be easily verified and related to the domain knowledge of a human expert. In particular, it is easy to verify if the acquired knowledge expresses new and interesting relations about the data; also, the acquired knowledge can be refined and integrated with expert knowledge.
2. The use of natural language as a mean for knowledge communication enables the possibility of interaction between the user and the system. Interactivity is meant to explore the acquired knowledge; in practice, it can be done at symbolical level (by adding new rules or modifying existing ones) and at numerical level (by modifying the fuzzy sets denoted by linguistic terms, or by adding new linguistic terms denoting new fuzzy sets).
3. The acquired knowledge can be easily validated against common-sense knowledge and domain-specific knowledge. This capability enables the detection of semantic inconsistencies that may have different causes (misleading data involved in the inductive process, local minimum where the inductive process may have been trapped, data overfitting, etc.). This kind of anomaly detection is important to drive the inductive process towards a qualitative improvement of the acquired knowledge.
4. The most important reason to adopt interpretable fuzzy models is their inherent ability to convince end-users about the reliability of a system (especially those users not concerned with knowledge acquisition techniques). An interpretable fuzzy rule-based model is endowed with the capability of explaining its inference process so that users may be confident on how it produces its outcomes. This is particularly important in such domains as medical diagnosis, where a human expert is the ultimate responsible of critical decisions.

3   How to Ensure Interpretability?

Interpretability is a quality of fuzzy systems that is not immediate to quantify. Nevertheless, a quantitative definition is required both for assessing the interpretability of a fuzzy system and for designing new fuzzy systems. A common approach for a quantitative definition of interpretability is based on the adoption of a number of constraints and criteria that, taken as a whole, provide for a (at least partial) definition of interpretability.

In literature a large number of interpretability constraints and criteria can be found [4,5]. An usual approach is to organize the interpretability constraints in a hierarchical fashion (fig. 1), which starts from the most basic components of a fuzzy system, namely the involved fuzzy sets, and goes on toward more complex levels, such as fuzzy partitions, fuzzy rules, up to considering the model as a whole.

At the lowest level, interpretability concerns each single fuzzy set, with the role of expressing an elementary yet imprecise concept that can be denoted by a linguistic term. Thus, fuzzy sets are the building blocks to translate a numerical domain into a linguistically quantified domain that can be used to communicate knowledge. However, not

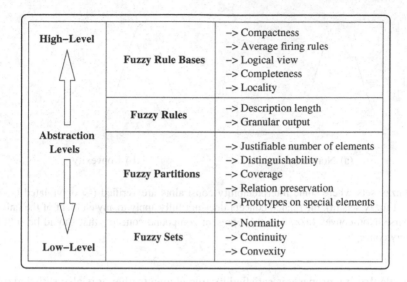

High–Level	Fuzzy Rule Bases	–> Compactness –> Average firing rules –> Logical view –> Completeness –> Locality
	Fuzzy Rules	–> Description length –> Granular output
Abstraction Levels	Fuzzy Partitions	–> Justifiable number of elements –> Distinguishability –> Coverage –> Relation preservation –> Prototypes on special elements
Low–Level	Fuzzy Sets	–> Normality –> Continuity –> Convexity

Fig. 1. Interpretability constraints and criteria in different abstraction levels

all fuzzy sets can be related to elementary concepts, since the membership function of a fuzzy set may be very awkward but still legitimate from a mathematical viewpoint. Actually, a sub-class of fuzzy sets should be considered, so that its members can be easily associated to elementary concepts and tagged by the corresponding linguistic labels. Fuzzy sets of this sub-class must verify a number of basic interpretability constraints, including the following:

One-Dimensionality. Usually fuzzy systems are defined on multidimensional domains characterized by several features. However, each fuzzy set being denoted by a linguistic term should be defined on a single feature, whose domain becomes the universe of discourse, which is assumed as a closed interval on the real line. Relations among features are represented as combinations of one-dimensional fuzzy sets, which can be linguistically interpreted as compound propositions.

Normality. At least one element of the universe of discourse is a prototype for the fuzzy set, i.e. it is characterized by a full membership degree. A normal fuzzy set represents a concept that fully qualifies at least one element of the universe of discourse, i.e. the concept has at least one example that fulfills it (fig. 2(a)).

Continuity. The membership function is continuous on the universe of discourse. As a matter of fact, most concepts that can be naturally represented through fuzzy sets derived from a perceptual act, which comes from external stimuli that usually vary in continuity. Therefore, continuous fuzzy sets are better in accordance with the perceptive nature of the represented concepts.

Convexity. In a convex fuzzy set, given three elements of the universe of discourse, the degree of membership of the middle element is always greater than or equal to the minimum membership degrees of the side elements. This constraint encodes

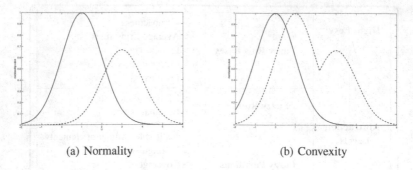

(a) Normality   (b) Convexity

Fig. 2. Fuzzy sets where some interpretability constraints are verified (–) or violated (- -). In subnormal fuzzy sets (a), the related concept does not fully apply to any element of the universe of discourse. Non-convex fuzzy sets (b) represent compound concepts that should be split into elementary concepts.

the rule that if a property is satisfied by two elements, then it is also satisfied by an element settled between them (fig. 2(b)).

A collection of fuzzy sets defined on the same universe of discourse forms a fuzzy partition, which defines in the very essence the semantics of a linguistic variable. A fuzzy partition defines a relation among fuzzy sets. Such a relation must be co-intensive with the relation connecting the elementary concepts represented by the fuzzy sets involved in the fuzzy partition. That is the reason why the design of fuzzy partitions is so crucial for the overall interpretability of a fuzzy system. The most critical interpretability constraints for fuzzy partitions are:

Justifiable Number of Elements. The number of fuzzy sets included in a linguistic variable must be small enough so that they can be easily remembered and recalled by users. Psychological studies suggest at most nine fuzzy sets or even less. Usually, three to five fuzzy sets are convenient choices to set the partition cardinality.

Distinguishability. Since fuzzy sets are denoted by distinct linguistic terms, they should refer to well distinguished concepts. Therefore, fuzzy sets in a partition should be well separated, although some overlapping is admissible because usually perception-based concepts are not completely disjoint (fig. 3(a)).

Coverage. Each element of the universe of discourse must belong to at least one fuzzy set of the partition with a membership degree not less than a threshold. This requirement involves that each element of the universe of discourse has some quality that is well represented in the fuzzy partition (fig. 3(b)).

Relation Preservation. The concepts that are represented by the fuzzy sets in a fuzzy partition are usually cross-related (e.g., LOW preceding MEDIUM, this preceding HIGH, and so on). Relations of this type must be preserved by the corresponding fuzzy sets in the fuzzy partition (see fig. 4 for a subtle violation of this constraint).

Prototypes on Special Elements. In many problems some elements of the universe of discourse have some special meaning. A common case is the meaning of the bounds of the universe of discourse, which usually represent some extreme qualities (e.g.,

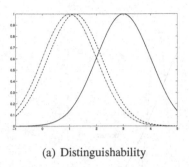
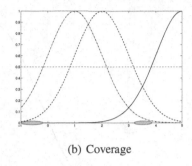

(a) Distinguishability   (b) Coverage

Fig. 3. Fuzzy partitions where some interpretability constraints are verified or violated. (a) It is easy to assign distinct fuzzy sets that are distinguishable (continuous line), while a fuzzy set that overlaps with another (dashed line) almost has the same semantics (hence the same linguistic label). (b) Some elements in the universe of discourse are under-represented by the fuzzy sets of the partition (grey areas). Usually the coverage threshold is set to 0.5.

VERY LARGE or VERY SMALL). Other examples are possible, which are more problem-specific (e.g., the typical human body temperature). In all these cases, the prototypes of some fuzzy sets of the partition must coincide with such special elements.

In most problems a number of linguistic variables must be defined, one for each feature. Different assignments of linguistic variables can be combined together to form fuzzy rules. A fuzzy rule is a unit of knowledge that has the twofold role of determining the system behavior and communicating this behavior in a linguistic form. Some of the most general interpretability constraints and criteria for fuzzy rules are the following:

Description Length. The description length of a fuzzy rule is the number of linguistic variables involved in the rule. A small number of linguistic variables in a rule implies both high readability and semantic generality, hence short rules should be preferred in fuzzy systems.

Granular Outputs. The main strength of fuzzy systems is their ability to represent and process imprecision in both data and knowledge. Imprecision is part of fuzzy inference, therefore the inferred output of a fuzzy system should carry information about the imprecision of its knowledge. This can be accomplished by using fuzzy sets as outputs. Defuzzification collapses fuzzy sets into single scalars; it should be therefore used only when strictly necessary and in those situations where outputs are not subject of user interpretation.

The set of rules that defines the behavior of a fuzzy system is named rule base. As previously stated, the interpretability of a rule base taken as a whole has two facets: (i) a structural facet (*readability*), which is mainly related to the easiness of reading the rules, and (ii) a semantic facet (*comprehensibility*), which is related to the information conveyed to the users to understand the system behavior. The following interpretability constraints and criteria are commonly defined to ensure the structural and semantic interpretability of fuzzy rule bases:

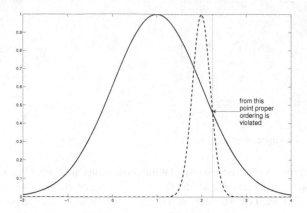

Fig. 4. A subtle case where relation preservation can be violated. Two Gaussian fuzzy sets are defined with different width: if the two fuzzy sets are denoted by implicitly ordered linguistic labels (e.g. MEDIUM and HIGH), then a point exists beyond which the implicit order is violated (in the example, the rightmost elements are more MEDIUM than HIGH even though the contrary is expected by the implicit semantics of the linguistic terms).

Compactness. A compact rule base is defined by a small number of rules. This is a typical structural constraint that advocates for simple representation of knowledge in order to allow easy reading and understanding.

Average Firing Rules. When an input is applied to a fuzzy system, the rules whose conditions are verified to a degree greater than zero are "firing", i.e. they contribute to the inference of the output. On the average, the number of firing rules should be as small as possible, so that users are able to understand the contributions of the rules in determining the output.

Logical View. Fuzzy rules resemble logical propositions when their linguistic description is considered. Since linguistic description is the main mean for communicating knowledge, it is necessary that logical laws are applicable to fuzzy rules; otherwise, the system behavior may result counter-intuitive. Therefore the validity of some basic laws of the propositional logic (like *Modus Ponens*) and the truth-preserving operations (e.g., application of distributivity, reflexivity, etc.) should be verified also for fuzzy rules.

Completeness. The behavior of a fuzzy system is well defined for all inputs in the universe of discourse; however when the maximum firing strength determined by an input is too small, it is not easy to justify the behavior of the system in terms of the activated rules. It is therefore required that for each possible input at least one rule is activated with a firing strength greater than a threshold.

Locality. Each rule should define a local model, i.e. a fuzzy region in the universe of discourse where the behavior of the system is mainly due to the rule and only marginally by other rules that are simultaneously activated. A moderate overlapping of local models is admissible in order to enable a smooth transition from a local model to another when the input values gradually shift from one fuzzy region to another.

On summary, a number of interpretable constraints and criteria apply to all levels of a fuzzy system. Sometimes interpretability constraints are conflicting (e.g. distinguishability vs. coverage) and, in many cases, they conflict with the overall accuracy of the system. A balance is therefore required, asking in its turn for a way to assess interpretability in a qualitative but also a quantitative way. This is the main subject of the next Section.

4   How to Assess Interpretability?

Assessing interpretability represents is hard because the analysis of interpretability is extremely subjective. In fact, it clearly depends on the background knowledge and experience of who is in charge of making the evaluation. Hence, it is necessary to consider both objective and subjective indexes. On the one hand, objective indexes are aimed at making feasible fair comparisons among different fuzzy models designed for solving the same problem. On the other hand, subjective indexes are thought for guiding the design of customized fuzzy models, thus making easier to take into account users' preferences and expectations during the design process [6]. Gacto et al. [7] proposed a double axis taxonomy regarding semantic and structural properties of fuzzy systems, at both partition and rule base levels. Accordingly, they pointed out four groups of indexes (see fig. 5).

Structural indexes are mainly designed to assess the readability of a fuzzy system, while semantic indexes concern the quantification of its comprehensibility. Accordingly, structural indexes at the partition level relate the number of features and the number of membership functions per feature to the readability of a fuzzy partition; at the rule-base level the structural indexes relate readability with the number of rules and the total rule-length (i.e. the sum of all linguistic variables used in each rule).

The indexes that try to assess the comprehensibility of a fuzzy system are far more complex. At the partition level it is worth mentioning the Context-Adaptation index [8], which is based on fuzzy ordering relations. As another example, the GM3M index [9] combines three indexes that assess how much a single fuzzy set changed after a tuning process. The Semantic Cointension index [10] belongs to the set of indexes at the rule-base level. For classification problems, this index evaluates the degree of fulfillment of a number of logical laws exhibited by a given fuzzy rule base. Finally, the CO-Firing based Comprehensibility Index [11] measures the complexity of understanding the fuzzy inference process in terms of information related to co-firing rules, i.e. rules firing simultaneously with a given input.

Even though there has been a great effort in the last years to propose new interpretability indexes, a universal index is still missing. Hence, defining such an index remains an open problem.

	Fuzzy Partition Level	Fuzzy Rule Base Level
Structural–based Interpretability	**Q1** Number of features Number of membership functions	**Q2** Number of rules Number of conditions
Semantic–based Interpretability	**Q3** Context–adaptation based index GM3M index	**Q4** Semantic–cointencion based index Co–firing based comprehensibility index

Fig. 5. Some interpretability indexes organized in a double-axis taxonomy (adapted from [7]).

5   How to Design Interpretable Fuzzy Systems?

The behavior of a fuzzy system directly depends on two aspects, the composition of the knowledge base (fuzzy partitions and fuzzy rules) and the way in which it implements the fuzzy inference process. Therefore, the design process of a fuzzy system includes two main tasks: (i) generation of the rule base, and (ii) definition of the inference engine.

As concerning the generation of the rule base, usually two objectives are addressed: accuracy and interpretability. These two objectives are conflicting, especially because of the readability facet of interpretability, which introduces a strong bias in the definition of the rule base. Accordingly, different design strategies could be devised [12]:

Linguistic Fuzzy Modeling with Improved Accuracy. A fuzzy system is firstly defined by taking into account interpretability criteria only (e.g. by defining fuzzy partitions regardless of the available data); as a successive step, its accuracy can be improved, e.g. by fine tuning the fuzzy sets in each partition. In essence, two ways of improving the accuracy in linguistic models can be considered by performing the improvement: by slightly changing the rule structure to make it more flexible, or by extending the model design to other components beyond the rule base, such as the fuzzy partitions, operators, etc. [13].

Precise Fuzzy Modeling with Improved Interpretability. This design strategy gives high priority to accuracy, ofter resulting in mostly incomprehensible fuzzy systems that need a post-processing step aimed at improving interpretability by minimizing the loss of accuracy. This fact is usually attained by merging or removing fuzzy sets in order to reduce redundancy and the presence of irrelevant information. Furthermore, an efficient way to improve the interpretability is to select a subset of significant fuzzy rules that represent in a more compactly way the behavior to be modeled. Finally, actions can be undertaken to improve interpretability of specific models, e.g. by enforcing locality of rules in Takagi-Sugeno systems [14].

Multi-objective Design. As an alternative approach, the multi-objective design takes into account both objectives simultaneously: the result is a set of fuzzy systems, characterized by different levels of accuracy and interpretability, which are proposed to the user for a final choice that depends on her needs [15]. Multi-objective design is usually carried out through evolutionary computation, according to different approaches, including fine tuning the parameters of an existing fuzzy system or generating fuzzy partitions and/or rules from scratch [16].

Ad-hoc Algorithms. Often, the interpretability/accuracy tradeoff is accomplished in a two stage approach: first, one objective is maximized (either accuracy or interpretability), then, the model is tuned so as to maximize the other objective. A different approach consists in employing ad-hoc algorithms that intrinsically embody a number of interpretability constraints in their scheme for generating fuzzy systems from data. Such algorithms are aimed at generating fuzzy systems that maximize accuracy: because of their nature, the resulting fuzzy systems are interpretable and maximally accurate (relatively to the constraints they verify). The DC* algorithm [17] is an example of ad-hoc algorithm specialized for classification problems.

As concerning the definition of the inference engine, although there are studies analyzing the behavior of the existing fuzzy operators for different purposes, unfortunately this question has not been considered yet as a whole from the interpretability point of view. Keeping in mind the interpretability requirement, the implementation of the inference engine must address a number of design choices, such as the logical operators, the implication function, the inference mechanism (First Aggregate Then Infer, or vice-versa) and the defuzzification operator, if necessary. Some preliminary studies [18] aim at relating the choice of operators with the interpretability objective; however the research in this direction is still open.

6   Real-World Applications

The usefulness of interpretable fuzzy systems is appreciable in all application areas that put humans at the center of computing. As an example, environmental issues are often challenging because of the complex dynamics, the high number of variables and the consequent uncertainty characterizing the behavior of subjects under study. Real-world environmental applications of interpretable fuzzy systems include: harmful bioaerosol detection [19]; modeling habitat suitability in river management [20]; modeling pesticide loss caused by meteorological factors in agriculture [21] and so on.

One of the most prominent application domains where interpretable fuzzy systems could be successfully used is Medicine (and health-care). In almost all medical contexts intelligent systems can be invaluable decision support tools, but people are the ultimate actors in any decision process. As a consequence, people need to rely on intelligent systems, whose reliability can be enhanced if their outcomes may be explained in terms that are comprehensible by human users. Interpretable fuzzy systems could play a key role in this area because of the concrete possibility of acquiring knowledge from data and communicating it to users. In literature several approaches have been proposed to apply interpretable fuzzy systems in different medical problems, like assisted diagnosis [22], prognosis prediction [23], patient subgroup discovery [24], etc.

Finance is a sector where human-computer cooperation is very tight. Cooperation is carried out in different ways, including the use of computers to provide business intelligence for decision support in financial operations. In many cases financial decisions are ultimately made by experts, who can benefit from automated analyses of big masses of data flowing daily in markets. To this pursuit, Computational Intelligence approaches are spreading among the tools used by financial experts in their decisions, including interpretable fuzzy systems for stock return predictions [25], exchange rate forecasting [26], portfolio risk monitoring [27], etc.

Industrial applications could take advantage from interpretable fuzzy systems when there is the need of explaining the behavior of complex systems and phenomena, like in fault detection [28]. Also, control plans for systems and processes can be designed with the aid of fuzzy rule-based systems. In such cases, a common practice is to start with an initial expert knowledge (used to design rules which are usually highly interpretable) that is then tuned to increase the accuracy of the controller. However, any unconstrained tuning could destroy the original interpretability of the knowledge base, whilst, by taking into account interpretability, the possibility of revising and modifying the controller (or the process manager) can be enhanced [29].

The advantages of interpretability in integrating expert knowledge and enabling user interaction can be appreciated in very specific sectors like robotics. As a matter of fact, the complexity of robot behavior modeling can be tackled by an integrated approach where a first modeling stage is carried out by combining human expert and empirical knowledge acquired from experimental trials. This integrated approach requires that the final knowledge base is provided to experts for further maintenance: this task could be done effectively only if the acquired knowledge is interpretable by the user. Some concrete applications of this approach can be found in robot localization systems [30] and motion analysis [31,32].

Finally, the focus of intelligent systems on social issues has noticeably increased in recent years. For reasons that are common to all the previous application areas, interpretable fuzzy systems have been applied in a wide variety of scopes, including Quality of Service improvement [33], data mining with privacy preservation [34], social network analysis [11], and so on.

7 Future Trends

The blur nature of interpretability requires continuous investigations on possible definitions that enable a computable treatment of this quality in fuzzy systems. As an example, the problem of interpretability of fuzzy systems can be intended as a particular instance of the more general problem of communication between granular worlds [35], where many aspects of interpretability could be treated in a more abstract way.

On a more concrete scale, a prominent objective is the adoption of a common framework for characterizing and assessing interpretability, where novel metrics could be devised (especially for assessing subjective aspects of interpretability) and integrated with objective interpretability measures to define more significant interpretability indexes.

Interpretability assessment is tightly related to designing interpretable fuzzy systems. A current research trend in designing interpretable fuzzy models makes use of multi-objective genetic algorithms in order to deal with the conflicting design objectives of accuracy and interpretability. The effectiveness and usefulness of these approaches require a verification process, especially for highly dimensional problems. In this case the combination of linguistic and graphical approaches could be a promising approach for descriptive and exploratory analysis of interpretable fuzzy systems [36].

Finally, the use of novel forms of representation may help in representing very complex relationships in comprehensible ways, thus yielding a valid aid in designing interpretable fuzzy systems. A multi-level representation could enhance the interpretability of fuzzy systems by providing different granularity levels for knowledge representation, whereas the highest granulation levels give a coarse —yet immediately comprehensible— description of knowledge, while lower levels provide for more detailed knowledge. Besides representation levels, other forms of representation, different from the classical rule-based, may be of help in representing complex relationship in comprehensible ways.

8 Conclusions

Interpretability is a very complex requirement for designing fuzzy systems, yet it is fundamental if such systems have to be accessible to users that use computers as tools for decision making, strategy planning, etc. The very essence of this paper is to arise questions and give some tentative answers to the issue of interpretability. In particular, the paper aims at viewing interpretability also from the semantic viewpoint, which departs from the commonplace belief that often confuses interpretability with structural simplicity. Based on this different viewpoint, new forms of quantification, assessment and design of interpretable fuzzy systems are topics of current scientific investigation.

As a final remark, it is worth observing that interpretability is one aspect of the multi-faceted problem of *human-centered* design of fuzzy systems [37]. Other facets include acceptability (e.g., according to ethical rules), interestingness of fuzzy rules, applicability (e.g., with respect to Law), etc. Many of them are not yet in the research mainstream but they clearly represent promising future trends.

Acknowledgements. The author is grateful to Dr. José M. Alonso and Dr. Ciro Castiello for their support in relation to the work presented in the paper.

References

1. Zadeh, L.A.: Is there a need for fuzzy logic? Information Sciences 178(13), 2751–2779 (2008)
2. Michalski, R.S.: A theory and methodology of inductive learning. Artificial Intelligence 20, 111–161 (1983)
3. Miller, G.A.: The Magical Number Seven, Plus or Minus Two: Some Limits on Our Capacity for Processing Information. The Psychological Review 63, 81–97 (1956)
4. Mencar, C., Fanelli, A.M.: Interpretability constraints for fuzzy information granulation. Information Sciences 178(24), 4585–4618 (2008)
5. Zhou, S., Gan, J.: Low-level interpretability and high-level interpretability: A unified view of data-driven interpretable fuzzy system modelling. Fuzzy Sets and Systems 159(23), 3091–3131 (2008)
6. Alonso, J.M., Magdalena, L., González-Rodríguez, G.: Looking for a good fuzzy system interpretability index: An experimental approach. International Journal of Approximate Reasoning 51(1), 115–134 (2009)
7. Gacto, M.J., Alcalá, R., Herrera, F.: Interpretability of linguistic fuzzy rule-based systems: An overview of interpretability measures. Information Sciences 181(20), 4340–4360 (2011)

8. Botta, A., Lazzerini, B., Marcelloni, F., Stefanescu, D.C.: Context adaptation of fuzzy systems through a multi-objective evolutionary approach based on a novel interpretability index. Soft Computing 13(5), 437–449 (2009)
9. Gacto, M.J., Alcalá, R., Herrera, F.: Integration of an index to preserve the semantic interpretability in the multiobjective evolutionary rule selection and tuning of linguistic fuzzy systems. IEEE Transactions on Fuzzy Systems 18(3), 515–531 (2010)
10. Mencar, C., Castiello, C., Cannone, R., Fanelli, A.M.: Interpretability assessment of fuzzy knowledge bases: A cointension based approach. International Journal of Approximate Reasoning 52(4), 501–518 (2011)
11. Alonso, J.M., Pancho, D.P., Cordón, O., Quirin, A., Magdalena, L.: Social network analysis of co-fired fuzzy rules. In: Yager, R.R., Abbasov, A.M., Reformat, M., Shahbazova, S.N. (eds.) Soft Computing: State of the Art Theory. STUDFUZZ, vol. 291, pp. 113–128. Springer, Heidelberg (2013)
12. Casillas, J., Cordón, O., Herrera, F., Magdalena, L.: Interpretability issues in fuzzy modeling. STUDFUZZ, vol. 128. Springer, Heidelberg (2003)
13. Casillas, J., Cordón, O., Herrera, F., Magdalena, L.: Accuracy improvements in linguistic fuzzy modeling. STUDFUZZ, vol. 129. Springer, Heidelberg (2003)
14. Riid, A., Rüstern, E.: Identification of transparent, compact, accurate and reliable linguistic fuzzy models. Information Sciences 181(20), 4378–4393 (2011)
15. Fazzolari, M., Alcalá, R., Nojima, Y., Ishibuchi, H., Herrera, F.: A review of the application of multi-objective evolutionary fuzzy systems: Current status and further directions. IEEE Transactions on Fuzzy Systems 21(1), 45–65 (2013)
16. Ducange, P., Marcelloni, F.: Multi-objective evolutionary fuzzy systems. In: Fanelli, A.M., Pedrycz, W., Petrosino, A. (eds.) WILF 2011. LNCS (LNAI), vol. 6857, pp. 83–90. Springer, Heidelberg (2011)
17. Lucarelli, M., Castiello, C., Fanelli, A.M., Mencar, C.: Automatic Design of Interpretable Fuzzy Partitions with Variable Granularity: An Experimental Comparison. In: Rutkowski, L., Korytkowski, M., Scherer, R., Tadeusiewicz, R., Zadeh, L.A., Zurada, J.M. (eds.) ICAISC 2013, Part I. LNCS, vol. 7894, pp. 318–328. Springer, Heidelberg (2013)
18. Cannone, R., Castiello, C., Mencar, C., Fanelli, A.M.: A Study on Interpretability Conditions for Fuzzy Rule-Based Classifiers. In: IEEE Ninth International Conference on Intelligent Systems Design and Applications, ISDA 2009, Pisa, Italy, pp. 438–443 (November 2009)
19. Pulkkinen, P., Hytonen, J., Koivisto, H.: Developing a bioaerosol detector using hybrid genetic fuzzy systems. Engineering Applications of Artificial Intelligence 21(8), 1330–1346 (2008)
20. Vanbroekhoven, E., Adriaenssens, V., Debaets, B.: Interpretability-preserving genetic optimization of linguistic terms in fuzzy models for fuzzy ordered classification: An ecological case study. International Journal of Approximate Reasoning 44(1), 65–90 (2007)
21. Guillaume, S., Charnomordic, B.: Interpretable fuzzy inference systems for cooperation of expert knowledge and data in agricultural applications using FisPro. In: IEEE International Conference on Fuzzy Systems, pp. 2019–2026 (2010)
22. Gadaras, I., Mikhailov, L.: An interpretable fuzzy rule-based classification methodology for medical diagnosis. Artificial Intelligence in Medicine 47(1), 25–41 (2009)
23. Alonso, J.M., Castiello, C., Lucarelli, M., Mencar, C.: Modelling interpretable fuzzy rule-based classifiers for medical decision support. In: Magdalena, R., Soria, E., Guerrero, J., Gómez-Sanchis, J., Serrano, A. (eds.) Medical Applications of Intelligent Data Analysis: Research Advancements, pp. 254–271. IGI Global (2012)
24. Carmona, C.J., Gonzalez, P., del Jesus, M.J., Navio-Acosta, M., Jimenez-Trevino, L.: Evolutionary fuzzy rule extraction for subgroup discovery in a psychiatric emergency department. Soft Computing 15(12), 2435–2448 (2011)

25. Kumar, A.: Interpretability and mean-square error performance of fuzzy inference systems for data mining. Intelligent Systems in Accounting, Finance and Management 13(4), 185–196 (2005)
26. Cheong, F.: A hierarchical fuzzy system with high input dimensions for forecasting foreign exchange rates. International Journal of Artificial Intelligence and Soft Computing 1(1), 15 (2008)
27. Ghandar, A., Michalewicz, Z., Zurbruegg, R.: Enhancing profitability through interpretability in algorithmic trading with a multiobjective evolutionary fuzzy system. In: Coello, C.A.C., Cutello, V., Deb, K., Forrest, S., Nicosia, G., Pavone, M. (eds.) PPSN 2012, Part II. LNCS, vol. 7492, pp. 42–51. Springer, Heidelberg (2012)
28. Altug, S., Chow, M.Y., Trussell, H.J.: Heuristic constraints enforcement for training of and rule extraction from a fuzzy/neural architecture. II. Implementation and application. IEEE Transactions on Fuzzy Systems 7(2), 151–159 (1999)
29. Riid, A., Rustern, E.: Interpretability of fuzzy systems and its application to process control. In: IEEE International Conference on Fuzzy Systems, pp. 1–6 (2007)
30. Alonso, J.M., Ocaña, M., Hernandez, N., Herranz, F., Llamazares, A., Sotelo, M.A., Bergasa, L.M., Magdalena, L.: Enhanced WiFi localization system based on Soft Computing techniques to deal with small-scale variations in wireless sensors. Applied Soft Computing 11(8), 4677–4691 (2011)
31. Alonso, J.M., Magdalena, L., Guillaume, S., Sotelo, M.A., Bergasa, L.M., Ocaña, M., Flores, R.: Knowledge-based intelligent diagnosis of ground robot collision with non detectable obstacles. Journal of Intelligent and Robotic Systems 48(4), 539–566 (2007)
32. Mucientes, M., Casillas, J.: Quick design of fuzzy controllers with good interpretability in mobile robotics. IEEE Transactions on Fuzzy Systems 15(4), 636–651 (2007)
33. Barrientos, F., Sainz, G.: Interpretable knowledge extraction from emergency call data based on fuzzy unsupervised decision tree. Knowledge-Based Systems 25(1), 77–87 (2011)
34. Troiano, L., Rodríguez-Muñiz, L.J., Ranilla, J., Díaz, I.: Interpretability of fuzzy association rules as means of discovering threats to privacy. International Journal of Computer Mathematics 89(3), 325–333 (2012)
35. Bargiela, A., Pedrycz, W.: Granular computing: an introduction. Kluwer Academic Publishers, Boston (2003)
36. Alonso, J., Cordon, O., Quirin, A., Magdalena, L.: Analyzing interpretability of fuzzy rule-based systems by means of fuzzy inference-grams. In: 1st World Conference on Soft Computing, San Francisco, CA, USA, pp. 181.1–181.8 (2011)
37. Bargiela, A., Pedrycz, W.: Human-Centric Information Processing Through Granular Modelling. Springer Publishing Company, Incorporated (2009)

Feature Selection Based on Fuzzy Mutual Information

Michela Antonelli, Pietro Ducange, and Francesco Marcelloni

Dipartimento di Ingegneria dell'Informazione, University of Pisa
Pisa, Italy

Abstract. In the framework of fuzzy rule-based models for regression problems, we propose a novel approach to feature selection based on the minimal-redundancy-maximal-relevance criterion. The relevance of a feature is measured in terms of a novel definition of fuzzy mutual information between the feature and the output variable. The redundancy is computed as the average fuzzy mutual information between the feature and the just selected features. The approach results to be particularly suitable for selecting features before designing fuzzy rule-based systems (FRBSs). We tested our approach on twelve regression problems using Mamdani FRBSs built by applying the Wang and Mendel algorithm. We show that our approach is particularly effective in selecting features by comparing the mean square errors achieved by the Mamdani FRBSs generated using the features selected by a state of the art feature selection algorithm and by our approach.

Keywords: Feature Selection, Fuzzy Mutual Information, Regression Problems, High Dimensional Datasets.

1 Introduction

Nowadays, several real-world applications require to identify regression models from input-output instances generally described by a large number of features. Often, some of these features are irrelevant or redundant, thus making the most popular learning algorithms inefficient and inaccurate. Thus, a lot of research activity has been devoted to design techniques for reducing dimensionality.

In the literature, dimensionality reduction is usually performed by feature selection. In general, feature selection algorithms are characterized by a search strategy that finds the optimal subset of features and by an evaluation criterion that assesses the relevance of each feature. Sequential search algorithms are among the most popular heuristic search strategies: they add (forward sequential selection (FSS)) or subtract (backward sequential selection (BSS)) features at each iteration in order to find the optimal subset [9]. As regards the evaluation criterion, several measures have been proposed: they can be grouped into distance, information and dependency measures [3]. *Mutual Information* (MI) is an information measure that quantifies the dependence of two variables: the value of MI is equal to zero for independent variables and increases with the increase

F. Masulli, G. Pasi, and R. Yager (Eds.): WILF 2013, LNAI 8256, pp. 36–43, 2013.

of the dependence between the variables. MI has been extensively used as evaluation measure for feature selection in classification problems [7]. In [2] MI is used to measure both the relevance and the redundancy of a feature in the framework of the minimal-redundancy-maximal-relevance criterion (mRMR) adopted in the feature selection process. In particular, the relevance is measured as the MI between the feature and the target class, and the redundancy is computed as the average MI between the feature and the just selected features.

There are a few approaches that use the MI for feature selection in regression problems. In [8] the authors study the behavior of MI as a relevance measure on several regression problems. In [11] MI is used for selecting relevant spectral variables in an FSS algorithm. To the best of our knowledge, no approach to feature selection based on MI has been proposed when the regression problems are tackled by fuzzy rule-based models. In this context, we propose a new filter approach for feature selection which extends to the fuzzy case the mRMR criterion proposed in [4]. In particular, we introduce a definition of fuzzy MI between linguistic variables based on the fuzzy entropy proposed in [10]. This definition differs from the MI between a random variable and a fuzzy random variable proposed in [12] for classification problems. Indeed, we compute the fuzzy MI between two fuzzy variables rather than between a crisp and a fuzzy variable.

In order to evaluate the effectiveness of the proposed feature selection approach, we use as comparative approach a similar method that uses a measure of crisp correlation as evaluation criteria, namely the Correlation Feature Selection algorithm (CFS) [6]. The subsets of features selected by the two algorithms are evaluated by applying the Wang and Mendel (WM) algorithm [14] to the dataset characterized by the selected features (we recall that this algorithm generates an FRBS from numerical data) and comparing the accuracies achieved by the two generated FRBSs. Using twelve high dimensional regression datasets, we show that our method selects features that produce FRBSs more accurate than the ones generated with the subset of features selected by CFS. We statistically validate this result applying the Wilcoxon signed-rank test.

2 Fuzzy Mutual Information

Let $\mathbf{X} = \{X_1, \ldots, X_f, \ldots, X_F\}$ be the set of input variables, X_{F+1} be the output variable and $P_f = \{A_{f,1}, \ldots, A_{f,T_f}\}$ be a strong fuzzy partition of T_f fuzzy sets defined on variable X_f.

The mutual information between two variables S and T, is defined as [2]:

$$MI(S,T) = H(S) + H(T) - H(S,T) \tag{1}$$

where $H(S)$ and $H(T)$ are the entropy of the variables S and T, respectively, and $H(S,T)$ is the joint entropy of S and T.

Similar to (1), we define the *Fuzzy Mutual Information* (FMI) of two fuzzy variables X_s and X_t as:

$$FMI(X_s, X_t) = H(X_s) + H(X_t) - H(X_s, X_t) \tag{2}$$

Let us assume that P_s and P_t are strong fuzzy partitions consisting of T_s and T_t fuzzy sets, respectively, defined on X_s and X_t. Then, the fuzzy entropy $H(X_s)$ of the variable X_s can be computed as [10]:

$$H(X_s) = -\sum_{i=1}^{T_s} P(A_{s,i}) \cdot \log P(A_{s,i}) \tag{3}$$

where $P(A_{s,i})$ is the probability of the fuzzy set $A_{s,i}$ and is defined for a distribution $\{x_1, \ldots, x_N\}$ with respect to a probability distribution $P = \{p_1, \ldots, p_N\}$ as $P(A_{s,i}) = \sum_{i=1}^{N} \mu_{A_{s,i}}(x_i) \cdot p_i$ where $\mu_{A_{s,i}}(x_i)$ is the membership degree of x_i to the fuzzy set $A_{s,i}$.

Similarly, the fuzzy joint entropy $H(X_t, X_s)$ can be computed as:

$$H(X_t, X_s) = -\left(\sum_{i=1}^{T_t} \sum_{j=1}^{T_s} P(A_{t,i}, A_{s,j}) \cdot \log P(A_{t,i}, A_{s,j})\right) \tag{4}$$

The joint probability $P(A_{t,i}, A_{s,j})$ is computed as in [5]:

$$P(A_{t,i}, A_{s,j}) = \sum_{k=1}^{N_1} \sum_{h=1}^{N_2} \mu_{A_{t,i} \cap A_{s,j}}(x_{k,t}, x_{h,s}) \cdot p(x_{k,t}, x_{h,s}) \tag{5}$$

where N_1 and N_2 are the numbers of different values for the variables X_s and X_t in the dataset, respectively, and $\mu_{A_{t,i} \cap A_{s,j}} = \mu_{A_{t,i}}(x_{k,t}) \cdot \mu_{A_{s,j}}(x_{h,s})$.

3   The Fuzzy Mutual Information Feature Selection Algorithm

Our feature selection method is based on an FSS scheme: starting from the empty feature subset $G = \{\varnothing\}$, it sequentially adds to G the feature that maximizes the evaluation criterion when combined with the features that have already been selected and therefore included in G. As regards the evaluation process, we asses each feature on the basis of the mRMR criterion. This criterion measures the relevance of a feature X_i by considering the FMI between X_i and the output variable X_{F+1}, and its redundancy by considering the FMI between X_i and the subset of previously selected features. Actually, in order to avoid bias toward multivalued features, in [4] the Normalized Mutual Information (NMI) is used in place of MI. The NMI between two variables S and T is defined as the MI between S and T normalized by the lowest value of the entropies of S and T.

We extend this concept to two fuzzy variables by defining the Normalized Fuzzy Mutual Information (NFMI) as:

$$NFMI(X_s, X_t) = \frac{FMI(X_s, X_t)}{\min\{H(X_s), H(X_t)\}} \tag{6}$$

Accordingly, the relevance of the feature X_i to be added to the subset $G = \{X_g\}$, $g = 1, \ldots, |G|$, of selected features is evaluated by $NFMI(X_i, X_{F+1})$ and its redundancy is computed as the average value of $NFMI(X_i, X_g)$, computed for all $X_g \in G$. The evaluation function used at each iteration is a fuzzy extension of the index proposed in [4]. We denote this index as Fuzzy Index (FI) and define FI as:

$$FI(X_i) = NFMI(X_i, X_{F+1}) - \frac{1}{|G|} \sum_{X_j \in G} NFMI(X_i, X_j) \qquad (7)$$

The minuend in (7) measures the relevance of the feature X_i in terms of NFMI between the feature and the output variable, while the subtrahend assesses the amount of redundancy between the feature X_i and the just selected features contained in subset $G = \{X_g\}$, $g = 1, \ldots, |G|$. At each iteration, the feature with the highest value of FI is selected and added to subset G.

The complete fuzzy mutual information feature selection (FMIFS) algorithm can be summarized as follows:

1. Let X and G be the set $X = \{X_1, \ldots, X_f, \ldots, X_F\}$ containing all the features and the subset $G = \{\varnothing\}$ of selected features;
2. For each feature $X_i \in X$, $i = \{1, \ldots, F\}$, compute $NFMI(X_i, X_{F+1})$;
3. Select the feature $\hat{X}_i$ that maximizes $NFMI(X_i, X_{F+1})$;
4. Remove $\hat{X}_i$ from the set X and add $\hat{X}_i$ to the set G;
5. Repeat until stopping condition is false
   (a) For each $X_i \in X$ calculate $FI(X_i)$
   (b) Select the feature $\hat{X}_i$ that maximizes the index FI
   (c) Remove $\hat{X}_i$ from the set X and add $\hat{X}_i$ to the set G;

In our experiments we choose as stopping criterion the cardinality of the subset G: we fix the desired number NF of features and stop the feature selection algorithm when the cardinality $|G|$ of the subset G is equal to NF.

4   Experimental Results

We tested our feature selection algorithm on twelve high dimensional regression datasets extracted from three repositories, namely the KEEL repository, the UCI Machine Learning Repository and the Torgo's repository. The first column of Table 1 shows the name of each dataset, the number of instances (NI) and the overall number of features (F).

In order to evaluate the effectiveness of the feature selection algorithm, we generate an FRBS from the data characterized only by the selected features. The FRBS generation can be performed by using several different approaches. For the sake of simplicity, in this paper we adopted the well-known WM algorithm [14]. We are conscious that this heuristic approach does not guarantee high accuracies. However, the aim of using the WM algorithm is to compare different filter feature selection approaches and not to achieve the highest values of accuracy. To compare different feature selection algorithms we generate the FRBSs by applying the WM algorithm to the dataset characterized by the selected features and then we compute the accuracy in terms of mean square error

(MSE) as $MSE = \frac{1}{2 \cdot |N|} \sum_{l=1}^{|N|} (F(x^l) - y^l)^2$ where $|N|$ is the size of the dataset, $F(x^l)$ is the output obtained from the MFRBS when the lth input pattern is considered, and y^l is the desired output.

We compare the results obtained by our algorithm with a similar approach, namely the CFS algorithm [6]. CFS uses an FSS scheme to generate the candidate feature subsets, and ranks these subsets by considering the correlation between each feature and the output variable, along with the degree of redundancy between them. At each iteration, each feature that has not been already included in the current subset is tentatively added to it and the resulting set of features is evaluated, thus producing a numeric measure. The feature that allows obtaining the highest value of this measure is selected. If no improvement is produced by adding the feature to the current subset, the FSS process ends and the current subset of features is provided.

The objective of our experiment is twofold. First we aim to show how the MSE varies with the increase of the number of features selected by both FMIFS and CFS. Second, we aim to prove the effectiveness of introducing fuzziness in the concept of mutual information. We carried out a 5-fold cross validation. In Figure 1, due to space limits, for only four datasets, we show the average MSEs (y axis) calculated on both the training set and the test set for the two feature selection algorithms, against the number NF (x axis) of selected features. As regards FMIFS, we consider NF ranging from 1 to the total number of features (we recall that FMIFS stops when a pre-fixed number of selected features is achieved). Since CFS stops if no feature produces an improvement when it is added to the current subset, NF ranges from 1 to the number of features computed by CFS. From the figure, we can observe that for most of the datasets, at the same number NF of features, FMIFS finds subsets of features that produce FRBSs with a lower MSE than the ones produced using the subsets found by CFS on both the training and test sets. In order to compare the numerical results of CFS and FMIFS, since the stopping criteria of the two methods are different, for each dataset we fix the value of NF in FMIFS as the value of the number of features found by CFS on the corresponding fold. In this way we can compare the MSEs of FRBSs built using subsets of features of the same cardinality. In Table 1 we show the mean values of the MSEs obtained on both the training and test sets and the number NF of features found by CFS. From this table, we can derive that the subsets of features generated by FMIFS produce FRBSs more accurate than the ones generated with the subsets produced by CFS.

To statistically verify this observation, we apply the Wilcoxon signed-rank test, a non-parametric statistical test that detects significant differences between two sample means [13]. Since this test is based on the ranking of the differences of two sample means, in order to make this difference comparable, in regression problems where the MSEs can be characterized by a different order of magnitude, we adopt a normalized difference $DIFF = \frac{MSE_{CFS} - MSE_{FMIFS}}{MSE_{CFS}}$ [1].

Table 2 shows the results of the Wilcoxon test on both the training and the test sets. In both cases, since the p-value is lower than the level of significance $\alpha = 0.05$, the null hypothesis is rejected, thus testifying that the two distributions

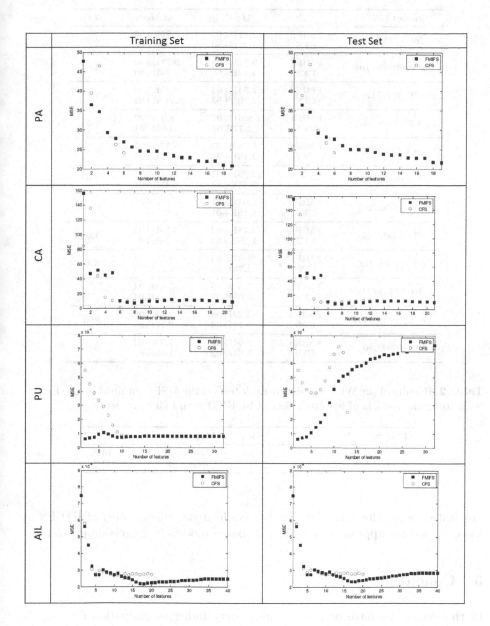

Fig. 1. *MSEs* versus the number *NF* of selected features

Table 1. MSEs obtained on the training and test sets by the FRBSs built using the subsets of features selected by FMIFS and CFS, respectively

Dataset (NI/F)		MSE_{TR}	MSE_{TS}	NF
WI (1461/9)	FMIFS	2.81E+00	2.89E+00	3.0
	CFS	3.27E+00	3.36E+00	
MV (40768/10)	FMIFS	3.71E+00	3.71E+00	4.0
	CFS	4.13E+00	4.13E+00	
FO (517/12)	FMIFS	1.54E+03	3.00E+03	4.8
	CFS	2.60E+03	2.80E+03	
TR (1049/15)	FMIFS	8.61E-02	8.95E-02	2.0
	CFS	2.77E-01	2.88E-01	
BA (337/16)	FMIFS	1.78E+05	3.13E+05	6.8
	CFS	2.14E+05	3.53E+05	
PA (5875/19)	FMIFS	2.69E+01	2.77E+01	6.0
	CFS	2.41E+01	2.43E+01	
CA (8192/21)	FMIFS	1.07E+01	1.10E+01	11.8
	CFS	1.18E+01	1.21E+01	
PT (14998/26)	FMIFS	3.78E+02	3.79E+02	4.0
	CFS	1.28E+03	1.28E+03	
BK (8192/32)	FMIFS	3.67E-03	4.98E-03	6.4
	CFS	3.75E-03	4.93E-03	
PU (8192/32)	FMIFS	7.55E-05	5.09E-04	11.8
	CFS	7.93E-05	6.76E-04	
AIL (13750/40)	FMIFS	2.22E-08	2.40E-08	20.0
	CFS	2.71E-08	2.77E-08	
CR (1994/101)	FMIFS	8.01E-03	1.23E-02	9.8
	CFS	7.61E-03	1.15E-02	

Table 2. Results of the Wilcoxon signed-rank test on the MSEs obtained by the FRBSs built using the subsets of features selected by FMIFS and CFS, respectively

FMIFS vs CFS	R+	R-	**Hypotesis**	p-value
Training Set	70	8	Rejected	0.013
Test Set	66	12	Rejected	0.033

are statistically different. These results confirm the effectiveness of FMIFS as feature selection approach for fuzzy rule-based models in regression problems.

5   Conclusion

In this paper, we have proposed a new fuzzy index as evaluation function in the process of feature selection for high dimensional regression problems tackled by fuzzy rule-based models. The proposed index is based on the minimal-redundancy-maximal-relevance criterion. Further, we have used a forward sequential selection scheme to perform the feature selection. To evaluate the effectiveness of the proposed method, we have adopted a heuristic approach, namely the Wang and Mendel algorithm, to generate FRBSs from the data described by the selected features. Then, we have computed the mean square error obtained by the FRBSs. We have adopted twelve regression datasets. We have compared the accuracies obtained by the FRBSs generated by using the features selected by both our approach and a similar forward feature selection method, namely CFS. The results show that for most of the datasets our method finds subsets of features that produce FRBSs with a lower MSE than the ones produced by the subsets selected by CFS on both the training and test sets. We have statistically validated this statement by applying the Wilcoxon signed-rank test to the distribution of the MSEs: the null hypothesis is rejected with a level of significance $\alpha = 0.05$, thus confirming that on average our method outperforms CFS.

References

1. Alcala, R., Ducange, P., Herrera, F., Lazzerini, B., Marcelloni, F.: A multiobjective evolutionary approach to concurrently learn rule and data bases of linguistic fuzzy-rule-based systems. IEEE Transactions on Fuzzy Systems 17(5), 1106–1122 (2009)
2. Battiti, R.: Using mutual information for selecting features in supervised neural net learning. IEEE Transactions on Neural Networks 5, 537–550 (1994)
3. Dash, M., Liu, H.: Feature selection for classification. Intelligent Data Analysis 1, 131–156 (1997)
4. Estévez, P., Tesmer, M., Perez, C., Zurada, J.: Normalized mutual information feature selection. IEEE Transaction on Neural Networks 20(2), 189–201 (2009)
5. Gerontidis, I., Petasakis, I.E.: Lumpability of absorbing markov chains and replacement chains on fuzzy partitions. In: FUZZ-IEEE, pp. 1–8 (2010)
6. Hall, M.A., Smith, L.A.: Practical Feature Subset Selection for Machine Learning (1998)
7. Huawen, L., Jigui, S., Lei, L., Huijie, Z.: Feature selection with dynamic mutual information. Pattern Recogn. 42(7), 1330–1339 (2009)
8. Kojadinovic, I.: Relevance measures for subset variable selection in regression problems based on k-additive mutual information. Comput. Stat. Data Anal. 49(4), 1205–1227 (2005)
9. Kudo, M., Sklansky, J.: Comparison of algorithms that select features for pattern classifiers. Pattern Recognition 33(1), 25–41 (2000)
10. Kuriyama, K.: Entropy of a finite partition of fuzzy sets. Journal of Mathematical Analysis and Applications 94, 38–43 (1983)
11. Rossi, F., Lendasse, A., François, D., Wertz, V., Verleysen, M.: Mutual information for the selection of relevant variables in spectrometric nonlinear modelling. Chemometrics and Intelligent Laboratory Systems 80(2), 215–226 (2006)
12. Sánchez, L., Suárez, M.R., Villar, J.R., Couso, I.: Mutual information-based feature selection and partition design in fuzzy rule-based classifiers from vague data. Int. J. Approx. Reasoning 49(3), 607–622 (2008)
13. Sheskin, D.J.: Handbook of Parametric and Nonparametric Statistical Procedures, 4th edn. Chapman & Hall/CRC (2007)
14. Wang, L., Mendel, J.: Generating fuzzy rules by learning from examples. IEEE Transactions on Systems Man and Cybernetics 22(6), 1414–1427 (1992)

A New Heuristic Function for DC*

Marco Lucarelli, Corrado Mencar, Ciro Castiello, and Anna Maria Fanelli

Department of Informatics, University of Bari "A. Moro", Bari, Italy

Abstract. DC* (Double Clustering with A*) is an algorithm capable of generating highly interpretable fuzzy information granules from pre-classified data. These information granules can be used as bulding-blocks for fuzzy rule-based classifiers that exhibit a good tradeoff between interpretability and accuracy. DC* relies on A* for the granulation process, whose efficiency is tightly related to the heuristic function used for estimating the costs of candidate solutions. In this paper we propose a new heuristic function that is capable of exploiting class information to overcome the heuristic function originally used in DC* in terms of efficiency. The experimental results show that the proposed heuristic function allows huge savings in terms of computational effort, thus making DC* a competitive choice for designing interpretable fuzzy rule-based classifiers.

1 Introduction

Several real world problems require more than just accurate solutions. In many cases, users (physicians, managers, etc.) have to be convinced about the reliability of the knowledge base, and hence they may be interested in systems capable to offer good support in terms of both accuracy and comprehensibility of the knowledge base. When intelligent systems are used to acquire knowledge from data, a methodology is required to derive interpretable knowledge that final users can easily understand. To this aim, the Theory of Fuzzy Information Granulation provides ways for summarizing data into Fuzzy Information Granules (FIGs), which are the building blocks of interpretable knowledge bases [1]. The interpretability requirement is (partially) achieved by fulfilling a number of constraints in the granulation process [2].

To achieve interpretable granulation, some algorithms have been proposed, like HFP [3], fuzzy decision trees [4], or more complex methodologies, such as HILK++ [5] and complete systems like FISPRO [6] and GUAJE [7]. In this scenario we proposed the DC* (Double Clustering with A*) algorithm [8,9], derived from the more general Double Clustering Framework DCf [10]. DC* generates an interpretable Fuzzy Rule Base (FRB) based on FIGs, from a dataset of numerical pre-classified data. In particular, DC* identifies the minimal number of information granules in the problem space and exploits them to build the final FRB. The granularity level, i.e. the maximum number of FIGs, is set by the user.

DC* is based on A*, a search algorithm which has exponential complexity in the worst case. Furthermore, its efficiency heavily relies on the heuristic function involved in the search process. In this paper we improve the original version of

F. Masulli, G. Pasi, and R. Yager (Eds.): WILF 2013, LNAI 8256, pp. 44–51, 2013.
© Springer International Publishing Switzerland 2013

DC* with a new heuristic function, which exploits class information to accelerate the search process. As shown by the experimental results, the new proposed heuristic function highly improves the efficiency of DC* without compromising the quality of the derived solutions. In section 2 an overview of DC* is provided. Section 3 is dedicated to the heuristic functions: the original heuristic is overviewed (3.1) and the new heuristic is presented in more details (3.2). Comparative experimental results are discussed in section 4. Finally, section 5 draws some conclusive remarks.

2   The Double Clustering with A* (DC*)

DC* is an instance of the Double Clustering Framework [10]. Given a multidimensional numerical dataset of pre-classified data, the aim of DC* is to automatically generate an interpretable FRB that describes data through linguistic terms. As implied by the name, DC* is mainly composed by two clustering steps: the clustering on multi-dimensional data and the clustering over each input feature. Those two steps define an optimal partition of the feature space in terms of the number of information granules. A final step of fuzzy granulation, based on Strong Fuzzy Partitions (SFPs), transforms the resulting input space partition into a FRB that fulfills a number of general-purpose interpretability constraints, such as: normality, convexity, continuity, distinguishability, completeness, leftmost/rightmost fuzzy sets [2].

The first step of DC* is aimed at data compression, which is performed by the class-aware quantization algorithm LVQ1 [11]. Given a (user-defined) number of prototypes, LVQ1 moves the prototypes into the feature space with an iterative process, aiming at best representing the dataset class distribution.

The second step of DC* performs the clustering over each input feature (one-dimensional clustering). Firstly, the prototypes are projected over each feature carrying class information. The concept of *cut* must be introduced to understand the working mechanism of DC*. A *cut* is the boundary of an information granule, defined on an input feature; in practice, a cut is defined by the midpoint between two prototype projections belonging to different classes. All the identifiable cuts over the problem space are named *candidate cuts*. The objective of the one-dimensional clustering is to select a subset of cuts that is optimal. In order to define optimality, the concept of *hyper-box* (HB) must be introduced. Given the feature space and a subset of cuts, a HB is a subspace of the feature space delimited by cuts. A HB can include zero or more multi-dimensional prototypes: a HB is said *pure* if it is empty or all its prototypes belong to the same class; otherwise it is said *impure* (fig. 1). A pure and non-empty HB is a "surrogate" for an information granule. Since the prototypes contained in a HB are surrounded by data samples, then most of these samples are also contained in the HB.

The main objective of the second step of DC* is therefore to find a minimal subset of cuts producing pure HBs. It is worth to mention that this process takes into account both the prototype class information and all the input features simultaneously. This clustering problem has exponential complexity. To tackle

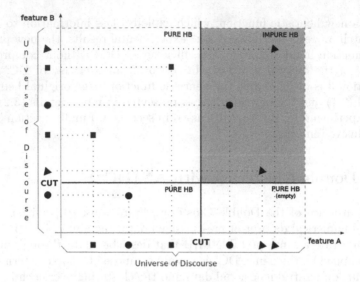

Fig. 1. A bi-dimensional input space with six prototypes of three different classes (square, circle, triangle). The prototype projections labeled with class information are also shown. The application of two cuts (chosen among all the possible candidate cuts) provides a partition of the feature space in four HBs: three pure HBs (one of them is empty) and one impure HB.

the problem, DC* exploits a strategy based on the A* search algorithm, which operates an informed search on the solution space defined by the set of all possible clustering configurations, i.e. all the possible subsets of cuts from the candidate cuts. A specific design of the components of A* is required, namely the goal test, the successor operator, the cost function (including the heuristic function) and the priority queue. In this paper we focus on the heuristic function; for further details on the other components, the reader is referred to [9,12].

The last DC* step is the fuzzy granulation of the input features exploiting the optimal partition derived by A*. The cuts included in the optimal partition are used to define SFPs (the process is described in detail in [13]), and each fuzzy set is labeled with a linguistic term (fig. 2).

Each non-empty HB (in a solution they are all pure) corresponds to a fuzzy information granule defined as the Cartesian product of one-dimensional fuzzy sets included in the SFPs. These fuzzy information granules can be used to define fuzzy classification rules that are collected in a highly interpretable FRB.

3   Heuristic Functions

In this section the heuristic function used in the original version of DC* and the proposed heuristic function are presented in detail. In general, a heuristic function is an estimation of the distance from a state to the closest goal state. In

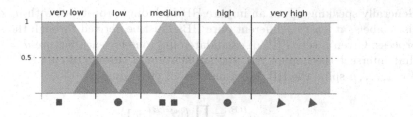

Fig. 2. Example of fuzzy partition of an input feature obtained from four cuts

order to be used in A*, a heuristic function has to be admissible or optimistic, i.e. it never overestimates the cost to reach a goal state from a current state. The admissibility property ensures that A* will reach the goal state visiting fewer states than other search algorithms. This must hold in DC* where, in particular, states correspond to subsets of candidate cuts and the heuristic value is an optimistic estimation of the number of cuts to be added to a state in order to reach a goal state, i.e. a subset of cuts that generates pure HBs only. The heuristic function contributes to the cost function, which is defined as the sum of the number of cuts in a state and the heuristic value, and deeply influences the order in which A* explores states in the solution space.

3.1 Original Heuristic Function

This section describes the heuristic function used in the original version of DC*. We first note that each HB in a state is identified as a Cartesian product of intervals, being each interval delimited by two cuts. Given two (impure) HBs, they are *connected* if they share the same interval on at least one feature. This implies that at least a single cut is necessary to split the two connected HBs into pure HBs. All impure HBs are collected and grouped by connections. It is worth to notice that a HB can belong to more than one set. The algorithm for computing the heuristic value selects the largest set of connected HBs, increases the heuristic value by 1 (the needed cut) and then removes the HBs from all the sets. This process is repeated until there are no more impure HBs to be processed. At the end of this iterative process the value of the heuristic function is provided. It corresponds to the *minimal* estimation of the number of cuts needed to move from a state to a goal state.

3.2 The New Heuristic Function

In this section the new proposed heuristic function is presented. The main idea is to exploit prototype class information included in an *impure* HB to optimistically estimate the minimum number of cuts needed to separate prototypes of different classes. By definition, in an impure HB there are at least two prototypes with two *different* class labels. It means that there is the need of at least one cut to split the impure HB into two new *pure* HBs (i.e. one HB for each class label).

Generally speaking, given an impure HB including prototypes with n_c different class labels, at least n_c different pure HBs must be derived through the splitting process. Given n sets T_d^{HB} of candidate cuts (one for each feature $d = 1, \ldots, n$) that intersect the impure HB, the application of subsets of cuts $S_d^{HB} \subseteq T_d^{HB}$, $d = 1, \ldots, n$ splits the HB into a number of HBs equal to:

$$n^{HB} = \prod_{d=1}^{n} \left(|S_d^{HB}| + 1 \right)$$

being n the total number of features and $|S_d^{HB}|$ the cardinality of S_d^{HB}. To ensure the split of an impure HB into pure HBs, the relation $n^{HB} \geq n_c$ must be satisfied. In particular, due to the admissibility property of the heuristic function, the number of cuts needed to define the minimum number of HBs, is defined as

$$n_{T_{heur}}^{HB} = \sum_{d=1}^{n} |S_d^{HB}|$$

such that $n^{HB} \geq n_c$ and n^{HB} is minimal (see also fig. 3). It is worth to mention that $n_{T_{heur}}^{HB}$ is an estimation that refers to an *impure* HB only, and *not* to all impure HBs in a state σ. To extend this idea to the whole input space, and hence to improve the heuristic informative power without loosing the admissibility property, the concept of connected HBs is exploited. Roughly speaking, taking into account an impure HB and calculating the value of $n_{T_{heur}}^{HB}$, it must be noted that the applied cuts can intersect other HBs that are connected. Therefore, to preserve the admissibility property of the heuristic function, the heuristic values of connected HBs cannot be simply summed together. Thus, to compute the heuristic value for a non-goal state σ (typically composed by more than one impure HB) satisfying the admissibility property, the following procedure is adopted:

1. $h(\sigma) \leftarrow 0$
2. $HB_{impure} \leftarrow \{hb | hb \in \sigma \land hb \text{ is impure}\}$
3. $hb_{maxClass} \leftarrow \max_{n_c} HB_{impure}$
4. $h(\sigma) \leftarrow h(\sigma) + n_{T_{heur}}^{hb_{maxClass}}$
5. $HB_{conn} \leftarrow \{hb | hb \in HB_{impure} \land connected(hb, hb_{maxClass})\}$
6. $HB_{impure} \leftarrow HB_{impure} \setminus HB_{conn}$
7. repeat from 3 until $HB_{impure} = \emptyset$

The final value of $h(\sigma)$ is provided as the heuristic value for the state σ.

4   Experimentation Results and Discussion

The experimental objective is to provide a performance comparison between the original and the proposed heuristic functions. In particular, for a fair comparison, two versions of A* (one for each heuristic function) are applied on the same

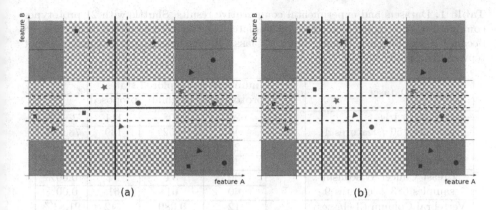

Fig. 3. Example of two non-goal states. In white, two impure HBs with four different classes are depicted. For both the HBs $n_{T_{heur}}^{HB} = 2$. The HB in (a) requires two cuts while the HB in (b) requires three cuts for splitting into pure HBs. HBs in checked white/gray are connected to the white HBs (dashed lines indicate other candidate cuts in T_d^{HB}).

prototypes obtained by the first DC* step (the data compression phase). The performances of the two heuristic functions are tested on seven different datasets selected from the UCI repository[1]; all these datasets include only numerical, pre-classified data without missing values. Two different numbers of prototypes are tested for each dataset (prototypes are proportionally assigned to the classes according to the class distribution in the dataset).

The key information that shows the different efficiency of the heuristic functions is the number of states explored by A*, which is the most expensive operation in DC*. In table 1 the summarized results of the experiments are shown. (For the Shuttle dataset with 21 prototypes computed by the original version of DC* we stopped the execution after 6 hours of execution time and reported the number of explored states.)

Due to the optimality of A*, for each dataset both the versions returned the same solution (i.e. the same cut configurations), but through a different number of explored states. It is possible to observe that for datasets with two classes there is no gain in efficiency because the two heuristic functions work in the same way. On the other hand, for datasets with more than two classes, the ability of the proposed heuristic in exploiting class information is apparent: the proposed heuristic function allows huge savings by exploring a very small number of states.

The proposed heuristic function proved to considerably boost the efficiency of DC*, making it a competitive alternative of other well known algorithms for extracting interpretable knowledge from data. In fact, in the worst case scenario considered in the experimentation (namely, the case of Statlog-Shuttle data with

---

[1] http://archive.ics.uci.edu/ml/

Table 1. Datasets and experimental comparative results. Shuttle with 21 prototypes computed by the original heuristic is incomplete. *The second feature has been removed because it exhibits a constant value. **Class "4" has been removed since it is not represented by any sample.

Dataset	classes	numb. of prototypes	explored states original	explored states proposed	% saving
Iris	3	21	408	111	72.79%
samples 150 / features 4		42	652	139	78.68%
Wine	3	20	5,454	1,026	81.19%
samples 178 / features 13		40	23,053	3,451	85.03%
Breast Cancer Wisconsin	2	30	34	34	0.00%
samples 683 / features 9		60	61	61	0.00%
Vertebral Column (3 classes)	3	12	9,089	742	91.84%
samples 310 / features 6		24	53,727	13,556	74.77%
Ionosphere	2	10	97	97	0.00%
samples 351 / features 33(34)*		20	23,143	23,143	0.00%
Glass Identification	6(7)**	9	10,720	1,095	89.79%
samples 214 / features 9		18	257,854	38,826	84.94%
Statlog-Shuttle	7	12	276,842	5,533	98.00%
samples 58,000 / features 9		21	>2,827,876	120,487	>95.74%

21 prototypes), the generation of the information granules required about 15 minutes to complete[2]. Furthermore, as concerning the accuracy/interpretability tradeoff —which is indepenent from the heuristic function— recent results show that DC* is competitive with other interpretability-oriented algorithms, such as HFP [12].

5   Conclusions

The experimental results show that DC* is a good candidate for automatically designing fuzzy rule-based classifiers that exhibit high interpretability and good accuracy. It is also easy to tune because it requires the specification of just one hyper-parameter, namely the number of prototypes for the first step, which has a clear semantics as it regulates the level of granularity of the derived knowledge base. Therefore, DC* can be used both to generate few fuzzy information granules for a rough description of data and, alternatively, to design an accurate classifier through a greater number of fuzzy information granules.

Future research is aimed at further improving the efficiency of DC* so that it can be applied to large-scale problems. This affects both steps of DC*; for the second one, in particular, we aim at exploiting the advantages of both A* and Evolutionary Computation to derive a hybrid approach to generate optimal solutions in reasonable time. This approach is under current investigation.

---

[2] Experiments have been conducted on a virtual machine (VMware) equipped with four x86 vCPUs @ 2.35GHz and 8GB of vRAM.

References

1. Zadeh, L.A.: Toward a theory of fuzzy information granulation and its centrality in human reasoning and fuzzy logic. Fuzzy Sets and Systems 90(2), 111–127 (1997)
2. Mencar, C., Fanelli, A.M.: Interpretability constraints for fuzzy information granulation. Information Sciences 178(24), 4585–4618 (2008)
3. Guillaume, S., Charnomordic, B.: Generating an Interpretable Family of Fuzzy Partitions From Data. IEEE Transactions on Fuzzy Systems 12(3), 324–335 (2004)
4. Weber, R.: Fuzzy-ID3: A class of methods for automatic knowledge acquisition. In: The Second International Conference on Fuzzy Logic and Neural Networks, pp. 265–268 (1992)
5. Alonso, J.M., Magdalena, L.: HILK++: an interpretability-guided fuzzy modeling methodology for learning readable and comprehensible fuzzy rule-based classifiers. Soft Computing 15(10), 1959–1980 (2011)
6. Guillaume, S., Charnomordic, B.: Learning interpretable fuzzy inference systems with FisPro. Information Sciences 181(20), 4409–4427 (2011)
7. Alonso, J.M., Magdalena, L.: Generating Understandable and Accurate Fuzzy Rule-Based Systems in a Java Environment. In: Fanelli, A.M., Pedrycz, W., Petrosino, A. (eds.) WILF 2011. LNCS (LNAI), vol. 6857, pp. 212–219. Springer, Heidelberg (2011)
8. Castellano, G., Fanelli, A.M., Mencar, C., Plantamura, V.L.: Classifying data with interpretable fuzzy granulation. In: Proceedings of the 3rd International Conference on Soft Computing and Intelligent Systems and 7th International Symposium on Advanced Intelligent Systems 2006, Tokyo, Japan, pp. 872–877 (2006)
9. Mencar, C., Consiglio, A., Castellano, G., Fanelli, A.M.: Improving the Classification Ability of DC* Algorithm. In: Masulli, F., Mitra, S., Pasi, G. (eds.) WILF 2007. LNCS (LNAI), vol. 4578, pp. 145–151. Springer, Heidelberg (2007)
10. Castellano, G., Fanelli, A.M., Mencar, C.: DCf: A Double Clustering framework for fuzzy information granulation. In: 2005 IEEE International Conference on Granular Computing, pp. 397–400 (2005)
11. Kohonen, T.: Self-organizing maps. Information Sciences, vol. 30. Springer (2001)
12. Lucarelli, M., Castiello, C., Fanelli, A.M., Mencar, C.: Automatic design of interpretable fuzzy partitions with variable granularity: An experimental comparison. In: Rutkowski, L., Korytkowski, M., Scherer, R., Tadeusiewicz, R., Zadeh, L.A., Zurada, J.M. (eds.) ICAISC 2013, Part I. LNCS, vol. 7894, pp. 318–328. Springer, Heidelberg (2013)
13. Mencar, C., Lucarelli, M., Castiello, C., Fanelli, A.M.: Design of strong fuzzy partitions from cuts. In: The 8th Conference of the European Society for Fuzzy Logic and Technology, EUSFLAT 2013 (in press, 2013)

Learning Membership Functions for Fuzzy Sets through Modified Support Vector Clustering

Dario Malchiodi[1] and Witold Pedrycz[2]

[1] Università degli Studi di Milano, Italy
malchiodi@di.unimi.it
[2] University of Alberta, Canada
wpedrycz@ualberta.ca

Abstract. We propose an algorithm for inferring membership functions of fuzzy sets by exploiting a procedure originated in the realm of support vector clustering. The available data set consists of points associated with a quantitative evaluation of their membership degree to a fuzzy set. The data are clustered in order to form a core gathering all points definitely belonging to the set. This core is subsequently refined into a membership function. The method is analyzed and applied to several real-world data sets.

1 Introduction

Designing fuzzy sets has been one of the pivotal problems in the methodology and practice of the technology of fuzzy sets. Fuzzy sets come with different interpretations, cf. [1]. There are several general approaches ranging from expert-driven methods to data-driven techniques and an entire spectrum of hybrid-like strategies combining these two development modes, cf. [2]. Various shapes of membership functions are proposed [3], sometimes being directly linked with the ensuing computational facets of fuzzy sets; here we can refer to triangular fuzzy sets and their role in fuzzy modeling and a degranulation process [2,4]. Intensive pursuits in the construction of membership functions are not surprising at all: evidently fuzzy sets form a backbone of fuzzy models, fuzzy classifiers and fuzzy reasoning schemes. Fuzzy sets used in these constructs directly impact their performance as well as contribute to the interpretability (readability) of these modeling constructs. Fuzzy sets formed through an expert-driven approach are reflective of the perception of concepts captured by humans; however the estimation process could exhibit some inconsistencies associated with the elicitation process itself (bottleneck of knowledge acquisition). On the other hand, data-driven approaches rely on available experimental data and fuzzy sets obtained in this manner are reflective of the nature of the available experimental evidence (which is going to be used intensively when forming fuzzy predictors or classifiers). In this domain, we encounter techniques using which fuzzy sets (treated as information granules) arise as a summarization of numeric data; one can refer here to fuzzy clustering or other mechanisms of vector quantization [5]. With this regard a prudent formulation of the optimization process and its relevance *vis-à-vis* the semantics of fuzzy set(s) to be developed is of paramount relevance.

F. Masulli, G. Pasi, and R. Yager (Eds.): WILF 2013, LNAI 8256, pp. 52–59, 2013.
© Springer International Publishing Switzerland 2013

Having this mind, we propose a modified support vector clustering in which we take advantage of the formulation and the nonlinear nature of the optimization problem falling within the realm of well-established methods of support vector machines. This formulation supports a construction of diversified membership functions.

A thorough parametric analysis of the resulting construct is presented. We demonstrate how the parameters (and a tradeoff of their values) of the method impact the shape (trapezoidal, quadratic, and bimodal) of membership function of the fuzzy set being formed. A series of illustrative examples is provided to visualize the flexibility of the construct considered here.

The paper is structured as follows: we start with a suitable modification of the support vector clustering algorithm and elaborate on a selection of numeric values of the essential parameters of the method. Subsequently, we present a series of experiments showing in detail on how membership functions are constructed.

2   Modifying the SV Clustering Algorithm

Let a sample $\{x_1, \ldots, x_m\}$ in a domain X be given, together with an associated set of membership grades $\{\mu_1, \ldots, \mu_m\}$ to some unknown fuzzy set A. The problem of inferring μ_A can be divided into two parts, namely: i) determining the *shape* of A, and ii) inferring the *parameters* of the membership function μ_A. These tasks are addressed by starting from the following hypothesis.

- Set $A_1 = \{x \in X \text{ s. t. } \mu_A(x) = 1\}$ contains all points in X whose images through a mapping Φ belong to a sphere of unknown center a and radius R.
- The membership $\mu_A(x)$ only depends on the distance between $\Phi(x)$ and a.

It has been shown that the set A_1 can be estimated through a modified support-vector clustering procedure [6] provided with $x_1, \ldots, x_m$ and $\mu_1, \ldots, \mu_m$: the problem is concerned with searching for the smallest sphere, having a and R respectively as center and radius, enclosing the images of $x_1, \ldots, x_m$ produced through a transformation Φ. More precisely, we use from a starting point the typical relaxation of this problem based on slack variables $\xi_1, \ldots, \xi_m$. As our target is that of learning a fuzzy set having as inputs some points $x_1, \ldots, x_m$ and their membership values $\mu_1, \ldots, \mu_m$, we consider the constraints in the form:

$$\mu_i \|\Phi(x_i) - a\|^2 \leq \quad \mu_i R^2 + \xi_i \ , \tag{1}$$

$$(1 - \mu_i)\|\Phi(x_i) - a\|^2 \geq (1 - \mu_i)R^2 - \tau_i \ , \tag{2}$$

$$\xi_i \geq 0, \tau_i \geq 0 \ . \tag{3}$$

It is easy to see that when $\mu_i = 1$ the constraints read in the same way as those in the problem of support vector clustering. In other words, we try to confine the images of x_i through Φ within a sphere centered at a and having radius R. On the other hand, when $\mu_i = 0$, the same set of constraint model the opposite target, i.e., exclusion of $\Phi(x_i)$ from the sphere.

Thus we can consider the following extension of the support vector clustering procedure: minimize $R^2 + C\sum(\xi_i + \tau_i)$ under constraints (1-3). Its Wolfe dual formulation is concerned with the maximization of $\sum_{i=1}^m (\alpha_i\mu_i - \beta_i(1 - \mu_i))k(x_i, x_i) - \sum_{i,j=1}^m (\alpha_i\mu_i - \beta_i(1 - \mu_i))(\alpha_j\mu_j - \beta_j(1 - \mu_j))k(x_i, x_j)$ subject to the constraints $\sum_{i=1}^m (\alpha_i\mu_i - \beta_i(1-\mu_i)) = 1$ and $0 \le \alpha_i, \beta_i \le C$, where k denotes the kernel function associated to the dot product computation in the image of Φ (that is, $k(x_i, x_j) = \Phi(x_i) \cdot \Phi(x_j)$). Denoting with a star the optimal value for a variable, Karush-Kuhn-Tucker (KKT) conditions [7] read

$$\alpha_i^* \left(R^{*2}\mu_i + \xi_i^* - \mu_i\|\Phi(x_i) - a^*\|^2 \right) = 0 , \tag{4}$$

$$\beta_i^* \left((1 - \mu_i)\|\Phi(x_i) - a^*\|^2 - R^{*2}(1 - \mu_i) + \tau_i^* \right) = 0 , \tag{5}$$

$$\gamma_i^*\xi_i^* = 0, \quad \delta_i^*\tau_i^* = 0 . \tag{6}$$

It is easy to show that when either $0 < \alpha_i^* < C$ or $0 < \beta_i^* < C$ it will necessary hold both $\xi_i^* = 0$ and $\|\Phi(x_i) - a^*\| = R^{*2}$. Thus the corresponding x_i has an image through Φ lying on the border of the learnt sphere S and will be called *support vector*. KKT conditions show that:

- $\alpha_i^* = 0$ implies $\xi_i^* = 0$ and $R^2(x) \le R^{*2}$, so $\Phi(x_i)$ lies in S or in its surface,
- $\alpha_i^* = C$ implies $R^2(x) = R^{*2} + \frac{\xi_i^*}{\mu_i}$, thus $\Phi(x_i)$ doesn't lie inside S,
- $\beta_i^* = 0$ implies $\tau_i^* = 0$, so that $R^2(x) \ge R^{*2}$, thus $\Phi(x_i)$ doesn't lie inside S,
- $\beta_i^* = C$ implies $R^2(x) = R^{*2} - \frac{\tau_i^*}{1-\mu_i}$, thus $\Phi(x_i)$ doesn't lie outside S,

where $R^2(x) = \|\Phi(x) - a^*\|^2$. Given any point $x \in X$, it can be shown that $R^2(x) = k(x, x) - 2\sum_{i=1}^m (\alpha_i^*\mu_i - \beta_i^*(1 - \mu_i))k(x, x_i) + \sum_{i,j=1}^m (\alpha_i^*\mu_i - \beta_i^*(1 - \mu_i))(\alpha_j^*\mu_j - \beta_j^*(1 - \mu_j))k(x_i, x_j)$ so that it is possible to compute the distance between the center of the learnt sphere and the image of the given point x. In particular, all points x with membership $\mu_A(x) = 1$ satisfy $R^2(x) \le R_1^2$, where $R_1^2 = R^2(x_i)$ for any support vector x_i. Moreover, as R^2 spans between a minimum and a maximum value when the membership value of its argument decreases from 1 to 0, the membership function μ_A can then be reconstructed in the following way:

- scaling R^2 to $R'(x) = \frac{M - R^2(x)}{M - R_1^2}$, where $M = \max_x R^2(x)$, so that R' approaches 0 and 1, respectively, when R^2 approaches its maximum and R_1^2;
- approximating μ_A with the function

$$\widehat{\mu}(x) = \begin{cases} 1 & \text{if } R'(x) \ge 1 , \\ R'(x) & \text{otherwise} . \end{cases} \tag{7}$$

The proposed procedure can produce membership functions of different shape. Figure 1 shows examples of the output for three different unidimensional membership functions, namely a trapezoidal, a quadratic and a bimodal one. In all

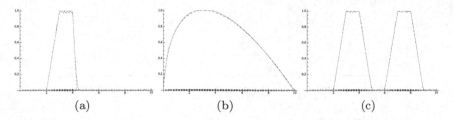

Fig. 1. Output of the proposed procedure (dashed curves) for different unidimensional membership functions (plain curves), inferred from samples of 50 item each (each sample point is drawn as a bullet colored according to its membership value, ranging from gray to black)

experiments we used a sample of $m = 50$ points uniformly distributed across the universe of discourse, associated with the corresponding membership value.

Inferring a membership function requires to strike the trade-off parameter C, as well as additional kernel parameters, an operation which is known in the literature as *model selection* [8]. In order to suitably select among the available methodologies it is worth studying the properties of parameters and their relations with the problem under study.

Figure 2 shows the results of an experiment aimed at understanding the role of involved parameters: having fixed: (i) a membership function (the dashed trapezoid in all graphs), (ii) a labeled sample, and (iii) a Gaussian kernel of parameter $\sigma = 0.12$ (see the beginning of Sect. 3), the learning procedure has been run several times using different values for C. The graphs in Fig. 2(a)–(c) highlight how an increase in C causes an enlargement of the inferred fuzzy set's *core*, intended as the subset of X whose elements are assigned unit membership. In particular, as C reaches the unit value the fuzzy set tends to a regular set enclosing all points in the labeled sample having non-zero membership values.

Similarly, we can start from the same membership function and labeled sample, set C to the best value found during the previous run, and change σ. The results, summarized in Fig. 2(d)–(f), show how the role of this parameter is that of modifying the *shape* of the membership function, which becomes more plastic as σ decreases toward zero. This experiment suggests a three-phase procedure for finding the optimal values for C and σ consisting in: 1. selecting a value C_0 in order to include in the inferred fuzzy set's core all points having unit membership; 2. selecting a value σ_0 in order to reasonably fit the data; 3. performing a fine-grained grid search centered around C_0 and σ_0.

3 Experiments

In all applications described in this paper the procedure relied on the Gaussian kernel defined by $k(x_1, x_2) = \exp\left(-||x_1 - x_2||^2/(2\sigma^2)\right)$. When using this kind of kernel [9] the optimization problem simplifies to the minimization of $\sum_{i,j=1}^{m}(\alpha_i\mu_i - \beta_i(1-\mu_i))(\alpha_j\mu_j - \beta_j(1-\mu_j))k(x_i, x_j)$; indeed, a Gaussian kernel

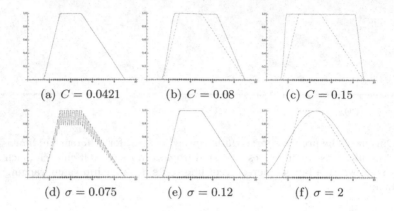

(a) $C = 0.0421$ (b) $C = 0.08$ (c) $C = 0.15$

(d) $\sigma = 0.075$ (e) $\sigma = 0.12$ (f) $\sigma = 2$

Fig. 2. (a)–(c): Increasing C has the effect of enlarging the learnt membership function core. (d)–(f): Increasing σ has the effect of changing the learnt membership function shape. Each graph is labelled with the corresponding parameter value.

k satisfies $k(x, x) = 1$, so that the constraints insure the equivalence between the original objective function and $1 - \sum_{i,j=1}^{m}(\alpha_i\mu_i - \beta_i(1 - \mu_i))(\alpha_j\mu_j - \beta_j(1 - \mu_j))k(x_i, x_j)$.

The computation of M was carried out used a Monte Carlo maximization and choosing a suitable number of samples in each experiment.

3.1 Inferring Membership Functions from Real-World Data

As a first example consider the body mass index (BMI) defined as the ratio between the weight and the squared height of a person, respectively measured in kilograms and meters. The World Health organization uses this quantity as an age- and gender-independent index for classification of weight categories in adult people, according to Table 1 [10]. Focusing on the category of *normal weight* we selected two mappings μ^1 and μ^2, shown in the table, associating each BMI range to a membership value. Subsequently we drew samples of 150 BMI values located uniformly in the interval $[10, 45]$ and computed their membership value.

Table 1. Classification of weight in function of the BMI, according to the World health organization [10]. Columns μ^1 and μ^2 show the values giving rise to the learnt membership functions shown in Fig. 3(a) and (b), respectively.

Classification	BMI range	μ^1	μ^2	Classification	BMI range	μ^1	μ^2
Severe thinness	BMI < 16	0	0	Pre-obese	25 ≤ BMI < 30	0.5	0.7
Moderate thinness	16 ≤ BMI < 17	0.2	0.4	Obese class I	30 ≤ BMI < 35	0.2	0.4
Mild thinness	17 ≤ BMI < 18.5	0.5	0.7	Obese class II	35 ≤ BMI < 40	0.1	0.2
Normal range	18.5 ≤ BMI < 25	1	1	Obese class III	BMI ≥ 40	0	0

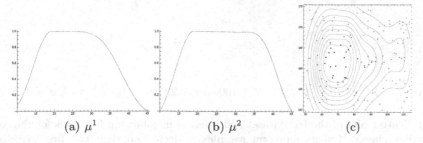

$$\text{(a) } \mu^1 \qquad\qquad \text{(b) } \mu^2 \qquad\qquad \text{(c)}$$

Fig. 3. (a)–(b): Learnt membership functions for normal weight according to Table 1, respectively referring to the values shown in columns μ^1 and μ^2 of the table. (c): Inferred membership function for the fuzzy set expressing the notion of normal physique in adult women in the US, in function of weight (X axis, measured in kilograms) and height (Y axis, measured in centimeters).

This allowed us to infer the membership functions (one for each mapping) shown in Fig. 3(a)–(b), setting $\sigma = 4$ and $C = 0.05$. Note how learnt membership function's shape is affected by the way categories are associated to numeric values for memberships. This is a key aspect for accommodating available domain knowledge coming from the experts in the field.

The proposed methodology is not confined to single-dimensional problems. Indeed, the kernel trick allows the inference to consider fuzzy sets defined on any space over which a kernel can be defined. Consider for instance the fuzzy notion of *normal physique* defined in terms of weight and height of a person. Figure 3(c) shows the results of a toy experiment aimed at capturing this notion, having as a starting point the distribution of weight and height, respectively measured in kilograms and centimeters, in adult women in the US [11]. Dividing the observation range in function of the data percentiles it is possible to obtain two functions μ_{weight} and μ_{height} approximating the corresponding memberships. Finally, considering a sample of 150 points uniformly drawn in $[50, 114] \times [150, 175]$ (the Cartesian product of the operational ranges in observed data) and building the membership value of each of its element (w, h) as $\mu(w, h) = \mu_{\text{weight}}(w)\mu_{\text{height}}(h)$, the proposed procedure learnt the membership function shown in Fig. 3(c).

3.2 Inferring Membership Functions in Absence of Membership Values

The method is also applicable to datasets not explicitly mentioning membership values. Consider for instance the Iris dataset [12], introduced by Fisher in 1936 and gathering 150 samples from three different species of the iris flower (namely, *Iris setosa*, *Iris virginica* and *Iris versicolor*). The observations, described through length and width of the petal and the sepal, are assigned to one of the previously mentioned species. The proposed learning procedure can be applied as follows: focusing on a given class, say *Iris setosa*, denote $\{x_1, \ldots, x_{150}\}$ the dataset observations and set $\mu_i = 1$ if x_i belongs to class *Iris setosa*, and 0

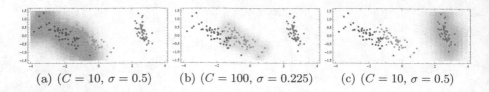

$$(a)\ (C = 10,\ \sigma = 0.5) \qquad (b)\ (C = 100,\ \sigma = 0.225) \qquad (c)\ (C = 10,\ \sigma = 0.5)$$

Fig. 4. Scatter plot of the Iris dataset and inferred membership functions for the corresponding classes. Bullets represent samples projected on their two first principal components, and colored according to their classes (in blue, green and red respectively for *Iris virginica*, *Iris versicolor*, and *Iris setosa*). Each graph also shows the density plot of the inferred membership function.

otherwise. Apply subsequently the learning procedure in order to infer a membership function μ_{setosa}. Idem for membership functions $\mu_{\mathrm{virginica}}$ and $\mu_{\mathrm{versicolor}}$. Given an observation x, assign it to the class it belongs to with maximal membership grade. Figure 4 shows a density plot of the membership functions inferred after application of the PCA procedure [13] selecting the first two principal components, for sake of visualization, and using a Gaussian kernel. Each plot shows the class it refers to, as well as the used values for parameters C and σ, chosen through a trial and error procedure.

We performed a more extensive experiment involving a repeated holdout scheme, in which 70% of a random permutation of the sample was used in order to infer the three membership functions, using the parameters highlighted in Fig. 4; the latter were subsequently tested on the remaining 30% of the data. Table 2 resumes average and standard deviation of the obtained error both in the training and the testing phase of 500 such procedures, starting each time from a different permutation and analyzing two, three and four principal components. These results show how even a very simple learning strategy (no complex procedures for fine tuning the parameters' choice such as a cross-validation) lead to an average test performance around 95%.

Table 2. Results of 500 holdout procedures on the Iris dataset. Each row shows average and standard deviation (columns Avg. and Stdev., respectively) of train and test error, in function of the number of principal components extracted from the original sample.

N. of principal	Train error		Test error	
components	Avg.	Stdev.	Avg.	Stdev.
2	0.00488	0.00653	0.04720	0.03143
3	0.00152	0.00349	0.06067	0.03128
4	0.00169	0.00374	0.05738	0.03347

4 Conclusions

This paper introduced a method for inferring the membership function to a fuzzy set on the basis of partial information, consisting in two finite sets: the former containing a sample of points, and the latter gathering measurements of the membership grades for points in the former set. The method relies on a special support vector clustering for the provided points, which is subsequently transformed into the inferred membership function.

References

1. Dubois, D., Prade, H.: The three semantics of fuzzy sets. Fuzzy Sets and Systems 90, 141–150 (1997)
2. Pedrycz, W.: Granular Computing: Analysis and Design of Intelligent Systems. CRC Press/Francis Taylor, Boca Raton (2013)
3. Nguyen, H., Walker, E.: A First Course in Fuzzy Logic. Chapman Hall, CRC Press, Boca Raton (1999)
4. Pedrycz, W.: Why triangular membership functions? Fuzzy Sets & Systems 64, 21–30 (1994)
5. Linde, Y., Buzo, A., Gray, R.: An algorithm for vector quantizer design. IEEE Transactions on Communications COM-28(1), 84–95 (1988)
6. Ben-Hur, A., Horn, D., Siegelmann, H.T., Vapnik, V.: Support vector clustering. Journal of Machine Learning Research 2, 125–137 (2001)
7. Fletcher, R.: Practical methods of optimization, 2nd edn. Wiley-Interscience, New York (1987)
8. Guyon, I., Saffari, A., Dror, G., Cawley, G.: Model selection: Beyond the bayesian/frequentist divide. J. of Machine Learning Research 11, 61–87 (2010)
9. Evangelista, P.F., Embrechts, M.J., Szymanski, B.K.: Some properties of the gaussian kernel for one class learning. In: Marques de Sá, J., Alexandre, L.A., Duch, W., Mandic, D.P. (eds.) ICANN 2007. LNCS, vol. 4668, pp. 269–278. Springer, Heidelberg (2007)
10. Consultation, W.E.: Appropriate body-mass index for asian populations and its implications for policy and intervention strategies. Lancet 363(9403), 157–163 (2004)
11. McDowell, M.A., Fryar, C., Ogden, C.L., Flegal, K.M.: Anthropometric reference data for children and adults: United states, 2003–2006. National health statistics reports, vol. 10. National Center for Health Statistics, Hyattsville, MD (2008), http://www.cdc.gov/nchs/data/nhsr/nhsr010.pdf accessed (May 2012)
12. Fisher, R.A.: The use of multiple measurements in taxonomic problems. Annals of Eugenics 7(2), 179–188 (1936)
13. Abdi, H., Williams, L.J.: Principal component analysis. Wiley Interdisciplinary Reviews: Computational Statistics 2, 433–459 (2010)

Using Fuzzy Multilayer Perceptrons for the Classification of Time Series

Toni Pimentel, Fernando M. Ramos, and Sandra Sandri

Instituto Nacional de Pesquisas Espaciais
12201-970, São José dos Campos, SP
tonipimentel@gmail.com, {fernando.ramos,sandra.sandri}@inpe.br

Abstract. In the last decades, rainforests all over the world have been subjected to high rates of land use change due to deforestation. Tracking and understanding the trends and patterns of these changes is crucial for the creation and implementation of effective policies for sustainable development and environment protection. Here we propose the use of Fuzzy Multilayer Perceptrons (Fuzzy MLP) for classification of land use and land cover patterns in the Brazilian Amazon, using time series of vegetation index, taken from NASA's MODIS (Moderate Resolution Imaging Spectroradiometer) sensor. Results show that the combination of degree of ambiguity and fuzzy desired output, two of the Fuzzy MLP techniques implemented here, provides an overall accuracy ranging from 89% to 96%.

1 Introduction

Statistics in the real world are often based on a sequence of pieces of data indexed by time. This compound type of data is referred to as *time series* and occur in all types of activities, from human-related ones, such as financial markets, company sales, demographic information of a geographical entity, etc, to those related to natural phenomena, such as the appearance of sunspots in a star or the decay of atoms in a piece of matter.

The basis of time series analysis is that repetitive behavior patterns can be identified and modeled. The repetition, occurring in either smooth or turbulent behavior, is essential for generalization [11]. Time series are invariably non-stationary, and the assumptions about their structures made by traditional methods are difficult to verify [7], making the use of such methods unsuitable even for "moderately entangled" systems [2]. In addition, real world data may show an overlap of many processes, exhibiting different dynamics.

Time series analysis focuses on three basic objectives: prediction of short-term progressions, modeling long-term behavior and characterization of underlying properties [2]. Conventional models – to test the hypothesis that complex and potentially causal relationships exist between various elements of a time series – based on parametric methods, express these relationships in a variety of ways. The most popular is the autoregressive model based on the hypothesis that causality connects the value of the series at a given moment of time to the values of the time series at some of the previous moments. On the other hand, computational intelligence techniques such as fuzzy systems, genetic algorithms, artificial neural networks and hybrid systems, do not make

F. Masulli, G. Pasi, and R. Yager (Eds.): WILF 2013, LNAI 8256, pp. 60–67, 2013.

assumptions about the structure of the data, and provide a "universal approach" to the nonlinear mapping of complex functions [15] [16].

The combination of Fuzzy Inference Systems (FIS) [17] [14] and Neural Networks (NN) [3] [6] incorporate strengths of both, such as machine learning and generalization ability, from NN, and qualitative reasoning and capability of uncertainty modeling, from FIS [11]. Fuzzy Neural Networks names a class of such hybrid approaches, that incorporate fuzzy concepts in a neural network [9]. It includes Fuzzy Multilayer Perceptrons [8] [5] [9], based on a classic Multilayer Perceptron neural network (MLP).

In the last decades, rainforests all over the world have been subjected to high rates of land use change due to deforestation. Tracking and understanding the trends and patterns of these changes is crucial for the creation and implementation of effective policies for sustainable development and environment protection. In the particular case of Brazil, there exists, on the one hand, a large amount of data derived from satellite images that can be used for the classification of temporal patterns of land use change on rainforest areas. On the other hand, there is, however, a shortage of professionals trained for satellite image interpretation, able to convert this mass of data into useful knowledge, what makes the use of automated techniques imperative to deal with the problem.

Here we investigate the use of Fuzzy MLPs in classification of land use and land cover temporal patterns in the Brazilian Amazon. For this, we use time series of vegetation indices recorded in images taken from MODIS (Moderate Resolution Imaging Spectroradiometer) sensor, on board of NASA's Aqua and Terra satellites. We compare the basic MLP algorithm with two extensions, one involving the concept of fuzzy desired output [8] and another involving a degree of ambiguity [9]. We also propose a classification confidence index for the system, that can help improve the quality of decision-making by the end user.

2   Fuzzy Multilayer Perceptrons

Multilayer Perceptrons (MLPs) using the *Backpropagation* learning mechanism are the most common neural networks found in the literature [6] [3], and have been used in a wide range of applications, including pattern recognition. Essentially, a MLP network is a feedforward multilayer mechanism that utilizes a supervised learning model based on the adjustment of its parameters (weights) according to the error between the actual and desired outputs of the network [12].

There exists a vast literature about the combination of fuzzy systems and multilayer perceptrons (see, for example, [13], [8] and [5] and references therein). In the conventional approaches for pattern classification using MLPs ([3], [12]), the number of nodes of the output layer in an application usually corresponds to the number of classes considered in that application. A method commonly used to produce the network output is the winner-take-all, which allocates value 1 (one) for the winner neuron and 0 (zero) to its competitors. Thus, the winner neuron represents the network prediction about the class to which the input pattern belongs.

In Fuzzy MLPs, each desired output of the modified multilayer perceptron is in the range $[0, 1]$, and refers to the degree of membership of the input pattern to its corresponding output class (fuzzy desired output) [8], [9]. Consequently, the errors can be propagated back regarding the exact likeness, which is reflected in the desired output.

In [8], a Fuzzy MLP has been proposed, here called MLP-D, which makes use of two parameters: the mean and standard deviation vectors of the training set. Let $C = \{c_1, ..., c_l\}$ be a set of classes, and $X = \{x_1, ..., x_m\}$ be a set of training patterns, with each $x_i \in X$ described as a feature vector $x_i = (x_{i,1}, ..., x_{i,n})$. Let $\mu_k : X \to [0, 1]$ denote the membership function that describes how much a pattern in X is compatible with the k-th class in C. According to [8], the following steps should be executed, in order to obtain the fuzzy desired output:

- Calculate the weighted distance between each input pattern and each class in C, taking into account the mean and standard deviation vectors of the training patterns. The weighted distance of training pattern x_i to the k-th class is defined by:

$$z_{ik} = \sqrt{\sum_{j=1}^{n} (\frac{x_{ij} - o_{kj}}{\sigma_{kj}})^2}, \tag{1}$$

where o_{kj} and σ_{kj} respectively denote the average and standard deviation of the values for the j-th feature of the elements in the training set of the k-th class (when all the training data are the same, σ_{kj} is set to 1);
- Once the weighted distance is defined, calculate the membership values with respect to each class (μ_k for $k \in C$), using the following equation:

$$\mu_k(x_i) = \frac{1}{1 + (\frac{z_{ik}}{f_d})^{f_e}}, \tag{2}$$

where f_e and f_d are fuzzy parameters that control the amount of imprecision for this class and z_{ik} is calculated in Equation (1).

The idea behind the membership function is that the greater the distance of an input pattern to class c_k, the less similar is the pattern to class c_k, and thus the lower will be the output value of the function membership function.

One of the learning methods of conventional MLP network is by minimizing the mean square error (LMS) between the desired output and the output vector calculated by the network. In this training process, each pattern has the same importance. However, it is reasonable to decrease the importance of patterns that are in areas of overlapping classes, and which are primarily responsible for misclassification. One way to implement that is to consider the amount of correction in the weight vector produced by the input pattern, according to the degree of ambiguity of a pattern.

In [9], a method incorporating a degree of ambiguity Fuzzy MLPs has been proposed, here called MLP-G. The degree of ambiguity is defined as follows:

$$A = (\mu_{(1)}(x_i) - \mu_{(2)}(x_i))^m, \tag{3}$$

where $\mu_{(1)}(x_i)$ (respec. $\mu_{(2)}(x_i)$) highest (respec. second highest) class membership degree for a pattern x_i in X and m is a enhancement/reduction fuzzy parameter. Parameter m increases ($m < 1$), maintains ($m = 1$) or decreases ($m > 1$) the influence of the ambiguity of a pattern training, as well as determines the strength of this increase/decrease.

Based on the techniques described above, we implemented four classification techniques: i) the usual MLP, ii) MLP with ambiguity degree (MLP-G), iii) MLP with fuzzy desired output (MLP-D), and iv) MLP with ambiguity and fuzzy desired output (MLP-GD). In the next section, we present their application to the problem of classification of land use and land cover temporal patterns in the Brazilian Amazon, using time series of vegetation index.

3   Application in Time Series of Vegetation Index

The time series selected for study in this work were obtained from the work of Freitas [1], available at the site https://www.dsr.inpe.br/laf/series/ (see Figure 1 for an illustrative example). The study area is a rectangle comprising approximately $10.5 km^2$ at the east of the state of Mato Grosso, Brazil, whose geographical opposite coordinates are situated at $(-12.331945, -52.422560)$ and $(-12.372355, -52.458480)$. Within this study area we selected a representative sample of 168 pixels in images taken from MODIS (Moderate Resolution Imaging Spectroradiometer) sensor, on board of NASA's Aqua and Terra satellites. Each pixel corresponds to a $250m^2$ area.

Fig. 1. Time series using vegetation index EV1-2, showing patterns of land cover and use [1]

The time series correspond to 11 years worth of EVI-2 vegetation index observations, from August 2000 to June 2011, totaling 1848 (168×11) annual patterns. We have used MODIS 16-days product, i.e. a composite image is generated every 16 days. Considering the total period of 11 years, the available data consists of 265 observations per pixel recorded by the satellites.

We have chosen to use exactly 23 (approximately 365/16) observations per year per pixel. This yields a total of 253 (23×11) observations per pixel, considering the whole period. Therefore, in order to run our experiments, we disregarded 12 of the 265 original observations from the original data.

Once the patterns were chosen, it was necessary to classify them into classes of land use and land cover. Having neither an available expert to precisely classify a significant amount of samples nor the ground truth, we adopted the following procedure.

First, by visual inspection, based on the classifications shown in [1], we pre-classified the 1848 patterns into four large classes: forest, deforestation, pasture and agriculture. Second, for each class, we computed the average pattern and the corresponding variance, and then selected only those patterns fully contained within the envelope defined by the mean value plus or minus k standard deviations ($k * \sigma$). The procedure has been validated in [10]. Figure 2 illustrates this filtering procedure for k=1.

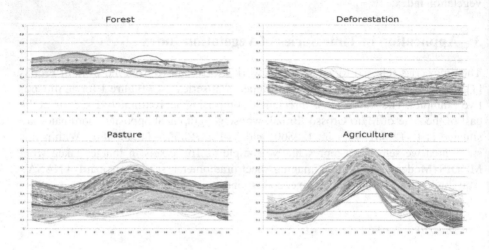

Fig. 2. Vegetation index time series for classes with indication of means and one standard deviation

From the initial 1848 patterns, we have created two sets of patterns: set I contains the 205 patterns obtained using $k = 1$, and set II contains 1363 patterns obtained with $k = 2$. Values $k = 1$ and $k = 2$ correspond to more or less conservative attitudes, respectively, considering an absence of solid expertise and/or ground truth. Set I contains 139 patterns of forest, 18 of deforestation, 35 of pasture and 13 of agriculture. Set II contains 641 patterns of forest, 100 of deforestation, 279 of pasture and 343 of agriculture.

We performed a series of tests on sets I and II, using a 4-folder cross-validation process (3 parts for training and 1 part for validation). We applied 4 methods on the data: the original MLP neural network (MLP), MLP using the degree of ambiguity (MLP-G), MLP using fuzzy desired output (MLP-D) and MLP using the degree of ambiguity and fuzzy desired output (MLP-GD). For both (MLP-D) and (MLP-GD), we obtained the best results with $f_d = f_d = 2$ in a series of trial-and-error experiments. Table 1 presents the results for sets I and II, showing the mean rates for each method used in the 4 folders, considering the individual classes and the overall results.

We see that all methods produced very good results in general, for both sets I and II. Set I produced better results than set II for individual accuracies of classes forest (F) and pasture (P), whereas set II produced better results for deforestation (D). In relation to agriculture, set II was better than set I, except for method MLP-GD, which is

Table 1. Mean individual accuracy for classes F (forest), D (deforestation), P (pasture) and A (agriculture) and mean global accuracy, for sets I and II, for methods MLP, MLP-G, MLP-D and MLP-GD

System	Accuracy									
	Individual								Global	
	I				II				I	II
	F	D	P	A	F	D	P	A		
MLP	100.00%	94.74%	94.63%	67.52%	98.33%	98.20%	86.40%	89.73%	89.22%	93.16 %
MLP-G	100.00%	93.91%	96.57%	83.33%	98.95%	97.47%	88.12%	89.45%	93.45%	93.50%
MLP-D	100.00%	95.29%	95.10%	79.62%	99.83%	97.67%	89.83%	80.86%	92.50%	92.05%
MLP-GD	100.00%	94.58%	96.84%	92.78%	99.47%	97.80%	86.86%	90.08%	96.05%	93.55%

also the best result for that class. In what regards individual accuracies, method MLP-GD was either better than its counterparts for all classes in both sets I and II, or with results closely resembling the best ones. In what regards the global results, method MLP-GD fared better, for both sets I and II. For global results, set I fared better than set II for methods MLP-GD and MLP-D and worse for methods MLP and MLP-G. The best global results were produced by method MLP-GD for set I. In conclusion, method MLP-GD and set I were more appropriate in the treatment of the data.

Using the fuzzy membership functions derived by the classifiers, we obtain a system classification confidence index, by applying Shannon entropy on the normalized membership functions. This index is illustrated in Figure 3, that indicates the vegetation index evolution inside each of the 11 yearly patterns for a set of selected pixels, considering both sets I (left side) and II (right side), using MLP-GD. In the figure, the difference in tonality in each pattern indicates the system confidence in its own judgment; the darkest the color, the highest the confidence.

The figure shows a uniform series of forest patterns for the first pixel. We can see that the difference between sets I and II is the confidence of the system on its own classification: set I produces results with higher confidence. The same tendency can be seen for the other pixels in the figure.

In what regards the second pixel in the figure, the system considers that, according to set I, the area was a forest in the first two years, suffered deforestation in the third year, became pasture on the fourth year, and was then used for agriculture in the remaining 7 years, thus following a logical order. In set II, however, the second year was classified as pasture, before becoming deforestation on the third year and again pasture on the fourth year, which is not consistent in terms of temporal evolution of patterns in the region.

The third pixel in the figure illustrates a less satisfactory result. We see that, according to set I, after pasture begins on the 6th year, it becomes forest on the 10th year to return to pasture on the 11th year. On the 10th year, the region was probably also covered by pasture, albeit possibly a dirtier pasture than the other pasture years. Note, however, that the system gives low confidence for that assessment. Using set II, only a sequence of forest patterns followed by a sequence of pasture patterns are detected, bypassing the expected deforestation step between them.

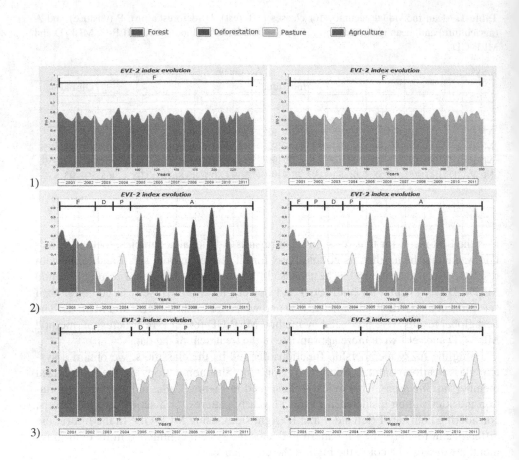

Fig. 3. Results of experiments of for 3 pixels, using sets I (left side) and II (right side)

4   Conclusions

The use of products and techniques of remote sensing and GIS in environmental analysis has become increasingly common. In the case of land use and land cover, these techniques contribute expressively for speed, efficiency and reliability in analyses involving the processes of degradation of natural vegetation, monitoring of forest resources, development of conservation policies, as well as several other factors that can cause changes in vegetation.

In this work, we investigated the combination of fuzzy and neural systems for classifying land use and land cover patterns in the Brazilian Amazon region, using time series of vegetation indices from NASA's MODIS sensor. For this, we implemented a Fuzzy Multilayer Perceptrons (MLP) using four approaches: MPL alone, MLP with degree of ambiguity, MLP with fuzzy desired output and MLP with degree of ambiguity and fuzzy desired output. We have obtained very good overall results. In particular, the combination of degree of ambiguity and fuzzy desired output provided the best results, ranging from 89% to 96%.

The application of a pattern filtering procedure to the raw data proved to be useful in the absence of ground truth. However, this technique has also its limitations, illustrated by the difficulty in distinguishing between forest and dirty pasture in some pixels.

Last but not least, we have used the fuzzy classification results to derive classification confidence to help the end user improve the quality of decision making.

References

1. de Freitas, R.M.: Laboratório virtual para visualizão e caracterização do uso e cobertura da terra utilizando imagens de sensoriamento remoto. PhD Thesis, INPE, Brazil (2012)
2. Gershenfeld, N.A., Weigend, A.S.: The future of time series: Learning and understanding, Working Papers, Santa Fe Inst (1993)
3. Haykin, S.S.: Neural Networks and Learning Machines. Prentice Hall (2009)
4. Jang, J.S.R.: ANFIS: Adaptive-network-based fuzzy inference system. IEEE Trans. on SMC 23(3), 665–685 (1993)
5. Keller, J.M., Hunt, D.J.: Incorporating fuzzy membership functions into the perceptron algorithm. IEEE Trans. on PAMI 6, 693–699 (1985)
6. Mehrotra, K., Mohan, C.K., Ranka, S.: Elements of artificial neural networks. MIT Press (1996)
7. Moorthy, M., Cellier, F.E., LaFrance, J.T.: Predicting US food demand in the 20th century: A new look at system dynamics. In: Proc. SPIE, vol. 3369, p. 343 (1998)
8. Pal, S.K., Mitra, S.: Multilayer perceptron, fuzzy sets, and classification. IEEE Trans. on Neural Networks 3(5), 683–697 (1992)
9. de Paula Canuto, A.M.: Combining neural networks and fuzzy logic for applications in character recognition. PhD Thesis Electronic Engineering, Un. of Kent at Canterbury (2001)
10. Pimentel, T., Ramos, F., Sandri, S.: Uso de Perceptrons Multicamadas Difusos para a Classificação de Padrões em Séries Temporais (submitted, 2013) (in Portuguese)
11. Popoola, A.O.: Fuzzy-Wavelet Method for Time Series Analysis. PhD Thesis, University of Surrey, UK (2007)
12. Rumelhart, D.E., Hinton, G.E., Williams, R.J.: Learning representations by back-propagating errors. Cognitive Modeling 1, 213 (2002)
13. Stoeva, S., Nikov, A.: A fuzzy backpropagation algorithm. Fuzzy Sets and Systems 112(1), 27–39 (2000)
14. Takagi, T., Sugeno, M.: Fuzzy identification of system and its applications to modeling and control. IEEE Trans. SMC 1(5) (1985)
15. Wang, L.X., Mendel, J.M.: Generating fuzzy rules by learning from examples. IEEE Trans. on SMC 22(6), 1414–1427 (1992)
16. Ying, H.: General SISO Takagi-Sugeno fuzzy systems with linear rule consequent are universal approximators. IEEE Trans. on Fuzzy Systems 6(4), 582–587 (1998)
17. Zadeh, L.A.: Fuzzy sets. Information and Control 8(3), 338–353 (1965)

Imputation of Possibilistic Data for Structural Learning of Directed Acyclic Graphs

Maroua Haddad[1], Nahla Ben Amor[1], and Philippe Leray[2]

[1] LARODEC Laboratory ISG, University of Tunis Tunisia, 2000
maroua.haddad@gmail.com, nahla.benamor@gmx.fr
[2] LINA Laboratory UMR 6241, PolytechNantes, France
philippe.leray@univ-nantes.fr

Abstract. One recent focus of research in graphical models is how to learn them from imperfect data. Most of existing works address the case of missing data. In this paper, we are interested by a more general form of imperfection i.e. related to possibilistic datasets where some attributes are characterized by possibility distributions. We propose a structural learning method of Directed Acyclic Graphs (DAGs), which form the qualitative component of several graphical models, from possibilistic datasets. Experimental results show the efficiency of the proposed method even in the particular case of missing data regarding the state of the art *Closure under tuple intersection* (CUTS) method [1].

1 Introduction

Over the last three decades, a lot of effort has been put into learning graphical models from data but most of proposed methods are relative to probabilistic models and especially Bayesian networks [2]. Such methods depend chiefly on data nature i.e. perfect or imperfect data. Learning from imperfect data addresses the particular case of missing data via the standard Expectation Maximization method [3]. In this paper, we are interested in learning networks structure from a more general form of imperfect data: possibilistic data in which some attributes are characterized by possibility distributions. Such a data were handled essentially to learn possibilistic classifiers namely *naive possibilistic networks*[4, 5], *possibilistic decision trees* [6] and *possibilistic clustering* [7]. The idea to learn possibilistic networks [1, 8], which are the possibilistic counterpart of Bayesian networks [2], from possibilistic datasets seems to be natural. Nevertheless, despite the multitude of works related to propagation in possibilistic networks [1, 8, 9], as far as we know, the unique attempt to learn them from data was carried out by Borgelt et al. [1] from missing data and not possibilistic ones. This paper addresses the problem of learning networks structure from possibilistic datasets which presents a part of the learning process of possibilistic networks. In fact, we only address the structure learning problem i.e. the output of the proposed method is a DAG which is not characterized by any numerical data even if the proposed learning process is ensured in the possibilistic framework. Semantically, the resultant structure is closest to a qualification via

F. Masulli, G. Pasi, and R. Yager (Eds.): WILF 2013, LNAI 8256, pp. 68–76, 2013.
© Springer International Publishing Switzerland 2013

possibilistic conditional distributions, in the same spirit of the work of Borgelt et al. [1].

This paper is organized as follows: Section 2 recalls basics of possibility theory and briefly introduces possibilistic networks. Section 3 proposes a new approach to learn networks structure from possibilistic datasets. Finally, Section 4 reports and analyzes experimental results.

2 Background on Possibility Theory and Possibilistic Networks

We first give the necessary background on possibility theory. For more details, we refer to [10]. Let $X_1, ..., X_n$ be a set of state variables whose values are ill-known such that $D_1, ..., D_n$ are their respective domains. We denote by x_i instances of a variable X_i. The joint domain of $X_1, ..., X_n$ is the universe of discourse $\Omega = D_1 \times ... \times D_n$. The agents knowledge about the value of X_i can be encoded by a possibility distribution π corresponding to a mapping from the universe of discourse Ω to the unit interval $[0, 1]$. For any state $\omega \in \Omega$, $\pi(\omega) = 1$ means that ω realization is totally possible for variables $X_1, ..., X_n$ and $\pi(\omega) = 0$ means that ω is an impossible state. The particularity of the possibilistic scale is that it can be interpreted in two-fold: in an ordinal manner i.e. the possibility degrees reflect only an ordering between the possible values and in a numerical interpretation i.e. the possibility degrees make sense in the ranking scale. Given a possibility distribution π, we can define for any subset $A \subseteq \Omega$ two dual measures $\Pi(A) = \max_{\omega \in A} \pi(\omega)$ and $N(A) = 1 - \Pi(\bar{A})$ where Π assesses at what level A is consistent with our knowledge represented by π whereas N evaluates at what level $\bar{A}$ is impossible.

Possibilistic networks [1, 8] represent the possibilistic counterpart of Bayesian networks [2] having similarly two components: a *graphical component* composed of a DAG which encodes a set of independence relations (i.e. each variable $X_i \in V$ is conditionally independent of its non-descendent given its parents) and a *numerical component* corresponding to the set of conditional possibility distributions relative to each node $X_i \in V$ in the context of its parents. The two interpretations of the possibilistic scale lead naturally to two different ways to define possibilistic networks [1, 8]: qualitative also called *min-based* possibilistic networks based on *min-based* conditioning and quantitative also called *product-based* possibilistic networks based on the *product-based* conditioning [10].

Several researchers were interested by possibilistic networks since they provide an interesting alternative to Bayesian networks especially in some situations when the probabilistic reasoning is controversial, like the case of total ignorance. The vast majority of these works concern propagation algorithms [1, 8, 9] and the unique attempt to learn possibilistic networks from data was proposed by Borgelt et al. [1] and it is restricted to datasets with missing values. Our goal in this work is to consider the more general case of possibilistic datasets as described in next section.

3 New Approach to Learn Networks Structure from Possibilistic Datasets

To learn DAG structure from possibilistic datasets, we propose two phases namely, possibilistic data imputation and learning. Before detailing our approach, we first define these latters. A possibilistic dataset D is defined as a collection of tuples (denoted by t_i) which can be dispatched into p certain tuples, denoted by CT, and q uncertain ones, denoted by UT, where attributes are characterized by possibility distributions. Each tuple t_i is characterized by its frequency, denoted by $fr(t_i)$ i.e. number of occurrence in the dataset.

Example 1. Let us consider Table 1 presenting an example of a possibilistic dataset with three variables (A, B, C) such that A and C are ternary and B is binary. The first five tuples are certain and the last five ones are uncertain. Tuple 1 (resp. 2,3,4,5) corresponds to $a_1 b_2 c_3$ (resp. $a_3 b_1 c_2$, $a_1 b_2 c_1$, $a_2 b_1 c_3$, $a_3 b_1 c_3$).

3.1 Possibilistic Data Imputation

Given a possibilistic dataset, the first phase is to impute uncertain tuples. More precisely, we start by computing the similarity between certain and uncertain tuples. There are several measures in literature that can be applied to reflect closeness between two objects (tuples in our case), we propose to use *information affinity* [6]. This choice is justified by the fact that this measure satisfies main properties of similarity measures [6]. Moreover, it has been successfully applied in the context of possibilistic learning of decision trees [6]. Let t_i and t_j be two distinct tuples each characterized by n attributes. Let π_i^k (resp. π_j^k) be the possibility distribution relative to the kth attribute of t_i (resp. t_j) such that m is the number of its values, then the information affinity between t_i and t_j is expressed by:

$$InfoAff(t_i, t_j) = \frac{\sum_{k=1}^{n} Aff(\pi_i^k, \pi_j^k)}{n} \qquad (1)$$

where $Aff(\pi_i^k, \pi_j^k)$ is the similarity degree between π_i^k and π_j^k based on two quantities: inconsistency degree, $Inc(\pi_i^k, \pi_j^k) = 1 - \max_{\omega \in \Omega} \{\pi_i^k(\omega) \wedge \pi_j^k(\omega)\}$ where $\wedge$ can be taken as min or product operator[1] and Manhattan distance i.e.
$d(\pi_i^k, \pi_j^k) = \frac{\sum_{l=1}^{m} |\pi_i^k(\omega_l) - \pi_j^k(\omega_l)|}{m}$. Formally, $Aff(\pi_i^k, {}_j^k)$ is expressed by:

$$Aff(\pi_i^k, \pi_j^k) = 1 - \frac{\kappa * d(\pi_i^k, \pi_j^k) + \lambda * Inc(\pi_i^k, {}_j^k)}{\kappa + \lambda} \qquad (2)$$

where $\kappa > 0$ and $\lambda > 0$. In the remaining, we take $\lambda = \kappa = 1$ and $\wedge$ is the min operator. Once the similarity between uncertain and certain tuples is computed, we can integrate uncertain tuples into the certain set updating thereby certain

---

[1] Using the min operator instead of the product means that we give less importance to the inconsistency degree.

tuples frequencies. Let t_u be an uncertain tuple and $NCT(t_u)$ be its nearest certain tuples i.e. tuples having the highest information affinity. Then, we propose two methods to handle t_u:

1. *Maximum frequency method*: The idea is to search the most frequent tuple among $NCT(t_u)$, denoted by t_c^u, to which we affect the uncertain tuple as follows:

$$fr(t_c^u) = fr(t_c^u) + InfoAff(t_u, t_c^u) * fr(t_u) \qquad (3)$$

   Note that if several tuples have the same maximum frequency, then, we choose randomly one of them as t_c^u.

2. *Dispatching method*: The idea, here, is to dispatch the information affinity value between t_u and $NCT(t_u)$ as follows:

$$\forall t_c \in NCT(t_u), fr(t_c) = fr(t_c) + \frac{InfoAff(t_u, t_c)}{|NCT(t_u)|} * fr(t_u) \qquad (4)$$

If $|NCT(t_u)| = 1$, *Maximum frequency* and *Dispatching* become identical.

Example 2. Let us consider the possibilistic dataset in Table 1. Table 2 presents information affinity values between certain and uncertain tuples and Table 3 presents the updated dataset applying *Dispatching* and *Maximum frequency*.

Table 2. Computing similarities between certain and uncertain tuples

CT \ UT	6	7	8	9	10
1	0.44	0.32	0.41	0.44	0.36
2	**0.79**	0.5	0.53	**0.77**	0.63
3	0.5	0.54	**0.68**	0.44	0.36
4	0.51	**0.77**	0.4	**0.77**	**0.91**
5	0.59	0.38	0.53	**0.77**	0.36

Table 1. An example of a possibilistic dataset

	a_1	a_2	a_3	b_1	b_2	c_1	c_2	c_3	$fr(t_i)$
	A			B		C			
1	1	0	0	0	1	0	0	1	3
2	0	0	1	1	0	0	1	0	4
3	1	0	0	0	1	1	0	0	1
4	0	1	0	1	0	0	1	0	2
5	0	0	1	1	0	0	0	1	1
6	0.1	0	1	0.7	1	0.5	1	0.3	2
7	0	1	0	1	0.8	1	0.6	0.2	1
8	1	0	0.5	1	0.2	1	0	0	1
9	1	1	1	1	0	1	1	1	1
10	0	1	0	1	1	0	1	0	1
								n	16

Table 3. Updating frequencies using *Dispatching* and Maximum frequency

CT		Dispatching $fr(t_i)$	Max frequency $fr(t_i)$
1	$a_1 b_2 c_3$	3	3
2	$a_3 b_1 c_2$	5.84	6.36
3	$a_1 b_2 c_1$	1.68	1.68
4	$a_2 b_1 c_2$	3.95	3.68
5	$a_3 b_1 c_3$	1.25	1
$\sum$		15.72	15.72

3.2   Learning Structure Phase

At this level, we proceed to learn networks structure using the updated dataset denoted by D' and we can apply any algorithm, originally proposed to learn Bayesian networks. In this paper, we propose using two score-based algorithms which have been already applied in the possibilistic framework [1].

- *Maximum Weight Spanning Tree* (MWST) [11]: This algorithm associates a weight (local score) to each pair of variables X_i, $X_j \in V$. MWST finds a subset of edges where the total of their weights is maximized.
- *Greedy Parent Search algorithm* (GPS) [12]: This algorithm requires a topological order to reduce the search space. At the beginning, the value of the score is computed for a variable X_i. Then, in turn, each of the parent candidates X_j is temporarily added and the score is recomputed. The parent candidate that yields the highest value of the scores is selected as a first parent and is permanently added.

These two algorithms are based on local scores to guide the search in graph candidates. In the current work, we retain two scores, namely, *possibilistic mutual information* and *possibilistic χ^2 measure* which are direct adaptations of probabilistic independence tests mutual information [13] and χ^2 [14]. In fact, Borgelt et al. showed that these adaptations yield to good structure in the context of learning possibilistic networks [1]. Given two variables X_i and X_j in V, then:

- *Possibilistic mutual information* is expressed by:

$$d_{mi}(X_i, X_j) = - \sum_{\substack{x_i \in D_i \\ x_j \in D_j}} \Pi(x_i, x_j).log_2 \frac{\Pi(x_i, x_j)}{\min\left(\Pi(x_i), \Pi(x_j)\right)} \tag{5}$$

- *Possibilistic χ^2 measure* is expressed by:

$$d_{\chi^2}(X_i, X_j) = \sum_{\substack{x_i \in D_i \\ x_j \in D_j}} \frac{(min(\Pi(x_i), \Pi(x_j)) - \Pi(x_i, x_j))^2}{min(\Pi(x_i), \Pi(x_j))} \tag{6}$$

Note that these scores are computed in a binary manner which fit well with MWST that generates trees. A generalization to more than two variables is also easy to achieve for the case of GPS. In fact, the score between a variable X_i and any set of candidate parents, denoted by Z, can be computed by a projection of each tuple t_i in the updated dataset D' into an instance z of Z in order to retain those matching to it. The possibility degree of z can be computed as follows. Let $Proj_z(D')$ be this tuple set then:

$$\Pi(z) = \frac{\max\limits_{t_i \in Proj_z(D')} fr(t_i)}{\sum\limits_{l_i \in D'} fr(t_i)} \tag{7}$$

4   Experimental Study

To evaluate *Dispatching* and *Maximum frequency* methods, we propose two sets of experiments:

- CUTS vs *Dispatching* and *Maximum frequency*: this experiment allows us to compare proposed methods with the state of the art one i.e. CUTS [1]. To this end, we should consider the particular case of datasets with missing values since this is the unique case where we can apply the three methods.
- *Dispatching* vs *Maximum frequency*: in this second experiment, we are interested by comparing *Dispatching* and *Maximum frequency* methods. We propose, in particular, to study the impact of data quality (% of missing data and possibilistic data) on the learned structures.

The evaluation consists in assessing quality of learned structures applying MWST and GPS with possibilistic mutual information and possibilistic χ^2 using the global score *weighted sum of possibility degrees* [1]. This evaluation schema has been already applied in the same context in [1]. Weighted sum of possibility degrees of a DAG G given a dataset D, denoted by $Q(G, D)$, consists in summing possibility distributions of possible tuples t_i in D determined from G, weighted with their number of occurrence denoted by $w(t_i)$. This quantity is expressed by:

$$Q(G, D) = \sum_{t \in D} w(t_i).\pi(t_i) \tag{8}$$

Weighted sum of possibility degrees can easily be computed if all tuples are certain because their possibility distributions are unique. Nevertheless, in the case of uncertain tuples, we use an aggregate: in the case of datasets with missing values we may use *min*, *mean* or *max* of possibility distributions of certain tuples that are compatible with it (i.e. a possible certain tuple that can be derived from it e.g. if we consider tuple 9 in Table 1, then a possible compatible tuple is $\{0, 0, 1, 1, 0, 0, 0, 1\}$) as proposed by Borgelt et al. in [1]. However, in the case of possibilistic datasets, the compatibility between tuples is meaningless. So, we propose to use the maximum of possibility degrees of nearest certain tuples as aggregate. Note that weighted sum of possibility degrees should be minimized.

As an example of dataset, we consider for all experiments, *Danish Jersey cattle blood type determination* dataset which contains 500 sample cases described by 21 attributes. This dataset also contains an important number of missing data ($\approx 10\%$ of values). In each experiment, we generate 10 bootstrap samples by selecting randomly 40% of the entire dataset. Each algorithm is evaluated by calculating the mean and the standard deviation of weighted sum of possibility degrees of learned networks structures. The order used in GPS corresponds to the one cited in *Danish Jersey cattle blood type determination* dataset.

4.1   CUTS vs Dispatching and Maximum Frequency Methods

The first experiment concerns the comparison between CUTS and *Dispatching* and *Maximum frequency* in the particular case of missing data. Table 4 shows results relative to this experiment. As we have mentioned, to treat uncertain tuples in weighted sum of possibility degrees, we may choose the *min*, *mean* or *max* of compatible tuples of possibility degrees. Table 4 shows that *Dispatching* and *Maximum frequency*yield better results than CUTS. This is an obvious result

Table 4. Weighted sum of possibility degrees of learned structures using min, mean and maxi aggregations

			max	mean	min	execution time
MWST	d_{mi}	CUTS	2+/- 0.2	1,8+/-0.1	1,7+/-0.1	2.5+/-0.2
		Dispatching	**1,9**+/-0.1	1,8+/-0.1	**1,6**+/-0.1	2.8+/-0.2
		Maximum frequency	**1,9**/-0.1	**1,7**+/-0.1	**1,6**+/-0.1	2.8+/-0.2
	d_{χ^2}	CUTS	2+/-0.2	1,9+/-0.1	1,8+/-0.1	2.7+/-0.4
		Dispatching	2+/-0.1	**1,8**+/-0.1	**1,7**+/-0.1	2.9+/-0.1
		Maximum frequency	2+/-0.1	**1,8**+/-0.1	**1,7**+/-0.1	2.8+/-0.1
GPS	d_{mi}	CUTS	1,9+/-0.2	1,7+/-0.2	1,5+/-0.1	18.5+/-0.2
		Dispatching	1,9+/-0.1	1,7+/-0.1	1,5+/-0.1	17+/-0.3
		Maximum frequency	1,9+/-0.1	1,7+/-0.1	1,5+/-0.1	18 +/-0.7
	d_{χ^2}	CUTS	1,9+/-0.2	1,7+/-0.1	1,5+/-0.1	33.7+/-0.6
		Dispatching	1,9+/-0.1	1,7+/-0.1	1,5+/-0.1	38.3+/-0.2
		Maximum frequency	1,9+/-0.1	**1,6**+/-0.1	1,5+/-0.1	38.1+/-0.2

due to the way in which uncertain tuples are handled, in fact, in *Dispatching* and *Maximum frequency*, their frequency corresponds to their similarity (less than 1) and not their real frequency (1) as it is the case in CUTS. By this way, we can deflate considerably possibility distributions and thereby, we make them more informative for discovering dependencies between attributes. Table 4 (last column) shows also that these three methods run in approximately equal time durations. The complexity of *Dispatching* and *Maximum frequency* is O(p*q).

4.2   Dispatching vs Maximum Frequency

The first experiment shows a very close behavior of *Dispatching* and *Maximum frequency*. Thus, we focus now on comparing them by varying the percentage of missing and possibilistic data in the dataset. Thus, we generate four synthetic datasets by randomly removing 10%, 20%, 30% and 40% of values. Figure 1 shows that adding missing data reduces learned structures quality. In fact, this operation introduces noise to the dataset which allows the emergence of corrupted dependencies. Obviously, in this situation, both methods perform less better but, we remark that they remain stable i.e. not very sensitive to noise. The last experiment covers four synthetic datasets generated by varying the percentage of missing data in the dataset replaced by possibility distributions (possibilistic data). Figure 1 gives results of this experiment. Unsurprisingly, the quality of learned structures is better when we replace missing data with possibility distributions in both methods *Dispatching* and *Maximum frequency*. This is due to the fact that possibility distributions are more specific than missing data (total ignorance). We also note that *Dispatching* and *Maximum frequency* behave almost the same way regarding missing and possibilistic data except in the case of MWST where *Maximum frequency* leads to slightly better learned structures. *Maximum frequency* is based on most frequent observations excluding dependencies discovered from very rare observations generally not relevant to the problem.

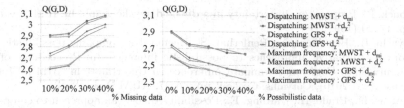

Fig. 1. Weighted sum of possibility degrees of learned structures from missing and possibilistic data

5   Conclusion

This paper addresses the problem of structural learning of DAGs from possibilistic datasets. The proposed approach is first based on imputation to handle uncertain tuples. To this end, two solutions are proposed: *Dispatching* and *Maximum frequency*. Then, we proceed to the learning phase where we can apply any of the learning structure algorithms. Experimental study shows that both *Dispatching* and *Maximum frequency* yield better structures than the closest existing method to our work i.e. CUTS [1]. It also shows that they have almost the same behavior with GPS and MWST learning algorithms with a slight advantage to *Maximum frequency* with MWST. The output of the proposed approach is a DAG without any numerical data which may represent the qualitative component of several graphical models. That said, the semantic of generated structures fits better with possibilistic networks and more precisely *product-based* ones. Future work concerns evaluation methods of learned networks structure to make it more specific to the possibilistic framework. We also tend to learn possibilistic networks parameters from data which remains a real challenge.

References

[1] Borgelt, C., Steinbrecher, M., Kruse, R.: Graphical models: representations for learning, reasoning and data mining, vol. 704. Wiley (2009)
[2] Pearl, J.: Probabilistic reasoning in intelligent systems: networks of plausible inference. Morgan Kaufmann (1988)
[3] Lauritzen, S.: The EM algorithm for graphical association models with missing data. Computational Statistics & Data Analysis 19(2), 191–201 (1995)
[4] Haouari, B., Ben Amor, N., Elouedi, Z., Mellouli, K.: Naïve possibilistic network classifiers. Fuzzy Sets and Systems 160(22), 3224–3238 (2009)
[5] Bounhas, M., Mellouli, K., Prade, H., Serrurier, M.: From Bayesian classifiers to possibilistic classifiers for numerical data. In: Deshpande, A., Hunter, A. (eds.) SUM 2010. LNCS, vol. 6379, pp. 112–125. Springer, Heidelberg (2010)
[6] Jenhani, I., Amor, N., Elouedi, Z.: Decision trees as possibilistic classifiers. International Journal of Approximate Reasoning 48(3), 784–807 (2008)
[7] Ammar, A., Elouedi, Z., Lingras, P.: K-modes clustering using possibilistic membership. In: Greco, S., Bouchon-Meunier, B., Coletti, G., Fedrizzi, M., Matarazzo, B., Yager, R.R. (eds.) IPMU 2012, Part III. CCIS, vol. 299, pp. 596–605. Springer, Heidelberg (2012)

[8] Fonck, P.: Propagating uncertainty in a directed acyclic graph. In: IPMU, vol. 92, pp. 17–20 (1992)

[9] Ayachi, R., Ben Amor, N., Benferhat, S., Haenni, R.: Compiling possibilistic networks: Alternative approaches to possibilistic inference. In: Proceedings of the Twenty-Sixth Conference Annual Conference on Uncertainty in Artificial Intelligence (UAI 2010), Corvallis, Oregon, pp. 40–47. AUAI Press (2010)

[10] Dubois, D., Prade, H., Harding, E.: Possibility theory: an approach to computerized processing of uncertainty, vol. 2. Plenum Press, New York (1988)

[11] Chow, C., Liu, C.: Approximating discrete probability distributions with dependence trees. IEEE Transactions on Information Theory 14(3), 462–467 (1968)

[12] Cooper, G., Herskovits, E.: A Bayesian method for the induction of probabilistic networks from data. Machine Learning 9(4), 309–347 (1992)

[13] Shannon, E.: A mathematical theory of evidence: Bellsyt. Techn. Journal 27, 379–423 (1948)

[14] Chernoff, H., Lehmann, E.: The use of maximum likelihood estimates in χ^2 tests for goodness of fit. The Annals of Mathematical Statistics 25(3), 579–586 (1954)

Adding Real Coefficients to Łukasiewicz Logic: An Application to Neural Networks

Antonio Di Nola[1], Brunella Gerla[2], and Ioana Leustean[3]

[1] Università di Salerno, Via Ponte don Melillo 84084 Fisciano, Salerno, Italy
adinola@unisa.it
[2] Università dell'Insubria, Via Mazzini 5, 21100 Varese, Italy
brunella.gerla@uninsubria.it
[3] University of Bucharest, Academiei 14, sector 1, C.P. 010014, Bucharest, Romania
ioana@fmi.unibuc.ro

Abstract. In this paper we shall deal with an extension of Łukasiewicz propositional logic obtained by considering scalar multiplication with real numbers, and we focus on the description of its Lindenbaum algebra, i.e., the algebra of truth functions. We show the correspondence between truth tables of such logic and multilayer perceptrons in which the activation function is the truncated identity.

Keywords: Many-valued logic, Łukasiewicz logic, McNaughton functions, Neural Networks, MV-algebras, Riesz MV-algebras.

1 Introduction

Many-valued logics are the logical instrument to use when dealing with more than two truth values. In particular, in the big class of many-valued logics a leading role belongs to Łukasiewicz logic that has truth values in the real interval $[0, 1]$ and whose connectives are the Łukasiewicz t-norm

$$x \odot y = \max(x + y - 1, 0)$$

as interpretation of conjunction, and the involution $\neg x = 1 - x$ as interpretation of negation.

The importance of Łukasiewicz logic is mainly due to the fact that it is a deductive system that is logically sound and complete with respect to interpretations in the interval $[0, 1]$ and, further, when interpreted in $[0, 1]$ all connectives become continuous functions.

Differently from what happens in classical propositional logic, a functional completeness theorem does not hold: not all the functions from $[0, 1]^n$ to $[0, 1]$ are *truth tables* of some Łukasiewicz formula. But a characterization of such functions exists: McNaughton theorem [13] ensures that they are exactly the class of continuous piecewise linear functions with integer coefficients. Then a natural question arises: how to modify the logic in order to obtain, as truth functions, all the continuous piecewise linear functions. The answer has been

F. Masulli, G. Pasi, and R. Yager (Eds.): WILF 2013, LNAI 8256, pp. 77–85, 2013.

given in [8,9] where a logical system $\mathbb{R}\mathcal{L}$ corresponding to Riesz MV-algebras (unit interval of vector lattices) is given.

Many-valued logic has been proposed in [5] to model neural networks: it is shown there that, by taking as activation function ϱ the identity truncated to zero and one (i.e., $\varrho(x) = (1 \wedge (x \vee 0)))$, it is possible to represent the corresponding neural network as combination of propositions of Łukasiewicz calculus. In [2], formulas of Rational Łukasiewicz logic have been studied in correspondence with multilayer perceptrons.

In this paper we extend the latter result and we show that multilayer percep-trons whose activation function is the identity truncated to zero and one, can be fully interpreted as logical objects, since they are equivalent to (equivalence classes of) formulas of $\mathbb{R}\mathcal{L}$. This result can be seen as a generalization of the well known correspondence between boolean circuits and formulas of classical propo-sitional logic (see also [7]). On one hand to have a logical representation (in a given logic) of neural networks could widen the interpretability, amalgamability and reuse of these objects. On the other hand, neural networks could be used to learn formulas from data and as circuital counterparts of (functions represented by) formulas.

2   MV-Algebras, Riesz MV-Algebras and Related Logical Systems

The algebraic structures related with Łukasiewicz infinite-valued logic are called *MV-algebras*. An MV-algebra is a structure $(A, \oplus, ^*, 0)$, where $(A, \oplus, 0)$ is an abelian monoid and the following identities hold for all $x, y \in A$:

MV(1) $(x^*)^* = x$,
MV(2) $0^* \oplus x = 0^*$,
MV(3) $(x^* \oplus y)^* \oplus y = (y^* \oplus x)^* \oplus x$.

The real unit interval $[0, 1]$ equipped with the operations
$$x^* = 1 - x \text{ and } x \oplus y = \min(1, x + y)$$
for any $x, y \in [0, 1]$ (the *standard* MV-algebra) generates the verity of MV-algebras, i.e. an equation holds in any MV-algebra if and only if it holds in $[0, 1]$. We refer to [6] for all the unexplained notions concerning MV-algebras. On any MV-algebra A the following operations are defined for any $x, y \in A$:

$$1 = 0^*, \; x \odot y = (x^* \oplus y^*)^*, \; x \to y = x^* \oplus y$$
$$0x = 0, \; mx = (m-1)x \oplus x \text{ for any } m \geq 1.$$

We recall that an *ℓ-group* is a structure $(G, +, 0, \leq)$ such that $(G, +, 0)$ is a group, $(G, \leq)$ is a lattice and any group translation is isotone [3]. If G is an abelian ℓ-group and $u \in G$, we define $[0, u] = \{x \in G \mid 0 \leq x \leq u\}$ and

$$x \oplus y = (x + y) \wedge u, \; x^* = u - x \text{ for any } x, y \in [0, u].$$

Then $[0, u]_G = ([0, u], \oplus, \neg, 0)$ is an MV-algebra [6, Proposition 2.1.2]. So for example, from the abelian ℓ-group $\mathbb{R}$ of real numbers (equipped with the usual linear ordering) and considering the unit element 1, one obtain the standard MV-algebra $[0, 1]$.

In [15] Mundici proved that MV-algebras are categorically equivalent with abelian lattice-ordered groups with strong unit (i.e. an element $u \in G$ such that $u \geq 0$ and for any $x \in G$ there is a natural number n such that $x \leq nu$.). Hence any MV-algebra is the unit interval of some abelian ℓ-group.

A *Riesz space (vector lattice)* [12] is a structure $(V, \cdot, +, 0, \leq)$ such that $(V, +, 0, \leq)$ is an abelian ℓ-group, $(V, \cdot, +, 0)$ is a real vector space and, in addition, $x \leq y$ implies $r \cdot x \leq r \cdot y$, for any $x, y \in V$ and $r \in \mathbb{R}$, $r \geq 0$. A Riesz space is *unital* if the underlaying ℓ-group has strong unit.

A simple example of Riesz space is once again the set of real numbers with operations of sum and multiplication and with the usual linear ordering.

If (V, u) is a Riesz space with strong unit then the unit interval $[0, u]_V$ is closed with respect to the scalar multiplication with scalars from $[0, 1]$. The structure

$$[0, u]_V = ([0, u], \cdot, \oplus, ^*, 0),$$

where $([0, u], \oplus, ^*, 0)$ is the MV-algebra defined as above and $\cdot : [0, 1] \times [0, u]_V \to [0, u]_V$ satisfies the axioms of the scalar product is the fundamental example in the theory of *Riesz MV-algebras*, initiated in [9].

Definition 1. *A* Riesz MV-algebra *is a structure*

$$(R, \cdot, \oplus, ^*, 0),$$

where $(R, \oplus, ^*, 0)$ *is an MV-algebra and the operation* $\cdot : [0, 1] \times R \to R$ *satisfies the following identities for any* $r, q \in [0, 1]$ *and* $x, y \in R$:

(RMV1) $r \cdot (x \odot y^*) = (r \cdot x) \odot (r \cdot y)^*$,
(RMV2) $(r \odot q^*) \cdot x = (r \cdot x) \odot (q \cdot x)^*$,
(RMV3) $r \cdot (q \cdot x) = (rq) \cdot x$,
(RMV4) $1 \cdot x = x$.

In the following we write rx instead of $r \cdot x$ for $r \in [0, 1]$ and $x \in R$. Note that rq is the real product for any $r, q \in [0, 1]$.

Theorem 1. *An equation* σ *in the theory of Riesz MV-algebras holds in all Riesz MV-algebras if and only if it holds in the standard Riesz MV-algebra* $[0, 1]$.

2.1   The Propositional Calculus $\mathbb{R}\mathcal{L}$

We denote by $\mathcal{L}_\infty$ the ∞-valued propositional Lukasiewicz logic. Recall that $\mathcal{L}_\infty$ has $\neg$ (unary) and $\to$ (binary) as primitive connectives and, for any φ and ψ we have the following derived connectives:

$$\varphi \oplus \psi := \neg\varphi \to \psi \qquad \varphi \odot \psi := \neg(\neg\varphi \oplus \psi)$$
$$\varphi \vee \psi := (\varphi \to \psi) \to \psi \qquad \varphi \wedge \psi := \neg(\neg\varphi \vee \neg\psi)$$
$$\top := (\varphi \to \varphi) \qquad \bot := \neg\top.$$

The language of $\mathbb{R}\mathcal{L}$ contains the language of $\mathcal{L}_\infty$ and a family of unary connectives $\{\nabla_r | r \in [0,1]\}$. We denote by $Form(\mathbb{R}\mathcal{L})$ the set of formulas defined inductively as usual.

Let R be a Riesz MV-algebra. An *evaluation* is a function $e : Form(\mathbb{R}\mathcal{L}) \to R$ which satisfies the following conditions for any $\varphi, \psi \in Form(\mathbb{R}\mathcal{L})$ and $r \in [0,1]$:
(e1) $e(\varphi \to \psi) = e(\varphi)^* \oplus e(\psi)$,
(e2) $e(\neg\varphi) = e(\varphi)^*$,
(e3) $e(\nabla_r\varphi) = (re(\varphi)^*)^*$.
As a consequence of Theorem 1, the propositional calculus $\mathbb{R}\mathcal{L}$ is complete with respect to $[0,1]$. In order to define the scalar multiplication we introduce new connectives $\Delta_r\varphi := \neg(\nabla_r\neg\varphi)$. Note that $e(\Delta_r\varphi) = re(\varphi)$.

Definition 2. *The term function* $\tilde{\varphi} : [0,1]^n \to [0,1]$ *associated with a formula* $\varphi(v_1, \ldots, v_n)$ *is the uniquely defined function such that* $\tilde{\varphi}(x_1, \ldots, x_n) = e(\varphi)$, *where* e *is an evaluation such that* $e(v_i) = x_i$ *for any* $i \in \{1, \ldots, n\}$.

The set $\{\tilde{\varphi} \mid \varphi \in Form(\mathbb{R}\mathcal{L})\}$ is a Riesz MV-algebra with operations defined pointwisely.

2.2   Term Functions and Continuous Piecewise Linear Functions

In the following, we characterize the class of functions that can be defined by formulas in $\mathbb{R}\mathcal{L}$.

Recall that $f : \mathbb{R}^n \to \mathbb{R}$ is a linear function if $f(x_1, \ldots, x_n) = a_1 x_1 + \ldots + a_n x_n + b$ with $a_i, b \in \mathbb{R}$.

Definition 3. *Let* $n > 1$ *be a natural number. A function* $f : \mathbb{R}^n \to \mathbb{R}$ *is a* piecewise linear function *if there exists a finite number of linear functions*

$$q_1 \ldots, q_k : \mathbb{R}^n \to \mathbb{R}$$

such that for any $(x_1, \ldots, x_n) \in \mathbb{R}^n$ *there is* $i \in \{1, \ldots, k\}$ *such that* $f(x_1, \ldots, x_n) = q_i(x_1, \ldots, x_n)$.

We denote by PL_n the set of continuous piecewise linear functions $f : [0,1]^n \to [0,1]$. The following can be proved by structural induction on the formulas.

Theorem 2. *If* φ *is a formula of* $\mathbb{R}\mathcal{L}$ *with propositional variables from* $\{v_1, \cdots, v_n\}$ *then* $\tilde{\varphi} \in PL_n$.

The continuous piecewise linear functions $f : [0,1]^n \to [0,1]$ with *integer coefficients* are called *McNaughton functions* and they are in one-one correspondence with the formulas of Łukasiewicz logic by McNaughton theorem [13]. The continuous piecewise linear functions with *rational coefficients* correspond to formulas of Rational Łukasiewicz logic, a propositional calculus developed in [10] that has divisible MV-algebras as models. In Theorem 3 we prove that any continuous piecewise linear function with *real coefficients* $f : [0,1]^n \to [0,1]$ is the term function of a formula from $\mathbb{R}\mathcal{L}$.

For now on we define $\varrho : \mathbb{R} \to [0,1]$ by

$$\varrho(x) = (x \vee 0) \wedge 1 \text{ for any } x \in \mathbb{R}.$$

Proposition 1. *For any linear function* $f : [0,1]^n \to \mathbb{R}$ *there exists a formula* φ *of* $\mathbb{R}\mathcal{L}$ *such that* $\varrho \circ f = \widetilde{\varphi}$.

Proof of this proposition can be found in [9]. For a comparison on the case of McNaughton functions and McNughton functions with rational coefficients, we refer the reader to [1].

Following the proof in [9], we define here a recursive function whose input is a linear function $f : [0,1]^n \to \mathbb{R}$ and whose output is a formula φ of $\mathbb{R}\mathcal{L}$ such that $\varrho \circ f = \widetilde{\varphi}$. If $f : [0,1]^n \to \mathbb{R}$ is a linear function, then

$$f(x_1, \ldots, x_n) = c_n x_n + \cdots + c_1 x_1 + c_0$$

with $c_0, \ldots, c_n \in \mathbb{R}$. Note that for any $c \in \mathbb{R}$ there is a natural number m such that $c = r_1 + \cdots + r_m$ where $r_1, \ldots, r_m \in [-1,1]$. Hence

$$f(x_1, \ldots, x_n) = r_m y_m + \cdots r_{p+1} y_{p+1} + r_p + \cdots + r_1$$

where $m \geq 1$ and $0 \leq p \leq m$ are natural numbers, $r_j \in [-1,1] \setminus \{0\}$ for any $j \in \{1, \ldots, m\}$ and $y_j \in \{x_1, \ldots, x_n\}$ for any $j \in \{p+1, \cdots, m\}$.

In the sequel we represent a monomial $r x_i$ as a pair (r,i) so, in consequence, a linear function is represented as a list of pairs (r,i) where $c \in [-1,1]$ and $i \in \{0, \ldots, n\}$. In this representation a pair $(r,0)$ will represent the free term r. The input of the recursive function **Formula** is a nonempty list of pairs.

```
function Formula((r₁,i₁),...,(rₘ,iₘ))
{
(F1) if rₖ ≤ 0 for any k ∈ {1,...,m} then return(⊥);
(F2) find k ∈ {1,...,m} such that rₖ > 0;
     if iₖ = 0 then ψ := Δ_{rₖ}⊤ else ψ := Δ_{rₖ}x_{iₖ};
(F3) if m = 1 then return(ψ);
(F4) φ =Formula((r₁,i₁),...,(r_{k-1},i_{k-1}),(r_{k+1},i_{k+1}),...,(rₘ,iₘ)) ;
     χ =Formula((-r₁,i₁),...,(-r_{k-1},i_{k-1}),(-r_{k+1},i_{k+1}),...,(-rₘ,iₘ)) ;
     return((φ ⊕ ψ) ⊙ ¬χ)
}
```

Note that in the above algorithm $\Delta_1 \varphi$ can be replaced by φ for any formula φ, since $\vdash \varphi \leftrightarrow \Delta_1 \varphi$ in $\mathbb{R}\mathcal{L}$. Further simplifications in $\mathbb{R}\mathcal{L}$ can be done, but they are beyond the scope of the above algorithm.

Example 1. We illustrate how the algorithm works on a simple example.
If $f : [0,1]^2 \to [0,1]$, $f(x_1, x_2) = x_2 - 0.3 x_1$ then we call the function

```
function Formula((1,2),(-0.3,1))
{
(F2) k = 1, rₖ = 1, iₖ = 2; ψ := Δ₁x₂;
(F4) φ =Formula((-0.3,1)) ; χ =Formula((0.3,1)) ;
return((φ ⊕ ψ) ⊙ ¬χ)
}
```

One can easily see that $\varphi = \bot$ and $\chi = \Delta_{0.3}x_1$, so the function returns

$$(\varphi \oplus \psi) \odot \neg\chi = (\bot \oplus \Delta_1 x_2) \odot \neg\Delta_{0.3}x_1$$

which is logically equivalent with $x_2 \odot \neg\Delta_{0.3}x_1$.

Theorem 3. *For any $f : [0,1]^n \to [0,1]$ from PL_n there is a formula φ of $\mathbb{R}\mathcal{L}$ such that $f = \widetilde{\varphi}$.*

Proof. Let $f : [0,1]^n \to [0,1]$ be a continuous piecewise linear function and let $p_1, \ldots, p_u$ be the linear functions that are the *pieces* of f in the sense that for every $\mathbf{x} \in [0,1]^n$ there exists $i \in \{1, \ldots, u\}$ such that $f(\mathbf{x}) = p_i(\mathbf{x})$.

Let Σ denote the set of permutations of $\{1, \ldots, u\}$ and for every $\sigma \in \Sigma$ let

$$P_\sigma = \{\mathbf{x} \in [0,1]^n \mid p_{\sigma(1)}(\mathbf{x}) \leq \ldots \leq p_{\sigma(u)}(\mathbf{x})\}.$$

In other words P_σ is a polyhedron such that the set of restrictions of linear functions $p_1, \ldots, p_u$ to P_σ is totally ordered, increasingly with respect to $\{\sigma(1), \ldots, \sigma(u)\}$. We denote by i_σ the index such that

$$f(\mathbf{x}) = p_{\sigma(i_\sigma)}(\mathbf{x}) \qquad \text{for every } \mathbf{x} \in P_\sigma.$$

Using the Max-Min representation from [16] (see also [13,14])

$$f = \bigwedge_{\sigma \in \Sigma} \bigvee_{j=1}^{i_\sigma} p_{\sigma(j)},$$

where we stress that $p_{\sigma(j)} : [0,1]^n \to \mathbb{R}$ are linear functions. We note that

$$f = \varrho \circ f = \bigwedge_{\sigma \in \Sigma} \bigvee_{j=1}^{i_\sigma} \varrho \circ p_{\sigma(j)}.$$

By Proposition 1, for any $\sigma \in \Sigma$ and $j = 1, \ldots, i_\sigma$ there is a formula $\varphi_{\sigma j}$ such that $\varrho \circ p_{\sigma(j)} = \widetilde{\varphi_{\sigma j}}$. In consequence, if we set $\varphi = \bigwedge_{\sigma \in \Sigma} \bigvee_{j=1}^{i_\sigma} \varphi_{\sigma j}$ then $f = \widetilde{\varphi}$. □

For any $n \geq 1$, the set PL_n is a Riesz MV-algebra with the operations defined componentwise. If RL_n is the Lindenbaum-Tarski algebra of $\mathbb{R}\mathcal{L}$ defined on formulas with variables from $\{v_1, \ldots, v_n\}$, then RL_n is the free Riesz MV-algebra with n free generators by standard results in universal algebra (see [4] and [1] for the case of free algebras related to many-valued logics) . Since the function $[\varphi] \mapsto \widetilde{\varphi}$ is obviously an isomorphism between RL_n and PL_n the following corollary is straightforward.

Corollary 1. *PL_n is the free Riesz MV-algebra with n free generators.*

Elements of PL_n will be also called $\mathbb{R}\mathcal{L}$ *functions.*

3   Neural Networks

Among the many possible neural networks typologies and structures, we focus our attention on multilayer perceptrons. These are feedforward neural networks with one or more hidden layers. A multilayer perceptron with l hidden layers [11], n inputs and one output can be represented as a function $F : [0,1]^n \to [0,1]$ such that $F(x_1,\ldots,x_n) =$

$$\phi\left(\sum_{k=1}^{n^{(l)}} \omega_{ok}^l \phi\left(\sum_{j=1}^{n^{(l-1)}} \omega_{kj}^{l-1}\phi\left(\ldots\left(\sum_{i=1}^{n} \omega_{li}^1 x_i + b_i\right)\ldots\right)\right)\right), \tag{1}$$

where $\phi : \mathbb{R} \to [0,1]$ is a monotone-nondecreasing continuous function (referred to as activation function), ω_{ok}^l is the synaptic weight from neuron k in the l-th hidden layer to the single output neuron o, ω_{kj}^{l-1} is the synaptic weight from neuron j in the $(l-1)$-th hidden layer to neuron k in the l-th hidden layer, and so on for the other synaptic weights.

In the simplest case, a multilayer perceptron has exactly one hidden layer. This network can be represented as a function $G : [0,1]^n \to [0,1]$:

$$G(x_1,\ldots,x_n) = \phi\left(\sum_{1=1}^{\bar{n}} \alpha_i \phi\left(\sum_{j=1}^{n} w_{ij}x_j + b_i\right)\right), \tag{2}$$

where $\bar{n}$ is the number of neurons in the hidden layer.

Let $\mathcal{N}$ be the class of multilayer perceptrons where the activation function is the continuous piecewise linear function $\varrho(x) = \max(\min(1,x),0)$, and the synaptic weights are real numbers.

3.1 $\mathbb{RL}$ and Neural Networks

In order to establish a correspondence between neural networks and $\mathbb{RL}$ functions, we need the following

Lemma 1. *The activation function ϱ maps any finite weighted sum of functions in PL_n into a function in PL_n.*

We want now to associate a neural network to each $\mathbb{RL}$ formula of n variables.

By using neural networks we can express linear combinations, but we need to define networks corresponding to minimum and maximum.

Proposition 2. *For every $x,y \in [0,1]$, one-layer neural networks*

$$F_1(x,y) = \varrho(y) - \varrho(y-x)$$
$$F_2(x,y) = \varrho(y) + \varrho(x-y)$$

coincide respectively with $\min(x,y)$ and $\max(x,y)$.

Proof. If $x \leq y$ then $\varrho(y) = y$, $\varrho(y - x) = y - x$ and $\varrho(x - y) = 0$, hence $F_1(x, y) = x$ and $F_2(x, y) = y$.

If $y \leq x$ then $\varrho(y) = y$, $\varrho(y - x) = 0$ and $\varrho(x - y) = x - y$, hence $F_1(x, y) = y$ and $F_2(x, y) = x$.

We can hence describe neural representation of $\mathbb{R}\mathcal{L}$ functions.

Theorem 4. *(i) For every $l, n, n^{(2)}, \ldots, n^{(l)} \in \mathbb{N}$, and $\omega_{ij}, b_i \in \mathbb{R}$, the function $F : [0, 1]^n \longmapsto [0, 1]$ defined as $F(x_1, \ldots, x_n) =$*

$$\varrho \left(\sum_{k=1}^{n^{(l)}} \omega_{ok} \varrho \left(\sum_{j=1}^{n^{(l-1)}} \omega_{kj} \varrho \left(\cdots \left(\sum_{i=1}^{n} \omega_{li} x_i + b_i \right) \cdots \right) \right) \right),$$

is a $\mathbb{R}\mathcal{L}$ function.
(ii) For any $\mathbb{R}\mathcal{L}$ function f, there exist $l, n, n^{(2)}, \ldots, n^{(l)} \in \mathbb{N}$, and $\omega_{ij}, b_i \in \mathbb{R}$ such that $f(x_1, \ldots, x_n) =$

$$\varrho \left(\sum_{k=1}^{n^{(l)}} \omega_{ok} \varrho \left(\sum_{j=1}^{n^{(l-1)}} \omega_{kj} \varrho \left(\cdots \left(\sum_{i=1}^{n} \omega_{li} x_i + b_i \right) \cdots \right) \right) \right).$$

Proof. (i) By Lemma 1.
(ii) By Theorem 3 we have

$$f(\mathbf{x}) = \min_{\sigma \in \Sigma} \max_{1 \leq j \leq i_\sigma} \varrho(p_{\sigma(j)}(\mathbf{x})).$$

For every σ and j, the function $\varrho(p_{\sigma(j)}(\mathbf{x}))$ is a network with one hidden layer. Then applying networks as in Proposition 2 we get the claim.

By using a simple variation of Weierstrass theorem it is possible to show that continuous piecewise linear functions are able to approximate every continuous function with an error as low as desired. Then we have the following

Corollary 2. *The class $\mathcal{N}$ of functions associated with multilayer perceptrons as in Equation 1, with $\omega_{ij} \in \mathbb{R}$ and $\phi = \varrho$ truncated identity, is dense in the class of continuous functions.*

From the corollary it follows that the use of only truncated identity ϱ as activation function is not a severe restriction on the class of neural networks which can be obtained; they can approximate every neural network representing a continuous function.

References

1. Aguzzoli, S., Bova, S., Gerla, B.: Free Algebras and Functional Representation for Fuzzy Logics. In: Cintula, P., Hájek, P., Noguera, C. (eds.) Handbook of Mathematical Fuzzy Logic. Studies in Logic, vol. 38, pp. 713–791. College Publications, London (2011)

2. Amato, P., Di Nola, A., Gerla, B.: Neural networks and rational McNaughton functions. Journal of Multiple-Valued Logic and Soft Computing 11, 95–110 (2005)
3. Bigard, A., Keimel, K., Wolfenstein, S.: Groupes et anneaux réticulés. Lecture Notes in Mathematics, vol. 608. Springer (1977)
4. Burris, S., Sankappanavar, H.P.: A Course in Universal Algebra. Springer (1982)
5. Castro, J.L., Trillas, E.: The logic of neural networks. Mathware and Soft Computing 5, 23–27 (1998)
6. Cignoli, R., D'Ottaviano, I.M.L., Mundici, D.: Algebraic Foundations of many-valued Reasoning. Kluwer, Dordrecht (2000)
7. Dhompongsa, S., Kreinovich, V., Nguyen, H.T.: How to interpret Neural Networks in terms of fuzzy logic? In: Proceedings of VJFUZZY 2001, pp. 184–190 (2001)
8. Di Nola, A., Leuştean, I.: Riesz MV-algebras and their logic. In: Proceedings of EUSFLAT-LFA 2011, pp. 140–145 (2011)
9. Di Nola, A., Leuştean, I.: Łukasiewicz logic and Riesz spaces. Soft Computing (accepter for publication)
10. Gerla, B.: Rational Łukasiewicz logic and Divisible MV-algebras. Neural Networks World 11, 159 (2001)
11. Haykin, S.: Neural Neworks – A Comprehensive Foundation. Prentice-Hall, Englewood Cliffs (1999)
12. Luxemburg, W.A.J., Zaanen, A.C.: Riesz Spaces I. North-Holland, Amsterdam (1971)
13. McNaughton, R.: A theorem about infinite-valued sentential logic. The Journal of Symbolic Logic 16, 1–13 (1951)
14. Mundici, D.: A constructive proof of McNaughton's theorem in infinite-valued logics. Journal of Symbolic Logic 59, 596–602 (1994)
15. Mundici, D.: Averaging the truth value Łukasiewicz logic. Studia Logica 55, 113–127 (1995)
16. Ovchinnikov, S.: Max-Min Representation of Piecewise Linear Functions. Beiträge zur Algebra und Geometrie Contributions to Algebra and Geometry 43, 297–302 (2002)

Possibilistic Graphical Models:
From Reasoning to Decision Making

Nahla Ben Amor

Laboratoire de Recherche Opérationnelle, de Décision et de Contrôle de processus
(LARODEC), Institut Supérieur de Gestion Tunis, Université de Tunis, Tunisia
nahla.benamor@gmx.fr

Abstract. Graphical models are important tools to efficiently represent and analyze uncertain information in knowledge-based systems. The most prominent representatives of these models refer to probability theory. In particular, Bayesian networks [27, 29] have been largely developed and used in real world applications. However, such networks are only appropriate when all numerical data are available, which is not always the case. Indeed, there are some situations such as the case of total ignorance, which are not well handled and which can make the probabilistic reasoning unsound. Therefore non-probabilistic graphical modeling has recently emerged as a promising new area of research. In particular, possibilistic networks [4, 8, 21] appear as noteworthy alternative to probabilistic networks whenever it is necessary to model both uncertainty and imprecision. In fact possibility theory [15] offers a natural and simple model to handle such data and presents an appropriate framework for experts to express their opinions numerically or qualitatively. This leads to two variants of possibilistic networks: *product-based networks* and *min-based networks* (also known as qualitative possibilistic networks). The first part of this talk adresses the reasoning problem in possibilistic networks. Several propagation algorithms will be presented with a focus on qualitative networks. The second part concerns the decisional aspect in possibility theory and in particular the sequential decision making in possibilistic decision trees. In fact, the development of possibilistic decision theory has lead to the proposition of a series of possibilistic criteria, namely: optimistic and pessimistic possibilistic qualitative criteria [17], possibilistic likely dominance [14, 20], binary possibilistic utility [23] and possibilistic Choquet integrals [32]. Thus a theoretical study on the complexity of the problem of finding an optimal strategy depending on the monotonicity property of the optimization criteria will be proposed. Details about different parts of this talk can be found in [1–5].

Keywords: Graphical models, Possibility theory, Causality, Propagation algorithms, Decision making, Possibilistic decision trees.

1   Background on Possibility Theory

Possibility theory, issued from Fuzzy Sets theory, was introduced by Zadeh [35] and further developed by Dubois and Prade [15]. This subsection briefly recalls some basic elements, for more details we refer to [15].

Let $V = \{X_1, X_2, ..., X_N\}$ be a set of variables. We denote by x_i any instance of X_i and by D_{X_i} the domain associated with X_i. $\Omega = D_{X_1} \times \cdots \times D_{X_N}$ denotes the universe

F. Masulli, G. Pasi, and R. Yager (Eds.): WILF 2013, LNAI 8256, pp. 86–99, 2013.
© Springer International Publishing Switzerland 2013

of discourse, which is the Cartesian product of all variable domains V. Vectors $\omega \in \Omega$ are often called realizations or simply "states" (of the world). The agent's knowledge about the value of the x_i's can be encoded by a possibility distribution $\pi : \Omega \to [0,1]$; $\pi(\omega) = 1$ means that realization ω is totally possible and $\pi(\omega) = 0$ means that ω is an impossible state. It is generally assumed that there exist at least one state ω which is totally possible - π is said then to be *normalized*. Extreme cases of knowledge are presented by:

- *complete knowledge* i.e. $\exists \omega_0$ s.t. $\pi(\omega_0) = 1$ and $\forall \omega \neq \omega_0, \pi(\omega) = 0$.
- *total ignorance* i.e. $\forall \omega \in \Omega, \pi(\omega) = 1$ (all values in Ω are possible).

From π, one can describe the uncertainty about the occurrence of an event $A \subseteq \Omega$ via two dual measures: the possibility $\Pi(A)$ and the necessity $N(A)$ expressed by:

$$\Pi(A) = \sup_{\omega \in A} \pi(\omega). \tag{1}$$

$$N(A) = 1 - \Pi(\bar{A}) = 1 - \sup_{\omega \notin A} \pi(\omega). \tag{2}$$

Measure $\Pi(A)$ evaluates to which extend A is *consistent* with the knowledge represented by π while $N(A)$ corresponds to the extent to which $\neg A$ is impossible and thus evaluates at which level A is certainly implied by the π.

The particularity of the possibilistic scale is that it can be interpreted twofold: when the possibilistic scale is interpreted in an *ordinal* manner, i.e. when the possibility degree reflects only an ordering between the possible values, the *minimum* operator is used to combine different distributions.

Conditioning is a crucial notion when studying independence relations. It consists in modifying our initial knowledge, encoded by the possibility distribution π by the arrival of a new fully *certain* piece of information e. Let us denote $\phi = [e]$ the set of models of e. The initial distribution π is then replaced by another one denoted by $\pi' = \pi(. \mid \phi)$ (we generally assume that $\phi \neq \emptyset$ and that $\Pi(\phi) > 0$). One important and natural postulate for possibilistic conditioning stipulates that π' should be normalized. This can be ensured in two different ways depending on whether we are in a qualitative or numerical setting leading to two possible definitions of possiblistic conditioning:

- In an ordinal setting, we assign to the best elements of ϕ, the maximal possibility degree (i.e. 1), then we obtain:

$$\pi(\omega \mid \phi) = \begin{cases} 1 & if \ \pi(\omega) = \Pi(\phi) \ and \ \omega \in \phi \\ \pi(\omega) & if \ \pi(\omega) < \Pi(\phi) \ and \ \omega \in \phi \\ 0 & otherwise. \end{cases} \tag{3}$$

This corresponds to the *min-based* conditioning.
- In a numerical setting , we proportionally shift up all elements of ϕ:

$$\pi(\omega \mid \phi) = \begin{cases} \frac{\pi(\omega)}{\Pi(\phi)} & if \ \omega \in \phi \\ 0 & otherwise. \end{cases} \tag{4}$$

This corresponds to the *product-based* conditioning.

These two definitions of conditioning satisfy a unique equation close to the Bayesian rule, of the form:

$$\forall \omega, \ \pi(\omega) = \pi(\omega \mid \phi) \otimes \Pi(\phi). \tag{5}$$

respectively for $\otimes$ are the **minimum** (for (3)) and the **product** (for (4)) operators. The min-based conditioning (3) corresponds to the least specific solution of Equation (5) first proposed by Hisdal [25]. If $\Pi(\phi) = 0$ then, by convention$\pi(\omega \mid_m \phi) = \pi(\omega \mid_p \phi) = 1$.

2   Possibilistic Networks

Possibilistic networks are defined as counterparts of Bayesian networks [29] in the context of possibility theory. They share the same basic components, namely:
(i) a *graphical component* which is a DAG (Directed Acyclic Graph) $\mathcal{G} = (V, E)$ where $V = \{X_1, X_2, ..., X_N\}$ denotes a set of nodes representing variables and E a set of edges encoding conditional (in)dependencies between them.
(ii) a *numerical component* associating a local normalized conditional possibility distribution to each variable $X_i \in V$ in the context of its parents (denoted by U_i).

The two definitions of possibilistic conditioning lead to two variants of possibilistic networks: in the numerical context, we get *product-based networks*, while in the ordinal context, we get *min-based networks* (also known as qualitative possibilistic networks). Let $\Pi G_\otimes$ be a possibilistic network (where $\otimes$ is either the min or the $product$ operator $*$ depending on the semantic underlying it), then we can compute the joint possibility distribution encoded by $\Pi G_\otimes$ using the following chain rule:

$$\pi_\otimes(X_1, \ldots, X_N) = \otimes_{i=1..N} \ \Pi(X_i \mid U_i). \tag{6}$$

For example, Table 1 gives local distributions ($\Pi(A)$ and $\Pi(B \mid A)$) relative to a small network $\Pi G_\otimes$ with two binary variable A and B such that A is the parent of B and the joint possibility distributions relative to ΠG_* and ΠG_{min} (i.e. π_* and π_{min})

Table 1. Example of the numerical component of a possibilistic network

A	B	$\mathbf{\Pi(A)}$	$\mathbf{\Pi(B \mid A)}$	π_*	π_{min}
a_1	b_1	1	1	1	1
a_1	b_2	1	0.8	0.8	0.8
a_2	b_1	0.4	0.8	0.32	0.4
a_2	b_2	0.4	1	0.4	0.4

It is important to note that the semantic behind edges in the graphical component can be generalized to direct causal relationships instead of simple (in)dependencies between variables. In such a case we talk about *causal possibilistic networks* [7] which are possibilistic counterparts of probabilistic causal networks [30]. Clearly, a causal possibilistic network is a proper possibilistic network but the contrary is not always true.

This means that its structure is more meaningful and more expressive. For instance, although the two networks $A \to B$ and $B \leftarrow A$ are equivalent (i.e. they encode the same joint distribution), only one of them is a correct causal network. In fact, if we consider the first network A causes B, then, manipulating the value of A affects B which is not true with the second structure (i.e. $B \leftarrow A$) where B is a cause of A, then manipulating A will not affect B. It is important to note that exactly as possibilistic networks, the two interpretations of the possibilistic scale lead to two kinds of possibilistic causal networks: min-based ones in an ordinal setting and product-based ones in a numerical setting.

The main purpose of building possibilistic networks or possibilistic causal networks is to use them for inference (or propagation) i.e. studying how the realization of specific values of some variables affects the remaining ones. Obviously this process depends on the semantic of the network at hand. More precisely, given a possibilistic network, we can determine how the observation of specific values of some variables (i.e. evidence, also called observation) affects remaining ones while if we deal with causal networks, network's information can be updated by the presence of two types of information: *observations* or *interventions* which represent external events, coming from outside the system and forcing some variables to take some specific values.

Similarly to the probabilistic case [12], possibilistic propagation (causal or not) is an NP-complete problem in both product and min based networks. The first possibilistic propagation algorithms were simple adaptations of standard message passing algorithms initially designed for Bayesian networks [27, 29]. We can mention, in particular, the adaptation of Pearl's algorithm and Junction tree algorithm [8, 21]. These adaptations show that product-based networks are very close to Bayesian networks sharing the same features (especially the product operator) and having the same theoretical and practical results. This is not the case with min-based networks due to the specificity of the minimum operator (e.g. idempotency property) and this motivates us to develop several new propagation algorithms for such networks. In what follows, we first detail the anytime possibilistic propagation algorithm which is an approximate approach that avoids the transformation of the initial network into a junction tree, then we present some variants of compilation-based propagation algorithms (also available for the causal inference) showing, specifically the power of the qualitative setting with the compilation technique recently proposed by Darwiche et al. for Bayesian networks [13, 28].

2.1 Anytime Possibilistic Propagation Algorithm

This algorithm (detailed in [4]) is inspired from the junction tree algorithm [27] with the crucial difference that it avoids the transformation step of the initial network into a junction tree which is known to be a hard problem [12]. Thus given a min-based possibilistic network ΠG_{min}, this algorithm locally computes for any instance a of a variable of interest A the possibility distribution $\Pi(a)$ inferred from ΠG_{min} according to the following major steps:
- *Initialization.* This first step transforms the initial DAG into an equivalent secondary structure, called *moral graph* by associating to each variable X_i a cluster C_i grouping X_i with its parents U_i. Then for each edge connecting two nodes X_i and X_j, we add

an undirected edge in the moral graph between the clusters C_i and C_j labeled with a separator S_{ij} corresponding to their intersection. The moral graph is quantified by associating to each cluster C_i a potential using the initial conditional distributions. Lastly, we should incorporate the instance of interest a in the cluster relative to A.

- *One-parent stability.* This step ensures that any cluster agrees with each of its parents on the distributions defined on common variables. This procedure is performed via a message passing mechanism between different clusters. Each separator *collects* information from its corresponding clusters, then *diffuses* it to each of them, in order to update them by taking the minimum between their initial potential and the one diffused by their separator. This operation is repeated until there is no modification on the cluster's potentials. It can be shown that the one-parent stability is reached after a finite number of message passes, and hence it is a *polynomial* procedure.
- *n-parents stability.* The previous step does not always guarantee local computations (from clusters) of the possibility measure $\Pi(A)$. Thus, the aim of n-parents stability is to improve the resulted possibility degree by considering stability with respect to a greater number of parents. Therefore, we will increase the parents number by first considering two parents, then three parents until reaching n parents where n is the cardinality of the parent set relative to each cluster. Obviously, the higher the number of parents considered in the stability procedure, the better the quality of results.
- *Handling the evidence.* Given any new evidence e, the computation of $\Pi(a \mid e)$ is performed via two calls of the previous steps in order to compute successively $\Pi(e)$ and $\Pi(a \wedge e)$. Then using the min-based conditioning (Equation 3), we get $\Pi(a \mid e)$.

This algorithm is said to be anytime since the longer it runs, the closer to the exact marginals it gets. In order to study the efficiency of this algorithm, we test the quality of generated marginals from different stability procedures by comparing them with exact ones (generated by the exact junction tree algorithm [8, 21]). This experimental study [4] was carried on random possibilistic networks (varying the number of nodes, their cardinalities and the maximum number of parents) and it shows that the stability degree, even at one-parent, is a good estimation of exact marginals (96,42%). This result is interesting since it means that with networks having complex structures with a great number of nodes, we can use efficiently the one-parent stability which is a polynomial procedure. Indeed, in such cases the exact algorithm generates huge clusters where local computations are impossible and blocks. Moreover, experimental study shows that the refined stability procedures improve the rate of correct exact marginals (for instance n-nodes stability provides 99.87% of exact marginals), without a huge increasing of running time (e.g. with a DAG having 60 nodes, the additional running time is between 10 and 60 seconds).

2.2   Compilation-Based Propagation in Min-based Possibilistic Networks

Recently, inference has been studied using new techniques, namely *knowledge compilation* [13, 28] which consists in preprocessing a propositional theory only once in an off-line phase, in order to make frequent on-line queries efficient [10]. The basic idea of compilation-based inference methods consists in encoding the initial network into a propositional base, usually a *conjunctive normal form (CNF)* and compiling it into a target compilation language that guarantees a polynomial inference.

In [3], we propose a possibilistic adaptation of the standard probabilistic inference approach of [13] and a purely possibilistic inference method based on the transformation of possibilistic networks into possibilistic knowledge bases [6]. The possibilistic adaptation does not take into account any numerical value in the encoding phase. In other terms, it associates a propositional variable per parameter, regardless of its value. Consequently, we propose to refine such encoding by dealing with specific values of parameters. In fact, two types of encoding strategies are explored. The first one, named *local structure* and used in both probabilistic and possibilistic networks, consists in assigning one propositional variable per equal parameters per possibility table. This encoding strategy does not take into account specific features of possibility theory such as the ordinal nature of uncertainty scale, which motivates us to propose a new encoding strategy, named *possibilistic local structure* and dealing with equal parameters from a global point of view. This latter is exclusively useful for min-based possibilistic networks since it exploits the idempotency property of the min operator. Our experimental results point out that the possibilistic local structure is the most compact one in terms of CNF parameters since it requires less variables and clauses than local structure [1]. In fact, the purely possibilistic encoding strategy, which takes advantage of the idempotency property of the min operator, allows us to associate a unique propositional variable per equal parameters per all possibility conditional tables. This means that possibilistic local structure deals with equal parameters globally per all tables, while local structure is only restricted to a local point of view, i.e., per a unique table. However, this reduction of CNF parameters generates compiled bases with higher edges. This is especially due to the higher number of shared variables incurring several interactions among clauses. This study points out that the inference time relies strongly on the compiled base size, i.e., the smaller the compiled base is the faster inference will be.

Moreover, in [2] we deal with *interventions* in possibilistic causal networks under a compilation framework. More precisely, we explored two different techniques: the most intuitive one, called *mutilation*, consists in ignoring relations between the intervened variable and its direct causes. The rest of the network remains intact. Hence, causal inference resides in applying the inference algorithm to the mutilated possibilistic network. A different but equivalent approach to represent intervention in possibilistic causal networks, called *augmentation*, is to consider it as an additional variable into the system. We proposed mutilated-based approaches and augmented-based approaches aiming to compute the effect of both observations and interventions in an efficient manner in possibilistic causal networks. Mutilated-based approaches are not sensitive to the number of interventions since the compiled base is mutilated instead of the initial possibilistic network, which enables the handling of a set of interventions without the need for re-compiling the network each time an intervention occurs. This is not the case of augmented-based approaches since the augmented network is compiled after performing the set of interventions. Our study shows that augmented-based approaches outperform mutilated-based approaches even in the extreme case in which an extra node is associated for each network variable.

2.3   Possibilistic Decision Trees

For several decades, there has been a growing interest in Operation Research and more recently in Artificial Intelligence towards the foundations and computational methods of decision making under uncertainty. This is especially relevant for applications to sequential decision making under uncertainty, where a suitable strategy needs to be found, that associates a decision to each state of the world. Several representation formalisms can be used for sequential decision problems, such as decision trees [31] and influence diagrams [26]. We focus here on decision trees, since this framework is simple and allows an explicit representation of the decision problem. Even in this simple, explicit, case, the set of potential strategies is combinatorial (i.e., its size increases exponentially with the size of the tree). The determination of an optimal strategy for a given representation and a given decision criterion is then an algorithmic issue in itself.

Decision trees are graphical representations of sequential decision problems under the assumption of full observability. This framework proposes an explicit modeling of sequential decision problems, by representing each possible scenario by a path from the root to the leaves of the tree. Formally, the graphical component of a decision tree $\mathcal{T}$ is composed of a set of nodes $\mathcal{N}$ and a set of edges $\mathcal{E}$ such that the set $\mathcal{N}$ contains three kinds of nodes:

- $\mathcal{D} = \{D_0, \ldots, D_m\}$ is the set of decision nodes (represented by rectangles). The labeling of the nodes is supposed to be in accordance with the temporal order i.e. if D_i is a descendant of D_j, then $i > j$. The root node of the tree is necessarily a decision node, denoted by D_0.
- $\mathcal{LN} = \{LN_1, \ldots, LN_k\}$ is the set of leaves, also called utility leaves: $\forall LN_i \in \mathcal{LN}$, $u(LN_i)$ is the utility of being eventually in node LN_i. For the sake of simplicity we assume that only leave nodes lead to utilities.
- $\mathcal{C} = \{C_1, \ldots, C_n\}$ is the set of chance nodes represented by circles.
  For any $X_i \in \mathcal{N}$, $Succ(X_i) \subseteq \mathcal{N}$ denotes the set of its children. Moreover, for any $D_i \in \mathcal{D}$, $Succ(D_i) \subseteq \mathcal{C}$: $Succ(D_i)$ is the set of actions that can be decided when D_i is observed. For any $C_i \in \mathcal{C}$, $Succ(C_i) \subseteq \mathcal{LN} \cup \mathcal{D}$: $Succ(C_i)$ is indeed the set of outcomes of the action C_i - either a leaf node is observed, or a decision node is reached (and then a new action should be executed).

In classical, probabilistic, decision trees [31] the uncertainty pertaining to the possible outcomes of each $C_i \in \mathcal{C}$, is represented by a conditional probability distribution p_i on $Succ(C_i)$, such that $\forall N \in Succ(C_i), p_i(N) = P(N|path(C_i))$ where $path(C_i)$ denotes all the value assignments to chance and decision nodes on the path from the root to C_i. In the present work, we obviously use a possibilistic labeling (for illustration see Figure 1). More precisely, for any $C_i \in \mathcal{C}$, the uncertainty pertaining to the more or less possible outcomes of each C_i is represented by a conditional possibility distribution π_i on $Succ(C_i)$, such that $\forall N \in Succ(C_i), \pi_i(N) = \Pi(N|path(C_i))$.

Solving a decision tree amounts at building a *strategy* that selects an action (i.e. a chance node) for each reachable decision node. Formally, we define a strategy as a function δ from $\mathcal{D}$ to $\mathcal{C} \cup \{\bot\}$. $\delta(D_i)$ is the action to be executed when a decision node D_i is observed. $\delta(D_i) = \bot$ means that no action has been selected for D_i (because either D_i cannot be reached or the strategy is partially defined). Admissible strategies

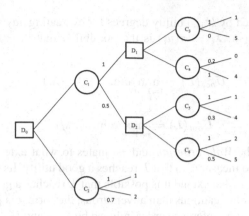

Fig. 1. Example of a possibilistic decision tree with $\mathcal{C} = \{C_1, C_2, C_3, C_4, C_5, C_6\}$, $\mathcal{D} = \{D_0, D_1, D_2\}$ and $\mathcal{LN} = U = \{0, 1, 2, 3, 4, 5\}$

should be: *sound*[1] and *complete*[2]. Let Δ be the set of sound and complete strategies that can be built from the decision tree. Any strategy $\delta \in \Delta$ can be viewed as a connected subtree of the decision tree whose arcs are of the form $(D_i, \delta(D_i))$ i.e. there being exactly one decision arc left at each decision node.

Strategies can be evaluated and compared thanks to the notion of lottery reduction. Recall indeed that leaf nodes in $\mathcal{LN}$ are labeled with utility degrees. Then a chance node can be seen as a simple lottery (for the rightmost chance nodes) or as a compound lottery (for the inner chance nodes). This means that each strategy $\delta \in \Delta$ is a compound lottery that can be reduced to an equivalent simple one (denoted by $Reduction(\delta)$) and compared to remaining strategies so that to define the optimal one.

A popular criterion to compare decisions under risk is the expected utility (*EU*) model axiomatized by Von Neumann and Morgenstern [34]. This model relies on a probabilistic representation of uncertainty. Thus for standard probabilistic decision trees, where the goal is to maximize expected utility, an optimal strategy can be computed in polytime (with respect to the size of the tree) thanks to an algorithm of *Dynamic Programming* which builds the best strategy backwards, optimizing the decisions from the leaves of the tree to its root. The completeness of such an algorithm is possible since the EU model satisfies the *monotonicity* property.

When the information about uncertainty cannot be quantified in a simple, probabilistic way, the topic of possibilistic decision theory is often a natural one to consider. The development of possibilistic decision theory has lead to the proposition and often of the characterization of a series of possibilistic criteria, namely:
- *Qualitative possibilistic utilities (U_{pes}, U_{opt}, PU)*: Under the assumption that the utility scale and the possibility scale are commensurate and purely ordinal, Dubois and Prade [17] have proposed the following qualitative pessimistic (denoted by U_{pes})

---

[1] $\forall D_i \in \mathcal{D}, \delta(D_i) \in Succ(D_i) \cup \{\bot\}$.
[2] (i) $\delta(D_0) \neq \bot$ and (ii)$\forall D_i$ s.t. $\delta(D_i) \neq \bot, \forall N \in Succ(\delta(D_i))$, either $\delta(N) \neq \bot$ or $N \in \mathcal{LN}$.

and optimistic (denoted by U_{opt}) utility degrees for evaluating any simple lottery $L = \langle \lambda_1/u_1, \ldots, \lambda_n/u_n \rangle$ (s.t. $\lambda_i = \pi(u_i)$ is the possibility that the decision leads to an outcome of utility u_i):

$$U_{pes}(L) = \min_{i=1..n} \max(u_i, 1 - \lambda_i). \tag{7}$$

$$U_{opt}(L) = \max_{i=1..n} \min(u_i, \lambda_i). \tag{8}$$

U_{pes} generalizes the *Wald criterion* and estimates to what extend it is certain (i.e. necessary according to measure N) that L reaches a good utility. Its optimistic counterpart, U_{opt}, estimates to what extend it is possible that L reaches a good utility. Because decision makers are rather cautious than adventurous, the former is generally preferred to the latter. Note that the preference order induced by U_{opt} and U_{pes} is transitive [17].

Claiming that the lotteries realized in the best prize or in the worst prize play an important role in decision making, Giang and Shenoy [23] have proposed a bipolar model (PU) in which the utility of an outcome is a pair $u = \langle \overline{u}, \underline{u} \rangle$ where $\max(\overline{u}, \underline{u}) = 1$: the utility is binary in this sense that $\overline{u}$ is interpreted as the possibility of getting the ideal, good reward (denoted $\top$) and $\underline{u}$ is interpreted as the possibility of getting the anti ideal, bad reward (denoted $\bot$). The normalization constraint $\max(\overline{u}, \underline{u}) = 1$, implies that the set $U = \{\langle \overline{u}, \underline{u} \rangle \in [0,1]^2, \max(\lambda, \mu) = 1\}$ is totally ordered by the relation $\succeq_{pu}$ defined by:

$$\langle \overline{u}, \underline{u} \rangle \succeq_{pu} \langle \overline{v}, \underline{v} \rangle \iff \begin{cases} \overline{u} = \overline{v} = 1 \text{ and } \underline{u} \leq \underline{v} \\ or \\ \overline{u} \geq \overline{v} \text{ and } \underline{u} = \underline{v} = 1 \\ or \\ \overline{u} = \underline{v} = 1 \text{ and } \overline{v} < 1 \end{cases} \tag{9}$$

Each $u_i = \langle \overline{u_i}, \underline{u_i} \rangle$ in the utility scale is thus understood as a small lottery $\langle \overline{u_i}/\top, \underline{u_i}/\bot \rangle$. A lottery $\langle \lambda_1/u_1, \ldots, \lambda_n/u_n \rangle$ can be viewed as a compound lottery, and its $\overline{PU}$ utility is computed by reduction:

$$\begin{aligned} PU(&\langle \lambda_1/u_1, \ldots, \lambda_n/u_n \rangle) \\ &= Reduction(\lambda_1/\langle \overline{u_1}/\top, \underline{u_1}/\bot \rangle, \ldots, \lambda_n/\langle \overline{u_n}/\top, \underline{u_n}/\bot \rangle) \\ &= \langle \max_{j=1..n}(\min(\lambda_j, \overline{u_j}))/\top, \max_{j=1..n}(\min(\lambda_j, \underline{u_j}))/\bot \rangle \end{aligned} \tag{10}$$

We thus get, for any lottery L a binary utility $PU(L) = \langle \overline{u}, \underline{u} \rangle$ in U. Lotteries can then be compared according to Equation (9):

$$L \succeq_{PU} L' \iff Reduction(L) \succeq_{pu} Reduction(L'). \tag{11}$$

In [24] Giang and Shenoy show that the order induced by PU is transitive and that it collapses with the one induced by U_{opt} (resp. U_{pes}) whenever for any lottery, the possibility $\underline{u}$ (resp. $\overline{u}$) of getting the worst (resp. the best) utility is equal to 1.

- *Possibilistic likely dominance (LΠ, LN)*: When the scales evaluating the utility and the possibility of the outcomes are not commensurate, [14, 20] propose to prefer, among two possibilistic decisions, the one that is more likely to overtake the other. Such a rule does not assign a utility degree to the decisions, but draws a pairwise comparison. Although designed on a Savage-like framework rather than on lotteries, it can be translated on lotteries. This rule states that given two lotteries $L_1 = \langle \lambda_1^1/u_1^1, \ldots, \lambda_n^1/u_n^1 \rangle$ and $L_2 = \langle \lambda_1^2/u_1^2, \ldots, \lambda_n^2/u_n^2 \rangle$, L_1 is as least as good as L_2 as soon as the likelihood (here, the necessity or the possibility) of the event *"The utility of L_1 is as least as good as the utility of L_2"* is greater or equal to the likelihood of the event *"The utility of L_2 is as least as good as the utility of L_1"*. Formally:

$$L_1 \succeq_{LN} L_2 \ iff \ N(L_1 \succeq L_2) \geq N(L_2 \succeq L_1). \tag{12}$$

$$L_1 \succeq_{L\Pi} L_2 \ iff \ \Pi(L_1 \succeq L_2) \geq \Pi(L_2 \succeq L_1). \tag{13}$$

where $\Pi(L_1 \succeq L_2) = \sup\limits_{u_i^1, u_j^2 \text{s.t. } u_i^1 \geq u_j^2} (\lambda_i^1 \otimes \lambda_j^2)$ and

$N(L_1 \succeq L_2) = 1 - \sup\limits_{u_i^1, u_j^2 \text{s.t. } u_i^1 < u_j^2} (\lambda_i^1 \otimes \lambda_j^2),$

such that $\otimes = min$ for ordinal setting and $\otimes = *$ for numerical setting.

The preference order induced on the lotteries is not transitive, but only quasi-transitive [14]. Note that contrary to U_{pes}, U_{opt} and PU, which are purely ordinal, possibilistic likely dominance can be defined in the ordinal setting or the numerical setting of possibility theory.

- *Order of Magnitude Expected Utility (OMEU)*: *Order of Magnitude Expected Utility* theory relies on a qualitative representation of beliefs, initially proposed by Spohn [33], via *Ordinal Conditional Functions*, and later popularized under the term *kappa-rankings*. Formally, $\kappa : 2^\Omega \rightarrow Z^+ \cup \{+\infty\}$ is a kappa-ranking if and only if it obeys to the following axioms:

(S1) $\min\limits_{w \in \Omega} \kappa(\{w\}) = 0,$

(S2) $\kappa(A) = \begin{cases} min\limits_{w \in A} \kappa(\{w\}) & if \ A \neq \emptyset \ and \ A \subseteq \Omega \\ +\infty & otherwise. \end{cases}$

Note that an event A is more likely than an event B if and only if $\kappa(A) < \kappa(B)$: kappa-rankings have been termed as *disbelief functions*. As pointed out by [16], there exists a close link between kappa-rankings and possibility measures, insofar as any kappa-ranking can be represented by a possibility measure, and vice versa. An *Order of Magnitude Expected Utility* (OMEU) model can then be defined. Considering that an order of magnitude lottery $L = \langle \kappa_1/\mu_1, \ldots, \kappa_n/\mu_n \rangle$ represents some probabilistic lottery, it is possible to compute its order of magnitude of the expected utility: $OMEU(L) = \min_{i=1,n}\{\kappa_i + \mu_i\}$. Given two lotteries L_1 and L_2, the preference relation $\succeq_{OMEU}$ is thus defined by:

$$L_1 \succeq_{OMEU} L_2 \ iff \ OMEU(L_1) \geq OMEU(L_2). \tag{14}$$

The preference order induced on the lotteries is transitive [22].

- *Possibilistic Choquet integrals (Ch_N, Ch_Π)*: In presence of heterogeneous information, i.e. when the knowledge about the state of the world is possibilistic while the utility degrees are numerical and compensatory Choquet integrals appear as a right way to extend expected utility to non-Bayesian models [11]. Like the EU model, this model is a numerical, compensatory, way of aggregating uncertain utilities. But it does not necessarily resort on a Bayesian modeling of uncertain knowledge. Indeed, this approach allows the use of any monotonic set function μ also called capacity or fuzzy measure. Such measure captures probability measures, necessity and possibility measures and belief functions etc. as particular cases.

$$Ch_\mu(L) = u_1 + \sum_{i=2,n} (u_i - u_{i-1}) \cdot \mu(L \geq u_i). \tag{15}$$

If μ is a probability measure then $Ch_\mu(L)$ is simply the expected utility of L. In the possibilistic framework, we should consider for cautious decision makers the necessity measure N and for adventurous ones, the possibility measure Π [32] which give the following expressions:

$$Ch_N(L) = u_1 + \sum_{i=2,n} (u_i - u_{i-1}) \cdot N(L \geq u_i). \tag{16}$$

$$Ch_\Pi(L) = u_1 + \sum_{i=2,n} (u_i - u_{i-1}) \cdot \Pi(L \geq u_i). \tag{17}$$

Let O be one of the possibilistic decision criteria presented above (i.e. U_{pes}, U_{opt}, PU, $L\Pi$, LN, OMEU, Ch_N, Ch_Π), a strategy $\delta \in \Delta$, is said to be optimal w.r.t. the preference order $\succeq_O$ iff $\forall \delta' \in \Delta$, $Reduction(\delta) \succeq_O Reduction(\delta')$. Formally, for any criterion O, the corresponding decision problem can be defined as follows:
[DT-OPT-O] (Strategy optimization w.r.t. an optimization criterion O in possibilistic decision trees)
INSTANCE: A possibilistic Decision Tree $\mathcal{T}$, a level α.
QUESTION: Does there exist a strategy $\delta \in \Delta$ such that $Reduction(\delta) \geq_O \alpha$?

The complexity of this problem depends on the monotonicity property - when the criterion is transitive, this property indeed allows a polytime solving of the problem by Dynamic Programming. In [5, 19], we show that most possibilistic decision criteria, except possibilistic Choquet integrals, satisfy monotonicity and that the corresponding optimization problems can be solved in polynomial time by Dynamic Programming (Table 2 summarizes different complexity results).

For the particular case of possibilistic Choquet integrals, we proved that the the problem is NP-hard and that it can be solved by implicit enumeration via a Branch and Bound algorithm that extends the use of Dynamic Programming. This algorithm takes as argument a partial strategy δ and an upper bound of the Choquet value Ch_N or Ch_Π of the best extension of the partial strategy. It returns the Choquet value of the best strategy found so far. As initial value for δ we retain the empty strategy ($\delta(D_i) = \bot, \forall D_i$). For δ^{opt}, we can start with the strategy provided by the Dynamic Programming algorithm: indeed, even not necessarily providing an optimal strategy, this algorithm generally provides a good one. At each step, the current partial strategy, δ, is developed by the choice of an action for some unassigned decision node. When several decision nodes are candidate, the one with the minimal rank (i.e. the former one according to the temporal order) is developed first. The recursive procedure backtracks when either the

Table 2. Results about the complexity of $DT - OPT - O$

U_{pes}	U_{opt}	PU	$LΠ$	LN	OMEU	Ch_N	$Ch_Π$
P	P	P	P	P	P	NP-complete	NP-complete

current strategy is complete (then $δ^{opt}$ may be updated) or proves to be worst than the current $δ^{opt}$ in any case. Our first experiments suggest that this approach is computationally sustainable.

So, it appears that the use of possibilistic decision criteria does not lead to an increase in complexity, except for Choquet integrals. This is an interesting result that allows the extension of our work to more sophisticated decisional graphical models as possibilistic influence diagrams [18].

3 Conclusion and Future Work

In this work, we addressed two key challenges related to a new research area relative to possibilitic graphical models. We focus on *reasoning* and *decision* showing the specificities of the possibilistic framework especially in its ordinal interpretation. It is important to note that possibilitic graphical models should not be seen as competitive with *standard* probabilistic graphical models but as complementary tools that should be used according to the problem at hand and to the available data. There are many more issues for further research about possibilistic graphical models. In particular, the unique attempt to learn such models from data was proposed by Borgelt et al. in [9] with a restriction to datasets with missing values. Thus we recently investigate this topic by considering the more general case of possibilistic datasets.

References

1. Ayachi, R., Ben Amor, N., Benferhat, S.: A generic framework for a compilation-based inference in probabilistic and possibilistic networks. To appear in Information Sciences (2013)
2. Ayachi, R., Ben Amor, N., Benferhat, S.: Inference using compiled min-based possibilistic causal networks in the presence of interventions. To appear in Fuzzy Sets and Systems (2013)
3. Ayachi, R., Ben Amor, N., Benferhat, S., Haenni, R.: Compiling possibilistic networks: Alternative approaches to possibilistic inference. In: Uncertainty on Artificial Intelligence (UAI), pp. 40–47 (2010)
4. Ben Amor, N., Benferhat, S., Mellouli, K.: Anytime propagation algorithm for min-based possibilistic graphs. Soft Computing a Fusion of Foundations, Methodologies and Applications 8, 150–161 (2003)
5. Ben Amor, N., Fargier, H., Guezguez, W.: Possibilistic sequential decision making. In: Technical report LARODEC/2013. Laboratoire de Recherche Opérationnelle, de Décision et de Contrôle de processus (LARODEC), Institut Supérieur de Gestion Tunis (2013)
6. Benferhat, S., Dubois, D., Garcia, L., Prade, H.: On the transformation between possibilistic logic bases and possibilistic causal networks. International Journal on Approximate Reasoning 29 (2002)
7. Benferhat, S., Smaoui, S.: Possibilistic causal networks for handling interventions: A new propagation algorithm. In: American Association for Artificial Intelligence Conference (AAAI), pp. 373–378 (2007)

8. Borgelt, C., Gebhardt, J., Kruse, R.: Possibilistic graphical models. In: International School for the Synthesis of Expert Knowledge (ISSEK), Udine, Italy (1998)
9. Borgelt, C., Steinbrecher, M., Kruse, R.R.: Graphical models: representations for learning, reasoning and data mining, vol. 704. Wiley (2009)
10. Cadoli, M., Donini, F.M.: A survey on knowledge compilation. AI Communications–The European Journal for Artificial Intelligence (10), 137–150 (1998)
11. Choquet, G.: Théorie des capacités. Technical report, Annales de l'institut Fourier, Grenoble (1953)
12. Cooper, G.F.: Computational complexity of probabilistic inference using bayesian belief networks. Artificial Intelligence 42, 393–405 (1990)
13. Darwiche, A.: A logical approach to factoring belief networks. In: Knowledge Representation, pp. 409–420. ACM (2002)
14. Dubois, D., Fargier, H., Perny, P.: Qualitative decision theory with preference relations and comparative uncertainty: An axiomatic approach. Artificial Intelligence 148(1-2), 219–260 (2003)
15. Dubois, D., Prade, H.: Possibility theory: An approach to computerized, Processing of uncertainty. Plenum Press, New York (1988)
16. Dubois, D., Prade, H.: Epistemic entrenchment and possibilistic logic. Artificial Intelligence 50, 223–239 (1991)
17. Dubois, D., Prade, H.: Possibility theory as a basis for qualitative decision theory. In: International Joint Conference on Artificial Intelligence (IJCAI), pp. 1924–1930 (1995)
18. Garcia, L., Sabbadin, R.: Possibilistic influence diagrams. In: Brewka, G., et al. (eds.) ECAI, Italie, Riva del Garda, pp. 372–376 (2006)
19. Fargier, H., Ben Amor, N., Guezguez, W.: On the complexity of decision making in possibilistic decision trees. In: Uncertainty in Artificial Intelligence (UAI 2011), pp. 203–210 (2011)
20. Fargier, H., Perny, P.: Qualitative models for decision under uncertainty without the commensurability assumption. In: Uncertainty in Artificial Intelligence (UAI), pp. 188–195 (1999)
21. Fonck, P.: Propagating uncertainty in a directed acyclic graph. In: International Conference on Information Processing of Uncertainty in Knowledge Based Systems (IPMU), Palma de Mallorca, pp. 17–20 (1992)
22. Giang, P.H., Shenoy, P.P.: A qualitative linear utility theory for spohn's theory of epistemic beliefs. In: Uncertainty in Artificial Intelligence (UAI), pp. 220–229 (2000)
23. Giang, P.H., Shenoy, P.P.: A comparison of axiomatic approaches to qualitative decision making using possibility theory. In: Uncertainty in Artificial Intelligence (UAI), pp. 162–170 (2001)
24. Giang, P.H., Shenoy, P.P.: Two axiomatic approaches to decision making using possibility theory. European Journal of Operational Research 162(2), 450–467 (2005)
25. Hisdal, E.: Conditional possibilities independence and non interaction. Fuzzy Sets and Systems 1, 283–297 (1978)
26. Howard, R.A., Matheson, J.E.: Influence diagrams. The Principles and Applications of Decision Analysis 2, 720–761 (1984)
27. Jensen, F.V.: Introduction to Bayesien networks. UCL Press, University College, London (1996)
28. Mark, C., Darwiche, A.: Compiling bayesian networks with local structure. In: International Joint Conference on Artificial Intelligence (IJCAI), pp. 1306–1312 (2005)
29. Pearl, J.: Probabilistic Reasoning in Intelligent Systems: Networks of Plausible Inference. Morgan Kaufmann Publishers Inc., San Francisco (1988)
30. Pearl, J.: Causality: Models, reasoning and inference. MIT Press (2000)

31. Raiffa, H.: Decision analysis. Addison-Welsley Publishing Company, Toronto (1968)
32. Rebille, Y.: Decision making over necessity measures through the choquet integral criterion. Fuzzy Sets and Systems 157(23), 3025–3039 (2006)
33. Spohn, W.: A general non-probabilistic theory of inductive reasoning. In: Uncertainty in Artificial Intelligence (UAI), pp. 315–322. Elsevier Science (1990)
34. von Neumann, J., Morgenstern, O.: Theory of games and economic behavior. Princeton University Press (1948)
35. Zadeh, L.A.: Fuzzy sets as a basis for a theory of possibility. Fuzzy Sets and Systems 1, 3–28 (1978)

Ranking Triangular Fuzzy Numbers Using Fuzzy Set Inclusion Index

Azedine Boulmakoul[1], Mohamed Haitam Laarabi[2], Roberto Sacile[2], and Emmanuel Garbolino[3]

[1] LIM/IST Lab., Computer Sciences Department, Mohammedia Faculty of Sciences and Technology (FSTM), Morocco
azedine.boulmakoul@yahoo.fr
[2] Department of Computer science, Bioengineering, Robotics and Systems Engineering (DIBRIS), University of Genoa, Italy
{haitam.laarabi,roberto.sacile}@unige.it
[3] Crisis Research Centre (CRC), Mines ParisTech, Sophia Antipolis, France
emmanuel.garbolino@mines-paristech.fr

Abstract. In this paper, an original ranking operator is introduced for Triangular Fuzzy Numbers. The purpose is to elaborate fast and efficient algorithms dealing with complicated operations and big data in fuzzy decision-making. The proposed ranking operator takes advantage of the topological relationship of two triangles, besides the Inclusion Index concept — which is an index indicating the Degree of Inclusion in the MIN of two Fuzzy Numbers, a way to approach the "strongly included in". Consequently, the ranking result can mostly be deduced directly, allowing an efficient ranking process.

Keywords: Fuzzy Ranking, Triangular Fuzzy Numbers, Inclusion Index, Degree of Inclusion, Decision Making.

1 Introduction

In many applications of the fuzzy set theory to decision making, we are faced with the problem of selecting one from a collection of possible solutions, and in general we want to know which is the best one [1]. Therefore, several propositions emerged whilst addressing this issue: [2] proposed a signed distance-based ranking, which allowed the distance evaluation between two fuzzy numbers; [3] suggested a centroid-based distance method; [4] introduced the user viewpoint-based evaluation of fuzzy sets as a pre-step to ordering using a satisfaction function; and several other approaches. These methods may not be adequately efficient when processing large amounts of data; since we are interested by risk fuzzification in decision-making on dangerous goods transport such in [5–9]. We propose a ranking method that ensures the reduction of operations and steps; to the point of making decisions directly without comparison operations.

This work is based mainly on five papers: [10] provided the mathematical foundations of operations on fuzzy numbers, while [11, 12] fully exploited the

F. Masulli, G. Pasi, and R. Yager (Eds.): WILF 2013, LNAI 8256, pp. 100–108, 2013.

properties of the operator MIN of fuzzy numbers, especially for TFNs. Those proposed in [13, 14] concern the fuzzy inclusion. The structure of this paper is organized as follows: in Section 2, the main concepts on which the proposed approach is based are introduced; in Section 3, the results obtained by the classification of the different topological relationship of two TFNs. Finally, conclusions, perspective and questions are drawn in Section 4.

2 Methodology

2.1 Background

Triangular Fuzzy Number. TFNs are represented as $\langle k, \alpha, \beta \rangle$. Its mathematical definition is:

Definition 1 (TFN Membership Function). *A TFN denoted by* $\Lambda = \langle k, \alpha, \beta \rangle$ *or* $\left(\Lambda^-, \Lambda^0, \Lambda^+ \right)$ *, has the membership function*

$$\Lambda\left(x\right) = \begin{cases} 0 & \text{for } x \leq \Lambda^- \\ 1 - \frac{k-x}{\alpha} & \text{for } \Lambda^- < x < \Lambda^0 \\ 1 & \text{for } x = \Lambda^0 \\ 1 - \frac{x-k}{\beta} & \text{for } \Lambda^0 < x < \Lambda^+ \\ 0 & \text{for } x \geq \Lambda^+ \end{cases} \tag{1}$$

with $\Lambda^0 = k$, $\Lambda^- = k - \alpha$ *and* $\Lambda^+ = k + \beta$. *k is called the kernel (or mean) value fo the TFN since its membership value is 1.* α, β *are the left and right hand spreads of* Λ *respectively.*

In addition to different shapes of fuzzy sets, Puri and Ralescu [15] introduced, in 1986, the Fuzzy Random Variables, which covers random experiments whose outcomes are neither numbers or vectors in $\mathbb{R}^n$. As for fuzzy numbers, the statistical aspect of Fuzzy Random Variables lacks of arithmetic linearity. However, the ordering of these variables are not a part of the scope of this paper.

Lattice Operators MIN **and** MAX. The method proposed, hereinafter, for ranking the TFNs is based mainly on the lattice operators MIN and MAX [11, 16]. Indeed, Dubois & Prade [10] and Klir [16] ensured that the triple $(\mathbb{R}, MIN, MAX)$ is a distributive lattice, in which MIN and MAX represented the meet and join, respectively. It is necessary to highlight therefore that the use of real numbers operators min and max are not applicable, since they are expressed by the terms of the pair $(\mathbb{R}, \leq)$. By extending min and max on TFNs, we can use them to formulate the proposed method. The lattice operator MIN definition is based on any two TFNs A and B as described by Klir [16]

$$MIN\left(A, B\right)\left(z\right) = \sup_{z = min(x,y)} min\left[A\left(x\right), B\left(y\right)\right] \tag{2}$$

for all $x, y, z \in \mathbb{R}$. Chiu and Wang introduced in [11] a Theorem pointing out the simplicity of the implementation MIN and MAX as follows,

Theorem 1 (Chiu-Wang-2002). *For any two TFNs A and B, defined on the universal set R, with continuous membership function and* $(A \cap B) \neq \varnothing$, *let* $x_m (\in R)$ *be the point such that* $(A \cap B)(x_m) \geqslant (A \cap B)(x)$ *for all* $x \in R$ *and* $A(x_m) = B(x_m)$, *moreover,* x_m *is between two mean values of A and B (if the number of* x_m *is not unique, any one point of those* x_m *is suitable). Then the operation MIN can be implemented as*

$$MIN(A, B)(z) = \begin{cases} (A \cup B)(z), \text{ as } z < x_m, \\ (A \cap B)(z), \text{ as } z \geqslant x_m, \end{cases} \tag{3}$$

where $z \in Z = R$, *and* $\cup$ *and* $\cap$ *denote the standard fuzzy intersection and union, respectively.*

The theorem given above provides a simple procedure for the implementation of MIN operator. It facilitates the quick checking of results promised by the ranking operator that have been built.

Inclusion Index (InI). It is a quantitative indicator expressing the *Degree of Inclusion*, whose definition consists in considering that $E \subseteq F \Leftrightarrow (Card(E \cap F) = Card(E))$ with E and F are fuzzy sets, as introduced by Dubois & Prade [10] and Bordogna [13]. Then the degree is given by:

Discrete Sets   Continuous Sets

$$\partial(E \subseteq F) = \frac{\sum \|E \cap F\|}{\sum \|E\|} \qquad \partial(E \subseteq F) = \frac{\int \|E \cap F\|}{\int \|E\|} \tag{4}$$

$$= \frac{\sum_{x \in X} T(\mu_E(x), \mu_F(x))}{\sum_{x \in X} \mu_E(x)} \qquad = \frac{\int_X T(\mu_E(x), \mu_F(x))}{\int_X \mu_E(x)}$$

where T is a triangular norm and $\| \|$ denote the standard fuzzy cardinal operator $Card$; μ_E and μ_F are respectively the membership function of E and F. Sometimes, we do not have to compute the *degree of inclusion* since $MIN(A, B) \in \{A, B\}$ — according to Dubois & Prade [10] and Klir [16]. Therefore, a partially ordering of so-called *comparable* fuzzy sets is obtained. Otherwise, when $MIN(A, B) \notin \{A, B\}$ they are called *non-comparable* fuzzy sets.

Intuitively, if the minimum of fuzzy sets A and B is neither A nor B, then the minimum will be one of the sets A and B where the fuzzy set $MIN(A, B)$ is *more strongly included*. Thus the InI will be used for this purpose.

In fact, Koczy and Hirota [17] introduced in 1993, the concept of similarity between two fuzzy terms, in order to reduce the number of rules in a fuzzy knowledge base. The similarity was measured with the index "degree of overlapping"; and from their distance, their closeness is derived.

The following subsection includes our proposal for a new ranking operator of TFNs.

2.2 The Proposed Approach for TFN Ranking

Proposed Operators. We introduce hereinafter the definition of the proposed ranking operators "$\prec$", "$\succ$" and "$\simeq$":

Definition 2 (Ranking Operators). *For every fuzzy sets A and B, the ranking operators are defined by the following implications:*

If $MIN \in \{A, B\}$ *Else*

$$\begin{cases} A \prec B & \Leftrightarrow MIN = A \\ A \succ B & \Leftrightarrow MIN = B \\ A \simeq B & \Leftrightarrow MIN = A \text{ and } MIN = B \end{cases} \qquad \begin{cases} A \prec B & \Leftrightarrow \partial\left(MIN \subseteq A\right) > \partial\left(MIN \subseteq B\right) \\ A \succ B & \Leftrightarrow \partial\left(MIN \subseteq A\right) < \partial\left(MIN \subseteq B\right) \\ A \simeq B & \Leftrightarrow \partial\left(MIN \subseteq A\right) = \partial\left(MIN \subseteq B\right) \end{cases} \quad (5)$$

In constrast, a majority of relative cases exists between two TFNs, where a direct deduction of the InI without any calculation has to be applied. Fig. 1 introduces the different situations that encompass all possibles cases [12].

3 Results Analysis

3.1 Classification Results

The InI application led to the classification of *10 different cases*. Indeed, since we have six points $\langle A^-, A^0, A^+ \rangle$ and $\langle B^-, B^0, B^+ \rangle$ for all TFN A, B, so the number of possibilities is equal to $\frac{1}{2}C_3^6 = \frac{6!}{2 \times 3!(6-3)!} = 10$. We divided by 2 to eliminate the 10 remaining possibilities that are *symmetric* to those presented hereinafter.

Fuzzy Disjoint: Obviously $A \prec B$ since $\forall x, A(x) < B(x)$ (see Fig. 2-C1).

Fuzzy Weak Overlapping: $A \prec B$, it is deduced from the Theorems 1 and (5) since $MIN\,(A, B) = A$ (see Fig. 2-C2).

Fuzzy Overlapping: Four possibles cases have been defined. The first three, C3, C4 and C5, in the Fig. 3 indicate, according to Theorems 1 and (5), that $A \prec B$. The fourth, C6, cannot be deduced directly by not being able to deduce *intuitively* the InI, since $MIN\,(A, B) \notin \{A, B\}$, $\{x \mid MIN\,(A, B)\,(x) > 0\} \nsubseteq \{x \mid A\,(x) > 0\}$ and $\{x \mid MIN\,(A, B)\,(x) > 0\} \nsubseteq \{x \mid B\,(x) > 0\}$, for all $x \in \mathbb{R}$. The comparison of the area of the Triangle B (TFN topology), with the area of the Triangle M indicated on the Fig. 3-C6, respectively S_B and S_M, allows the deduction of the results. In fact, the surface measurement of the two triangles A_{inc} and B_{inc} is adequate to deduce the InI; since $A_{inc}, B_{inc} \subseteq MIN\,(A, B)$ but $A_{inc}, B_{inc} \nsubseteq A \cap B$. By comparing S_B and S_M, which is similar to the comparison of $S_{A_{inc}}$ and $S_{B_{inc}}$, the ranking is carried out.

Fuzzy Inclusion: Finally, the Fig. 4 introduces the last four cases. The first two, C7 and C8, we have $MIN\,(A, B) \notin \{A, B\}$. However for all $x \in \mathbb{R}$, $\{x \mid MIN\,(A, B)\,(x) > 0\} \subseteq \{x \mid A\,(x) > 0\}$ and $\{x \mid MIN\,(A, B)\,(x) > 0\} \nsubseteq \{x \mid B\,(x) > 0\}$, therefore it is obvious that $A \prec B$ according to the *degree of inclusion* concept (5). As previously with the overlapping case, the ranking of C9 and CX can be inferred by comparing S_B with S_M.

3.2   Properties of the TFN Ranking Operators

Method Reasonableness Proof. Wang and Kerre [18] propose a reasonable axioms for ranking fuzzy numbers. We have proven the reasonableness of our ranking method by studying it according to the theorem introduced in [18]. However, due to constraints on the number of pages the axioms and proofs will not be detailed here.

Comparison with Other Ranking Methods. Thorough comparison have been undertaken with various major approaches. Notably the comparison with the maximizing and minimizing set method proposed by Chen [19], which is a commonly used approach, highly cited and has wide applications according to [20]. Hereinafter, we present some of the examples on which our studies took as a comparing means.

Example 1: Asady and Zendehnam [21] consider the three TFNs $A = (5, 6, 7; 1)$, $B = (5.9, 6, 7; 1)$ and $C = (6, 6, 7; 1)$ shown in Fig. 5-a. The application of most methods such Chen's approach [19], and the proposed method infer the following outcome: $A \prec B \prec C$. Whereas, with the Cheng method [22] infer $C \prec B \prec A$.

Example 2: The ranking of TFNs in the Fig. 5-b, $C = (-0.70, -0.40, -0.25; 1)$, $B = (-0.58, -0.32, -0.17; 1)$ and $A = (-0.50, -0.30, -0.20; 1)$ results in $C \prec B \prec A$. The same result is obtained by Choobineh [23] and Chu [24] methods, however the Cheng [22] and Chen [19] methods results in $A \prec B \prec C$.

Example 3: Consider the two TFNs — as in Ezzati et al. [25] — $A = (3, 6, 9; 1)$ and $B = (5, 6, 7; 1)$ shown in Fig. 5-c. It is a common problem, and yet a very controversial one. Indeed, A and B have the same symmetrical spread [26] and most existing methods fail to rank them properly [27]. By using the approaches in [2, 24, 28, 29], we obtain $A \simeq B$; and with [25] the ranking order resulted is $A \succ B$. Different ranking results are obtained when different indices of optimism are considered among the approaches [30]. Ezzati et al. [25] consider that the decision makers prefer the result $A \succ B$ and adds, it is intuitive. However, by applying our approach $A \prec B$ since A has a greater *degree of inclusion* in $MIN(A, B)$ than B. Therefore A has a greater tendency to be lower than B.

Example 4: Consider the followings set, see [25] and [2]: $A = (0.4, 0.5, 1; 1)$, $B = (0.4, 0.7, 1; 1)$, $C = (0.4, 0.9, 1; 1)$, see Fig. 5-d. With the proposed method we get $A \prec B \prec C$, as well as with most of approaches (such [19, 21–25, 28, 30]). But Cheng [31] obtains $A \prec C \prec B$.

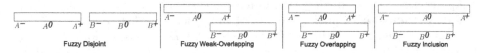

Fig. 1. All possible topological situations for two TFNs

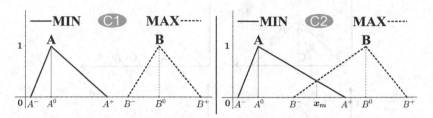

Fig. 2. Topological Representation of the Situation 1 & 2: Disjoint & Weak cases

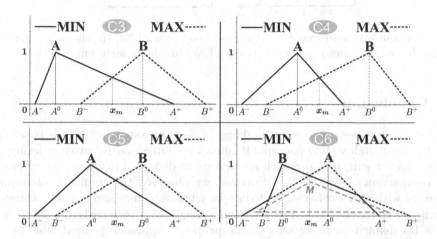

Fig. 3. Topological Representation of the Situation 3: overlapping cases

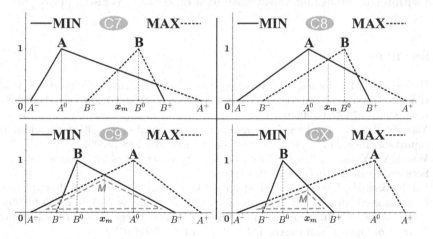

Fig. 4. Topological Representation of the Situation 4: inclusion cases

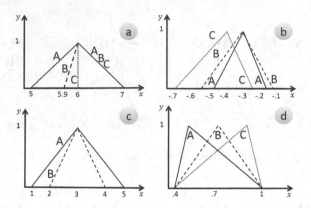

Fig. 5. 4 controversial examples: (a) shows 3 positives TFNs; (b) shows 3 negatives TFNs; (d) shows same symmetrical spread TFNs; (d) shows same support TFNs

4   Conclusion

In this paper, a new method for ranking TFNs is introduced, which is based on the Inclusion Index (InI) concept. It allows a simple and intuitive ordering of TFNs. As a result, our approach allowed us to deduce *directly* in 70% of cases the comparison of two TFNs. Moreover, we observed the similarity of results obtained with either other suggested approaches outcomes and human intuition, which proves its efficiency. However, some issues need to be asked: Can we use other InI defined on fuzzy sets? Is the proposed approach generalizable to all shapes of fuzzy numbers? Future developments of this work will address these issues in depth. Deployment of this approach for computing the fuzzy shortest path within hazardous materials transportation context, is also a priority in our research areas.

References

1. Detyniecki, M., Ronald, R.: Ranking fuzzy numbers using α-weighted valuations. International Journal of Uncertainty, Fuzziness and Knowledge-Based Systems 8(05), 573–591 (2000)
2. Yao, J., Wu, K.: Ranking fuzzy numbers based on decomposition principle and signed distance. Fuzzy Sets and Systems 116(2), 275–288 (2000)
3. Wang, Y., Yang, J., Xu, D., Chin, K.: On the centroids of fuzzy numbers. Fuzzy Sets and Systems 157(7), 919–926 (2006)
4. Lee-Kwang, H., Lee, J.: A method for ranking fuzzy numbers and its application to decision-making. IEEE Transactions on Fuzzy Systems 7(6), 677–685 (1999)
5. Boulmakoul, A.: Fuzzy graphs modelling for hazmat telegeomonitoring. European Journal of Operational Research 175(3), 1514–1525 (2006)
6. Boulmakoul, A.: Generalized path-finding algorithms on semirings and the fuzzy shortest path problem. Journal of Computational and Applied Mathematics 162(1), 263–272 (2004)

7. Boulmakoul, A., Laurini, A., Mouncif, H., Taqafi, G.: Path-finding operators for fuzzy multimodal spatial networks and their integration in mobile gis. In: Proceedings of the 2nd IEEE International Symposium on Signal Processing and Information Technology (2002)
8. Laarabi, M.H., Sacile, R., Boulmakoul, A., Garbolino, E., et al.: An overview of a multiagent-based simulation system for dynamic management of risk related to dangerous goods transport. In: Proceedings IEEE International Systems Conference in Engineering of Complex Systems, pp. 830–835 (April 2013)
9. Roncoli, C., Bersani, C., Sacile, R.: A decentralised control model for the risk-based management of dangerous good transport flows on road. In: 2012 IEEE International Systems Conference (SysCon), pp. 1–5. IEEE (April 2012)
10. Dubois, D., Prade, H.: Operations on fuzzy numbers. International Journal of Systems Science 9(6), 613–626 (1978)
11. Chiu, C., Wang, W.: A simple computation of min and max operations for fuzzy numbers. Fuzzy Sets and Systems 126(2), 273–276 (2002)
12. Boukezzoula, R., Galichet, S., Foulloy, L.: Min and max operators for fuzzy intervals and their potential use in aggregation operators. IEEE Transactions on Fuzzy Systems 15(6), 1135–1144 (2007)
13. Bordogna, G., Bosc, P., Pasi, G.: Fuzzy inclusion in database and information retrieval query interpretation. In: Proceedings of the 1996 ACM symposium on Applied Computing, pp. 547–551. ACM (1996)
14. Beg, I., Ashraf, S.: Fuzzy set of inclusion under kleene implicator. Applied and Computational Math. 10(1), 65–77 (2011)
15. Puri, M.L., Ralescu, D.A.: Fuzzy random variables. Journal of Mathematical Analysis and Applications 114(2), 409–422 (1986)
16. Klir, G., Yuan, B.: Fuzzy sets and fuzzy logic: Theory and Applications. Prentice Hall, New Jersey (1995)
17. Kóczy, L., Hirota, K.: Approximate reasoning by linear rule interpolation and general approximation. International Journal of Approximate Reasoning 9(3), 197–225 (1993)
18. Wang, X., Kerre, E.: Reasonable properties for the ordering of fuzzy quantities (i). Fuzzy Sets and Systems 118(3), 375–385 (2001)
19. Chen, S.: Ranking fuzzy numbers with maximizing set and minimizing set. Fuzzy Sets and Systems 17(2), 113–129 (1985)
20. Chou, S., Dat, L., Yu, V.: A revised method for ranking fuzzy numbers using maximizing set and minimizing set. Computers & Industrial Engineering 61(4), 1342–1348 (2011)
21. Asady, B., Zendehnam, A.: Ranking fuzzy numbers by distance minimization. Applied Mathematical Modelling 31(11), 2589–2598 (2007)
22. Cheng, C.: A new approach for ranking fuzzy numbers by distance method. Fuzzy Sets and Systems 95(3), 307–317 (1998)
23. Choobineh, F., Li, H.: An index for ordering fuzzy numbers. Fuzzy Sets and Systems 54(3), 287–294 (1993)
24. Chu, T., Tsao, C.: Ranking fuzzy numbers with an area between the centroid point and original point. Computers & Mathematics with Applications 43(1), 111–117 (2002)
25. Ezzati, R., Allahviranloo, T., Khezerloo, S., Khezerloo, M.: An approach for ranking of fuzzy numbers. Expert Systems with Applications 39(1), 690–695 (2012)
26. Wang, Y.: Centroid defuzzification and the maximizing set and minimizing set ranking based on alpha level sets. Computers & Industrial Engineering 57(1), 228–236 (2009)

27. Wang, Y., Luo, Y.: Area ranking of fuzzy numbers based on positive and negative ideal points. Computers & Mathematics with Applications 58(9), 1769–1779 (2009)
28. Abbasbandy, S., Hajjari, T.: A new approach for ranking of trapezoidal fuzzy numbers. Computers & Mathematics with Applications 57(3), 413–419 (2009)
29. Wang, Y., Lee, H.: The revised method of ranking fuzzy numbers with an area between the centroid and original points. Computers & Mathematics with Applications 55(9), 2033–2042 (2008)
30. Abbasbandy, S., Asady, B.: Ranking of fuzzy numbers by sign distance. Information Sciences 176(16), 2405–2416 (2006)
31. Cheng, C.: Evaluating weapon systems using ranking fuzzy numbers. Fuzzy Sets and Systems 107(1), 25–35 (1999)

Towards Categorical Fuzzy Logic Programming

Patrik Eklund[1], M. Ángeles Galán[2], Robert Helgesson[1], Jari Kortelainen[3], Ginés Moreno[4], and Carlos Vázquez[4]

[1] Department of Computing Science
Umeå University, SE-90187 Umeå, Sweden
{peklund,rah}@cs.umu.se
[2] Department of Applied Mathematics
University of Málaga, E-29071, Málaga, Spain
magalan@ctima.uma.es
[3] Department of Electrical Engineering and Information Technology
Mikkeli University of Applied Sciences, FIN-50100, Mikkeli, Finland
jari.kortelainen@mamk.fi
[4] Department of Computing Systems*
University of Castilla-La Mancha, E-02071, Albacete, Spain
gines.moreno@uclm.es, carlos.vazquez@alu.uclm.es

Abstract. In this paper we investigate the shift from two-valued to many-valued logic programming, including extensions involving functorial and monadic constructions for sentences building upon terms. We will show that assigning uncertainty is far from trivial, and the place where uncertainty should be used is also not always clear. There are a number of options, including the use of composed monads, and replacing the underlying category for monads with categories capturing uncertainty in a more canonic way. This is indeed important concerning terms and sentences, as classic logic programming, and also predicate logic for that matter, is not all that clear about the distinctive characters of terms and sentences. Classically, they are sets, and in our approach they are categorical objects subject to being transformed e.g. by transformations between functors. Naive set-theoretic approaches, when dealing e.g. with 'sets of sentences' and 'sets of ground atoms', may easily lead to confusion and undesirable constructions if generalizations are performed only as a shift from 'set' to 'fuzzy set'. We present some basic results on how adaptation of a strictly categorical framework enables us to be very precise about the distinction between terms and sentences, where predicates symbols become part of a signature which is kept apart from the signature for terms. Implication will not be included in signatures, but appears integrated into our sentence functors. Doing so we are able to relate propositional logic to predicate logic in a more natural way. Integration of uncertainty then becomes much more transparent.

Keywords: Fuzzy logic programming, fuzzy terms, fuzzy sentences.

* C. Vázquez and G. Moreno received grants for International mobility from the University of Castilla-La Mancha (CYTEMA project, Vicerrectorado de Profesorado).

F. Masulli, G. Pasi, and R. Yager (Eds.): WILF 2013, LNAI 8256, pp. 109–121, 2013.

1   Introduction

Intuitively speaking, terms are produced by signatures such that variables and constants are terms, and if $t_1, \ldots, t_n$ are terms then also $\omega(t_1, \ldots, t_n)$ is a term, where ω resides in the given signature. Categorically, it is well known that terms may be produced by functors that are extendible to monads (see e.g. [7,14]), whereas sentences are produced by functors. Indeed, variables may be substituted by terms, but sentence variables are dubious. For example, we may have terms $P(x)$ and $Q(y)$, where P and Q are predicate symbols residing in the signature, with x and y as variables. We might now produce a sentence in some abstract form like as a pair $(P(x), Q(x))$, intuitively then corresponding to "$P(x)$ is inferred by $Q(y)$" to check whether that sentence is valid or not. Here, the 'pairing operation' is not given in the underlying signature, but clearly appears within a sentence constructor. This indeed reveals that substitution with sentences makes no sense. The distinction between monads for representing terms and functors only to represent sentences makes the situation concerning substitution very transparent.

The overall scope of logic in this paper is that of generalized general logic [14], extending the frameworks of institutions [13] and general logic [24]. Morphisms between logics play an important role, and such morphisms are built up of morphisms respectively between underlying signatures, terms, sentences, and so on, all the way through all building blocks of logic. This means that the 'set of terms' and 'set of sentences' cannot be simple sets, so that we would have straightforward mappings between them. Categorically, they are based on functors and monads, which provides a richer algebraic structure and constraints morphisms between logics in a more canonic way. In logic programming, informal production of sets of terms and well-formed formulas in fact leads to confusion concerning the borderline between terms and sentences. In [21], notation and concepts mention 'signature', 'functions' (operators of formal universal algebra based signatures), and 'predicates'. In this conventional view, predicates are typically seen as different from operators in some underlying signature, and such treatments are also 'unsorted', or in fact one-sorted concerning the underlying set of terms.

In first-order logic based logic programming we are immediately confronted with the issue of the underlying signature. Informal treatments of first-order logic are not always clear about predicates being operator symbols or simply relations or functions, the latter confusing semantics with syntax in a way where the 'semantic jacket' acts as a 'dress code' for syntactic treatment of predicate symbols. Even more confusing is the adoption in [21] to say that operator symbols in signatures are 'function symbols', and the Boolean like operators representing predicates are called a 'predicate symbols'. Indeed, in [21], first-order logic is called a 'first order theory' consisting of alphabet, language, and so on, but these notion are not in harmony with the necessity to keep terms apart from sentences. Such verbose notations and names as used in [21] are not clear about the distinction between terms and sentences, and an alphabet is simply assumed to contain both operator as a well as predicate symbols. This means that terms and sentences are lumped together within that informal language description. The use of 'function' in this context is obviously misleading as ω is only a syntactic symbol, but its semantic counterpart is a function (in the sense of ZFC), which in [21] is called a 'mapping'.

In our categorical approach, 'alphabet' is the underlying signature of sorts and operators, and we are always many-sorted. In [21] the treatment is basically one-sorted, and operators are called 'constants' and 'functions'. The confusion concerning terms and sentences also leads to technicalities involving interpretations and models. The classical treatment of models is using sets rather than algebras, which in turns invites or even enforces [21] to say that "the identification of a Herbrand interpretation as a subset of the Herbrand base will be made throughout". Strictly speaking, we do not have subsets in this case.

In this paper we will have predicates as operators, so atoms are terms, but program clauses become sentences. Basically this means that conjunction of predicates are still terms, but clauses involving implication is not a term, since implication is not included as an operator in the underlying signature. We will categorically aim at being precise so that notions like 'ground terms', 'well-formed formulas' in predicate logic, 'predicates' or 'predicate symbols', and 'atoms' can be explained more strictly in the categorical machinery.

Preliminary notions used in this paper appear in a working version [10], and the categorical framework of our monad constructions appear in [7].

These monads make use of constructions in *categorical algebra* more broadly, which goes back to the study of natural equivalences [5]. Monoidal closed categories emerges more or less in [4], and attained its simple and clean formulation in [22]. This is the categorical realm of this paper, and the categorical notation adopted in this paper is the same as in [7].

2   Traditional Extensions from Two-Valued to Many-Valued Logic Programming

In traditional two-valued logic, and once negation is given, implication and conjunction are defined by one another. In the intuitionistic tradition, negation as a basic building block is avoided, and then implication and conjunction needs to be otherwise related, and this is done by the residuation property, which categorically is an adjoint situation, given as a Galois connection. This enables to define negation, if negation is desired. Residuated lattices have been extensively studied and are appealing algebraic structures for semantics of logic, and indeed because of the tight bound between implication and conjuction.

In many-valued logic, this 'semantic jacket' has been adopted in several approaches. E.g. in [2], this residuated situation appears in what is called 'implication algebras', and later on, e.g. in [23], where the name 'multi-adjoint' is used in this context. 'Multi-adjointness' in logic programming then refers to the use of residuated lattices that provides the desired semantic jacket that prescribes the behaviour of the truth values.

All this is, from the viewpoint of that semantic jacket, basically an extension of two-valued logic to many-valued logic using algebras of truth values.

The underlying language involving its terms and sentences remain traditional. It also follows the tradition of extending propositional calculus to predicate calculus, where the implication operator receives a similar semantic. Traditional predicate logic is set-theoretic, not functorial, about its 'set of sentences'. Many-valued logic programming has followed that same tradition, and then the semantics, which restricts to management of truth values, is adopted using this semantic jacket provided by that residuated situation. The acronym 'MALP' for multi-adjoint logic programming has then been quite widely adopted, and as an acronym is seen as a specific version of fuzzy logic programming. 'Adjointness' refers to the residuated situation, and 'multi' to the allowance of using particular lattices for each separate logic program. Much of this work basically keeps the classical constructions of logic programming as they are e.g. in [21], and many-valued extensions indeed focus on the many-valued extensions of the truth values. It does deal with uncertainty issues, but restricted to consequences of algebraic manipulation of truth values. It is also seen to represent 'approximate reasoning', which it certainly does, but as restricted to that focus on truth values, leaving all the other bits and pieces of logic as they are in a two-valued setting.

As mentioned before, our scope is logic as categorical object, that is constructed functorially and monadically, with morphisms between respective substructures in logic. Thus we do not propose to have a 'universal logic', and further, logic programs in our setting is the axiom system in a particular logic. This means e.g. that logic programs can have different inference rules, and morphisms between logic programs makes no sense unless we would have morphisms between their underlying logics, which in turn include appropriate transformations between their respective inference systems.

Resolution in these approaches eventually enters the scene, and theory developments are confronted e.g. with fixpoint issues and inference rules. This then is mostly ad hoc as typically seen e.g. in [1,3,15,19,20,25,28,34]. Essentially, they differ in the underlying notion of uncertainty theory and vagueness theory (probability theory, possibilistic logic, fuzzy logic and multi-valued logic) and how uncertainty/vagueness values, associated to rules, are managed. Annotated logic programming [17] also falls within adoption of such jackets.

Fixpoint considerations [33] are interesting in these settings, even if it cannot be expected that the relation between fixpoints and least Herbrand models appears as it is in a many-valued extension. Nevertheless, analyzing this fixpoint situation [30] reveals some crucial underlying structures that are important to consider in dealing with soundness and completeness issues. Operational and fix-point semantics are provided also in [23], and these considerations has been extended with a declarative semantics based on model-theory [16].

Further, there are a number of independently developed more general language based approaches to fuzzy logic programming, where there are less considerations involving first-order aspects, and more papers covering truth value considerations only. For the first-order aspects see [18,27] for some historically important contributions. Categories for logic programming enters the scene in

[29] with co-equalizers seen to correspond precisely to most general unifiers. A word of caution, however, is that co-equalizers as such do not suffice as categorical constructions when we move over to the many-valued setting. This then affects the resolution principle as an algorithm that has been subject of fuzzification e.g. in [1,19,23]. This mostly focuses on truth values more than extending the underlying language. Similarly for fixpoint considerations, interpretations are considered mostly as points in sets, and uncertainties are added [34]. The fixpoint semantics framework has been enriched with a declarative semantics based on model-theory as described in [16].

3   Signatures, Terms and Sentences

Throughout this paper we assume the readers are familiar with categorical concepts. However, this section starts with introducing some categorical concepts needed in the paper. Then, signatures and term monads are recalled and we introduce sentences in a logic programming context. Finally, we show how fixpoints can be considered.

3.1   Some Categorical Concepts and Notations

Let C be a category and S a set of sorts. Then, C_S is a category with objects $X_S = (X_s)_{s \in S}$ where each $X_s \in \mathrm{Ob}(C)$. The morphisms between X_S and Y_S are $f_S \colon X_S \to Y_S$ where $f_S = (f_s)_{s \in S}$ and each $f_s \in \hom_C(X_s, Y_s)$. The composition of morphisms is defined sortwise, thus, $f_S \circ g_S = (f_s \circ g_s)_{s \in S}$.

We may sometimes need to pick an object X_s in $\mathrm{Ob}(C)$ when X_S is given in a form or another. For this purpose we define a functor $\mathrm{arg}^s \colon C_S \to C$ such that $\mathrm{arg}^s X_S = X_s$ and $\mathrm{arg}^s f_S = f_s$. Especially, when working in Set_S, $\mathrm{card}(S) > 1$, we may define two emptifying functors: $\phi^{S \backslash s} \colon \mathrm{Set}_S \to \mathrm{Set}_S$ such that $\phi^{S \backslash s} X_S = X'_S$, where for all $t \in S \backslash \{s\}$ we have $X'_t = X_t$, and $X'_s = \varnothing$. Similarly we define the functor $\phi^s \colon \mathrm{Set}_S \to \mathrm{Set}_S$ as $\phi^s X_S = X'_S$, where for all $t \in S \backslash \{s\}$ we have $X'_t = \varnothing$, and $X'_s = X_s$. Actions on morphisms are defined in obvious way.

Clearly, a functor $F \colon C \to D$ may be extended to a functor $F_S = (F)_{s \in S} \colon C_S \to D_S$ (for all $s \in S$, the functor remains the same). For example, the powerset functor $P \colon \mathrm{Set} \to \mathrm{Set}$ as well as the many-valued powerset functor $L \colon \mathrm{Set} \to \mathrm{Set}$ both determine functors on Set_S, we write $P_S = (P)_{s \in S}$ and $L_S = (L)_{s \in S}$. Also functors $G_s \colon C_S \to D$, $s \in S$, are of interest, because we can determine a functor $G \colon C_S \to D_S$ such that for all $X_S \in \mathrm{Ob}(C_S)$ we have $G X_S = (G_s X_S)_{s \in S}$. Notice that we have now $G_s = \mathrm{arg}^s \circ G$.

Now, assume any two functors $F, G \colon C \to D$. A natural transformation τ between F and G, denoted by $\tau \colon F \to G$, assigns for each C-object X a D-morphism $\tau_X \colon FX \to GX$ satisfying $Gf \circ \tau_X = \tau_Y \circ Ff$ for all $f \in \hom_C(X, Y)$. Notice that C_S is also a category, thus we may have natural transformations, between functors on C_S, for example.

Finally, we recall a monad $\mathbf{F}$ over a category C, which is a triple (F, η, μ), where $F \colon C \to C$ is a (covariant) functor, and $\eta \colon \mathrm{id} \to F$ and $\mu \colon F \circ F \to F$ are natural transformations for which $\mu \circ F\mu = \mu \circ \mu F$ and $\mu \circ F\eta = \mu \circ \eta F = \mathrm{id}_F$ hold.

3.2   Signatures and the Term Monad Construction

A many-sorted signature $\Sigma = (S, \Omega)$ consists of a set S of sorts (or types), and a set Ω of operators. Here S as an index set, whereas Ω may be an object in Set_S. Operators in Ω_s are written as $\omega : s_1 \times \cdots \times s_n \to s$.

It is convenient to use the notation $\Omega^{s_1 \times \cdots \times s_n \to s}$ for the set, as an object in Set, of operators $\omega : s_1 \times \cdots \times s_n \to s \in \Omega_s$ with n given, and $\Omega^{\to s}$ for the set of constants $\omega :\to s$. With these notations we keep explicit track of operator sorts as well as their arities and we consider

$$\Omega_s = \coprod_{\substack{s_1, \ldots, s_n \\ n \leq k}} \Omega^{s_1 \times \cdots \times s_n \to s}.$$

On algebraic structures for truth values, we mostly prefer to use quantales as they play an important role when invoking the use of monoidal closed categories for the formal construction of signatures. Quantales fulfill the properties of residuated lattices, and complete residuated lattices are quantales. We further restrict to quantales $\mathfrak{Q}$ that are commutative and unital, as this makes the Goguen category[1] $\mathrm{Set}(\mathfrak{Q})$ to be a symmetric monoidal closed category and therefore also biclosed. This Goguen category carries all structure needed for modelling uncertainty using underlying categories for fuzzy terms over appropriate signatures, and as constructed by their term monads [7]. Note indeed that the signature, as a categorical object itself, also carries uncertainty, which is brought up partly to represent the overall uncertainties attached to fuzzy terms. Recall that $(A, \alpha) \otimes (B, \beta) = (A \times B, \alpha \odot \beta)$ provides the monoidal operation on objects in the Goguen category. If $\odot$ is the meet operator, then $\otimes$ is the categorical product.

A signature $(S, (\Omega, \alpha))$ over $\mathrm{Set}(\mathfrak{Q})$ then typically has S as a crisp set, and $\alpha : \Omega \to Q$ then assigns uncertain values to operators. For the term monad construction we need objects $(\Omega^{s_1 \times \cdots \times s_n \to s}, \alpha^{s_1 \times \cdots \times s_n \to s})$ for the operators $\omega : s_1 \times \cdots \times s_n \to s$ with n given, and $(\Omega^{\to s}, \alpha^{\to s})$ for the constants $\omega :\to s$. These objects are provided by respective pullbacks using (Ω, α).

In our general term functor construction we have

$$\Psi_{\mathtt{m},\mathtt{s}}((X_t)_{t \in S}) = \Omega^{s_1 \times \cdots \times s_n \to s} \otimes \bigotimes_{i=1,\ldots,n} X_{s_i},$$

and this specializes, in the case of the Goguen category, to

$$\Psi_{\mathtt{m},\mathtt{s}}(((X_t, \delta_t))_{t \in S}) = (\Omega^{s_1 \times \cdots \times s_n \to s}, \alpha^{s_1 \times \cdots \times s_n \to s}) \otimes \bigotimes_{i=1,\ldots,n} (X_{s_i}, \delta_{s_i})$$

$$= (\Omega^{s_1 \times \cdots \times s_n \to s} \times \prod_{i=1,\ldots,n} X_{s_i}, \alpha^{s_1 \times \cdots \times s_n \to s} \odot \bigodot_{i=1,\ldots,n} \delta_{s_i}).$$

The inductive steps start with $\mathsf{T}^1_{\Sigma,\mathtt{s}} = \coprod_{\mathtt{m} \in \hat{S}} \Psi_{\mathtt{m},\mathtt{s}}$, and, for $\iota > 1$, proceeds with $\mathsf{T}^\iota_{\Sigma,\mathtt{s}} X_{\mathtt{s}} = \coprod_{\mathtt{m} \in \hat{S}} \Psi_{\mathtt{m},\mathtt{s}}((\mathsf{T}^{\iota-1}_{\Sigma,\mathtt{t}} X_{\mathtt{s}} \sqcup X_t)_{t \in S})$, and $\mathsf{T}^\iota_{\Sigma,\mathtt{s}} f_{\mathtt{s}} = \coprod_{\mathtt{m} \in \hat{S}} \Psi_{\mathtt{m},\mathtt{s}}((\mathsf{T}^{\iota-1}_{\Sigma,\mathtt{t}} f_{\mathtt{s}} \sqcup f_t)_{t \in S})$.

---

[1] Objects in the Goguen category are pairs (A, α), where $\alpha : A \to Q$ is a mapping.

This then allows us to define the functors T_Σ^ι by $T_\Sigma^\iota X_S = (T_{\Sigma,s}^\iota X_S)_{s\in S}$, and $T_\Sigma^\iota f_S = (T_{\Sigma,s}^\iota f_S)_{s\in S}$. There is a natural transformation $\Xi_\iota^{\iota+1} : T_\Sigma^\iota \to T_\Sigma^{\iota+1}$ such that $(T_\Sigma^\iota)_{\iota>0}$ is an inductive system of endofunctors with $\Xi_\iota^{\iota+1}$ as its connecting maps. The inductive limit $F = \mathrm{ind}\varinjlim T_\Sigma^\iota$ exists, and the final term functor T_Σ is $T_\Sigma = F \sqcup \mathrm{id}_{\mathbf{Set}_S}$. We also have $T_\Sigma X_S = (T_{\Sigma,s} X_S)_{s\in S}$, and T_Σ is strictly not idempotent, but only "idempotent like", as there is a natural isomorphism between $T_\Sigma T_\Sigma$ and T_Σ.

For more detail concerning this term construction, see [7].

3.3   Sentences in a Logic Programming Context

Let then $\Sigma_0 = (S_0, \Omega_0)$ be a signature over $\mathbf{Set}$, and $\mathbf{T}_{\Sigma_0}$ be the term monad over $\mathbf{Set}_{S_0}$. For the variables in X_{S_0}, the set of terms $T_{\Sigma_0} X_{S_0}$, as an object of $\mathbf{Set}_{S_0}$, then correspond to the 'terms', and similarly $T_{\Sigma_0} \varnothing_{S_0}$ will be the set of so called 'ground terms' in the sense of [21].

In order to introduce predicates as operators in a separate signature, and then composing that resulting 'predicate' functor with the term functor, we assume that Σ contains a sort $\mathtt{bool}$, which does not appear in connection with any operator in Ω, i.e., we set $S = S_0 \cup \{\mathtt{bool}\}$, $\mathtt{bool} \notin S_0$, and $\Omega = \Omega_0$. This means that $T_{\Sigma,\mathtt{bool}} X_{\mathtt{bool}} = X_{\mathtt{bool}}$, and for any substitution $\sigma_S : X_S \to T_\Sigma X_S$, we have $\sigma_{\mathtt{bool}}(x) = x$ for all $x \in X_{\mathtt{bool}}$. The composition of the 'predicate' functor with T_Σ is intuitively expected to be the desired 'predicates as terms' functor.

We can now also separate propositional logic from predicate logic, and also decide whether or not to include negation. The key effect in doing this arrangement is that implication becomes 'sentential' where as conjunction (and negation, if included) produces terms from terms.

To proceed towards this goal, let $\Sigma_{PL} = (S_{PL}, \Omega_{PL})$ be the underlying *two-valued propositional logic* signature, where $S_{PL} = S$, and $\Omega_{PL} = \{\mathtt{F,T} :\to \mathtt{bool}, \& : \mathtt{bool} \times \mathtt{bool} \to \mathtt{bool}, \neg : \mathtt{bool} \to \mathtt{bool}\} \cup \{\mathtt{P}_i : \mathtt{s}_{i_1} \times \cdots \times \mathtt{s}_{i_n} \to \mathtt{bool} \mid i \in I, \mathtt{s}_{i_j} \in S\}$. Similarly as $\mathtt{bool}$ leading to no additional terms, except for additional variables being terms when using Σ, the sorts in S_{PL}, other than $\mathtt{bool}$, will lead to no additional terms except variables. Adding predicates as operators even if they produce no terms seems superfluous at first sight, but the justification is seen when we compose these term functors with T_Σ.

In the many-valued case we would have some sort $\mathtt{lat}$, so that $\mathfrak{A}(\mathtt{lat}) = L$, the underlying set of a complete lattice $\mathfrak{L}$. Now, $\mathfrak{L}$ could indeed more specifically be a residuated lattice, when conjunction is desired to be residuated with the implication operator (in the lattice), or a quantale, justifying the use of monoidal closed subcategories. The choice of the lattice or quantale is typically justified by the application context.

It is important also to notice indeed that it is possible to include the both sorts $\mathtt{bool}$ and $\mathtt{lat}$ in the same signature, if one needs to distinguish the two-valued case from the many-valued case also on the syntactic level.

In the *many-valued propositional logic* signature $\Sigma_{PL}^{mv} = (S_{PL}^{mv}, \Omega_{PL}^{mv})$ constants clearly map algebraically to uncertainty values. In what follows we will not explicitly distinguish between Σ^{mv} and Σ, so whenever we write Σ, the underlying lattice representing the algebra may be two-valued or many-valued. We now introduce the notation $\Sigma_{PL\backslash\neg}$ for the signature where the operator $\neg$ is removed, and $\Sigma_{PL\backslash\neg,\&}$ for the signature where both $\neg$ and $\&$ are removed.

The ZFC-set of 'terms' over Σ may now be given by

$$\bigcup_{s\in S}(\mathsf{T}_{\Sigma,s}\circ\phi^{S\backslash\mathbf{bool}})X_S,$$

and now the ZFC-set of propositional logic formulas are

$$\bigcup_{s\in S}(\mathbf{arg}^s\circ\mathsf{T}_{\Sigma_{PL}}\circ\phi^{\mathbf{bool}})X_S=(\mathbf{arg}^{\mathbf{bool}}\circ\mathsf{T}_{\Sigma_{PL}}\circ\phi^{\mathbf{bool}})X_S.$$

We use the expression $\mathbf{arg}^s\circ\mathsf{T}_{\Sigma_{PL}}$ instead of $\mathsf{T}_{\Sigma_{PL},s}$ for convenience. Note how

$$(\mathbf{arg}^{\mathbf{bool}}\circ\mathsf{T}_{\Sigma_{PL\backslash\neg,\&}}\circ\phi^{\mathbf{bool}})X_S=\{\mathbf{F},\mathbf{T}\}.$$

Sentences, i.e., formulas in propositional logic are now obviously given by the functor

$$\mathsf{Sen}_{PL}=\mathbf{arg}^{\mathbf{bool}}\circ\mathsf{T}_{\Sigma_{PL}}\circ\phi^{\mathbf{bool}},$$

and sentences in 'Horn clause logic' can now be given by the functor

$$\mathsf{Sen}_{HCL}=(\mathbf{arg}^{\mathbf{bool}})^2\circ(((\mathsf{T}_{\Sigma_{PL\backslash\neg,\&}}\circ\mathsf{T}_\Sigma)\times(\mathsf{T}_{\Sigma_{PL\backslash\neg}}\circ\mathsf{T}_\Sigma))\circ\phi^{S\backslash\mathbf{bool}})$$
$$=(\mathbf{arg}^{\mathbf{bool}})^2\circ((\mathsf{T}_{\Sigma_{PL\backslash\neg,\&}}\times\mathsf{T}_{\Sigma_{PL\backslash\neg}})\circ\mathsf{T}_\Sigma\circ\phi^{S\backslash\mathbf{bool}})$$

Note that $\mathsf{Sen}_{HCL}X_S$ is an object in $\mathbf{Set}$, and therefore the pair $(h,b)\in\mathsf{Sen}_{HCL}$ X_S, as a sentence representing the 'Horn clause', means that h is an 'atom' and b is a conjunction of 'atoms'. Further, $(h,\mathbf{T})$ is a 'fact', $(\mathbf{F},b)$ is a 'goal clause', and $(\mathbf{F},\mathbf{T})$ is a 'failure'.

This obviously relates to similar approaches for using sentence functors in other logics. Intuitively, the identity functor is the sentence functor for lambda terms as 'sentences' in λ-calculus, and id^2 is the sentence functor for equations as 'sentences' in equational logic [9].

Before proceeding, now note a fundamental appearance of the residuated situation. The quantale, as a residuated lattice, uses the residuation at least for the underlying signature to work properly in the setting of monoidal biclosed categories, but is in no way at that point necessarily related to 'implication' as appearing in Horn clauses. In our treatment we therefore clearly show where and how residuation can be introduced. Indeed, residuation as possibly used for uncertainty consideration in terms has nothing to do with residuation related properties as possible used for uncertainty on sentence level.

We are now in a position to introduce *variable substitutions*. Indeed, because we have a monad $\mathbf{T}_\Sigma=(\mathsf{T}_\Sigma,\eta,\mu)$, we may now perform a variable substitution $\sigma_S\colon\phi^{S\backslash\mathbf{bool}}X_S\to\mathsf{T}_\Sigma\phi^{S\backslash\mathbf{bool}}Y_S$, that is, variables $\phi^{S\backslash\mathbf{bool}}X_S$ are subsituted by terms $\mathsf{T}_\Sigma\phi^{S\backslash\mathbf{bool}}Y_S$. The substitution is defined sortwise $\sigma_S=(\sigma_s)_{s\in S}$ such that $\sigma_s\colon\mathbf{arg}^s(\phi^{S\backslash\mathbf{bool}}X_S)\to\mathsf{T}_{\Sigma,s}\phi^{S\backslash\mathbf{bool}}Y_S$. We have the following:

$$\mu \circ \mathsf{T}_\Sigma \sigma_S : \mathsf{T}_\Sigma \phi^{S \backslash \mathtt{bool}} X_S \to \mathsf{T}_\Sigma \phi^{S \backslash \mathtt{bool}} Y_S$$

$$\sigma_S^{head} = \mathsf{T}_{\Sigma_{PL \backslash \neg, \&}}(\mu \circ \mathsf{T}_\Sigma \sigma_S) : (\mathsf{T}_{\Sigma_{PL \backslash \neg, \&}} \circ \mathsf{T}_\Sigma)\phi^{S \backslash \mathtt{bool}} X_S$$
$$\to (\mathsf{T}_{\Sigma_{PL \backslash \neg, \&}} \circ \mathsf{T}_\Sigma)\phi^{S \backslash \mathtt{bool}} Y_S$$

$$\sigma_S^{body} = \mathsf{T}_{\Sigma_{PL \backslash \neg}}(\mu \circ \mathsf{T}_\Sigma \sigma_S) : (\mathsf{T}_{\Sigma_{PL \backslash \neg}} \circ \mathsf{T}_\Sigma)\phi^{S \backslash \mathtt{bool}} X_S$$
$$\to (\mathsf{T}_{\Sigma_{PL \backslash \neg}} \circ \mathsf{T}_\Sigma)\phi^{S \backslash \mathtt{bool}} Y_S$$

$$(\sigma_S^{head}, \sigma_S^{body}) = (\mathsf{T}_{\Sigma_{PL \backslash \neg, \&}} \times \mathsf{T}_{\Sigma_{PL \backslash \neg}})(\mu \circ \mathsf{T}_\Sigma \sigma_S) :$$
$$((\mathsf{T}_{\Sigma_{PL \backslash \neg, \&}} \times \mathsf{T}_{\Sigma_{PL \backslash \neg}}) \circ \mathsf{T}_\Sigma)\phi^{S \backslash \mathtt{bool}} X_S \to ((\mathsf{T}_{\Sigma_{PL \backslash \neg, \&}} \times \mathsf{T}_{\Sigma_{PL \backslash \neg}}) \circ \mathsf{T}_\Sigma)\phi^{S \backslash \mathtt{bool}} Y_S$$

Finally,

$$\sigma^{HC} = (\sigma_{\mathtt{bool}}^{head}, \sigma_{\mathtt{bool}}^{body}) : \mathsf{Sen}_{HCL} X_S \to \mathsf{Sen}_{HCL} Y_S$$

Notice that σ_S^{head}, σ_S^{body} and $(\sigma_S^{head}, \sigma_S^{body})$ are morphisms in Set_S but σ^{HC} is a morphism in Set.

It is now clear that a candidate for the underlying category can be the Goguen category $\mathsf{Set}(\mathfrak{Q})$. Further, and as will be explored in subsequent papers, replacement of T_Σ with the composed functor $\mathsf{Q} \circ \mathsf{T}_\Sigma$ [12], provides another style of fuzzy extension.

3.4 Algebras, Models and Fixpoints

In the two-valued case, $\mathfrak{A}(\mathtt{bool})$ is often $\{false, true\}$, so that $\mathfrak{A}(\mathtt{F}) = false$ and $\mathfrak{A}(\mathtt{T}) = true$. Further, $\mathfrak{A}(\&) : \mathfrak{A}(\mathtt{bool}) \times \mathfrak{A}(\mathtt{bool}) \to \mathfrak{A}(\mathtt{bool})$, is expected to be defined by the usual 'truth table'. Further $\mathfrak{A}(\mathtt{s}_0)$ is usually denoted by D so that the semantics for a (syntactic) n-ary operator $\omega : \mathtt{s}_0 \times \cdots \times \mathtt{s}_0 \to \mathtt{s}_0$ is an n-ary operation (function) $\mathfrak{A}(\omega) : D^n \to D$. Generally speaking, a many-sorted algebra is not a traditional algebra, not even a tuple of traditional algebras, since an operator ω may touch many sorts and then the semantics of ω is not an n-ary function on some set. For example, we may assign for a signature $\Sigma_{PL} = (S_{PL}, \Omega_{PL})$ a pair, the 'many-sorted algebra', $(\mathsf{T}_{\Sigma_{PL}} X_S, (\mathfrak{A}(\omega))_{\omega \in \Omega_{PL}})$, where $X_\mathtt{s} = \varnothing$ if $\mathtt{s} \neq \mathtt{bool}$. Then, $(\bigcup_{\mathtt{s} \in S}(\mathtt{arg}^\mathtt{s} \circ \mathsf{T}_{\Sigma_{PL}}) X_S, (\mathtt{F}, \mathtt{T}, \&, \neg))$ serves as a traditional Boolean algebra, when certain equational laws are given.

For a finite set of program clauses $\Gamma = \{(h_1, b_1), \ldots, (h_n, b_n)\} \subseteq \mathsf{Sen}_{HCL} X_S$, based on Σ and Σ_{PL}, we assign a Set_S object

$$(U_\Gamma)_S = \mathsf{T}_\Sigma \varnothing_S = (\mathsf{T}_{\Sigma, \mathtt{s}} \varnothing_S)_{\mathtt{s} \in S}$$

where $\mathsf{T}_{\Sigma, \mathtt{s}} \varnothing_S$ is the set of all ground terms of type $\mathtt{s}$, and indeed $\mathsf{T}_{\Sigma, \mathtt{bool}} \varnothing_S = \varnothing$. Note how $\bigcup_{\mathtt{s} \in S}(U_\Gamma)_\mathtt{s}$ corresponds to the traditional and unsorted view of the *Herbrand universe* as a ZFC-set.

We are also interested in the Set-object

$$B_\Gamma = (\mathsf{arg}^{\mathsf{bool}} \circ \mathsf{T}_{\Sigma_{PL \backslash \neg, \&}} \circ \mathsf{T}_\Sigma) \, \varnothing_S$$

corresponding to the *Herbrand base* in the traditional sense [21].

Herbrand interpretations of a program Γ are subsets $\mathcal{I} \subseteq B_\Gamma$, that is, $\mathcal{I} \in PB_\Gamma$.

For sake of convenience, when dealing with the immediate consequences operator for the fixpoint considerations, we will need the *Herbrand expression base*

$$B_\Gamma^\& = (\mathsf{arg}^{\mathsf{bool}} \circ \mathsf{T}_{\Sigma_{PL \backslash \neg}} \circ \mathsf{T}_\Sigma) \, \varnothing_S.$$

Note that a Herbrand interpretation $\mathcal{I}$ canonically extends to a *Herbrand expression interpretation* $\mathcal{I}^\& \subseteq B_\Gamma^\&$. Similarly, when $\mathcal{I} \in LB_\Gamma$, one might extend $\mathcal{I}$ to *Herbrand fuzzy expression interpretation* $\mathcal{I}^\&$ (semantically) as follows: for an element $b \in B_\Gamma^\&$ of the form $b = b_1 \& \cdots \& b_n$ we have $\mathcal{I}^\&(b) = \bigwedge\{\mathcal{I}(b_1), \ldots, \mathcal{I}(b_n)\}$ and for an atom element $b \in B_\Gamma^\&$, $\mathcal{I}^\&(b) = \mathcal{I}(b)$. However, it is questionable to call $\mathcal{I} \in LB_\Gamma$ to an interpretation.

Note that in this paper we avoid describing the informal passage [21] from 'interpretation' to 'Herbrand interpretation', which categorically means describing the shift from algebras to term algebras. The Herbrand interpretation is the 'ground term algebra' [21] in the universal algebra sense. This is the T_Σ-algebra, rather than the Σ-algebra which corresponds to 'interpretation', and in all case we are 'ground' in the sense of the variable sets in the tuples being empty sets.

The extension to the many-valued case is now a question about composing with the many-valued powerset functor L with term functors, producing a style of "logic with fuzzy" or having the term functors work over the Goguen category, producing a style of "fuzzy logic". It should therefore not be looked at simply from the viewpoint of replacing the functor P to L with $\mathfrak{L}$ as the underlying complete lattice, and extending the Herbrand interpretations to *Herbrand fuzzy interpretations* of a program Γ by $\mathcal{I} \in LB_\Gamma$. We will here look more into the first situation, as the "squeezing in" of L can indeed be done in two ways. Either we annotate it "outside", as mentioned above, with sentences in such a 'annotated fuzzy Horn clause logic' can be given by the sentence functor $L \circ \mathsf{Sen}_{HCL}$ and then proceed to produce interpretations for fuzzy sets of predicates

$$LB_\Gamma = (L \circ \mathsf{arg}^{\mathsf{bool}} \circ \mathsf{T}_{\Sigma_{PL \backslash \neg, \&}} \circ \mathsf{T}_\Sigma) \, \varnothing_S.$$

A fuzzy interpretation in this case is then just a mapping $\mathcal{I} : B_\Gamma \to L$, and uncertainties arising from terms and substitutions remain unaffected. On the other hand, we may go "inside" to produce the *substitution fuzzy Horn clause logic* with the sentence functor

$$\mathsf{Sen}_{SFHCL} = (\mathsf{arg}^{\mathsf{bool}})^2 \circ ((\mathsf{T}_{\Sigma_{PL \backslash \neg, \&}} \times \mathsf{T}_{\Sigma_{PL \backslash \neg}}) \circ \mathsf{L}_S \circ \mathsf{T}_\Sigma \circ \phi^{S \backslash \mathsf{bool}})$$

so that ground predicates over fuzzy sets of terms is the set

$$B_\Gamma^{\mathsf{L}} = (\mathsf{arg}^{\mathsf{bool}} \circ \mathsf{T}_{\Sigma_{PL \backslash \neg, \&}} \circ \mathsf{L}_S \circ \mathsf{T}_\Sigma) \, \varnothing_S$$

with the corresponding extension $B_\Gamma^{\mathsf{L},\&}$ being defined in the obvious way. The resulting fuzzy sets of ground predicates then comes about from considering the swapper

$$\varsigma : \mathsf{T}_{\Sigma_{PL\backslash\neg,\&}} \circ \mathsf{L}_S \to \mathsf{L}_S \circ \mathsf{T}_{\Sigma_{PL\backslash\neg,\&}}$$

which is given in [6] for the many-sorted case, and in [11] for the one-sorted case. Indeed we can use $\mathsf{arg^{bool}}_{\varsigma_{\mathsf{T}_\Sigma\varnothing_S}} : B_\Gamma^{\mathsf{L}} \to \mathsf{L}B_\Gamma$. Note also how $\mathsf{L}B_\Gamma^{\mathsf{L}}$ would correspond to a Herbrand base like the set with uncertainty considerations both for the sets of clauses, as well as sets of terms.

Moving to fixpoints, we first consider crisp *ground term substitution*, that is, a Set_S-morphism $\sigma_S \colon X_S \to \mathsf{T}_\Sigma\varnothing_S$. By the previous discussion, this induces a morphism $\sigma^{HC} \colon \mathsf{Sen}_{HCL}X_S \to \mathsf{Sen}_{HCL}\varnothing_S$. We can now define a mapping $\varpi : \mathsf{L}B_\Gamma \to \mathsf{L}B_\Gamma$, where the underlying lattice $\mathfrak{L}$ for the many-valued powerset functor L is a complete lattice, by

$$\varpi(\mathcal{I})(\sigma_{\mathsf{bool}}^{head}(h)) = \bigvee_{(h,b)\in\Gamma} \mathcal{I}^{\&}(\sigma_{\mathsf{bool}}^{body}(b)).$$

When $(h,b) \in B_\Gamma \times B_\Gamma$ is such that $(h,b) \notin R_{\sigma^{HC}}$ (the range of σ^{HC}), then $\varpi(\mathcal{I})(h) = \mathcal{I}(h)$ and $\varpi(\mathcal{I})(b) = \mathcal{I}(b)$.

Clearly, ϖ is monotonic, and it is now well-known that ϖ has the least and greatest fixpoints.

This, however, is a simpler approach to fuzzy models, as substitutions remain crisp. For fuzzy ground term substitution, that is, a Set_S-morphism of the form $\sigma_S^{\mathsf{L}} \colon X_S \to \mathsf{L}_S\mathsf{T}_\Sigma\varnothing_S$, corresponding $\sigma_S^{\mathsf{L},head}$ and $\sigma_S^{\mathsf{L},body}$ mappings can be provided with L_S "inside".

A mapping $\varpi^{\mathsf{L}} : \mathsf{L}B_\Gamma^{\mathsf{L}} \to \mathsf{L}B_\Gamma^{\mathsf{L}}$, considering the effect of substitutions with fuzzy sets of terms, can now, using $\mathsf{arg^{bool}}_{\varsigma_{\mathsf{T}_\Sigma\varnothing_S}} : B_\Gamma^{\mathsf{L}} \to \mathsf{L}B_\Gamma$, be considered in various forms, e.g., as

$$\varpi^{\mathsf{L}}(\mathcal{I})(\sigma_{\mathsf{bool}}^{\mathsf{L},head}(h)) = (\bigvee_{t\in B_\Gamma} (\mathsf{arg^{bool}}_{\varsigma_{\mathsf{T}_\Sigma\varnothing_S}}(h))(t)) \wedge \mathcal{I}^{\mathsf{L},\&}(\sigma_{\mathsf{bool}}^{\mathsf{L},body}(b)).$$

In this case, ϖ^{L} is also monotonic.

4   Conclusions

What is Logic? Logic is a structure containing signatures, terms, sentences, structured sets of sentences, entailments, algebras, satisfactions, axioms, theories and proof calculi. Signature have sorts (types) and operators, and algebras provide the meaning of the signature. All terms are constructed (syntactically) using operators in the signature, and sentences have terms as building blocks. Entailment is the relation between the structured sets of sentences, representing what we already know, and sentences representing knowledge we are trying to arrive at. Satisfaction is the semantic counterpart to entailment providing the notion of valid conclusions. Axioms prescribe what we take for granted at start, and act as the logic program. Inference rules say how we can jump to conclusions in a chain of entailments.

Further, unsortedness and many-sortedness are clearly different, and so are crisp and fuzzy cases. Moreover, we should distinguish between "fuzzy logic programming", which requires considerations of underlying categories [8], from "logic programming with fuzzy", which is more about composing with term monads using Set as the underlying category [12].

Fuzzy considerations in logic are then indeed similarly related to structures which contain fuzzy signatures, fuzzy terms, fuzzy sentences, fuzzy structured sets of sentences, fuzzy entailments, fuzzy algebras, fuzzy satisfactions, fuzzy axioms, fuzzy theories and fuzzy proof calculi.

Details related to generalized general logic appear in [14], and further developments in particular related to sentence constructions will appear in [9].

References

1. Baldwin, J.F., Martin, T.P., Pilsworth, B.W.: Fril - Fuzzy and Evidential Reasoning in Artificial Intelligence. John Wiley & Sons, Inc. (1995)
2. Viegas Damásio, C., Moniz Pereira, L.: Monotonic and Residuated Logic Programs. In: Benferhat, S., Besnard, P. (eds.) ECSQARU 2001. LNCS (LNAI), vol. 2143, pp. 748–759. Springer, Heidelberg (2001)
3. Ebrahim, R.: Fuzzy logic programming. Fuzzy Sets and Systems 117(2), 215–230 (2001)
4. Eilenberg, S., Kelly, G.M.: Closed categories. In: Eilenberg, S., et al. (eds.) Proceedings of the Conference on Categorical Algebra, La Jolla 1965, pp. 421–562. Springer (1966)
5. Eilenberg, S., MacLane, S.: General theory of natural equivalences. Transactions of the American Mathematical Society 58(2), 231–294 (1945)
6. Eklund, P., Galán, M.A., Helgesson, R., Kortelainen, J.: Paradigms for many-sorted non-classical substitutions. In: 2011 41st IEEE International Symposium on Multiple-Valued Logic (ISMVL 2011), pp. 318–321 (2011)
7. Eklund, P., Galán, M.A., Helgesson, R., Kortelainen, J.: Fuzzy terms. Fuzzy Sets and Systems (in press)
8. Eklund, P., Galán, M.Á., Helgesson, R., Kortelainen, J.: From Aristotle to Lotfi. In: Seising, R., Trillas, E., Moraga, C., Termini, S. (eds.) On Fuzziness. STUDFUZZ, vol. 298, pp. 147–152. Springer, Heidelberg (2013)
9. Eklund, P., Galán, M.A., Helgesson, R., Kortelainen, J.: Fuzzy sentences (in progress)
10. Eklund, P., Galán, M.A., Helgesson, R., Kortelainen, J., Moreno, G., Vázquez, C.: Towards a Categorical Description of Fuzzy Logic Programming. Working paper accepted for presentation in PROLE 2013 (2013)
11. Eklund, P., Ángeles Galán, M., Ojeda-Aciego, M., Valverde, A.: Set functors and generalised terms. In: Proc. IPMU 2000, 8th Information Processing and Management of Uncertainty in Knowledge-Based Systems Conference, pp. III:1595–III:1599 (2000)
12. Galán, M.A.: Categorical Unification. PhD thesis, Umeå University, Department of Computing Science (2004)

13. Goguen, J.A., Burstall, R.M.: INSTITUTIONS: Abstract Model Theory for Specification and Programming. J. ACM 39(1), 95–146 (1992)
14. Helgesson, R.: Generalized General Logics. PhD thesis, Umeå University, Department of Computing Science (2013)
15. Ishizuka, M., Kanai, N.: Prolog-ELF Incorporating Fuzzy Logic. In: Joshi, A.K. (ed.) Proc. of the 9th International Joint Conference on Artificial Intelligence (IJCAI 1985), pp. 701–703. Morgan Kaufmann, Los Angeles (1985)
16. Julián, P., Moreno, G., Penabad, J.: On the declarative semantics of multi-adjoint logic programs. In: Cabestany, J., Sandoval, F., Prieto, A., Corchado, J.M. (eds.) IWANN 2009, Part I. LNCS, vol. 5517, pp. 253–260. Springer, Heidelberg (2009)
17. Kifer, M., Subrahmanian, V.S.: Theory of generalized annotated logic programming and its applications. Journal of Logic Programming 12, 335–367 (1992)
18. Klawonn, F., Kruse, R.: A Łukasiewicz logic based prolog. Mathware and Soft Computing 1, 5–29 (1994)
19. Lee, R.C.T.: Fuzzy Logic and the Resolution Principle. Journal of the ACM 19(1), 119–129 (1972)
20. Li, D., Liu, D.: A fuzzy Prolog database system. John Wiley & Sons, Inc. (1990)
21. Lloyd, J.W.: Foundations of logic programming. Springer (1984)
22. MacLane, S.: Categories for the working mathematician. Springer (1971)
23. Medina, J., Ojeda-Aciego, M., Vojtáš, P.: Similarity-based Unification: a multi-adjoint approach. Fuzzy Sets and Systems 146, 43–62 (2004)
24. Meseguer, J.: General logics. In: Ebbinghaus, H.-D. (ed.) Logic Colloquium 1987, pp. 275–329. North-Holland, Granada (1989)
25. Muñoz-Hernández, S., Ceruelo, V.P., Strass, H.: RFuzzy: Syntax, semantics and implementation details of a simple and expressive fuzzy tool over Prolog. Information Sciences 181(10), 1951–1970 (2011)
26. Ng, R., Subrahmanian, V.S.: Stable semantics for probabilistic deductive databases. Information and Computation 110(1), 42–83 (1994)
27. Pavelka, J.: On fuzzy logic I, II, III. Zeitschrift für Math. Logik und Grundlagen der Math. 25, 45–52, 119–134, 447–464 (1979)
28. Rodríguez-Artalejo, M., Romero-Díaz, C.A.: Quantitative logic programming revisited. In: Garrigue, J., Hermenegildo, M.V. (eds.) FLOPS 2008. LNCS, vol. 4989, pp. 272–288. Springer, Heidelberg (2008)
29. Rydeheard, D.E., Burstall, R.M.: A categorical unification algorithm. In: Pitt, D.H., Abramsky, S., Poigné, A., Rydeheard, D.E. (eds.) CTCS. LNCS, vol. 240, pp. 493–505. Springer, Heidelberg (1985)
30. Sessa, M.I.: Approximate reasoning by similarity-based SLD resolution. Fuzzy Sets and Systems 275, 389–426 (2002)
31. Shapiro, E.Y.: Logic programs with uncertainties: A tool for implementing rule-based systems. In: Proc. of the 8th International Joint Conference on Artificial Intelligence, IJCAI 1983, Karlsruhe, pp. 529–532 (1983)
32. Subrahmanian, V.S.: On the Semantics of Quantitative Logic Programs. In: Proc. of International Symposium on Logic Programming, pp. 173–182 (1987)
33. van Emden, M.H.: Quantitative deduction and its fixpoint theory. Journal of Logic Programming 3(1), 37–53 (1986)
34. Vojtáš, P.: Fuzzy Logic Programming. Fuzzy Sets and Systems 124(1), 361–370 (2001)

Probability-Possibility Transformation:

Application to Bayesian and Possibilistic Networks

Yosra Ben Slimen, Raouia Ayachi, and Nahla Ben Amor

LARODEC, Institut Supérieur de Gestion Tunis 41 Avenue de la liberté, 2000 Le Bardo, Tunisie

Abstract. Probability-possibility transformation is a purely mechanical transformation of probabilistic support to possibilistic support and vice versa. In this paper, we apply the most common transformations to graphical models, i.e., Bayesian into possibilistic networks. We show that existing transformations are not appropriate to transform Bayesian networks to possibilistic ones since they cannot preserve the information incorporated in joint distributions. Therefore, we propose new consitency properties, exclusively useful for graphical models transformations.

Keywords: Probability-Possibility transformation, Bayesian networks, Possibilistic networks.

1 Introduction

Probability and possibility theories are two ways to express uncertainty. Several bridges between these two frameworks were established. Especially, several researches addressed the problem of transformation of possibilistic distributions into probabilistic ones and vice versa. The first interest underlying these transformations is to study the coherence between these frameworks and, more precisely, the consistency of derived distributions. Another interest is to make a benefit advantage of each framework. Following this idea, we are interested by transformations between Bayesian networks [13] and their adaptation in the possibilistic framework i.e. possibilistic networks [13]. In fact, these graphical models, which share the same graphical component i.e. Directed Acyclic Graph (DAG), are quantified using different distributions (i.e., probability distributions in the case of Bayesian networks and possibility ones in the case of possibilistic networks). Recently, the inference topic in possibilistic networks has been explored using compilation techniques [1]. It has been shown that the qualitative setting of possibility theory goes beyond the probabilistic framework and the quantitative possibilistic framework since it takes advantage of specific properties of the minimum operator. So, our objective in this paper is to study the possibility of switching from one model to another in order to reason in an efficient way.

This paper is organized as follows: Section 2 presents most common transformations. Section 3 presents some basics of Bayesian and possibilistic networks. Section 4 studies the particular case of transforming Bayesian networks into possibilistic ones.

F. Masulli, G. Pasi, and R. Yager (Eds.): WILF 2013, LNAI 8256, pp. 122–130, 2013.
© Springer International Publishing Switzerland 2013

2 Probability-Possibility Transformation

Possibility theory introduced by Zadeh [14] and developed by Dubois and Prade [6] lies at the crossroads between fuzzy sets, probability and non-monotonic reasoning. The basic building block in possibility theory is the notion of *possibility distribution* [6]: let $V = \{X_1, ..., X_N\}$ be a set of state variables whose values are ill-known such that $D_1 ... D_n$ are their respective domains. $\Omega = D_1 \times ... \times D_N$ denotes the universe of discourse, which is the cartesian product of all variable domains in V. Vectors $\omega \in \Omega$ are often called *realizations* or simply "states" (of the world). In what follows, we use x_i to denote possible instances of X_i. The agent's knowledge about the value of the x_i's can be encoded by a possibility distribution $\pi : \Omega \to [0, 1]$ where $\pi(\omega) = 1$ means that ω is totally possible and $\pi(\omega) = 0$ means that ω is an impossible state. It is generally assumed that there exist at least one state ω which is totally possible, π is then said to be *normalized*. We denote by $\top(\pi)$ the set of totally possible states in π. From π, one can compute, for any event $A \subseteq \Omega$, the possibility measure $\Pi(A) = \sup_{\omega \in A} \pi(\omega)$ that evaluates to which extend A is *consistent* with the knowledge represented by π. The particularity of the possibilistic scale is that it can be interpreted twofold: either in an *ordinal* manner, when the possibility degree reflects only an ordering between the possible values, so the *minimum* operator is used to combine different distributions, or, in a *numerical* manner, so possibility distributions are combined using the *product* operator.

Several researchers tackle different bridges between probability and possibility theory. When we deal with those transformations, two cases can be distinguished, those relative to subjective probabilities [8] and those relative to objective ones. In this paper, we focus on these latters which were used in several practical problems such as: *constructing a fuzzy membership function from statistical data* [11], *combining probabilities and possibilities information in expert systems* [9] and *reducing the computational complexity* [7]. Roughly speaking, transforming probabilistic distributions to possibilistic ones, denoted by $p \to \pi$, is useful when weak source of information makes probabilistic data unrealistic or to reduce the complexity of the solution or to combine different types of data. However, transformation, denoted by $\pi \to p$, is useful in the case of decision making. Interestingly enough, when transforming $p \to \pi$, some information is lost because we transform point value probabilities to interval values ones. In contrast, $\pi \to p$ adds information to some possibilistic incomplete knowledge.

2.1 Consistency Principle

In order to describe different transformations, several properties, called *consistency principle*, were proposed in literature. We retain, in particular, three of them:

Zadeh Consistency Principle: Zadeh [14] defined the probability-possibility consistency principle such as *"a high degree of possibility does not imply a high degree of probability, and a low degree of probability does not imply a low degree of possibility"*. The degree of consistency between p and π is defined by: $C(\pi, p) = \sum_{i=1...n} \pi_i * p_i$. Zadeh [14] pointed out that $C(\pi, p)$ is not a precise law or a relationship between possibility and probability distributions. It is an approximate formalization of the heuristic connection stating that lessening the possibility of an event tends to lessen its probability but not vice-versa.

Klir Consistency Principle: The concept of consistency condition was redefined by Klir [10]. Assume that the elements of Ω are ordered in such a way that $p_i > 0$ and $p_i \geq p_{i+1}, \ \forall \ i = \{1..n\}$. Any transformation should be based on these assumptions:
– A *scaling assumption* that forces each value π_i to be a function of p_i/p_1 (where $p_1 \geq \ldots \geq p_n$).
– An *uncertainty invariance assumption* according to which p and π must have the same amount of uncertainty.
– *Consistency condition:* $\pi_i \geq p_i$ stating that what is probable must be possible, so π can be seen as an upper-bound of p.
Dubois and Prade [5] gave an example to show that the scaling assumption of Klir may sometimes lead to violation of the consistency principle. The second assumption is also debatable because it assumes that possibilistic and probabilistic information measures are commensurate.

Dubois and Prade Consistency Principle: Dubois and Prade defined the consistency principle, differently, using these assumptions [4]:
– *Consistency condition:* $P_i < \Pi_i, \ \forall \ i = \{1..n\}$.
– *Preference preservation:* Assuming that π has the same form as p, then $\forall (\omega_1, \omega_2) \in \Omega^2, \ p(\omega_1) > p(\omega_2) \ \Rightarrow \ \pi(\omega_1) > \pi(\omega_2)$ and $p(\omega_1) = p(\omega_2) \ \Rightarrow \ \pi(\omega_1) = \pi(\omega_2)$.
– *Maximum specificity:* Let π_1 and π_2 be two possibility distributions, then π_2 is more specific than π_1 iff: $\forall \omega \in \Omega, \ \pi_2(\omega) \leq \pi_1(\omega)$.

2.2   Probability-Possibility Transformation Rules

Several transformation rules are proposed in literature. We present the most common ones, namely: *Klir transformation* (KT), *Optimal transformation* (OT), *Symmetric transformation* (ST) and *Variable transformation* (VT).

Klir Transformation (KT): Assume that the elements of Ω are ordered in such a way that: $\forall \ i = \{1..n\}, \ p_i > 0, \ p_i \geq p_{i+1}$ and $\pi_i > 0, \ \pi_i \geq \pi_{i+1}$ with $p_{n+1} = 0$ and $\pi_{n+1} = 0$. Klir has considered the principle of uncertainty preservation under two scales [10]:

  – *The ratio scale:* $p \rightarrow \pi$ and $\pi \rightarrow p$, named the normalized transformations, are defined by:
$$\pi_i = \frac{p_i}{p_1} \ , \ \ p_i = \frac{\pi_i}{n \sum_{i=1}^{n} \pi_i} \tag{1}$$
  – *The log-interval scale:* $p \rightarrow \pi$ and $\pi \rightarrow p$ are defined by:
$$\pi_i = \left(\frac{p_i}{p_1}\right)^\alpha \ , \ \ p_i = \frac{\pi_i^{\frac{1}{\alpha}}}{\sum_{i=1}^{n} (\pi_i)^{\frac{1}{\alpha}}} \tag{2}$$

where α is a parameter that belongs to the open interval $]0, 1[$.

Optimal Transformation (OT): proposed by Dubois and Prade [4] and also called "Asymmetric Transformation", is defined as follows:
$$\pi_i = \sum_{j/p_j \leq p_i} p_j, \ \ p_i = \sum_{j=1}^{n} \frac{\pi_j - \pi_{j+1}}{j} \tag{3}$$

OT is optimal because it gives the most specific possibility distribution i.e. that loses less information [7], and it's asymmetric since the two formulas in Equation (3) are not converse. Sandri et al. [7] suggested a *Symmetric Transformation* (ST) that needs less computation but it is quite far from the optimum. It is defined by:

$$\pi_i = \sum_{j=1}^{n} min(p_i, p_j) \tag{4}$$

Variable Transformation (VT): It's a $p \to \pi$ transformation proposed by Mouchaweh et al. [12] and expressed as follows: assume that the elements of Ω are ordered in such a way that: $\forall\ i = \{1..n\},\ p_i > 0,\ p_i \geq p_{i+1}$ and $\pi_i > 0,\ \pi_i \geq \pi_{i+1}$ with $p_{n+1} = 0$ and $\pi_{n+1} = 0$, then:

$$\pi_i = \left(\frac{p_i}{p_1}\right)^{k.(1-p_i)} \tag{5}$$

where k is a constant belonging to the interval: $0 \leq k \leq \frac{log p_n}{(1-p_n).\log(\frac{p_n}{p_1})}$.

Bouguelid [3] proposed VT_i, which is an improvement of VT, to make it as specific as OT. So, a parameter k_i is set for each π_i. Formally: $\forall\ i = \{1..n\}$,

$$\pi_i = \left(\frac{p_i}{p_1}\right)^{k_i.(1-p_i)} \tag{6}$$

where k_i belongs to the interval: $0 \leq k_i \leq \frac{log(p_i + p_{i+1} + ... + p_n)}{(1-p_i).\log(\frac{p_i}{p_1})},\ \forall i = \{2..n\}$.

Table 1 summarizes characteristics of KT, OT, ST, VT and VT_i. For each transformation, it is mentioned if it deals with discrete (D) and-or continuous case (C) and if it satisfies consistency principle (Cs), preference preservation (PP) and maximum specificity (MS). Clearly, OT and VT_i are the most interesting rules in the discrete case for $p \to \pi$.

Table 1. Summary of transformations

TR	$p \to \pi$	$\pi \to p$	Properties				
			D	C	Cs	PP	MS
KT	×	×	×	×		×	
OT	×	×	×	×	×	×	×
ST	×	×	×	×	×	×	
VT	×		×			×	
VTi	×		×		×	×	×

3   Basics on Bayesian and Possibilistic Networks

Bayesian networks [13] are powerful probabilistic graphical models for representing uncertain knowledge. Studying the possibilistic counterpart of Bayesian networks leads to two variants, namely: min-based possibilistic networks corresponding to the ordinal interpretation of the possibilistic scale and product-based possibilistic networks corresponding to the numerical interpretation [2]. It is well-known that product-based possibilistic networks are close to Bayesian networks since they share the same features (essentially the product operator) with almost the same theoretical and practical results [2]. This is not the case for min-based possibilistic networks due to the particularities of the min operator (e.g. the idempotency). Over a set of N variables $V = \{X_1, .., X_N\}$, Bayesian networks (denoted by BN) and possibilistic networks (denoted by $\Pi G_\otimes$ where $\otimes = min$ in the ordinal setting, and $\otimes = *$ in the numerical one) share the same two components:

– A *graphical component* composed of a DAG, $\mathcal{G} = (V, E)$ where V denotes a set of *nodes* representing variables and E a set of *edges* encoding links between nodes.

– A *numerical component* that quantifies different links. Uncertainty of each node X_i is represented by a local normalized conditional probability or possibility distribution in the context of its parents.

Given a Bayesian network BN on N variables, we can compute its joint probability distribution by the following chain rule :

$$p(X_1, \ldots, X_N) = *_{i=1..N} \ P(X_i \mid U_i) \tag{7}$$

In a similar manner, the joint possibility distribution of a possibilistic network $\Pi G_\otimes$ is defined by the $\otimes$-based chain rule, where $\otimes = min$ for the ordinal setting and $\otimes = *$ for the numerical one, expressed by:

$$\pi_\otimes(X_1, \ldots, X_N) = \otimes_{i=1..N} \ \Pi(X_i \mid U_i) \tag{8}$$

One of the most interesting treatments that can be applied for possibilistic networks is to evaluate the impact of a certain event on the remaining variables. Such process, called *inference*, consists on computing a-posteriori possibility distributions of each variable X_i given an evidence e.

Example 1. Let us consider the Bayesian network and the possibilistic network in Fig. 1(a) and Fig. 1 (b), respectively (sharing the same DAG). The joint distributions of BN and $\Pi G_\otimes$ using Equations (7) and (8) are presented in Fig. 1 (c).

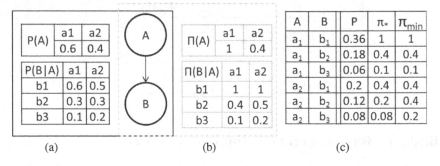

Fig. 1. A Bayesian network (a), a possibilistic network (b) and their joint distributions (c)

4   Transformation from Bayesian to Possibilistic Networks

Probability-possibility transformations can be useful to study the coherence between probabilistic and possibilistic frameworks and, more precisely, the consistency of derived distributions. Our idea consists in applying such transformations from Bayesian networks to possibilistic networks and interpreting their behavior on joint distributions. Formally, using existing transformations, we can define transformation from Bayesian to possibilistic networks in a local manner as follows:

Definition 1. *Let BN be a Bayesian network and p be its joint distribution. Let TR be a transformation rule. Let $BNto\Pi N$ be the function that transforms BN into $\Pi N_\otimes^{TR}$ using TR under the setting $\otimes$ s.t. $\otimes = \{*, min\}$. Let $PDto\Pi D$ be the function that transforms a probability distribution into a possibilistic one using TR. Formally, $\Pi N_\otimes^{TR}$ is the transformation of BN using TR if, $\forall X_i \in V$,*

$$\Pi(X_i \mid U_i) = PDto\Pi D(P(X_i \mid U_i), TR) \tag{9}$$

$$\Pi N_\otimes^{TR} = BNto\Pi N(BN, TR, \otimes) \tag{10}$$

Example 2. Table 2 depicts the transformation of conditional tables of the Bayesian network of Fig. 1 (a) using KT, OT, ST, VT and VT_i.

Table 2. Transformation of conditional distributions

$\Pi(A)$	Π^{KT}	Π^{OT,VT_i}	Π^{ST}	Π^{VT}
a_1	1	1	1	1
a_2	0.66	0.4	0.8	0.4

$\Pi(B \mid A)$	Π^{KT}	Π^{OT,VT_i}	Π^{ST}	Π^{VT}
$b_1 \mid a_1$	1	1	1	1
$b_2 \mid a_1$	0.5	0.4	0.7	0.5
$b_3 \mid a_1$	0.16	0.1	0.3	0.1
$b_1 \mid a_2$	1	1	1	1
$b_2 \mid a_2$	0.6	0.5	0.8	0.27
$b_3 \mid a_2$	0.4	0.2	0.6	0.2

This local transformation does not ensure the same results as a global one. In other words, the transformation of the joint distribution underlying the initial Bayesian network is not equivalent to the transformation of its local conditional distributions, which can affect the inference results. Let π_p^{TR} be the transformation of the joint distribution encoded by a Bayesian network BN using the transformation TR and let $\pi_\otimes^{TR}$ be the joint distribution relative to $\Pi N_\otimes^{TR}$ obtained using Definition 1. The following example illustrates the problem described above.

Example 3. Table 3 presents the transformation of global distributions of the Bayesian network of Fig. 1 (a) and of the resulted possibilistic network $\Pi N_\otimes$ using KT, OT, ST, VT and VT_i.

Table 3. Possibility distributions using different transformations

A	B	p	KT			OT, VT_i			ST			VT		
			π_p^{KT}	π_*^{KT}	π_{min}^{KT}	π_p^{OT,VT_i}	π_*^{OT,VT_i}	π_{min}^{OT,VT_i}	π_p^{ST}	π_*^{ST}	π_{min}^{ST}	π_p^{VT}	π_*^{VT}	π_{min}^{VT}
a_1	b_1	0.36	1	1	1	1	1	1	1	1	1	1	1	1
a_1	b_2	0.18	0.5	0.5	0.5	0.44	0.4	0.4	0.8	0.7	0.7	0.38	0.5	0.5
a_1	b_3	0.06	0.16	0.16	0.16	0.06	0.1	0.1	0.36	0.3	0.3	0.06	0.1	0.1
a_2	b_1	0.2	0.55	0.66	0.66	0.64	0.4	0.4	0.84	0.8	0.8	0.45	0.4	0.4
a_2	b_2	0.12	0.33	0.4	0.6	0.26	0.2	0.4	0.62	0.64	0.8	0.19	0.108	0.27
a_2	b_3	0.08	0.22	0.26	0.4	0.14	0.08	0.2	0.46	0.48	0.6	0.09	0.08	0.2

As depicted in Table 3, if we are in a numerical setting, the values of π_p^{TR} are different from those of π_*^{TR} and, if we deal with an ordinal setting, the order between π_*^{TR} and π_{min}^{TR} is not preserved, as well. For instance, for the transformation ST, more precisely for a_1b_2 and a_2b_2, we can see that $0.8 > 0.62$ while $0.7 < 0.8$. It is also the case of VT for a_1b_2 and a_2b_1. Suppose, now, that we have the evidence $B = b_2$, then for π_p^{ST} we have $a_1 > a_2$ while the same evidence implies $a_2 > a_1$ for π_{min}^{ST}. This means that, considering π_{min}^{ST} as the consistent transformation of the initial Bayesian network and using it to infer evidence can lead to erroneous results.

The question that may arise is the following: *Do all transformations suffer from the problem of information loss?* The answer can be found in the following example.

Example 4. Let us consider the BN of Fig. 2 (a) s.t $p > q$. This implies that $p > 0.5$ and $q < 0.5$, which in its turn implies that $0.5p > 0.5q > 0.25$. Fig. 2 (c) shows the joint distributions where $x < 1$, $y < 1$ and $z < 1$ and TR can be any transformation (i.e. KT, OT, ST, VT, VT_i).

We start by interpreting product-based networks which only rely on numerical values. It is obvious, from columns 4 and 5 of Fig. 2 (c), that there is a loss of information since values of π_p^{TR} and π_*^{TR} are different. When we deal with min-based networks, the focus is only on the order induced by values. In fact, the order of π_p^{TR} of the initial network BN is $\{a_1b_1 > a_1b_2 > (a_2b_1 = a_2b_2)\}$, while the order relative to π_{min}^{TR} is $\{(a_1b_1 = a_2b_1 = a_2b_2) > a_1b_2\}$.

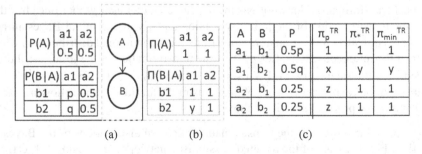

(a)   (b)   (c)

Fig. 2. A BN (a), its transformation into a possibilistic one (b) and their joint distributions (c)

Following this problem, we propose two new properties. The first one (resp. the second one), presented in Definition 2 (resp. Definition 3), is applicable for transforming Bayesian networks into min-based possibilistic networks (resp. product-based possibilistic networks). These properties should be seen as extensions of Dubois and Prade Consistency principle described above.

Definition 2. *Let TR be a transformation rule used in order to transform a Bayesian network BN into a min-based possibilistic network ΠN_{min}^{TR}. Let p be the joint distribution relative to BN computed using Equation (7) and π_p^{TR} be its transformation by TR. Let π_{min}^{TR} be the joint distribution relative to ΠN_{min}^{TR} using Equation (8) (s.t $\otimes = min$). Let $\delta(\pi_p^{TR})$ and $\delta(\pi_{min}^{TR})$ be the order underlying π_p^{TR} and π_{min}^{TR}, respectively. Then TR is said to be consistent iff: (i) $\delta(\pi_p^{TR}) = \delta(\pi_{min}^{TR})$ and (ii) $\top(\pi_p^{TR}) = \top(\pi_{min}^{TR})$*

Definition 3. *Let TR be a transformation rule used in order to transform a Bayesian network BN into a product-based possibilistic network ΠN_*^{TR}. Let p be the joint distribution relative to BN computed using Equation (7) and π_p^{TR} be its transformation by TR. Let π_*^{TR} be the joint distribution relative to ΠN_*^{TR} using Equation (8) (s.t $\otimes = *$). Then TR is said to be consistent iff: $\pi_p^{TR} = \pi_*^{TR}$*

Clearly, the formulas (ii) in Definition 2. guarantees the normalized values in both ordinal and numerical settings. We point out that this property is ensured by existing transformations.

5   Conclusion

Our objective in this paper is to study the transformation of Bayesian networks into possibilistic networks using existing transformations proposed in literature. We found out that switching from one model to another does not preserve the information incorporated in joint distributions (either numerical values for ΠN_* or the order induced by values for ΠN_{min}). Such result allows us to conclude that such transformations are inappropriate in the case of graphical models. Indeed, we have shown that it leads to erroneous inference results. A deep study on this behavior shows that this loss of information is due to the non-compatibility of product and min operators, in the ordinal setting. In our future work, we will deeply explore the impact of this loss of information on inference result for both product-based possibilistic networks and min-based possibilistic networks and propose two new transformations that respect the properties we proposed in order to transform Bayesian networks into possibilistic ones.

References

1. Ayachi, R., Ben Amor, N., Benferhat, S.: Possibilistic local structure for compiling min-based networks. In: SMPS, pp. 479–487 (2012)
2. Borgelt, C., Gebhardt, J., Kruse, R.: Possibilistic graphical models. In: Proceedings of the International School for the Synthesis of Expert Knowledge (1998)
3. Bouguelid, M.S.: Contribution à l'application de la reconnaissance des formes et la théorie des possibilités au diagnostic adaptatif et prédictif des systèmes dynamiques. PhD thesis, Université de Reims Champaghe-Ardenne (December 2007)

4. Dubois, D., Foulloy, L., Mauris, G., Prade, H.: Probability-Possibility Transformations, Triangular Fuzzy Sets, and Probabilistic Inequalities. Reliable Computing (2004)
5. Dubois, D., Prade, H.: Fuzzy Sets and Systems: Theory and Applications. Academic Press, New York (1980)
6. Dubois, D., Prade, H.: Possibility theory: An approach to computerized, Processing of uncertainty. Plenium Press, New York (1988)
7. Dubois, D., Prade, H., Sandri, S.: On possibility/probability transformations. Fuzzy Logic (1993)
8. Dubois, D., Prade, H., Smets, P.: A definition of subjective possibility. International Journal of Approximate Reasoning 48, 352–364 (2008)
9. Klir, G.J.: Probability-possibility transformations: a comparison. Int. J. General Systems 21, 291–310 (1992)
10. Klir, G.J.: Information-preserving probability-possibility transformations: recent developments. Fuzzy Logic, 417–428 (1993)
11. Mouchaweh, M.S.: Diagnosis in real time for evolutionary processes using pattern recognition and possibility theory. Invited paper in International Journal of Computational Cognition, 79–112 (2004)
12. Mouchaweh, M.S., Bouguelid, M.S., Billaudel, P., Riera, B.: Variable probability-possibility transformation. In: 25th European Annual Conference on Human Decision-Making and Manual Control (EAM 2006), pp. 417–428 (September 2006)
13. Pearl, J.: Probabilistic Reasoning in Intelligent Systems: Networks of Plausible Inference. Morgan Kaufmann Publishers Inc., San Francisco (1988)
14. Zadeh, L.A.: Fuzzy sets as a biaisis for a therory of possibility. Fuzzy Sets and Systems 1, 3–28 (1978)

The Equation $\mathcal{I}(\mathcal{S}(x,y),z) = \mathcal{T}(\mathcal{I}(x,z),\mathcal{I}(y,z))$ for t-representable t-conorms and t-norms Generated from Continuous, Archimedean Operations

Michał Baczyński

Institute of Mathematics, University of Silesia,
40-007 Katowice, ul. Bankowa 14, Poland
michal.baczynski@us.edu.pl

Abstract. In this article we continue investigations presented at previous WILF 2011 conference which are connected with distributivity of implication operations over t-representable t-norms and t-conorms. Our main goal is to show the general method of solving the following distributivity equation $\mathcal{I}(\mathcal{S}(x,y),z) = \mathcal{T}(\mathcal{I}(x,z),\mathcal{I}(y,z))$, when $\mathcal{S}$ is a t-representable t-conorm on $\mathcal{L}^I$ generated from two continuous, Archimedean t-conorms, $\mathcal{T}$ is a t-representable t-norm on $\mathcal{L}^I$ generated from two continuous, Archimedean t-norms and $\mathcal{I}$ is an unknown function.

Keywords: Interval-valued fuzzy sets, Triangular norm, Triangular conorm, Distributivity equations, Functional equations.

1 Introduction

Distributivity of (classical) fuzzy implications over different fuzzy logic connectives has been studied in the recent past by many authors (see chronologically [2], [32], [12], [29], [30], [11],[3],[8]). These equations have a very important role to play in efficient inferencing in approximate reasoning, especially in fuzzy control systems. Given an input "$\tilde{x}$ is A'", the role of an inference mechanism is to obtain a fuzzy output B' that satisfies some desirable properties. The most important inference schemas are fuzzy relational inference and similarity based reasoning. In the first case the inferred output B' is obtained either as

(i) $\sup -T$ composition, as in the compositional rule of inference (CRI) of Zadeh (see [33]), or

(ii) $\inf -I$ composition, as in the Bandler-Kohout Subproduct (BKS) (see [13]),

of A' and given rules. Since all the rules of an inference engine are exercised during every inference cycle, the number of rules directly affects the computational duration of the overall application.

F. Masulli, G. Pasi, and R. Yager (Eds.): WILF 2013, LNAI 8256, pp. 131–138, 2013.

To reduce the complexity of fuzzy "IF-THEN" rules, Combs and Andrews [16] proposed an equivalent transformation of the CRI to mitigate the computational cost. In fact, they required of the following classical tautology

$$(p \wedge q) \to r = (p \to r) \vee (q \to r).$$

so we see that the distributivity of fuzzy implications over t-norms (or t-conorms) play a major role in this transformation. Subsequently, there were many discussions (see [14], [15], [20], [28]), most of them pointed out the need for a theoretical investigation required for employing such equations. Later, the similar method but for similarity based reasoning was demonstrated by Jayaram [24]. For an overview of the most important methods that reduce the complexity of different inference systems and concrete examples see [10, Chapter 8].

Recently, in [4], [5], [6] (for the full article see [9]) and [7] we have discussed the distributivity equation of implications

$$\mathcal{I}(x, \mathcal{T}_1(y, z)) = \mathcal{T}_2(\mathcal{I}(x, y), \mathcal{I}(x, z))$$

over t-representable t-norms generated from continuous Archimedean t-norms, in interval-valued fuzzy sets theory. In these articles we have obtained the solutions for each of the following functional equations, respectively:

$$f(u_1 + v_1, u_2 + v_2) = f(u_1, u_2) + f(v_1, v_2), \tag{A}$$
$$g(\min(u_1 + v_1, a), \min(u_2 + v_2, a)) = g(u_1, u_2) + g(v_1, v_2), \tag{B}$$
$$h(\min(u_1 + v_1, a), \min(u_2 + v_2, a)) = \min(h(u_1, u_2) + h(v_1, v_2), b), \tag{C}$$
$$k(u_1 + v_1, u_2 + v_2) = \min(k(u_1, u_2) + k(v_1, v_2), b), \tag{D}$$

where $a, b > 0$ are fixed real numbers, $f \colon L^\infty \to [0, \infty]$, $g \colon L^a \to [0, \infty]$, $h \colon L^a \to [0, b]$, and $k \colon L^\infty \to [0, b]$ are unknown functions. The above we use the following notation

$$L^\infty = \{(u_1, u_2) \in [0, \infty]^2 \mid u_1 \geq u_2\},$$
$$L^a = \{(u_1, u_2) \in [0, a]^2 \mid u_1 \geq u_2\}.$$

More precisely, the solutions of Eq. (A) have been presented in [4, Proposition 3.2], the solutions of Eq. (B) have been presented in [5, Proposition 4.2], the solutions of Eq. (C) have been presented in [9, Proposition 5.2] and the solutions of Eq. (D) have been presented in [7, Proposition 3.2].

In this paper we continue these investigations, but for the following functional equation

$$\mathcal{I}(\mathcal{S}(x, y), z) = \mathcal{T}(\mathcal{I}(x, z), \mathcal{I}(y, z)), \tag{D-ST}$$

satisfied for all $x, y, z \in L^I$, when $\mathcal{S}$ is a t-representable t-conorm on $\mathcal{L}^I$ generated from two continuous, Archimedean t-conorms S_1, S_2, $\mathcal{T}$ is a t-representable t-norm on $\mathcal{L}^I$ generated from two continuous, Archimedean t-norms T_1, T_2 and $\mathcal{I}$ is an unknown function.

Please note that the solutions for this Eq. (D-ST) in the classical case, i.e. for classical continuous Archimedean t-norms and t-conorms have been presented by the author in [8].

2   Interval-Valued Fuzzy Sets

One possible extension of fuzzy sets theory is interval-valued fuzzy sets theory introduced, independently, by Sambuc [31] and Gorzałczany [23], in which to each element of the universe a closed subinterval of the unit interval is assigned – it can be used as an approximation of the unknown membership degree. Let us define

$$L^I = \{(x_1, x_2) \in [0,1]^2 : x_1 \le x_2\},$$
$$(x_1, x_2) \le_{L^I} (y_1, y_2) \Longleftrightarrow x_1 \le y_1 \wedge x_2 \le y_2.$$

In the sequel, if $x \in L^I$, then we denote it by $x = [x_1, x_2]$. One can easily observe that $\mathcal{L}^I = (L^I, \le_{L^I})$ is also a complete lattice with units $0_{\mathcal{L}^I} = [0,0]$ and $1_{\mathcal{L}^I} = [1,1]$.

Definition 2.1. *An interval-valued fuzzy set on X is a mapping $A : X \to L^I$.*

Another extension of fuzzy sets theory is intuitionistic fuzzy sets theory introduced in 1983 by Atanassov [1].

Definition 2.2. *An intuitionistic fuzzy set A on X is a set*

$$A = \{(x, \mu_A(x), \nu_A(x)) \; : \; x \in X\},$$

where μ_A, $\nu_A : X \to [0,1]$ are called, respectively, the membership function and the non-membership function. Moreover they satisfy the condition

$$\mu_A(x) + \nu_A(x) \le 1, \quad x \in X.$$

Let us define

$$L^* = \{(x_1, x_2) \in [0,1]^2 \; : \; x_1 + x_2 \le 1\},$$
$$(x_1, x_2) \le_{L^*} (y_1, y_2) \Longleftrightarrow x_1 \le y_1 \wedge x_2 \ge y_2.$$

It is important to notice that in [19] it is shown that interval-valued fuzzy sets theory is equivalent, from the mathematical point of view, to intuitionistic fuzzy sets theory (see [1] and [21]). In fact, we can see the point $(x_1, x_2) \in L^*$ as the interval $[x_1, 1 - x_2] \in L^I$ (and vice-verse). Since we are limited in number of pages, in this article we will discuss main results in the language of interval-valued fuzzy sets, but they can be easily transformed to the intuitionistic case.

3   Basic Fuzzy Connectives

We assume that the reader is familiar with the classical results concerning basic fuzzy logic connectives, but we briefly mention some of the results employed in the rest of the work.

Definition 3.1. *Let $\mathcal{L} = (L, \leq_L)$ be a complete lattice. An associative, commutative operation $\mathcal{T}: L^2 \to L$ is called a t-norm if it is increasing and $1_{\mathcal{L}}$ is the neutral element of $\mathcal{T}$. An associative, commutative operation $\mathcal{S}: L^2 \to L$ is called a t-conorm if it is increasing and $0_{\mathcal{L}}$ is the neutral element of $\mathcal{S}$.*

The following characterizations of classical t-norms are well-known in the literature.

Theorem 3.2 ([26], cf. [25, Theorem 5.1]). *For a function $T: [0,1]^2 \to [0,1]$ the following statements are equivalent:*

(i) *T is a continuous Archimedean t-norm, i.e., if for every $x, y \in (0,1)$ there is an $n \in \mathbb{N}$ such that $x_T^{[n]} < y$.*

(ii) *T has a continuous additive generator, i.e., there exists a continuous, strictly decreasing function $f: [0,1] \to [0, \infty]$ with $f(1) = 0$, which is uniquely determined up to a positive multiplicative constant, such that*

$$T(x, y) = f^{-1}(\min(f(x) + f(y), f(0))), \qquad x, y \in [0,1].$$

Theorem 3.3 ([26], cf. [25, Corollary 5.5]). *For a function $S: [0,1]^2 \to [0,1]$ the following statements are equivalent:*

(i) *S is a continuous and Archimedean t-conorm, i.e., if for every $x, y \in (0,1)$ there is an $n \in \mathbb{N}$ such that $x_S^{[n]} > y$.*

(ii) *S has a continuous additive generator, i.e., there exists a continuous, strictly increasing function $s: [0,1] \to [0, \infty]$ with $s(0) = 0$, which is uniquely determined up to a positive multiplicative constant, such that*

$$S(x, y) = s^{-1}(\min(s(x) + s(y), s(1))), \qquad x, y \in [0,1]. \tag{1}$$

In our article we shall consider the following special classes of t-norms and t-conorms on $\mathcal{L}^I$.

Definition 3.4 (see [17]).

(i) *A t-norm $\mathcal{T}$ on $\mathcal{L}^I$ is called t-representable if there exist t-norms T_1 and T_2 on $([0,1], \leq)$ such that $T_1 \leq T_2$ and*

$$\mathcal{T}([x_1, x_2], [y_1, y_2]) = [T_1(x_1, y_1), T_2(x_2, y_2)], \qquad [x_1, x_2], [y_1, y_2] \in L^I.$$

(ii) *A t-conorm $\mathcal{S}$ on $\mathcal{L}^I$ is called t-representable if there exist t-conorms S_1 and S_2 on $([0,1], \leq)$ such that $S_1 \leq S_2$ and*

$$\mathcal{S}([x_1, x_2], [y_1, y_2]) = [S_1(x_1, y_1), S_2(x_2, y_2)], \qquad [x_1, x_2], [y_1, y_2] \in L^I.$$

It should be noted that not all t-norms and t-conorms on $\mathcal{L}^I$ are t-representable (for counterexamples see [17]).

One possible definition of an implication on $\mathcal{L}^I$ is based on the well-accepted notation introduced by Fodor and Roubens [22] (see also [10], [18] and [27]).

Definition 3.5. *Let $\mathcal{L} = (L, \leq_L)$ be a complete lattice. A function $\mathcal{I}: L^2 \to L$ is called a fuzzy implication on $\mathcal{L}$ if it is decreasing with respect to the first variable, increasing with respect to the second variable and fulfills the following conditions: $\mathcal{I}(0_{\mathcal{L}}, 0_{\mathcal{L}}) = \mathcal{I}(1_{\mathcal{L}}, 1_{\mathcal{L}}) = \mathcal{I}(0_{\mathcal{L}}, 1_{\mathcal{L}}) = 1_{\mathcal{L}}$ and $\mathcal{I}(1_{\mathcal{L}}, 0_{\mathcal{L}}) = 0_{\mathcal{L}}$.*

4 On Eq. (D-ST) for t-representable t-conorms and t-norms

In this section we will show how we can use solutions discussed earlier in Section 1 to obtain all solutions of our main distributivity equations

$$\mathcal{I}(\mathcal{S}(x,y),z) = \mathcal{T}(\mathcal{I}(x,z),\mathcal{I}(y,z)), \qquad x,y,z \in L^I,$$

where $\mathcal{I}$ is an unknown function, $\mathcal{S}$ is a t-representable t-conorm on $\mathcal{L}^I$ generated from continuous, Archimedean t-conorms S_1, S_2 and $\mathcal{T}$ is a t-representable t-norm on $\mathcal{L}^I$ generated from continuous, Archimedean t-norms T_1, T_2.

Assume that projection mappings on $\mathcal{L}^I$ are defined as the following:

$$pr_1([x_1, x_2]) = x_1, \quad pr_2([x_1, x_2]) = x_2,$$

for $[x_1, x_2] \in L^I$. At this situation our distributivity equation has the following form

$$\mathcal{I}([S_1(x_1, y_1), S_2(x_2, y_2)], [z_1, z_2])$$
$$= [T_1(pr_1(\mathcal{I}([x_1, x_2], [z_1, z_2])), pr_1(\mathcal{I}([y_1, y_2], [z_1, z_2]))),$$
$$T_2(pr_2(\mathcal{I}([x_1, x_2], [z_1, z_2])), pr_2(\mathcal{I}([y_1, y_2], [z_1, z_2])))]$$

for all $[x_1, x_2], [y_1, y_2], [z_1, z_2] \in L^I$. As a consequence we obtain the following two equations

$$pr_1(\mathcal{I}([S_1(x_1, y_1), S_2(x_2, y_2)], [z_1, z_2]))$$
$$= T_1(pr_1(\mathcal{I}([x_1, x_2], [z_1, z_2])), pr_1(\mathcal{I}([y_1, y_2], [z_1, z_2]))),$$
$$pr_2(\mathcal{I}([S_1(x_1, y_1), S_2(x_2, y_2)], [z_1, z_2]))$$
$$= T_2(pr_2(\mathcal{I}([x_1, x_2], [z_1, z_2])), pr_2(\mathcal{I}([y_1, y_2], [z_1, z_2]))),$$

which are satisfied for all $[x_1, x_2], [y_1, y_2], [z_1, z_2] \in L^I$. Now, let us fix arbitrarily $[z_1, z_2] \in L^I$ and define two functions $g_1^{[z_1, z_2]}, g_2^{[z_1, z_2]} \colon L^I \to L^I$ by

$$g_1^{[z_1, z_2]}(\cdot) := pr_1 \circ \mathcal{I}(\cdot, [z_1, z_2]),$$
$$g_2^{[z_1, z_2]}(\cdot) := pr_2 \circ \mathcal{I}(\cdot, [z_1, z_2]).$$

Thus we have shown that if $\mathcal{S}$ and $\mathcal{T}$ on $\mathcal{L}^I$ are t-representable, then

$$g_1^{[z_1, z_2]}([S_1(x_1, y_1), S_2(x_2, y_2)]) = T_1(g_1^{[z_1, z_2]}([x_1, x_2]), g_1^{[z_1, z_2]}([y_1, y_2])),$$
$$g_2^{[z_1, z_2]}([S_1(x_1, y_1), S_2(x_2, y_2)]) = T_2(g_2^{[z_1, z_2]}([x_1, x_2]), g_2^{[z_1, z_2]}([y_1, y_2])).$$

Let us assume that $S_1 = S_2$ is a continuous, Archimedean t-conorm generated from continuous generator s and $T_1 = T_2$ is a continuous, Archimedean t-norm generated from continuous generator t. Using the representations of t-conorms

(Theorem 3.3) and t-norms (Theorem 3.3) we can transform our problem to the following equations:

$$g_1^{[z_1,z_2]}([t^{-1}(\min(t(x_1)+t(y_1),t(0))),t^{-1}(\min(t(x_2)+t(y_2),t(0)))])$$
$$= s^{-1}(\min(s(g_1^{[z_1,z_2]}([x_1,x_2]))+s(g_1^{[z_1,z_2]}([y_1,y_2])),s(1))).$$

Hence

$$s \circ g_1^{[z_1,z_2]}([t^{-1}(\min(t(x_1)+t(y_1),t(0))),t^{-1}(\min(t(x_2)+t(y_2),t(0)))])$$
$$= \min(s(g_1^{[z_1,z_2]}([x_1,x_2]))+s(g_1^{[z_1,z_2]}([y_1,y_2])),s(1)).$$

Let us put $t(x_1) = u_1$, $t(x_2) = u_2$, $t(y_1) = v_1$ and $t(y_2) = v_2$. Of course $u_1, u_2, v_1, v_2 \in [0, t(0)]$. Moreover $[x_1, x_2], [y_1, y_2] \in L^I$, thus $x_1 \leq x_2$ and $y_1 \leq y_2$. The generator t is strictly decreasing, so $u_1 \geq u_2$ and $v_1 \geq v_2$. If we put

$$f_{[z_1,z_2]}(u,v) := s \circ pr_1 \circ \mathcal{I}([t^{-1}(u),t^{-1}(v)],[z_1,z_2]),$$

where $u, v \in [0, t(0)]$, $u \geq v$, then we get the following functional equation

$$f_{[z_1,z_2]}(\min(u_1+v_1,t(0)),\min(u_2+v_2,t(0)))$$
$$= \min(f_{[z_1,z_2]}(u_1,u_2)+f_{[z_1,z_2]}(v_1,v_2),s(1)), \qquad (2)$$

satisfied for all $(u_1,u_2),(v_1,v_2) \in L^{t(0)}$. Of course function $f_{[z_1,z_2]} : L^{t(0)} \to [0,\infty]$ is unknown above. In a same way we can repeat all the above calculations, but for the function g_2, to obtain the following functional equation

$$f^{[z_1,z_2]}(\min(u_1+v_1,t(0)),\min(u_2+v_2,t(0)))$$
$$= \min(f^{[z_1,z_2]}(u_1,u_2)+f^{[z_1,z_2]}(v_1,v_2),s(1)), \qquad (3)$$

satisfied for all $(u_1,u_2),(v_1,v_2) \in L^{t(0)}$, where

$$f^{[z_1,z_2]}(u,v) := s \circ pr_2 \circ \mathcal{I}([t^{-1}(u),t^{-1}(v)],[z_1,z_2])$$

is an unknown function.

Observe that considering different values for $t(0)$ and $s(1)$, i.e., the following four cases:

- $t(0) = s(1) = \infty$,
- $t(0) < \infty$ and $s(1) = \infty$,
- $t(0) < \infty$ and $s(1) < \infty$,
- $t(0) = \infty$ and $s(1) < \infty$,

our equations (2) and (3) are becoming one of the previously considered equations (A) - (D). Therefore, using solutions already presented in the literature (cf. Section 1), we are able to obtain (separately) the description of the horizontal section $\mathcal{I}(\cdot,[z_1,z_2])$ for a fixed $[z_1,z_2] \in L^I$. Now, taking into account both equations (2) and (3), it is possible to find solutions $\mathcal{I}$ for which the range is L^I. Since we are limited in number of pages it is not possible to show all these solutions, in particular fuzzy implications, but it is our goal for the future work.

References

1. Atanassov, K.T.: Intuitionistic fuzzy sets. In: Sgurev, V. (ed.) VII ITKR's Session, volume deposed in Central Sci.-Technical Library of Bulg. Acad. of Sci., 1697/84, Sofia (June 1983)
2. Baczyński, M.: On a class of distributive fuzzy implications. Internat. J. Uncertain. Fuzziness Knowledge-Based Systems 9, 229–238 (2001)
3. Baczyński, M.: On the distributivity of fuzzy implications over continuous and Archimedean triangular conorms. Fuzzy Sets and Systems 161(10), 1406–1419 (2010)
4. Baczyński, M.: On the Distributivity of Implication Operations over t-Representable t-Norms Generated from Strict t-Norms in Interval-Valued Fuzzy Sets Theory. In: Hüllermeier, E., Kruse, R., Hoffmann, F. (eds.) IPMU 2010. CCIS, vol. 80, pp. 637–646. Springer, Heidelberg (2010)
5. Baczyński, M.: On the distributive equation for t-representable t-norms generated from nilpotent and strict t-norms. In: Galichet, S., Montero, J., Mauris, G. (eds.) Proc. EUSFLAT-LFA 2011, Aix-les-Bains, France, pp. 540–546 (July 2011)
6. Baczyński, M.: Distributivity of Implication Operations over t-Representable T-Norms Generated from Nilpotent T-Norms. In: Fanelli, A.M., Pedrycz, W., Petrosino, A. (eds.) WILF 2011. LNCS (LNAI), vol. 6857, pp. 25–32. Springer, Heidelberg (2011)
7. Baczyński, M.: Distributivity of Implication Operations over t-Representable T-Norms Generated from Continuous and Archimedean T-Norms. In: Greco, S., Bouchon-Meunier, B., Coletti, G., Fedrizzi, M., Matarazzo, B., Yager, R.R. (eds.) IPMU 2012, Part II. CCIS, vol. 298, pp. 501–510. Springer, Heidelberg (2012)
8. Baczyński, M.: On two distributivity equations for fuzzy implications and continuous, Archimedean t-norms and t-conorms. Fuzzy Sets and Systems 211, 34–54 (2013)
9. Baczyński, M.: Distributivity of implication operations over t-representable t-norms in interval-valued fuzzy set theory: the case of nilpotent t-norms. Inform. Sci. (2013), doi: http://dx.doi.org/10.1016/j.ins.2013.06.013
10. Baczyński, M., Jayaram, B.: Fuzzy Implications. STUDFUZZ, vol. 231. Springer, Heidelberg (2008)
11. Baczyński, M., Jayaram, B.: On the distributivity of fuzzy implications over nilpotent or strict triangular conorms. IEEE Trans. Fuzzy Syst. 17(3), 590–603 (2009)
12. Balasubramaniam, J., Rao, C.J.M.: On the distributivity of implication operators over T and S norms. IEEE Trans. Fuzzy Syst. 12(2), 194–198 (2004)
13. Bandler, W., Kohout, L.J.: Semantics of implication operators and fuzzy relational products. Internat. J. Man-Mach. Stud. 12, 89–116 (1980)
14. Combs, W.E.: Author's reply. IEEE Trans. Fuzzy Syst. 7(3), 371–373 (1999)
15. Combs, W.E.: Author's reply. IEEE Trans. Fuzzy Syst. 7(4), 477–478 (1999)
16. Combs, W.E., Andrews, J.E.: Combinatorial rule explosion eliminated by a fuzzy rule configuration. IEEE Trans. Fuzzy Syst. 6(1), 1–11 (1998)
17. Deschrijver, G., Cornelis, C., Kerre, E.E.: On the representation of intuitionistic fuzzy t-norms and t-conorms. IEEE Trans. Fuzzy Syst. 12(1), 45–61 (2004)
18. Deschrijver, G., Cornelis, C., Kerre, E.E.: Implication in intuitionistic and interval-valued fuzzy set theory: construction, classification and application. Internat. J. Approx. Reason. 35(1), 55–95 (2004)
19. Deschrijver, G., Kerre, E.E.: On the relationship between some extensions of fuzzy set theory. Fuzzy Sets and Systems 133(2), 227–235 (2003)

20. Dick, S., Kandel, A.: Comments on "Combinatorial rule explosion eliminated by a fuzzy rule configuration". IEEE Trans. Fuzzy Syst. 7(4), 475–477 (1999)
21. Dubois, D., Gottwald, S., Hájek, P., Kacprzyk, J., Prade, H.: Terminological difficulties in fuzzy set theory - the case of "Intuitionistic fuzzy sets". Fuzzy Sets and Systems 156(3), 485–491 (2005)
22. Fodor, J., Roubens, M.: Fuzzy Preference Modelling and Multicriteria Decision Support. Kluwer Academic Publishers, Dordrecht (1994)
23. Gorzałczany, M.B.: A method of inference in approximate reasoning based on interval-valued fuzzy sets. Fuzzy Sets and Systems 21(1), 1–17 (1987)
24. Jayaram, B.: Rule reduction for efficient inferencing in similarity based reasoning. Internat. J. Approx. Reason. 48, 156–173 (2008)
25. Klement, E.P., Mesiar, R., Pap, E.: Triangular Norms. Kluwer Academic Publishers, Dordrecht (2000)
26. Ling, C.H.: Representation of associative functions. Publ. Math. Debrecen 12, 189–212 (1965)
27. Mas, M., Monserrat, M., Torrens, J., Trillas, E.: A survey on fuzzy implication functions. IEEE Trans. Fuzzy Syst. 15(6), 1107–1121 (2007)
28. Mendel, J.M., Liang, Q.: Comments on "Combinatorial rule explosion eliminated by a fuzzy rule configuration". IEEE Trans. Fuzzy Syst. 7(3), 369–371 (1999)
29. Ruiz-Aguilera, D., Torrens, J.: Distributivity of strong implications over conjunctive and disjunctive uninorms. Kybernetika 42(3), 319–336 (2006)
30. Ruiz-Aguilera, D., Torrens, J.: Distributivity of residual implications over conjunctive and disjunctive uninorms. Fuzzy Sets and Systems 158(1), 23–37 (2007)
31. Sambuc, R.: Fonctions Φ-floues. Application l'aide au diagnostic en pathologie thyroidienne. PhD thesis, Univ. Marseille, France (1975)
32. Trillas, E., Alsina, C.: On the law $[(p \wedge q) \rightarrow r] = [(p \rightarrow r) \vee (q \rightarrow r)]$ in fuzzy logic. IEEE Trans. Fuzzy Syst. 10(1), 84–88 (2002)
33. Zadeh, L.A.: Outline of a new approach to the analysis of complex systems and decision processes. IEEE Trans. on Syst. Man and Cyber. 3, 28–44 (1973)

Evaluation and Ranking of Intuitionistic Fuzzy Quantities

Luca Anzilli[1], Gisella Facchinetti[2], and Giovanni Mastroleo[3]

[1] Department of Management, Economics, Mathematics and Statistics,
University of Salento, Italy
{luca.anzilli,gisella.facchinetti,giovanni.mastroleo}@unisalento.it
[2] Department of Management, Economics, Mathematics and Statistics,
University of Salento, Italy
[3] Department of Management, Economics, Mathematics and Statistics,
University of Salento, Italy

Abstract. We deal with the problem of evaluating and ranking intu-itionistic fuzzy quantities (IFQs). We call IFQ an intuitionistic fuzzy set (IFS) described by a pair of fuzzy quantities, where a fuzzy quantity is defined as the union of two, or more, convex fuzzy sets that may be non-normal. We suggest an evaluation defined by a pair index based on "value" & "ambiguity" and a ranking method based on them. This new formulation contains as particular cases the ones proposed by Fortemps and Roubens [13], Yager and Filev [24, 25] and follows a completely different approach.

Keywords: Fuzzy quantities, Intuitionistic fuzzy quantities, Evaluation, Ranking, Ambiguity.

1 Introduction

In many practical applications the available information corresponding to a fuzzy concept may be incomplete, that is the sum of the membership degree and the non-membership degree may be less than one. A possible solution is to use "Intuitionistic fuzzy sets" (IFSs) introduced by Atanassov [5, 6, 8]. Several proposals of "Intuitionistic fuzzy numbers" evaluation and ranking are present in literature [14, 11, 15, 17–21]. Due to the connection between IFSs and Interval type-2 fuzzy sets and industrial applications that have used interval type-2 fuzzy logic systems [16, 23, 10], we have thought that it may be interesting to work on a better characterization of particular IFSs in which the two memberships may be not normal and not fuzzy convex. In this direction the definition of Intuitionistic Fuzzy Quantities (IFQs) is present in a previous paper [2]. These fuzzy sets are defined by a pair of Fuzzy Quantities (FQs) that may be obtained as the union of N convex fuzzy sets with continuous membership functions. In the same paper we have introduced an IFQs evaluation formula that takes the cue from a previous definition introduced for FQs in [12], based on a geometrical approach with $N = 2$ components. The transition from two to more than two

F. Masulli, G. Pasi, and R. Yager (Eds.): WILF 2013, LNAI 8256, pp. 139–149, 2013.

requires to redefine all what we have done before, using a different approach that may be more useful in presence of a higher number of components. In this direction an approach based on total variation of bounded variation functions is introduced in [3]. To reach an evaluation and consequent ranking of IFQs, we work on FQs evaluation and ranking. The new proposed definition contains as particular case the heuristic proposal of Fortemps and Roubens [13] for FQs and the definition proposed by Yager and Filev [24, 25] and by Facchinetti and Pacchiarotti [12]. Using the same approach we introduce a general definition of ambiguity and by evaluation and ambiguity we introduce a way to rank IFQs.

In Section 2 we give basic definitions and notations. In Section 3 we introduce our definition of fuzzy quantity and illustrate our general evaluation method. In Section 4 we propose a definition of ambiguity for fuzzy quantities. In Section 5 and Section 6 we use the previous model to evaluate and rank intuitionistic fuzzy quantities.

2   Preliminaries and Notation

Let X denote a universe of discourse. A fuzzy set A in X is defined by a membership function $\mu_A : X \to [0,1]$ which assigns to each element of X a grade of membership to the set A. The height of A is $h_A = height\, A = \sup_{x \in X} \mu_A(x)$. The support and the core of A are defined, respectively, as the crisp sets $supp(A) = \{x \in X; \mu_A(x) > 0\}$ and $core(A) = \{x \in X; \mu_A(x) = 1\}$. A fuzzy set A is normal if its core is nonempty. The union of two fuzzy set A and B is the fuzzy set $A \cup B$ defined by the membership function $\mu_{A \cup B}(x) = \max\{\mu_A(x), \mu_B(x)\}$, $x \in X$. The intersection is the fuzzy set $A \cap B$ defined by $\mu_{A \cap B}(x) = \min\{\mu_A(x), \mu_B(x)\}$. A fuzzy number A is a fuzzy set of the real line $\mathbb{R}$ with a normal, convex and upper-semicontinuous membership function of bounded support (see, e.g., [9]). From the definition given above there exist four numbers $a_1, a_2, a_3, a_4 \in \mathbb{R}$, with $a_1 \le a_2 \le a_3 \le a_4$, and two functions $f_A, g_A : \mathbb{R} \to [0,1]$ called the left side and the right side of A, respectively, where f_A is nondecreasing and right-continuous and g_A is nonincreasing and left-continuous, such that

$$\mu_A(x) = \begin{cases} 0 & x < a_1 \\ f_A(x) & a_1 \le x < a_2 \\ 1 & a_2 \le x \le a_3 \\ g_A(x) & a_3 < x \le a_4 \\ 0 & a_4 < x. \end{cases}$$

The α-cut of a fuzzy set A, $0 \le \alpha \le 1$, is defined as the crisp set $A_\alpha = \{x \in X; \mu_A(x) \ge \alpha\}$ if $0 < \alpha \le 1$ and as the closure of the support if $\alpha = 0$. Every α-cut of a fuzzy number is a closed interval $A_\alpha = [a_L(\alpha), a_R(\alpha)]$, for $0 \le \alpha \le 1$, where $a_L(\alpha) = \inf A_\alpha$ and $a_R(\alpha) = \sup A_\alpha$.

In the following we will employ the mid-spread representation of intervals. The middle point and the spread of the interval $I = [a, b]$ will be denoted, respectively, by

$$mid(I) = \frac{a+b}{2}, \qquad spr(I) = \frac{b-a}{2}.$$

3   Evaluation of Fuzzy Quantities

In [4] we give a definition of fuzzy quantity and propose a general evaluation model. Furthermore, we show that the evaluation methods presented by Fortemps and Roubens [13] and Yager and Filev [24, 25] are special cases of our approach. In this section we review this model.

3.1   Fuzzy Quantities

Definition 1. *Let N be a positive integer and let $a_1, a_2, \ldots, a_{4N}$ be real numbers with $a_1 < a_2 \leq a_3 < a_4 \leq a_5 < a_6 \leq a_7 < a_8 \leq a_9 < \cdots < a_{4N-2} \leq a_{4N-1} < a_{4N}$. We call fuzzy quantity*

$$A = (a_1, a_2, \ldots, a_{4N};\ h_1, h_2, \ldots, h_N,\ h_{1,2}, h_{2,3}, \ldots, h_{N-1,N}) \tag{1}$$

where $0 < h_j \leq 1$ for $j = 1, \ldots, N$ and $0 \leq h_{j,j+1} < \min\{h_j, h_{j+1}\}$ for $j = 1, \ldots, N-1$, the fuzzy set defined by a continuous membership function $\mu : \mathbb{R} \to [0,1]$, with $\mu(x) = 0$ for $x \leq a_1$ or $x \geq a_{4N}$, such that for $j = 1, 2, \ldots, N$

   (i) μ is strictly increasing in $[a_{4j-3}, a_{4j-2}]$, with $\mu(a_{4j-3}) = h_{j-1,j}$ and $\mu(a_{4j-2}) = h_j$,
   (ii) μ is constant in $[a_{4j-2}, a_{4j-1}]$, with $\mu \equiv h_j$,
   (iii) μ is strictly decreasing in $[a_{4j-1}, a_{4j}]$, with $\mu(a_{4j-1}) = h_j$ and $\mu(a_{4j}) = h_{j,j+1}$,

and for $j = 1, 2, \ldots, N-1$

(iv) μ is constant in $[a_{4j}, a_{4j+1}]$, with $\mu \equiv h_{j,j+1}$,

where $h_{0,1} = h_{N,N+1} = 0$. Thus the height of A is

$$h_A = \max_{j=1,\ldots,N} h_j.$$

Remark 1. When $N = 1$ the fuzzy quantity $A = (a_1, a_2, a_3, a_4; h_1)$ defined in (1) is fuzzy convex, that is every α-cut A_α is a closed interval, with a continuous membership function of bounded support and with height $h_A = h_1$. Note that if $h_1 = 1$ then A is a fuzzy number.

When $N \geq 2$ the fuzzy quantity A defined in (1) is a non-convex fuzzy set with N humps and height $h_A = \max_{j=1,\ldots,N} h_j$. Such a fuzzy quantity can be obtained as the union of N convex fuzzy sets.

Proposition 1. *Let A be the fuzzy quantity defined in (1) with height h_A. Then each α-cut A_α, with $0 \leq \alpha \leq h_A$, is the union of a finite number of disjoint intervals. That is for each $\alpha \in [0, h_A]$ there exist an integer n_α, with $1 \leq n_\alpha \leq N$, and $A_1^\alpha, \ldots, A_{n_\alpha}^\alpha$ disjoint intervals such that*

$$A_\alpha = \bigcup_{i=1}^{n_\alpha} A_i^\alpha = \bigcup_{i=1}^{n_\alpha} [a_i^L(\alpha), a_i^R(\alpha)] \tag{2}$$

where we have denoted $A_i^\alpha = [a_i^L(\alpha), a_i^R(\alpha)]$. Thus n_α is the number of intervals producing the α-cut A_α.

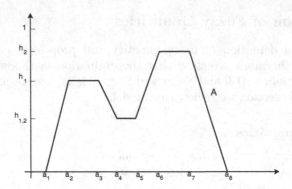

Fig. 1. Example of fuzzy quantity with $N = 2$

Proof. See [4].

For example, if $N = 1$, that is if A is a convex fuzzy quantity with height $h_A = h_1$, we have $n_\alpha = 1$ and α-cuts $A_\alpha = [a_L(\alpha), a_R(\alpha)] = [a_1^L(\alpha), a_1^R(\alpha)]$ for $0 \leq \alpha \leq h_A$.

Moreover, in the case $N = 2$ with $h_1 < h_2$ (see Fig. 2)

- for $0 < \alpha \leq h_{1,2}$ we have $n_\alpha = 1$ and $A_\alpha = A_1^\alpha = [a_1^L(\alpha), a_1^R(\alpha)]$,
- for $h_{1,2} < \alpha \leq h_1$ we have $n_\alpha = 2$ and

$$A_\alpha = A_1^\alpha \cup A_2^\alpha = [a_1^L(\alpha), a_1^R(\alpha)] \cup [a_2^L(\alpha), a_2^R(\alpha)]$$

- for $h_1 < \alpha \leq h_2$ we have $n_\alpha = 1$ and $A_\alpha = A_1^\alpha = [a_1^L(\alpha), a_1^R(\alpha)]$.

The following result shows a relation between the number of intervals producing each α-cut and the values $h_j, h_{j,j+1}$.

Proposition 2. *Let A be the fuzzy quantity defined in* (1) *with α-cuts given by* (2). *Then*

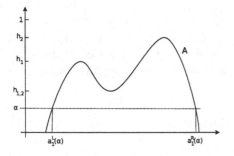
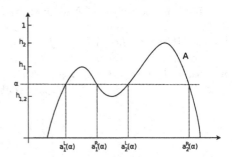

Fig. 2. α-cuts

$$\int_0^{h_A} n_\alpha \, d\alpha = \sum_{j=1}^N h_j - \sum_{j=1}^{N-1} h_{j,j+1} \tag{3}$$

where $h_A = \max_{j=1,\dots,N} h_j$.

Proof. See [4].

3.2 The Evaluation Model

In [13] Fortemps and Roubens propose an empiric approach to the evaluation of a particular fuzzy quantity. In [12] the authors give a general formula for the union of two convex fuzzy quantities. In [4] we formalize the model presented in [13] and provide the following expression for the value of the fuzzy quantity A defined in (1) with α-cuts given by (2) and height $h_A = \max_{j=1,\dots,N} h_j$

$$V_1(A) = \frac{1}{\int_0^{h_A} n_\alpha \, d\alpha} \int_0^{h_A} \sum_{i=1}^{n_\alpha} mid(A_i^\alpha) \, d\alpha. \tag{4}$$

The above formulation allows us to understand how the Fortemps and Roubens evaluation works on α-cuts. If we rewrite (4) as

$$V_1(A) = \frac{1}{\int_0^{h_A} n_\alpha \, d\alpha} \int_0^{h_A} \left(\frac{1}{n_\alpha} \sum_{i=1}^{n_\alpha} mid(A_i^\alpha) \right) n_\alpha \, d\alpha$$

we find that the value of A is calculated applying first a horizontal aggregation, in which the value of each α-cut A_α is the arithmetic mean of the midpoints of its intervals and by a vertical aggregation in which the evaluation of A is obtained as a weighted average of α-cuts values, where the weights are connected with the number of intervals producing every α-cut.

In [24, 25] Yager and Filev define the value of the fuzzy quantity A by

$$V_2(A) = \frac{1}{h_A} \int_0^{h_A} \frac{\sum_{i=1}^{n_\alpha} mid(A_i^\alpha) spr(A_i^\alpha)}{\sum_{j=1}^{n_\alpha} spr(A_\alpha^j)} \, d\alpha. \tag{5}$$

Thus, in Yager and Filev evaluation the value of A is calculated applying first a horizontal aggregation, in which the value of each α-cut A_α is a weighted average of the midpoints of its intervals, where the weights are connected with the interval spreads and by a vertical aggregation in which the evaluation of A is obtained as the arithmetic mean of α-cuts values.

In [4] we highlight some of the weaknesses of the previous methods and propose a new evaluation by the following definition.

Definition 2.

$$V_3(A) = \frac{1}{\int_0^{h_A} n_\alpha \, d\alpha} \int_0^{h_A} \frac{\sum_{i=1}^{n_\alpha} mid(A_i^\alpha) spr(A_i^\alpha)}{\sum_{j=1}^{n_\alpha} spr(A_j^\alpha)} n_\alpha \, d\alpha. \tag{6}$$

Thus, in our evaluation method the value of A is calculated applying first a horizontal aggregation, in which the value of each α-cut A_α is a weighted average of the midpoints of its intervals, where the weights are connected with the interval spreads and by a vertical aggregation in which the evaluation of A is obtained as a weighted average of α-cuts values, where the weights are connected with the number of intervals producing every α-cut.

Moreover, in [4] we propose a general formulation for the evaluation of a fuzzy quantity A with height h_A and α-cuts given by (2) by the following definition

Definition 3.

$$V(A) = \frac{1}{\int_0^{h_A} \phi(\alpha)\, d\alpha} \int_0^{h_A} \sum_{i=1}^{n_\alpha} mid(A_i^\alpha)\, p^i(\alpha)\, \phi(\alpha)\, d\alpha \tag{7}$$

where for each α the weights $p(\alpha) = (p^i(\alpha))_{i=1,\dots,n_\alpha}$ satisfy

$$\sum_{i=1}^{n_\alpha} p^i(\alpha) = 1$$

and the weight function $\phi : [0,1] \to [0, +\infty[$ satisfies

$$\int_0^{h_A} \phi(\alpha)\, d\alpha > 0\,.$$

Thus our general method performs a horizontal aggregation, level by level, with weights p and a vertical aggregation using a weight function ϕ. Note that we obtain $V(A) = V_1(A)$ if we choose (p, ϕ) as

$$\begin{cases} p^i(\alpha) = \frac{1}{n_\alpha} \\ \phi(\alpha) = n_\alpha, \end{cases} \tag{8}$$

we obtain $V(A) = V_2(A)$ if we choose

$$\begin{cases} p^i(\alpha) = \frac{spr(A_i^\alpha)}{\sum_{j=1}^{n_\alpha} spr(A_j^\alpha)} \\ \phi(\alpha) = 1, \end{cases} \tag{9}$$

and we obtain $V(A) = V_3(A)$ if we choose

$$\begin{cases} p^i(\alpha) = \frac{spr(A_i^\alpha)}{\sum_{j=1}^{n_\alpha} spr(A_j^\alpha)} \\ \phi(\alpha) = n_\alpha\,. \end{cases} \tag{10}$$

Remark 2. If $A = (a_1, a_2, a_3, a_4; h_1)$ is a convex fuzzy quantity with height $h_A = h_1$ and α-cuts $A_\alpha = [a_L(\alpha), a_R(\alpha)]$, $0 \le \alpha \le h_A$, we have $n_\alpha \equiv 1$ and

$$V(A) = \frac{1}{\int_0^{h_A} \phi(\alpha)\, d\alpha} \int_0^{h_A} \frac{a_L(\alpha) + a_R(\alpha)}{2} \phi(\alpha)\, d\alpha\,.$$

Moreover (taking into about that $n_\alpha \equiv 1$) we get

$$V_1(A) = V_2(A) = V_3(A) = \frac{1}{h_A} \int_0^{h_A} \frac{a_L(\alpha) + a_R(\alpha)}{2}\, d\alpha\,.$$

4   Ambiguity of Fuzzy Quantities

In this section we propose a definition of ambiguity for fuzzy quantities.

Definition 4. *Let A be the fuzzy quantity defined in* (1) *with α-cuts given by* (2) *and height $h_A = \max_{j=1,\dots,N} h_j$. We call ambiguity of the fuzzy quantity A with respect to (p, ϕ) the real number*

$$Amb(A) = \int_0^{h_A} \sum_{i=1}^{n_\alpha} spr(A_i^\alpha)\, p^i(\alpha)\, \phi(\alpha)\, d\alpha . \tag{11}$$

Thus, fixed (p, ϕ) we can assign to each fuzzy quantity A the pair $(V(A), Amb(A))$. In the following result we compute the ambiguity in some special cases.

Proposition 3. *(i) If (p, ϕ) are chosen as in* (8) *we have the evaluation $V_1(A)$ and the ambiguity*

$$Amb_1(A) = \frac{1}{2} \int_0^{h_A} \sum_{i=1}^{n_\alpha} |A_i^\alpha|\, d\alpha = \frac{1}{2} \int_0^{h_A} |A_\alpha|\, d\alpha$$

where $|\cdot|$ is the Lebesgue measure on the real line;
(ii) if (p, ϕ) are chosen as in (9) *we have the evaluation $V_2(A)$ and the ambiguity*

$$Amb_2(A) = \frac{1}{2} \int_0^{h_A} \sum_{i=1}^{n_\alpha} |A_i^\alpha|\, w_i(\alpha)\, d\alpha$$

where $w_i(\alpha) = |A_i^\alpha|/|A_\alpha|$;
(iii) if (p, ϕ) are chosen as in (10) *we have the evaluation $V_3(A)$ and the ambiguity*

$$Amb_3(A) = \frac{1}{2} \int_0^{h_A} \sum_{i=1}^{n_\alpha} |A_i^\alpha|\, w_i'(\alpha)\, d\alpha$$

where $w_i'(\alpha) = n_\alpha |A_i^\alpha|/|A_\alpha|$.

Proof. The assertions follow substituting (8), (9), (10) in (11), respectively, taking into about that $|A_i^\alpha| = 2\, spr(A_i^\alpha)$ and thus from (2)

$$|A_\alpha| = \sum_{i=1}^{n_\alpha} |A_i^\alpha| = 2 \sum_{i=1}^{n_\alpha} spr(A_i^\alpha) .$$

Remark 3. If we choose $p^i(\alpha) = 1/n_\alpha$ and $\phi(\alpha) = 1$ we obtain the evaluation

$$V_4(A) = \frac{1}{h_A} \int_0^{h_A} \left(\frac{1}{n_\alpha} \sum_{i=1}^{n_\alpha} mid(A_i^\alpha) \right) d\alpha$$

and the ambiguity

$$Amb_4(A) = \int_0^{h_A} \left(\frac{1}{n_\alpha} \sum_{i=1}^{n_\alpha} spr(A_i^\alpha) \right) d\alpha = \frac{1}{2} \int_0^{h_A} \sum_{i=1}^{n_\alpha} |A_i^\alpha|\, w_i''(\alpha)\, d\alpha$$

where $w_i''(\alpha) = 1/n_\alpha$.

Remark 4. If $A = (a_1, a_2, a_3, a_4; h_1)$ is a convex fuzzy quantity with height $h_A = h_1$ and α-cuts $A_\alpha = [a_L(\alpha), a_R(\alpha)]$, $0 \le \alpha \le h_A$, we have $n_\alpha \equiv 1$ and

$$Amb(A) = \int_0^{h_A} \frac{a_R(\alpha) - a_L(\alpha)}{2} \phi(\alpha) \, d\alpha \, .$$

In particular

$$Amb_i(A) = \int_0^{h_A} \frac{a_R(\alpha) - a_L(\alpha)}{2} \, d\alpha \qquad i = 1, 2, 3, 4 \, .$$

Remark 5. In [4] we introduced the approximation interval $\widehat{C}(A) = [\widehat{c}_L, \widehat{c}_R]$ of a fuzzy quantity A with respect to (p, ϕ) by

$$\widehat{C}(A) = \left[\frac{\int_0^{h_A} \sum_{i=1}^{n_\alpha} a_i^L(\alpha) \, p^i(\alpha) \, \phi(\alpha) \, d\alpha}{\int_0^{h_A} \phi(\alpha) \, d\alpha}, \frac{\int_0^{h_A} \sum_{i=1}^{n_\alpha} a_i^R(\alpha) \, p^i(\alpha) \, \phi(\alpha) \, d\alpha}{\int_0^{h_A} \phi(\alpha) \, d\alpha} \right] .$$

From definitions (7) and (11) we obtain $V(A) = mid(\widehat{C}(A))$ and

$$Amb(A) = spr(\widehat{C}(A)) \cdot H(A)$$

where $H(A) = \int_0^{h_A} \phi(\alpha) \, d\alpha$. If $\phi(\alpha) = 1$ then $H(A) = h_A$. If $\phi(\alpha) = n_\alpha$ from (3) we obtain $H(A) = \sum_{j=1}^{N} h_j - \sum_{j=1}^{N-1} h_{j,j+1}$. We note that these results are consistent with [1–3].

5   Evaluation of Intuitionistic Fuzzy Quantities

An intuitionistic fuzzy set (IFS) A in X is given by

$$A = \{< x, \mu_A(x), \nu_A(x) > ; \ x \in X\}$$

where $\mu_A : X \to [0, 1]$ and $\nu_A : X \to [0, 1]$ satisfy the condition $0 \le \mu_A(x) + \nu_A(x) \le 1$. The numbers $\mu_A(x), \nu_A(x) \in [0, 1]$ denote the degree of membership and a degree of non-membership of x to A, respectively. For each IFS A in X, we call $\pi_A(x) = 1 - \mu_A(x) - \nu_A(x)$ the degree of the indeterminacy membership of the element x in A, that is the hesitation margin (or intuitionistic index) of $x \in A$ which expresses a lack of information of whether x belongs to A or not. We have $0 \le \pi_A(x) \le 1$ for all $x \in X$. The support of A is defined by $supp \, A = \{x \in X; \nu_A(x) < 1\}$. An IFS A of the real line is called an intuitionistic fuzzy number if μ_A and $1 - \nu_A$ are membership functions of fuzzy numbers [14] (see also [7] for different definitions).

Definition 5. *We call IFQ an IFS $A = \langle \mu_A, \nu_A \rangle$ of the real line such that μ_A and $1 - \nu_A$ are membership functions of fuzzy quantities.*

If A is an IFQ we denote by A^+ the fuzzy quantity with membership function $\mu_{A^+} = \mu_A$ and by A^- the fuzzy quantity with membership function $\mu_{A^-} = 1 - \nu_A$. In the following an IFQ A will be indifferently denoted by $A = \langle \mu_A, \nu_A \rangle$ or $A = (A^+, A^-)$. The last formulation has supported us in the proposal of IFQ value based on a convex combination of the two evaluations of A^+ and A^-.

Definition 6. *Let A be an IFQ. We define the value of A with respect to the parameter $\rho \in [0, 1]$ as*

$$V_\rho(A) = (1 - \rho)V(A^+) + \rho V(A^-).$$

where the values $V(A^+)$ and $V(A^-)$ are defined by (7).

The choice of the parameter ρ reflects some attitude on the part of the decision maker [15].

Remark 6. For each $x \in X$ the degree of membership of x to the IFQ A is between $\mu_A(x)$ and $1 - \nu_A(x)$. The length of the interval $[\mu_A(x), 1 - \nu_A(x)]$, which is given by $\pi_A(x)$, is the hesitation between the two membership degrees. When ρ is zero the evaluation $V_\rho(A)$ of IFQ A is given by the evaluation of the fuzzy quantity A^+ whose membership function is $\mu_{A^+} = \mu_A$ and thus we don't consider the hesitation region. When ρ is one the evaluation $V_\rho(A)$ is given by the evaluation of the fuzzy quantity A^- whose membership function is $\mu_{A^-} = 1 - \nu_A = \mu_A + \pi_A$ and thus we consider the whole hesitation region. An intermediate value of the parameter ρ suggests the decision maker's will to consider some part of the wavering ones.

6   Ambiguity and Ranking of Intuitionistic Fuzzy Quantities

We now introduce the definition of ambiguity for an IFQ by using the notion of ambiguity of fuzzy quantities given in (11).

Definition 7. *We define the ambiguity of the IFQ $A = (A^+, A^-)$ as*

$$Amb_\rho(A) = (1 - \rho)Amb(A^+) + \rho Amb(A^-)$$

where the values $Amb(A^+)$ and $Amb(A^-)$ are defined by (11).

In order to compare two or more IFQs we introduce a function that maps the set of IFQs into $\mathbb{R}^2$ by assigning to every IFQ A the pair $(V(A), Amb(A))$ where $V(A)$ and $Amb(A)$ are, respectively, the value and ambiguity of A with respect to parameter ρ (fixed). The ranking method we propose can be summarized into the following steps:
1. For two IFQs A and B
   if $V(A) > V(B)$ then $A \succ B$; if $V(A) < V(B)$ then $A \prec B$;
   if $V(A) = V(B)$ then go to the next step.
2. Compare $Amb(A)$ and $Amb(B)$:
   if $Amb(A) < Amb(B)$ then $A \succ B$; if $Amb(A) > Amb(B)$ then $A \prec B$;
   if $Amb(A) = Amb(B)$ then $A \sim B$, that is A and B are indifferent.
The proposed ranking method satisfies axioms $A1 - A5$ proposed in [22] as reasonable properties for the rationality of a ranking method.

7 Conclusions

We have presented two new results that would be useful both in the evaluation and ranking of Intuitionistic Fuzzy Quantities. These sets are characterized by two fuzzy quantities obtained by the union of two or more convex fuzzy sets. The latter are non-normal fuzzy sets and their union produces non convex and non-normal fuzzy sets. The evaluation we propose is very general and contains as particular case other classic definitions. The connection between Intuitionistic fuzzy sets and type-2 fuzzy sets is easy to find. In fact if we think to a defuzzification problem of a type-2 inference control system, we, almost surely, meet with the problem to evaluate an Intuitionistic Fuzzy Quantities. In this direction many authors have proposed "centroid" definitions for interval type-2 fuzzy logic systems. The last ones have had a wide number of applications in many fields [16, 23]. In this direction we think that our paper may produce an interesting starting point. We may think either to propose the same ranking procedure or to evaluate them with the intent to connect every interval type-2 fuzzy quantities to a real number or an interval to face optimization problems in a type-2 fuzzy context.

References

1. Anzilli, L., Facchinetti, G.: Ambiguity of Fuzzy Quantities and a New Proposal for their Ranking. Przeglad Elektrotechniczny-Electrical Review 10b, 280–283 (2012)
2. Anzilli, L., Facchinetti, G.: A political scenario faced by a new evaluation of intuitionistic fuzzy quantities. In: Greco, S., Bouchon-Meunier, B., Coletti, G., Fedrizzi, M., Matarazzo, B., Yager, R.R. (eds.) IPMU 2012, Part IV. CCIS, vol. 300, pp. 54–63. Springer, Heidelberg (2012)
3. Anzilli, L., Facchinetti, G.: The total variation of bounded variation functions to evaluate and rank fuzzy quantities. International Journal of Intelligent Systems 28, 927–956 (2013)
4. Anzilli, L., Facchinetti, G., Mastroleo, G.: Evaluation and interval approximation of fuzzy quantities. Accepted for publication in Proceedings of EUSFLAT 2013. Atlantis Press (2013)
5. Atanassov, K.: Intuitionistic fuzzy sets. Fuzzy Sets and Systems 20, 87–96 (1986)
6. Atanassov, K.: Intuitionistic fuzzy sets. Theory and Applications. Physica-Verlag, Heidelberg (1999)
7. Atanassov, K.: Intuitionistic fuzzy sets: past, present and future. In: Proceedings of the Third Conference on Fuzzy Logic and Technology (Eusflat 2003), pp. 12–19 (2003)
8. Atanassov, K.T.: On Intuitionistic Fuzzy Sets Theory. STUDFUZZ, vol. 283. Springer, Heidelberg (2012)
9. Bede, B.: Mathematics of Fuzzy Sets and Fuzzy Logic. STUDFUZZ, vol. 295. Springer, Heidelberg (2013)
10. Castillo, O.: Type-2 Fuzzy Logic in Intelligent Control Applications. STUDFUZZ, vol. 272. Springer, Heidelberg (2012)
11. Dubey, D., Mehra, A.: Linear programming with Triangular intuitionistic fuzzy number. In: EUSFLAT-LFA, pp. 563–569 (2011)

12. Facchinetti, G., Pacchiarotti, N.: Evaluations of fuzzy quantities. Fuzzy Sets and Systems 157, 892–903 (2006)
13. Fortemps, P., Roubens, M.: Ranking and defuzzification methods based on area compensation. Fuzzy Sets and Systems 82, 319–330 (1996)
14. Grzegorzewski, P.: Distances and orderings in a family of intuitionistic fuzzy numbers. In: Proceedings of the Third Conference on Fuzzy Logic and Technology (Eusflat 2003), pp. 223–227 (2003)
15. Li, D.-F.: A ratio ranking method of triangular intuitionistic fuzzy numbers and its application to MADM problems. Computers and Mathematics with Applications 60, 1557–1570 (2010)
16. Mendel, J.M.: Advances in type-2 fuzzy sets and systems. Information Sciences 177, 84–110 (2007)
17. Mitchell, H.B.: Ranking intuitionistic fuzzy numbers. International Journal of Uncertainity, Fuzziness and Knowledge-Based Systems 12, 377–386 (2004)
18. Nan, J.X., Li, D.F.: A lexicographic method for matrix games with payoffs of triangular intuitionistic fuzzy numbers. International Journal of Computational Intelligence Systems 3, 280–289 (2010)
19. Nayagam, V.L., Vankateshwari, G., Sivaraman, G.: Ranking of intuitionistic fuzzy numbers. In: IEEE International Conference on Fuzzy Systems, pp. 1971–1974 (2008)
20. Nehi, H.M.: A new ranking method for intuitionistic fuzzy numbers. International Journal of Fuzzy Systems 12, 80–86 (2010)
21. Su, J.S.: Fuzzy programming based on intervalvalued fuzzy numbers and ranking. International Journal of Contempraroy Mathematical Sciences 2, 393–410 (2007)
22. Wang, X., Kerre, E.E.: Reasonable properties for the ordering of fuzzy quantities (I). Fuzzy Sets and Systems 118, 375–385 (2001)
23. Wu, D., Mendel, J.M.: Uncertainty measures for interval type-2 fuzzy sets. Information Sciences 177, 5378–5393 (2007)
24. Yager, R.R.: A procedure for ordering fuzzy subsets of the unit interval. Information Sciences 24, 143–161 (1981)
25. Yager, R.R., Filev, D.: On ranking fuzzy numbers using valuations. International Journal of Intelligent Systems 14, 1249–1268 (1999)

Approximation of Fuzzy Measures Using Second Order Measures: Estimation of Andness Bounds

Marta Cardin and Silvio Giove

Department of Economics,
University Cà Foscari of Venice

Abstract. In this paper we analyze the compensation property of a second order fuzzy measure in the context of a multi-attribute problem. In particular, we show that the disjunction/conjunction behavior (andness/orness) changes with the number of criteria to be aggregated. Interpreting the spread between the maximum and the minimum orness as a measure of the representation capability, we obtain two bounds in function of which asymptotically converge to a limit interval.

Keywords: Fuzzy measures, second order measures, Choquet integral, andness index, OWA.

1 Introduction

Non additive measures (fuzzy measures, capacities) and the Choquet integral are widely considered in multi attribute decision problems such as in sensor fusion, pattern recognition, classification, and so on. The main characteristic consists in the non linear nature of this approach, which makes it possible to include interactions among the criteria to be aggregated, as synergies or redundancy, modulating the compensation degree in function of the preference structure of the Decision Maker. Unlike from the usual linear approach (weighted averaging), this method produces an aggregation function whose result varies from a non complete compensative (andness) in the case of a conjunctive behavior, to the complete compensative one, in the opposite disjunctive case (orness). Given that the compensation can be continuously modulated in between the two extreme cases, an index was introduced (see[12]), to measure the compensative characteristic of the considered measure, the orness degree. This index varies from zero (completely non compensative) to one (completely compensative), and its complement to one, the andness degree, measure symmetrically the conjunctive nature of the measure. Anywise, the number of parameters of a fuzzy measure increases exponentially with the number of the criteria, and at the same time, as far as the preference structure of a Decision Maker is concerned, it has been experimentally verified (see[8]) that in most of the cases a reduced order measure, i.e. a measure which includes interactions only for subsets of limited cardinality, suffices to represent the preference structure. In other words, given the limited capability of the human brain to define interactions between a high number of

F. Masulli, G. Pasi, and R. Yager (Eds.): WILF 2013, LNAI 8256, pp. 150–160, 2013.
© Springer International Publishing Switzerland 2013

criteria, a reduced order can be considered, typically, a second order measure, which consider interactions between only a couple of criteria. This choice even if it drastically reduces the number of parameters to be elicited, in many applications is not a real limitation. But it is well known that such reduced order measures cannot represent the two extreme cases, the disjunction and the conjunction of the criteria, with the exception of the simplest case of the two two criteria. Thus the reduced order models limit preference representation. To this end we consider the spread between the maximum (resp.: minimum) and the minimum (resp.: maximum) orness (resp.: andness) as a measure of the information power of a measure, obtaining an inferior bound and a superior bound for the orness (andness) index in function of the number of criteria. As may be expected, the spread (difference between the two bounds) reduces with the criteria number, but asymptotically converge to a defined interval, and the reduction is not so crucial for low values of the number of criteria. Thus we can conclude that the capability representation of a reduced order model can be sufficient if the number of criteria is not too high, confirming the fact that for real problems, a second order measure can be sufficient.

2 Fuzzy Measures and the Choquet Integral in MCDA Problems

The Choquet integral was widely applied in multi-criteria decision problems, MCDA for brevity, such as sensors fusion and other real-world problems. The main reason is due to the capability to consider interaction among the criteria, thus to be a tool that reflects the preference structure of a Decision Maker or of the nature of the decision problem. The simpler and widely used Weighted Averaging (WA) cannot include interactions, given its linear nature, which require the satisfaction of the Preferential Independence axiom, rarely satisfied in practice. This implies that WA requires complete compensativeness, i.e. a low value of a criterion, can be compensated by an high value of another one and this can be undesirable. As an example, consider the Sustainability of a territorial unit (town, region, etc.) as a function of the three classical pillars, Economy, Environmental, Society; a high economic improvement cannot be paid for too drastic an environmental damage or social inequalities. In other words, an equilibrated scenario can be preferred, even if its average value is lower. Interactions among the criteria can be easily formalized using fuzzy measures (non additive measures, capacities) where a fuzzy measure is a generalization of WA.

Let us recall some well known definitions on Choquet integration (see [4], [5], [10], [12]). If we consider a finite index set of interacting criteria $N = \{1, \ldots, n\}$. a set function $v: 2^N \to \mathbb{R}$ is said to be a *fuzzy measure* if $v(\emptyset) = 0$ and if $S \subseteq T \subseteq N$ implies that $v(S) \leq v(T)$.

We note that if $S \subseteq N$ then $v(S)$ can be viewed as the importance of the set of elements S and the measure that is assigned to S can be different from the sum of the measures of the elements of a partition of S.

The fuzzy measure is said to be *additive* if $v(S \cup T) = v(S) + v(T)$ when $S, T \subseteq N$ and $S \cap T = \emptyset$. Moreover the fuzzy measure is *superadditive* (*subadditive*) if $v(S \cup T) \geqslant (\leqslant) v(S) + v(T)$ when $S, T \subseteq N$ and $S \cap T = \emptyset$.

If v is a fuzzy measure $v : 2^N \to \mathbb{R}$ and $\mathbf{x} \in \mathbb{R}^n$ let $(\cdot)$ be a permutation of N such that $x_{(1)} \leqslant x_{(2)} \ldots \leqslant x_{(n)}$ and $A_i = \{(i), \ldots, (n)\}$. Then the Choquet integral of $\mathbf{x}$ is:

$$\mathbf{C}_v(\mathbf{x}) = \sum_{i=1}^{n} \left(v(A_i) - v(A_{i+1}) \right) x_{(i)}. \tag{1}$$

The Choquet integral is an aggregation operator and obviously in the case of additive measure we have a WA operator

$$\mathbf{C}_v(\mathbf{x}) = \sum_{i=1}^{n} \omega_i x_i \tag{2}$$

where the weights are given by $\omega_i = v(\{i\})$. A fuzzy measure v is symmetric if it depends only on the cardinality of the set considered

$$v(T) = v(t) \quad \text{where} \quad t = |T| \quad \text{for every } T \subseteq N. \tag{3}$$

In this case it can be proved (see [1], [3], [6], [7] and [17]) that the Choquet integral reduces to an OWA operator. An OWA operator is defined by

$$\mathbf{C}_v(\mathbf{x}) = \sum_{i=1}^{n} \omega_i x_{(i)}. \tag{4}$$

If v is a fuzzy measure the Möbius transform associated with v is a function $m : 2^N \to \mathbb{R}$ defined by:

$$m(S) = \sum_{T \subseteq S} (-1)^{s-t} v(T) \quad \text{with} \quad S \subseteq N. \tag{5}$$

where $s = |S|$ and $t = |T|$. The inverse transformation is given by:

$$v(S) = \sum_{T \subseteq S} m(T) \quad \text{with} \quad S \subseteq N. \tag{6}$$

If we consider the Möbius representation the boundary conditions are:

$$m(\emptyset) = 0, \qquad \sum_{T \subseteq N} m(T) = 1 \tag{7}$$

while the monotonicity conditions can be expressed as

$$\sum_{T \subseteq S, i \in T} m(T) \geqslant 0 \quad \text{for every } S \subseteq N \text{ and } i \in S. \tag{8}$$

Using the Möbius representation m of v the Choquet integral $C_v : \mathbb{R}^n \to \mathbb{R}$ can be written as

$$C_v(\mathbf{x}) = \sum_{T \subseteq N} m(T) \bigwedge_{i \in T} x_i, \qquad \mathbf{x} \in \mathbb{R}^n. \tag{9}$$

To every measure some indices can be assigned. We limit ourselves to quote the Shapley index which captures the overall importance of a criterion, the inter-action index to compute the (average) interaction between two criteria, useful to measure the complementary/substitutivity between them. Again, we quote the andness (orness) degree, which to some extend measure how much the fuzzy measure is characterized by a greater or lesser tendency to a conjunctive (dis-junctive) behavior; for a completely conjunctive (disjunctive) case, the andness (orness) equals one (zero), and andness and orness degrees sum up to one. The andness (orness) degree gives a rough idea of the conjunctive/disjunctive prop-erty of the measure, i.e. the tendency to generate an output more or less close to the minimum or to the maximum of the inputs. The Choquet integral is a very general tool for aggregation, see [12] for an axiomatic approach, but the price to pay is an exponential increase in the necessary parameters, given that a value needs to be assigned to every subset of criteria, which are 2^n. For this reason, the literature proposed reduced order model, where interactions among the criteria can appear only for limited cardinality subsets.

3   Reduced Order Models and Parameters Elicitation

A k-order model (reduced order) is a set of fuzzy measures such that there are no interaction for every coalition with cardinality higher than k. In the Möbius space, all the parameters relating to coalition with cardinality higher than k are equal to zero. A reduced order model is usually a simplification, given that it avoids the possibility of interactions between coalitions with higher order cardi-nality. But in many real cases, the reduced order model can suffice to represent a rich preference structure, given the limited power of the human brain to consider too much complexity relationships. In many application, a second order model with $k = 2$ can be sufficient, implying that only interaction among couple of criteria are explicitly considered, and in the rest of the paper we remain inside this context. Elicitation of measures is a crucial item in Decision Making and two methods are usually applied; a direct approach, for which the measure values are directly assigned, and an indirect ore, where they are implicitly elicited, nor-mally using a questionnaire designed *ad hoc*. The direct method presents some difficulties for assigning a numeric value to every coalition of criteria, due to the presence of synergies. Conversely, the indirect one seems to me more suitable for real problems, and it has been widely applied, in different version, in the past literature(see [9], [11], [15]). Most of them concentrate on the elicitation for a second order model, avoiding the exponential complexity for a complete one, which also would imply too much huge number of complex questions for the DM, subjected to excessive mental effort. We refer to the specialized literature for the different methods used, such as entropy based, maximum split, least square, and so on.

Basic concepts about k-additive measures are formally defined below.

A fuzzy measure v is said to be k-*additive* if its Möbius transform is such that $m(T) = 0$ for all $T \subseteq N$ with $|T| > k$ and there exists at least one $T \subseteq N$ with

$m(T) \neq 0$. We consider in particular 2-additive measures while the 1-additive measures are obviously additive measures. It can be proved that a 2-additive fuzzy measure is entirely determined by the value on the singletons $\{i\}$ and on the pairs $\{i,j\}$ of 2^N.

We simplify our notation for the Möbius transform of a 2-additive fuzzy measures by using the following definitions $m_i = v(\{i\}), m_{i,j} = v(\{i,j\})$ for all i, j with $i \neq j$. Then we have the following decomposition formula

$$v(T) = \sum_{i \in T} m_i + \sum_{\{i,j\} \subseteq T, i \neq j} m_{i,j} \qquad \text{for every } T \subseteq N, \tag{10}$$

while the boundary conditions are

$$m(\emptyset) = 0, \qquad \sum_{i \in T} m_i + \sum_{\{i,j\} \subseteq N, i \neq j} m_{i,j} = 1 \tag{11}$$

and the monotonicity conditions can be written as

$$m_i \geqslant 0, \qquad m_i + \sum_{\{i,j\} \subseteq T, i \neq j} m_{i,j} \qquad \text{for every } T \subseteq N \text{ and } i \in T. \tag{12}$$

Moreover for 2-additive fuzzy measures the Choquet integral is

$$C_v(\mathbf{x}) = \sum_{i \in N} m_i x_i + \sum_{\{i,j\} \subseteq N, i \neq j} m_i(x_i \wedge x_j) \tag{13}$$

Now we consider second order OWA that are Choquet integral with respect to a 2-additive symmetric fuzzy measure that can be characterized by the following result (see [1]).

Proposition 1. *If we consider the second order OWA*

$$\sum_{i=1}^{n} \omega_i x_i$$

then the weights are given by

$$\omega_i = \alpha + (n - i)\beta \quad \text{for every } i = 1, \dots, n \tag{14}$$

where α, β are the measures of the subsets of cardinality one and two respectively.

As pointed to in the Introduction, even if for many real world applications a second order model is sufficient some information is lost. In particular, a second order model cannot the implement neither the conjunctive nor the disjunctive cases. In essence, these extremes, which are the bounds for every aggregation operators, can be too drastic. Considering again the example proposed in [16] even if, ceteris paribus for the worst case, higher values for other pillars are surely preferred. Thus the minimum operator can be too drastic and normally does not corresponds to the real preference function. Thus a second order model even if it considers interactions between a couple of criteria, can be considered adequate, if the andness (orness) degree is sufficiently high (small), but not necessarily equal to one (zero). So the question is which limit of orness (andness) behavior can be obtained when we use a second order model. In what follows the answer to this question is solved, analytically computing two bounds for a second order model, namely, an upper and a lower bound for a second order model.

The andness and orness degree express the relative location of a given aggregation function with respect to minimum and maximum, respectively. This notion was considered by Marichal [12] for the Choquet integral with respect to a fuzzy measure and by Yager [17] for reflecting the andlike or orlike of OWA operators. The orness index for a Choquet integral is

$$\text{orness}(C_v) = \frac{1}{n-1} \sum_{T \subseteq N} \frac{n-t}{t+1} m(T) \tag{15}$$

where $t = |T|$ and m is the Möbius transform associated with v.

The andness index is defined by andness $(C_v) = 1 - \text{orness}(C_v)$.

If we consider a second order model we get from (15)that

$$\text{orness}(C_v) = \frac{1}{n-1} \left(\frac{n-1}{2} \sum_{i=1}^{n} m_i + \frac{n-2}{3} \sum_{i=1}^{n-1} \sum_{j=i+1}^{n} m_{i,j} \right). \tag{16}$$

Now we use the spread between the maximum A_s and the minimum values of the andness in function of n, A_i, as a measure of representation power. If $n = 2$, the spread equals one $(A_s = 1, A_i = 0)$, and it decreases with n. The values of A_s, A_i can be interpreted as how much the second order can approximate the conjunction (disjunction) operator. For instance, a value of $A_s = 0.9$ means that the second order model is a very good approximation of a complete model, for what it concerns the conjunctive behavior.

Moreover, we define two fuzzy measures *orness-equivalent* if they are characterized by the same value of the orness index (they are also andness-equivalent).

Let us observe that it is easy to prove that the orness degree for a second order OWA is:

$$\text{orness}(C_v) = \frac{1}{n-1} \left(\frac{n(n-1)}{2} \alpha + \frac{n-2}{3} \cdot \frac{n(n-1)}{2} \beta \right) = \frac{n}{2} \left(\alpha + \frac{n-2}{2} \beta \right). \tag{17}$$

The following proposition proves that every second order fuzzy measures is orness-equivalent to an OWA, whose characterizing parameters are the averaging of the Möbius values.

Proposition 2. *For every second-order fuzzy measure it exists a second order OWA which is orness-equivalent to it and with*

$$\alpha = \frac{1}{n} \sum_{i=1}^{n} m_i, \qquad \beta = \frac{2}{n(n-1)} \sum_{i=1}^{n-1} \sum_{j=i+1}^{n} m_{i,j}. \tag{18}$$

Proof. In order to obtain the result we have to prove that we have defined a second order OWA and so we consider the weights $\omega_i = \alpha + (n-i)\beta$, $i = 1, \ldots, n$. By the monotonicity conditions we have that $m_i + \sum_{\{i,j\}\subseteq N, i\neq j} m_{i,j} \geq 0$ for every $i \in N$. Summing up with respect to i we get

$$\sum_{i=1}^{n} m_i + 2 \sum_{i=1}^{n-1} \sum_{j=i+1}^{n} m_{i,j} \geq 0. \tag{19}$$

If we prove that $\omega_1 = \alpha + (n-1)\beta \geq 0$ we can conclude that $\omega_i = \alpha + (n-i)\beta \geq 0$ for every $i = 1, \ldots, n$. We have that

$$\omega_1 = \alpha + (n-1)\beta = \frac{1}{n}\sum_{i=1}^{n} m_i + (n-1)\frac{2}{n(n-1)}\sum_{i=1}^{n-1}\sum_{j=i+1}^{n} m_{i,j} =$$

$$\frac{1}{n}\left(\sum_{i=1}^{n} m_i + 2\sum_{i=1}^{n-1}\sum_{j=i+1}^{n} m_{i,j}\right) \geq 0.$$

Moreover we get that

$$\sum_{i=1}^{n}\omega_i = \sum_{i=1}^{n}\alpha + (n-i)\beta = n\alpha + \frac{n(n-1)}{2}\beta = \sum_{i=1}^{n}\left(\frac{1}{n}\sum_{i=1}^{n} m_i\right) +$$

$$\frac{n(n-1)}{2}\left(\frac{2}{n(n-1)}\sum_{i=1}^{n-1}\sum_{j=i+1}^{n} m_{i,j}\right) = \sum_{i\in T} m_i + \sum_{\{i,j\}\subseteq N, i\neq j} m_{i,j} = 1 \tag{20}$$

by boundary condition. We conclude that the second order OWA and the second order fuzzy measure are orness-equivalent.

Of course, the proposition cannot be inverted and for any second order OWA there are infinite second order fuzzy measure characterized by the same orness degree.

4 Upper and Lower Bounds

The aim of this section consists into the assessment of the upper and of the lower bounds for a second order model in function of the number of criteria. Then we have considered the maximum and the minimum values for orness degree of the equivalent reduced order fuzzy measure need to be obtained. That is, the following constrained optimization problem has to be solved

$$\max/\min{}_{\alpha,\beta}\left(\alpha + \frac{n-2}{3}\beta\right) \tag{21}$$

$$0 \leqslant \alpha \leqslant 1, -1 \leqslant \beta \leqslant 1, \tag{22}$$

$$n\alpha + \frac{n(n-1)}{2}\beta = 1, \tag{23}$$

$$\alpha + k\beta \geqslant 0, \quad 1 \leqslant k \leqslant n-1. \tag{24}$$

The second equation represents the border constraints, while the last one the monotonicity constraints. Let us observe that the inequality constraints $\alpha + (n-1)\beta \geqslant 0$, implies all the previous ones.

We state the main result of the paper.

Proposition 3. *The minimum and the maximum orness of a 2-order OWA with respect to a, b are respectively*

$$morness = \frac{1}{3}\frac{n-2}{n-1}, \qquad Morness = \frac{2n-1}{3(n-1)}. \tag{25}$$

Proof. We consider the problem

$$\max/\min{}_{\alpha,\beta}\left(\alpha + \frac{n-2}{3}\right) \tag{26}$$

$$0 \leqslant \alpha \leqslant 1, -1 \leqslant \beta \leqslant 1, \tag{27}$$

$$n\alpha + \frac{n(n-1)}{2}\beta = 1, \tag{28}$$

$$\alpha + (n-1)\beta \geqslant 0. \tag{29}$$

By geometrical or algebraic considerations we can solve the constrained optimization problem with respect to α, β. We get that the maximum point is $\left(\frac{2}{n}, \frac{2}{n(1-n)}\right)$ and the minimum point is $\left(0, \frac{2}{n(n-1)}\right)$ then the minimum value is $m = \frac{1}{3}\frac{n-2}{n-1}$ while the maximum value is $M = \frac{2n-1}{3(n-1)}$.

Now it is possible to note that

$$\lim_{n\to\infty} Morness\,(n) = \frac{2}{3}, \tag{30}$$

and if we consider the minimum value of andness

$$\lim_{n\to\infty} mandness\,(n) = \frac{1}{3}. \tag{31}$$

Finally we note that

$$mandness + morness = 1 \text{ then } mandness = 1 - morness = Morness \tag{32}$$

and similarly $Mandness = morness$ so there is a sort of duality between the minimum and the maximum cases.

Finally and just to illustrate the practical usefulness of our approach, suppose that the Environmental Sustainability of a region has to be evaluated on the basis of five elementary indicators, each of them normalized into the common $[0, 1]$ scale, like the percentage of Co_2 emission over the primary energy consumption, the percentage of renewable energy over the total energy consumption, the endangered animals or plants over the total, and so on. Let $(x_1, x_2, \dots, x_5)$ be the normalized values of the five in indicators. As usual, a normalized value close to zero means an unacceptable situation, and conversely a value close to one a very good one. As for all the concept like well-being, happiness, sustainability etc. which are multi-dimensional, the construction of a composite indicator requires the introduction of a preference function by a Decision Makers, Stakeholders, Politicians, Experts. In this field, the Choquet integral approach has been showed as an efficient tool (see [15]). Again, we remark that the aggregation algorithm usually requires an andness-like operator, given that Sustainability implies only partial compensation. In the limit case, the andness operator will be used, meaning that no compensation at all is possible in the mind of the Decision Maker. Anywise, a pure andness computation can penalize too much the case where only one indicator is very low, while the other ones are completely satisfied. Thus a partial compensation can be the right solution. In this spirit, our proposal can be useful since permitting interactions only among couple of criteria, thus reducing as most as possible the number of the required parameters. At the same time it can include partial compensation. Coming back to the example consider the following two hypothetical scenarios, i.e. vector of the five normalized indicators:

$$S_1 = (1, 0.5, 0, 0, 0), \qquad S_2 = (1, 1, 1, 1, 0)$$

The two scenarios differ together for the normalized values of the indicators. In particular, the first is characterized by unsatisfied values for three indicators, a medium satisfied value for the second indicator but a completely satisfied values for the first one. While in the second scenario the first four indicators are completely satisfied but x_5 is completely unsatisfied. Thus let us observe that for a second order model, being $n = 5$, from the results of the Proposition 3 we obtain in the case of maximum andness $\alpha = 0, \beta = \frac{1}{10}$ and consequently:

$$\mathbf{C}(S_1) = 1/10(1 + 0.5 + 0.5 + 0 + 0.5 + 0.5 + 0 + 0.5 + 0 + 0) = 0.35$$

$$\mathbf{C}(S_2) = 1/10(1 + 1 + 1 + 0 + 1 + 1 + 0 + 1 + 0 + 0) = 0.6.$$

If a pure andness were applied, both in the cases we obtain zero, thus the two scenarios are equally judged, even if the differ a lot for some indicators. At the same time, a value of andness=3/4 is obtained, meaning that only a medium-low compensation is possible, as the two numerical results confirm.

5   Conclusions

Fuzzy measures and the Choquet integral are a general tool for multi attribute decision problems, possibly including interactions among the criteria. The aggregated result can continuously vary from a non compensative up to a compensative behavior, and suitably modulating the measures assigned to each coalition of criteria, can represent a wide spectrum of preference structure. Nevertheless, the number of parameters required for a general fuzzy measure increases exponentially with the number of the criteria. For this reason, reduced order measures were introduced, for which the number of parameters number is strongly reduced. Limiting the attention to a second order model, which admits interaction only between couple of parameters, for more than two criteria neither a complete disjunctive nor a conjunctive can be reached. The main contribution of this paper consists in the computation of a disjunctive-conjunctive spread in function of the number of criteria, i.e. the maximum andness (minimum orness) and the minimum andness (maximum orness) that can be achieved by a second order model. The inferior and superior bounds thus obtained can help the facilitator of process, to accept or not the possibility to use a second order model, or to design the criteria structure differently by means of a decision tree in such a way as to reduce the cardinality of criteria at the same level. This study can then contribute to confirm or not the suitability of a second order model, often accepted in real world applications. In a future step, we intend to perform the same analysis for higher order model.

Finally note that our approach is in the spirit of the paper of Yager [18] but differs in many aspects, in particular there is not a preliminary ranking of the criteria to be aggregated.

References

1. Bortot, S., Marques Pereira, R.A.: The Generalized Gini Welfare Function in the Framework of Symmetric Choquet Integration. In: Ventre, A.G.S., Maturo, A., Hošková-Mayerová, Š., Kacprzyk, J. (eds.) Multicriteria & Multiagent Decision Making. STUDFUZZ, vol. 305, pp. 15–26. Springer, Heidelberg (2013)
2. Calvo, T., De Baets, B.: Aggregation operators defined by k-order additive/maxitive fuzzy measures. International Journal of Uncertainty, Fuzzyness and Knowledge-Based Systems 6(6), 533–550 (1998)
3. Chateauneuf, A., Jaffray, J.Y.: Some characterizations of lower probabilities and other monotone capacities throught the use of Möbius inversion. Mathematical Social Sciences 17(3), 263–283 (1989)
4. Choquet, G.: Theory of capacities. Annales de l'Institut Fourier 5, 131–295 (1953)
5. Denneberg, D.: Non-additive measure and integral. Kluwer Academic Publisher, Dordrecht (1994)
6. Gilboa, I., Schmeidler, D.: Additive representations of non-additive measures and the Choquet integral. Annals of Operations Research 52(1), 43–65 (1994)
7. Gilboa, I., Schmeidler, D.: Canonical representation of set functions. Mathematics of Operations Research 20(1), 197–212 (1995)
8. Grabish, M.: k-order additive discrete fuzzy measures and their representation. Fuzzy Sets and Systems 92, 167–189 (1997)
9. Grabish, M., Kojadinovic, I., Meyer, P.: A review of capacity identification methods for Choquet integral based multi-attribute theory – Applications of the Kappalab R package. European Journal of Operations Research 186(2), 766–785 (1995)
10. Grabisch, M., Marichal, J.L., Mesiar, R., Pap, E.: Aggregation Functions, Encyclopedia of Mathematics and its Applications. Cambridge University Press, Cambridge (2009)
11. Kojadinovic, I.: Minimum variance capacity identification. European Journal of Operations Research 177(1), 498–514 (2007)
12. Marichal, J.L.: Aggregation operators for multicriteria decision aid. Ph.D. Thesis, University of Liège, Liège, Belgium (1998)
13. Mayag, B., Grabisch, M., Labreuche, C.: A representation of preferences by the Choquet integral with respect to a 2-additive capacity. Theory and Decision 71(3), 297–324 (2011)

14. Mayag, B., Grabisch, M., Labreuche, C.: A characterization of the 2-additive Choquet integral through cardinal information. Fuzzy Sets and Systems 184(1), 84–105 (2011)
15. Meyer, P., Ponthière, G.: Eliciting preferences on Multiattribute Societies with a Choquet Integral. Computational Economics 37(2), 133–168 (2011)
16. Pinar, M., Cruciani, C., Giove, S., Sostero, M.: Constructing the FEEM Sustainability Index: a Choquet integral application (submitted)
17. Yager, R.R.: On ordered weighted averaging aggregation operators in multicriteria decision making. IEEE Trans. on Systems, Man and Cybernetics 18(1), 183–190 (1988)
18. Yager, R.R.: Prioritized aggregations operators. International Journal of Approximate Reasoning 48, 263–274 (2008)

Neighbor-Based Similarities

Stefano Rovetta[1], Francesco Masulli[1,2], and Hassan Mahmoud[1]

[1] University of Genoa, Italy
[2] Temple University, Philadelphia PA, USA

Abstract. We present an overview of association criteria that build upon the relative position of a set of reference data items with respect to given query data items, and propose fuzzy generalizations that allows to use these criteria as real-valued similarity measures. Some experimental consistency tests are also presented.

1 Introduction

We have witnessed a shift from feature-based data representation, such as images, to similarity-based representation, exemplified by complex data in protein-protein interaction. This shift has prompted a renewed interest in methods based on similarities which are not evaluated as distances in some suitable space, but given as inputs obtained from some complex, costly, or unobservable source. In this paper we examine some proximity measures derived from the analysis of the ordered list of neighbors to data items.

As opposed to geometric distance, these criteria are applicable even when data are not Euclidean. We are interested in fuzzy data, since they are more realistic. For the sake of concreteness, fuzziness in this work is assumed to derive from measurement uncertainty in an Euclidean setting, similarly to the cases studied by Yager [1]. The methods studied can be applied in other cases.

These measures may be interesting even when a primary similarity is available. For popular methods such as kernel classifiers [2] and spectral clustering [3] a suitably sparse proximity (similarity) matrix has definite computational advantages. In addition, while nearest neighbor classification criteria are asymmetric, similarities based on *shared* neighbor lists are symmetric (and positive semidefinite), which makes them suitable in applications that require this property.

The rationale of the present work is that similarity can be considered a fuzzy generalization of identity, so it is possible to unify binary, discrete-valued, and continuous-valued similarity measures under a general fuzzy framework. A family of neighbor-based similarity measures is surveyed and some of them are experimentally compared.

2 Preliminaries

2.1 Notational Conventions and Background Assumptions

In the following, we assume a training or reference set $Y = \{y_j\}$ of m data points, either unlabeled or labeled with labels indicated by the (crisp or fuzzy) indicator vector $c(y_j)$

F. Masulli, G. Pasi, and R. Yager (Eds.): WILF 2013, LNAI 8256, pp. 161–170, 2013.
© Springer International Publishing Switzerland 2013

(of size C for C classes), and a query set X of n data points. An available $n \times m$ matrix D of pairwise primary similarities or distances is assumed, and R will be the $n \times m$ matrix whose row R_i contains the rank of each reference item $y_j \in Y$ sorted by decreasing similarity from query item $x_i \in X$. Ranks are integers from 1 (the nearest neighbor) to m. Definitions however will mainly use the index matrix I (again $n \times m$) whose row I_i contains the indexes of all reference points according to R_i, so that for instance if $R_{ij} = 1$, then $I_{i1} = j$ (this is the index of the nearest neighbor); more generally $I_{iR_{ij}} = R_{iI_{ij}} = j$. The self-relational case is also included. Here $Y \equiv X$ and $m = n$, therefore all matrices are square $n \times n$, and ranks 1 is that of the nearest point in X (that is, the query point itself), rank 2 that of the second nearest... up to n.

To simplify the treatment, we will assume that rows of D do not include repeated values, i.e., we assume no ties in ranking.

2.2 Fuzzy Equality and Inequality

We assume that each data item in X and Y is a fuzzy vector (a vector whose components are fuzzy numbers), with Gaussian membership of identical variance.

Crisp equality may be expressed by the following indicator function:

$$\delta(x,y) = \begin{cases} 1 & \text{for } x - y = 0, \\ 0 & \text{otherwise,} \end{cases} \tag{1}$$

so that $\delta(x,y) = 1 \iff x = y$, i.e., $\delta()$ indicates that its argument is exactly zero. A fuzzy generalization eq() of $\delta()$ can be interpreted as the indicator of the fuzzy number "about 0" computed for the value $x - y$. This is a fuzzy equivalence relation [4], and several choices are possible. For instance, in [5] interval values were used, and (in)equality tests compared the overlap between intervals. Our Gaussian membership assumption connects fuzzy knowledge and probabilistic uncertainty [1] (one very common source of imprecise knowledge). Equality may be defined as follows:

$$\text{eq}(a,b) = e^{-(a-b)^2/\gamma^2} \quad \text{for } a, b \text{ fuzzy number centroids,} \tag{2}$$

where the fuzziness parameter γ should be tuned to the range of the data under study.

We also need to "overload" the indicator eq() for vector arguments: a natural choice is based on the logical conjunction of equality for the N individual components,

$$\text{eq}(\mathbf{x},\mathbf{y}) = \left(\prod_{p=1}^{N} \text{eq}(\mathbf{x}_p, \mathbf{y}_p) \right)^{1/N} \quad \text{for } \mathbf{x}, \mathbf{y} \text{ fuzzy } N\text{-vectors.} \tag{3}$$

The geometric mean provides a normalization with respect to N, whereas the simple product would yield a smaller value for larger N. For scalars ($N = 1$), (3) reduces to (2).

To model *fuzzy inequality*, Yager [1] employs the probability distribution of the difference of two values. In [6] a similar approach was followed, but based on the probability distribution in a Gaussian dipole, a pair of equal variance Gaussian distributions, which yields a sigmoid:

$$\lambda(a,b) = \frac{1}{1 + e^{(a-b)/\gamma}}, \tag{4}$$

a natural generalization of the Heaviside indicator with fuzzification parameter γ. In the limit for $\gamma \to 0$ the inequality tends to become crisp. The value of $\lambda(a, b)$ represents the degree of truth of the statement "*a* is larger than *b*", with value 0 when $a \ll b$, 1 when $a \gg b$, and a value approaching 0.5 when $a \approx b$. We remark that, similarly to Yager's approach, the fuzzy indicator $\lambda()$ can be used to directly define fuzzy rankings [6].

3   A Taxonomy of Neighbor-Based Similarity Measures

To design neighbor-based similarity values, several choices are possible, although not all combinations make sense. Here we present these choices along with the naming conventions. Measures will be given a symbol indicating its supervised / unsupervised and crisp / fuzzy nature, and further choices will be specified by a subscript, a sequence of *key* characters chained in the same order as they are presented in the following. Some examples are given at the end of this section.

- **Supervised vs Unsupervised Measures**
  Measures based on neighbors assume the existence of a primary pairwise similarity information, and use it to define a new similarity. In the supervised case this primary information is given by a class labeling for Y. Classification in the same class is a kind of similarity measure, binary only in the crisp case, used for instance in correlation clustering [7].
  A base name will be given to each measure as follows: t is a supervised measure, s an unsupervised measure.
- **Crisp vs Fuzzy Measures**
  Depending on the availability of fuzzy information, measures can be either crisp or fuzzy. Symbols for crisp measures are plain: t, s; symbols for fuzzy measures have a "hat": $\hat{t}$, $\hat{s}$
- **Number k of Neighbors**
  The number k of neighbors considered can range from 1 to $|Y|$. In general we only distinguish the case $k = 1$ from $k > 1$. A subscript starting with 1 has $k = 1$; a subscript starting with k has $k \neq 1$, to be specified.
- **Near vs Far Neighbors**
  The neighbors considered for measuring similarities are usually the nearest to the items considered. However, some approaches use the *farthest* neighbors.
  A subscript that has 1 or k followed by n indicates that neighbors are the nearest; if followed by f, neighbors are farthest. Note that all remaining choices are meaningful only for $k > 1$, so subscripts starting with 1 end with either n or f.
- **List vs Set of Neighbors**
  Neighbors can conceptually be arranged in a list or in a set. Comparing two lists requires that all neighbors considered appear with the same rank in both lists. Comparing two sets does not take ranks into account, only the existence of points.
  The key l indicates list, while s stands for set. This choice does not apply for $k = 1$.
- **Measuring Strategy**
  There are several ways to evaluate similarity between two data items. Here we consider three approaches: The number of coincident neighbors or of neighbors

sharing the same class label can be used directly (this is indicated by the key c). Or, this number can be offset by a threshold ("ε-insensitive" count), so that if the shared items are less than this threshold the similarity is zero, and only the excess is counted (key e). Finally, a binary similarity is obtained by simply considering counts that are/are not above the threshold (key t).

Note that in the fuzzy case the concepts of "coincident items" and "larger than a threshold" must be suitably defined, as we did in Subsection 2.2, and give rise to a fuzzy truth degree rather than a binary value.

This choice does not apply for $k = 1$.

For instance, the measure $\hat{t}_{1n}$ is a supervised, fuzzy similarity based on the nearest neighbor only; s_{knst}, a crisp unsupervised similarity, is 1 if the count of the shared near neighbors among the nearest k (taken in any order) is above threshold t, where k and t must be specified; and $\hat{s}_{kflc}$, a fuzzy unsupervised similarity, is the count of fuzzy shared farthest neighbors taken with their ranks, where k must be specified.

4   A Survey of Some Supervised Measures

4.1 k Nearest Neighbor Classification

The well-known nearest neighbor classification rule [8,9] states that a point is attributed to the same class as its closest reference point:

$$c(x_i) = c(y_{I_{i1}}) .\tag{5}$$

Therefore, the nearest neighbor similarity between x_i and x_j is

$$t_{1n}(x_i, x_j) = \begin{cases} 1 & \text{if } c(y_{I_{i1}}) = c(y_{I_{j1}}) , \\ 0 & \text{otherwise.} \end{cases}\tag{6}$$

Nearest neighbor rules can be stated as a Bayes decision criterion working on a crude estimation of class-conditional data densities [8,10]. Using a set of k neighbors makes the nearest neighbor rule less sensitive to local variation in data distribution. A point is in the class that is most represented among the k nearest neighbors, or:

$$c(x_i) = \arg\max_c \left| \{ y_j : c(y_j) = c, R_{ij} \le k \} \right| ,\tag{7}$$

where $|S|$ = cardinality of S. Once a majority class is established, the k nearest neighbor similarity is again given by s_{1n} (6).

The number of majority class representatives can be used to introduce a degree of classification confidence [11], allowing to implement a rejection option in classification tasks. In the k-nearest neighbor distance, confidence can be used to grade the distance, making it non-binary. In [11], t_{knlc} is also used.

4.2 Fuzzy k Nearest Neighbors

Fuzzy supervised nearest neighbor criteria may be based on metrics $\hat{f}_{1n}$ and $\hat{f}_{knst}$. However Keller *et al.* proposed a fuzzy k nearest neighbor classification [12], based on the idea of applying the fuzzy c-means membership function to Y. The fuzzy k nearest neighbor classification is a C-vector of memberships $u(x_i) = [u_1(x_i), \ldots, u_C(x_i)]$, so that

$$u_h(x_i) = \frac{\sum_{j=1}^{k} c_h(y_{I_{i,1}})(1/D_{ij})^{2/(m-1)}}{\sum_{j=1}^{k}(1/D_{ij})^{2/(m-1)}}, \qquad h : 1 \ldots C \qquad (8)$$

and the nearest neighbor similarity between x_i and x_j can be computed as the degree of similarity between two modified membership vectors

$$\hat{s}'_{knlc}(x_i, x_j) = \frac{\sqrt{u'(x_i) \cdot u'(x_j)}}{k}, \qquad (9)$$

a variation of $\hat{s}_{knlc}$ where

$$u'(x) \begin{cases} u(x) & \text{if } u(x) \in \text{top } k \text{ memberships,} \\ 0 & \text{otherwise.} \end{cases} \qquad (10)$$

Note that, according to this model, the nearest neighbor ($k = 1$) criterion is always crisp, unless the target class indicators $c_h(y_j)$ are fuzzy to start with. This requirement is not usually satisfied.

When the y_j are the centroids of meaningful groupings in data, e.g., class centroids or centroids of convex components of classes, these criteria are called "nearest centroid". Usually, however, they are prototypes [13] or landmarks [14] in the data space, in a more generic sense. A similar representation, with $k \equiv m$, has been used in [15].

5   A Survey of Some Unsupervised Measures

5.1 Shared Near Neighbors

A binary similarity measure was proposed by Jarvis and Patrick [16]. The measure is inherently unsupervised. It assigns two points to the same cluster whenever, among the k nearest neighbors of each point, at least t are common to both ("shared"). In other words, it uses the s_{knst} measure: If $n_n(k) = \left| \{y_p : R_{ip} \leq k, R_{jp} \leq k\} \right|$ is the number of shared near neighbors among the nearest k,

$$s_{knst}(x_i, x_j) = \begin{cases} 1 & \text{if } \quad n_n \geq t, \\ 0 & \text{otherwise.} \end{cases} \qquad (11)$$

5.2 Shared Farthest Neighbors

Another binary, unsupervised similarity measure was presented in [17]. This measure assigns two points to the same cluster whenever the *farthest* neighbor of the two points is the same:

$$s_{1f}(x_i, x_j) = \begin{cases} 1 & \text{if } \quad I_{in} = I_{jn}, \\ 0 & \text{otherwise.} \end{cases} \qquad (12)$$

This measure can be applied recursively up to depth k, using s_{kfit} for a sequence of thresholds t. Similarly to the k nearest neigbors rule, we can apply this criterion to the set of k farthest neighbors.

5.3 Fuzzy Shared Near and Far Neighbors

Using the definitions of fuzzy equality and inequality given in Subsection 2.2, fuzzy neighbor-based similarities can be readily defined. These similarities measure the degree of overlap between the k nearest or farthest neighbors. If the lists of neighbors include similar, albeit not identical, points, these give some (reduced) contribution to the measure. The following is the definition of measures, for both nearest and farthest neighbors, using the "list" representation, i.e., keeping ranks into account:

$$\hat{s}_{knlc}(x_i,x_j) = \sum_{p=1}^{k} \text{eq}\left(y_{I_{ip}}, y_{I_{jp}}\right) ; \qquad \hat{s}_{kflc}(x_i,x_j) = \sum_{p=m-k+1}^{m} \text{eq}\left(y_{I_{ip}}, y_{I_{jp}}\right) . \qquad (13)$$

In measures using the "set" representation, data items are required to be included in the two lists of neighbors, but not necessarily with the same rank in both.

$$\hat{s}_{knsc}(x_i,x_j) = \sum \text{top}(k)\left\{\text{eq}\left(y_{I_{ip}}, y_{I_{jq}}\right), i=1\ldots k, j=i\ldots k\right\} ; \qquad (14)$$

$$\hat{s}_{kfsc}(x_i,x_j) = \sum \text{top}(k)\left\{\text{eq}\left(y_{I_{ip}}, y_{I_{jq}}\right), i=m-k+1\ldots m, j=i\ldots m\right\} . \qquad (15)$$

Here top(k) is the top-k query operator, applied to the fuzzy equality level eq() of $k(k+1)/2$ pairs of neighbors (either nearest or farthest).

Finally, threshold-based nearest and farthest neighbor measures, according to the ideas of Jarvis and Patrick, are defined as follows:

$$\hat{s}_{knst}(x_i,x_j) = \lambda(\hat{s}_{knsc}, t) ; \qquad \hat{s}_{kfst}(x_i,x_j) = \lambda(\hat{s}_{kfsc}, t) . \qquad (16)$$

6   Experiments

Due to the large number of variations and the resulting huge number of comparisons that would be needed, in this paper it is impossible to provide a complete experimental validation of the measures described and surveyed. Only selected experiments on some measures will be presented to illustrate a possible experimental approach.

The experiments have been performed on two datasets from the UCI Machine Learning Repository [18], Iris [19] and Seeds [20]. Both are simple and not very extensive, but both present a weak clustering structure, useful to gain understanding on the type of information revealed by similarity measures. we only take fuzzy unsupervised similarities into account, although data are labeled and supervised approaches are also possible.

The well-known Iris data (150 items with 4 attributes) are distributed in three equal-sized classes structured into two clusters. Centroid-based clustering methods can approximate the two touching classes because the resulting distribution is elongated and such methods make a globular cluster assumption that does not match the distribution

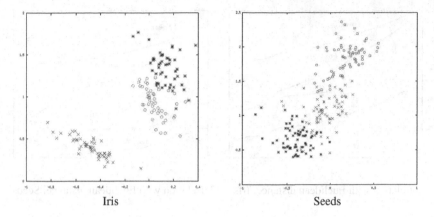

Iris   Seeds

Fig. 1. The datasets used in the experiments, projected onto their first two principal components

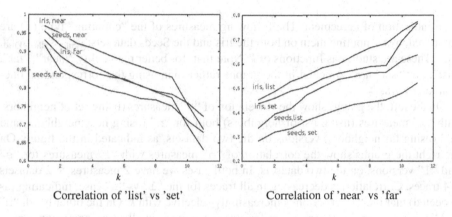

Correlation of 'list' vs 'set'   Correlation of 'near' vs 'far'

Fig. 2. Correlation coefficient between different measures as a function of k

very well. Methods that do not rely on this assumption (including heat-kernel based spectral clustering for a range of width parameters) may or may not be able to separate these classes on the basis of structure only (i.e., in an unsupervised setting). On the other hand, the first class is extremely well separated.

The Seeds data is 210 items with 7 attributes, in 3 classes, and is somewhat similar to two of the three classes of the Iris data in that there are no clear clusters; however the situation here is even worse, since cardinality is similar (70 items per class), dimensionality is higher, and all the three classes are overlapping in one cluster only.

Figure 1 shows the two datasets, projected on their first two principal components.

6.1   Consistency between Measures

Figure 2 shows the value of the correlation coefficient between the fuzzy measures, as a function of k. This is a consistency test for the measures considered, since correlation

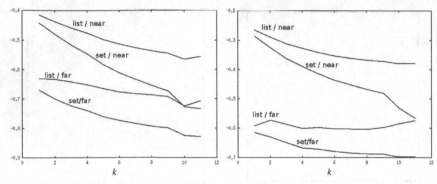

Correlation with Euclidean distance, Iris   Correlation with Euclidean distance, Seeds

Fig. 3. Correlation coefficient of measures with Euclidean distance, as a function of k

is an indication of agreement. The following measures of the "counting" type (c) are compared, by computing them on both the Iris and the Seeds data sets: $\hat{s}_{\text{knlc}}$, $\hat{s}_{\text{kflc}}$, $\hat{s}_{\text{knsc}}$, $\hat{s}_{\text{kfsc}}$. These are studies as functions of k. Note that, for better readability, "near", "far", "list", and "set" are explicited in the graphs rather than using the corresponding one-character keys.

On the left, the graphs show the correlation of "s" measures (using set of neighbors) with "l" measures (using list of neighbors) both for "n" (using near neighbors) and "f" (using far neighbors) versions on the two datasets, as indicated in the figure. On the right the graphs show the correlation of "n" measures with "f" measures for "s" and "l" versions, on the two datasets. In both cases we have 2 measures × 2 datasets = 4 traces. Correlation is decreasing in all traces for the "l" vs "s" case, indicating (as expected) that the "l" criterion is increasingly selective with k. On the other hand, "n" and "f" criteria are increasingly similar, with growing k, in all cases, again confirming a reasonable expectation.

6.2   Consistency with Euclidean Distance

Figure 3 shows the value of the correlation coefficient between fuzzy measures and Euclidean distance, as a function of k, another consistency test. The consistency is higher for *more negative* values of the correlation coefficient (since we compare similarities with distances).

Correlation grows with k, and, somewhat surprisingly, is stronger for measures based on farthest neighbors rather than on nearest neighbors. An expected result, instead, is that correlation for "s" measures is higher than for "l" measures.

6.3   Use in Spectral Clustering

A sample experiment on the Iris data is presented here to see the actual behavior of a similarity measure when used in spectral clustering, here defined as in [21]. Since

Table 1. Example spectral clustering results

Heat kernel, $\sigma = 0.1$ $\hat{s}_{knlc}, k = 20$

	Setosa	Versicolor	Virginica		Setosa	Versicolor	Virginica
cluster 1	50	0	0	cluster 1	50	0	0
cluster 2	0	26	43	cluster 2	0	27	33
cluster 3	0	24	7	cluster 3	0	23	17

(contrary to k-means) we are not enforcing a globular cluster assumption, we expect clusters to be found only for class 1 (Setosa), while the other classes should correspond much less precisely to clusters.

Confusion matrices between classes and clusters are presented in Table 1 for both heat kernel with parameter $\sigma = 1$ (a non-optimal value) and the $\hat{s}_{knlc}$ similarity (fuzzy unsupervised k-nearest neighbors, rank-sensitive match count). The heat kernel uses all the information available, while $\hat{s}_{knlc}$ uses only the list of the first 20 nearest neighbors; yet, the results are comparable if one does not take the additional effort to select a suitable heat kernel parameter, a task that in general is known to be tricky [22]. In particular, the well-clustered class is perfectly separated, while the other two classes are mixed in the two other clusters.

7 Conclusion and Perspectives of Work

The measures surveyed here can be applied even in the absence of an explicitly computable primary measure. They can be used to turn an asymmetric similarity structure into a symmetric, positive definite similarity matrix even for non-Euclidean, fuzzy data. The sample experiments seem to suggest (subject to further extensive verification) that these measure convey significant information, and are consistent both with each other and with Euclidean distance.

Since the methodology proposed disregards the nature of the actual primary similarity, requiring only that it induces an ordering in the reference data items, it is notably flexible and can be applied in several contexts.

References

1. Yager, R.R., Detyniecki, M., Bouchon-Meunier, B.: A context-dependent method for ordering fuzzy numbers using probabilities. Information Sciences 138(1), 237–255 (2001)
2. Cristianini, N., Shawe-Taylor, J.: An Introduction to Support Vector Machines (and Other Kernel-based Learning Methods). Cambridge University Press (2000)
3. Von Luxburg, U.: A tutorial on spectral clustering. Statistics and Computing 17(4), 395–416 (2007)
4. Zadeh, L.A.: Similarity relations and fuzzy orderings. Information Sciences 3(2), 177–200 (1971)
5. Ridella, S., Rovetta, S., Zunino, R.: IAVQ–interval-arithmetic vector quantization for image compression. IEEE Transactions on Circuits and Systems 47(12, Pt. II), 1378–1390 (2000)

6. Rovetta, S., Masulli, F.: Vector quantization and fuzzy ranks for image reconstruction. Image and Vision Computing 25(2), 204–213 (2006)
7. Bansal, N., Blum, A., Chawla, S.: Correlation clustering. Machine Learning 56(1-3), 89–113 (2004)
8. Fix, E., Hodges, J.L.: Discriminatory analysis. nonparametric discrimination: Consistency properties. Project Number 21-49-004 4, USAF School of Aviation Medicine, Randolph Field, Texas, USA (February 1951)
9. Cover, T.M., Hart, P.E.: Nearest neighbor pattern classification. IEEE Trans. Info. Theory IT-13, 21–27 (1967)
10. Duda, R.O., Hart, P.E.: Pattern Classification and Scene Analysis. John Wiley and Sons, Chichester (1973)
11. Ridella, S., Rovetta, S., Zunino, R.: K-winner machines for pattern classification. IEEE Transactions on Neural Networks 12(2), 371–385 (2001)
12. Keller, J.M., Gray, M.R., Givens, J.A.: A fuzzy k-nearest neighbor algorithm. IEEE Transactions on Systems, Man and Cybernetics (4), 580–585 (1985)
13. Duin, R.P., Pękalska, E.: The dissimilarity space: Bridging structural and statistical pattern recognition. Pattern Recognition Letters 33(7), 826–832 (2012)
14. de Silva, V., Tenenbaum, J.B.: Global versus local methods in nonlinear dimensionality reduction. In: Becker, S., Thrun, S., Obermayer, K. (eds.) Proceedings NIPS, vol. 15, pp. 721–728 (2003)
15. Filippone, M., Masulli, F., Rovetta, S.: Clustering in the membership embedding space. International Journal of Knowledge Engineering and Soft Data Paradigms 1(4), 363–375 (2009)
16. Jarvis, R.A., Patrick, E.A.: Clustering using a similarity measure based on shared near neighbors. IEEE Transactions on Computers C22, 1025–1034 (1973)
17. Rovetta, S., Masulli, F.: Shared farthest neighbor approach to clustering of high dimensionality, low cardinality data. Pattern Recognition 39(12), 2415–2425 (2006)
18. Asuncion, A., Newman, D.J.: UCI machine learning repository (2007)
19. Fisher, R.A.: The use of multiple measurements in taxonomic problems. Annual Eugenics 7(Pt. II), 179–188 (1936)
20. Charytanowicz, M., Niewczas, J., Kulczycki, P., Kowalski, P.A., Łukasik, S., Żak, S.: Complete gradient clustering algorithm for features analysis of X-ray images. In: Piętka, E., Kawa, J. (eds.) Information Technologies in Biomedicine. AISC, vol. 69, pp. 15–24. Springer, Heidelberg (2010)
21. Shi, J., Malik, J.: Normalized cuts and image segmentation. IEEE Transactions on Pattern Analysis and Machine Intelligence 22(8), 888–905 (2000)
22. Nadler, B., Galun, M.: Fundamental limitations of spectral clustering. In: Schölkopf, B., Platt, J., Hoffman, T. (eds.) Advances in Neural Information Processing Systems 19, pp. 1017–1024. MIT Press, Cambridge (2007)

Model-Based Image Interpretation under Uncertainty and Fuzziness

Isabelle Bloch

Institut Mines-Telecom - Telecom ParisTech - CNRS LTCI - Paris, France
`isabelle.bloch@telecom-paristech.fr`

Abstract. Structural models such as ontologies and graphs can encode generic knowledge about a scene observed in an image. Their use in spatial reasoning schemes allows driving segmentation and recognition of objects and structures in images. The developed methods include finding a best segmentation path in a graph, global solving of a constraint satisfaction problem, integrating prior knowledge in deformable models, and exploring images in a progressive fashion. Conversely, these models can be specified based on individual information resulting from the segmentation and recognition process. In particular models relying on spatial relations between structures are relevant and more flexible than shape models to be adapted to potential variations, multiple occurrences, or pathological cases. The problem of semantic gap is addressed by generating spatial representations (in the image space) of relations initially expressed in linguistic or symbolic form, within a fuzzy set formalism. This allows coping with uncertainty and fuzziness, which are inherent both to generic knowledge and to image information. Applications in medical imaging and remote sensing imaging illustrate the proposed paradigm.

Keywords: Image understanding, structural models, graphs, spatial relations, fuzzy modeling, model-based segmentation and recognition, constraint satisfaction problems.

1   Structural Models

Models constitute an important source of information for image understanding, that provides generic knowledge, complementary to the actual data and images. Such models may provide information regarding the objects contained in the scene, as well as their spatial arrangement. This aspect confers them a structural nature, in which spatial relations are of prime importance.

Let us consider medical image interpretation as an example. On the one hand, biological, anatomical or biomechanical models can be used to guide image interpretation. On the other hand, medical images can be exploited in order to build models of the human body, from an anatomical or functional point of view.

Iconic representations of anatomical knowledge can be found, such as anatomical atlases. Although their use for normal structure recognition is well acknowledged, they remain difficult to exploit in pathological cases. Anatomical

F. Masulli, G. Pasi, and R. Yager (Eds.): WILF 2013, LNAI 8256, pp. 171–183, 2013.
© Springer International Publishing Switzerland 2013

knowledge is also available in textbooks or dedicated web sites, and expressed mainly in linguistic form. These models involve concepts that correspond to anatomical objects, their characteristics, or the spatial relations between them. Human experts use intensively such concepts and knowledge to recognize visually anatomical structures in images. This motivates their use in computer aided image interpretation. Some attempts to formalize this knowledge have been performed, in particular in the form of ontologies (e.g. the Foundational Model of Anatomy [14]). Such linguistic or ontological descriptions can be found in other domains, such as remote sensing.

In several applications, shape is not a sufficient information to describe a scene, and models should involve higher level information, on the structure and spatial arrangement of the scene. Hence models of spatial relations have to be developed and included in the models. Graphs are often used to represent the structural information in image interpretation, where the vertices represent objects or image regions (and may carry attributes such as their shapes, sizes, and colors or grey levels), and the edges carry the structural information, such as the spatial relations among objects, or radiometric contrasts between regions.

In our work, we concentrate mainly on spatial relations, which are strongly involved in linguistic descriptions. We proposed mathematical models of several spatial relations, in the framework of fuzzy set theory [5]. Fuzziness is very important to model the intrinsic imprecision of spatial relations expressed in a linguistic way. The modeling relies on tools from mathematical morphology [7,9], which provides a strong algebraic framework. This allows deriving similar models, with the same properties, in various settings, either quantitative, semi-quantitative (fuzzy) or qualitative (logics) ones (see [6] for mathematical details), and thus reasoning at different levels and on different types of information. In particular, the fuzzy representations can enrich anatomical ontologies [21] and contribute to fill the semantic gap between symbolic concepts, as expressed in the ontology, and visual percepts, as extracted from the images. A symbolic concept representing a given spatial relation can be translated into semi-qualitative representation using the proposed fuzzy models. The parameters are tuned using learning procedures for each application domain[1] [3], leading to a representation in the image domain. Combination with image information can then be performed. These ideas were used in particular in our segmentation and recognition methods.

Interactions between models and images can be seen in different directions. A model can drive the exploration of an image, as described next. Conversely, the result of an image interpretation process can be used to modify a generic model to make it specific to the observed case. Moreover, results on several images can help building generic models. In the sequel, we focus on the first aspect.

---

[1] For instance, a relation such as "close to a given object" is intrinsically fuzzy, and moreover its concrete meaning depends on the domain. It is typically not the same for anatomical structures in medical images, and for man-made or natural objects in satellite images.

2 Model-Based Structure Recognition and Image Understanding

The methods we developed for segmentation and recognition of 3D structures in medical images can be seen as spatial reasoning processes. Two main components of this domain are spatial knowledge representation and reasoning.

In particular spatial relations constitute an important part of the knowledge we have to handle, as explained before, since they constitute relevant information to guide the recognition of structures embedded in a complex environment, and are more stable and less prone to variability (even in pathological cases) than object characteristics such as shape or size. Imprecision is often attached to spatial reasoning in images, and can occur at different levels, from knowledge to the type of question we want to answer.

The reasoning component includes fusion of heterogeneous spatial knowledge, decision making, inference, recognition. Two types of questions are raised when dealing with spatial relations:

1. given two objects (possibly fuzzy), assess the degree to which a relation is satisfied;
2. given one reference object, define the area of space in which a relation to this reference is satisfied (to some degree).

In order to answer these questions and address both representation and reasoning issues, we rely on three different frameworks and their combination:

- mathematical morphology, which is an algebraic theory that has extensions to fuzzy sets and to logical formulas, and can elegantly unify the representation of several types of relations;
- fuzzy set theory, which has powerful features to represent imprecision at different levels, to combine heterogeneous information and to make decisions;
- formal logics and the attached reasoning and inference power.

The association of these three frameworks for spatial reasoning is an original contribution of our work, and the lattice structure underlying each of these frameworks is a core feature, making the use of mathematical morphology relevant and powerful [6].

The interpretation of complex scenes in images often requires (or can benefit from) a model of the scene. The spatial arrangement of objects or structures is often crucial for differentiating among objects with similar appearances in the images, or disambiguating complex cases. Examples occur in many domains, including medical imaging, in which structural knowledge can help in the interpretation of the images. In magnetic resonance imaging (MRI), for instance, radiometry is often insufficient for recognizing individual anatomical structures, and their relative spatial configuration provides an important input into the recognition process [12]. Other examples occur in aerial and satellite imaging, robot vision, and video sequence interpretation, among other fields.

In our work, we often address the image interpretation problem as a joint problem of image segmentation and object recognition, based on structural information. The methods summarized in the next section address this question, and belong to a more general class of model-based or knowledge-based interpretation systems. Only a sketch of each of them is provided here, and mathematical and technical details can be found in the mentioned references.

3 A Few Approaches

3.1 Morphisms between Graphs

A first recognition approach, called global, uses the first type of question (1). The idea is to represent all available knowledge about the objects to be recognized. A typical example consists of graph-based representations. The model is then represented as a graph where nodes are objects and edges represent links between these objects. Both nodes and edges are attributed. Node attributes are characteristics of the objects, while edge attributes quantify spatial relations between the objects. A data graph is then constructed from each image where the recognition has to be performed, based on a preliminary segmentation into homogeneous regions. Each region of the image constitutes a node of this data graph, and edges represent spatial relations between regions, as for the model graph. The comparison between representations is performed through the computation of similarities between model graph attributes and data graph attributes. Note that it might not be straightforward to design an appropriate similarity function involving vertex and edge attributes for a specific application.

Although graph representations have become popular in the last 40 years [13], a number of open problems remain in their efficient implementation. In particular, when expressing the recognition problem as a graph matching problem between the image and model graphs, which is an annotation problem, this scheme often requires solving complex combinatorial problems [13]. Improvements can be achieved by suppressing iteratively inconsistent annotations using a constraint propagation procedure, as proposed e.g. in [29,36] for simple geometrical figures or in [24,32] for the annotation of image segmentations. However, the constraint propagation procedure does not guarantee a unique annotation. Moreover, all of these approaches assume a correct initial segmentation of the image. However, the segmentation problem is a known challenge in image processing, to which no universal solution exists. The segmentation is usually imperfect, and no isomorphism exists between the graphs being matched. An inexact matching must then be found, for instance by allowing several image regions to be assigned to one model vertex or by relaxing the notion of morphism to that of fuzzy morphism [10,28]. For example, previous studies [15,16] employ an over-segmentation of the image, which is easier to obtain. A model structure (i.e. a graph vertex) is then explicitly associated with a set of regions, and the recognition problem is expressed as a constraint satisfaction problem. To overcome the complexity issue, a weaker version of the model relations (encoded in the edges) is considered, and the problem is solved using a modified AC-4 propagation algorithm [25].

3.2 Progressive Exploration of the Image Using Graphs

A second type of approach relies on the second type of question (2), and is called here progressive or sequential [8,12,18]. In this approach, objects are recognized sequentially and their recognition makes use of knowledge about their relations with respect to other objects. This sequential segmentation framework allows decomposing the initial problem into several easier-to-solve sub-problems, using the generic knowledge about the scene. Relations with respect to previously obtained objects can be combined at two different levels of the procedure. First, fusion can occur in the spatial domain, using spatial fuzzy sets. The result of this fusion allows building a fuzzy region of interest in which the search of a new object will take place, in a process similar to focalization of attention, thus driving the image exploration. In a sequential procedure, the amount of available spatial relations increases with the number of processed objects. Therefore, the recognition of the most difficult structures, usually handled in the last steps, will be focused in a more restricted area. Another fusion level occurs during the final decision step, i.e. segmentation and recognition of a structure. For this purpose, spatial relations are introduced in the evolution scheme of a deformable model, in which they are combined with other types of numerical information, usually edge and regularity constraints.

This approach, as pointed out in [12], requires to define the order according to which the objects have to be recognized and the choice of the most appropriate order is a challenging issue. This was addressed in [18], with two original contributions:

- First, we extended the sequential segmentation framework by introducing a pre-attentional mechanism based on saliency [22], which is used, in combination with spatial relations, to derive a criterion for the optimization of the segmentation order.
- Secondly, we introduced criteria and a data structure which allow us to detect the potential errors and control the ordering strategy.

The proposed framework has two levels. The first level is a generic bottom-up module which allows selecting the next structure to segment. This level does not rely on an initial segmentation or classification, but instead on a focus of attention and a map of generic features. The sequential approach allows this level to use two types of knowledge: generic and domain independent features in unexplored area of the image to segment, and high-level knowledge such as spatial relations linked to the already recognized structures. The selection criterion is used to optimize the segmentation order and to select the next structure to segment at each step. The second level achieves recognition and segmentation of the selected structure, as well as the evaluation of the segmentation. The recognition of the structure is achieved at the same time as the segmentation. This level is composed by the segmentation method defined in [12], integrating spatial relations in a deformable model, and an original evaluation method. It uses two types of a priori information: the spatial information which allows us to reduce the search area, and a radiometric estimation of the intensity of the structure.

Therefore, the radiometric estimation needs to discriminate the intensity of the structure only in the search area and not in the whole image. Once a structure is segmented and recognized, this level also evaluates the quality of the result and proposes a strategy to guarantee the spatial consistency of the result and to potentially backtrack on the segmentation order.

This approach is illustrated in Figure 1.

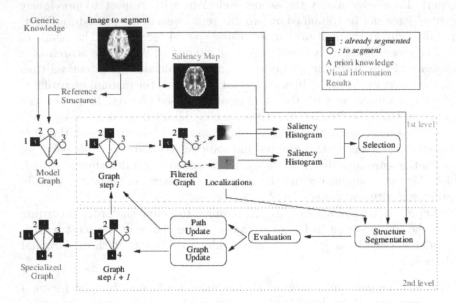

Fig. 1. General scheme of the sequential segmentation framework (figure reproduced from [18]). The graph initially represents only the generic knowledge (here about the brain) and the reference structures. At each step, a structure is selected according to the saliency of its localization and its relations to other structures. This structure is then segmented and the result is evaluated. In case of success, the graph is updated and the process is iterated until the graph is completely specialized or no more structure can be segmented. In case of failure, the system is constrained to select another path to segment and the process is iterated.

3.3   Global Method Based on Graphs and CSP

To overcome the problems raised by sequential approaches while avoiding the need for an initial segmentation, we proposed in [27] an original method that still employs a structural model, but solves the problem in a global fashion. Our definition of a solution is the assignment of a spatial region to each model object, in a way that satisfies the constraints expressed in the model. We propose a progressive reduction of the solution domain for all objects by excluding assignments that are inconsistent with the structural model. Constraint networks [30] constitute an appropriate framework for both the formalization of the problem and the optimization. An original feature of the proposed approach is that the regions are not predetermined, but are instead constructed during the reduction process. The image segmentation and recognition algorithm therefore differs from an annotation procedure, and no prior segmentation of the image into meaningful or homogeneous regions is required. This feature overcomes the limitations of many previous approaches (such as [15,16]). More precisely, a constraint network is constructed from the structural model, and a propagation algorithm is then designed to reduce the search space, which is an adaptation of AC-3 algorithm [30] with an ordering of constraints to reduce the computational cost and reduce the domains as much as possible. Finally, an approximate solution is extracted from the reduced search space. Once the propagation process terminates, the solution space is typically reduced substantially for all of the model structures. The final segmentation and recognition results can then be obtained using any segmentation method that is constrained by this solution space.

This approach is illustrated in Figure 2.

3.4 Global Method Based on Nested Conceptual Graphs and Fuzzy CSP

In this section, we summarize a hybrid method, relying on a preliminary segmentation of the image, which does not need to be perfect, and on a recognition step to identify the concepts represented in the model [33]. In some applications, for instance to interpret Earth observation images, multiple instantiations of some objects should be taken into account (e.g. several boats in a harbor).

In this case, the interpretation relies on a generic model of the scene to be recognized, encoding objects and groups of objects, spatial relations between between objects or between groups, along with the imprecision and uncertainty attached to the formal representations of such relations (this includes complex relations such as alignment, parallelism, etc. [34,35]). The model is formalized as a nested conceptual graph [31], which allows representing internal and external information, zooming, partial description of an entity, or specific contexts. Identifying possibly multiple instances of the model in an image is formalized as a graph homomorphism.

Finding the best homomorphism is performed by solving a fuzzy constraint satisfaction problems (FCSP) [17], using arc-consistency checking [11]. FCSP and arc-consistency checking have been extended in [33] to deal with relations having an arity greater than two and with complex objects. The main contribution in this work concerns the adaptation of the algorithm to deal with groups of objects which can be related among them or have a spatial property such as being aligned. A methodology is then proposed to find the instantiations of a nested conceptual graph in an unlabeled image. Experimental results on high resolution satellite images show that the proposed approach successfully recognizes a given spatial configuration (such as harbor or airport) and is robust to image segmentation errors. The results demonstrate the interest of using complex spatial relations for the interpretation of images.

This approach is summarized in Figure 3.

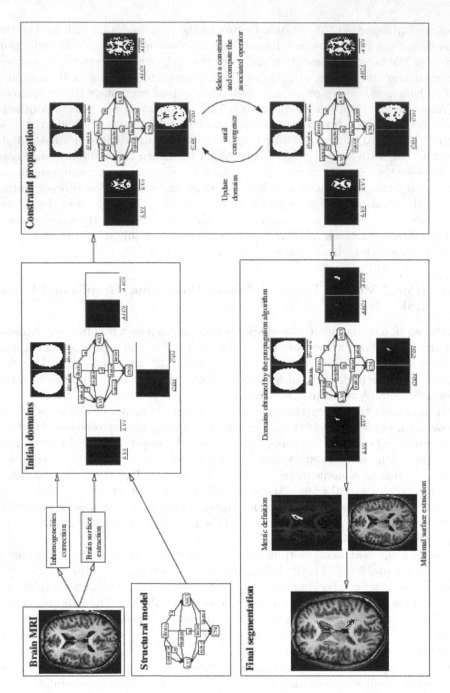

Fig. 2. Overview of the CSP approach for the brain structures example (figure reproduced from [27]). For instance, the solution space of the left caudate nucleus (CNl) is reduced based on the constraint that "the left caudate nucleus (CNl) is exterior (i.e. to the right in the image) to the left lateral ventricle (LVl)".

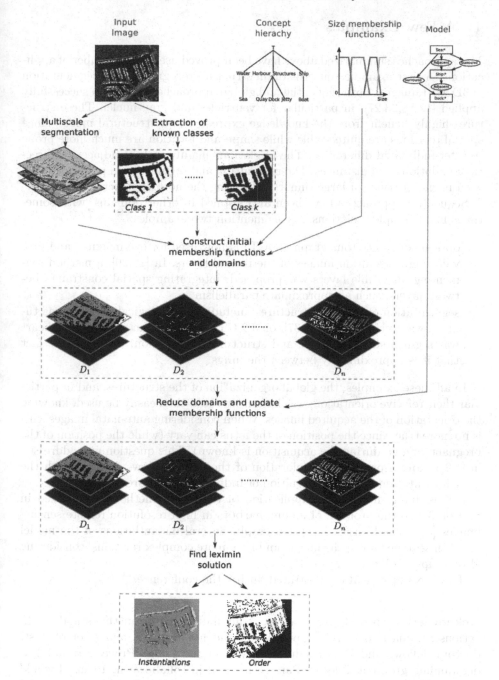

Fig. 3. Summary of the method for determining the model's instantiations using nested conceptual graphs and FCSP (figure reproduced from [33])

4   A Few Examples

The approaches summarized above have been proved useful in a number of applications. A first example concerns brain structure recognition and segmentation in 3D MRI images. Both sequential and global approaches have been successfully applied [12,18,23,27], in particular for ventricles and grey nuclei. These structures highly benefit from the knowledge expressed in a structural model, since spatial relations are quite stable while shape and location are much more prone to inter-individual differences. These relations mainly include adjacency, directional relations and distances. The recognition and segmentation performed well even in the presence of large tumors deforming the normal structures.

Sequential approaches have been also applied in other domains, with sometimes more complex relations. Let us mention two examples:

- optical coherence tomography (OCT) is now used for eye imaging, and provides high resolution images of the retinal layers. In [19,20], a method segmenting all visible layers was proposed, integrating spatial constraints between layers, such as approximate parallelism;
- segmentation of thoracic structures, including pathological ones such as tumors, was performed in [26,37], on 3D CT images. As an example, the heart was segmented using shape and structural information, modeling the fact that it is approximately between the lungs.

In all these examples, the global organization of the structures, and in particular their relative orientation, was known. It could then easily be used, knowing the orientation of the acquired images. When considering ante-natal images, this is no more true, since the position of the fetus can vary (while the position of the pregnant woman during the acquisition is known). This question was addressed in [1,2,4], and a progressive exploration of the images allows deriving both the global orientation and the recognition of individual structures.

Let us finally mention an application of the FSCP method summarized in Section 3.4 to the problem of finding harbors in high resolution remote sensing images [33], based on a conceptual graph. Several instantiations of the model are then searched for in the image, and here more complex relations, considering also groups of objects, are used.

These examples will be illustrated during the conference.

Acknowledgments. Several persons contributed to the methods and applications summarized in this paper (a few faculty members and a lot of post-doctoral fellows and PhD candidates), within the Image Processing and Understanding group at Telecom ParisTech[2], and in collaborating teams. I would like to thank them all, and in particular Elsa Angelini, Jérémie Anquez, Jamal Atif, Endika Bengoetxea, Lazar Bibin, Tamy Boubekeur, Oscar Camara, Roberto Cesar, Olivier Colliot, Geoffroy Fouquier, Thierry Géraud, Itebeddine

---

[2] http://perso.telecom-paristech.fr/~bloch/tii/staff.html

Ghorbel, Jordi Inglada, Céline Hudelot, Hassan Khotanlou, Henri Maître, Antonio Moreno, Olivier Nempont, Aymeric Perchant, Florence Rossant, Carolina Vanegas, Julien Wojak.

These developments also benefited from fundings from ANR (French National Research Agency) and industrial collaborations. I would like also to thank the collaborating hospitals for the applications in medical imaging, and the CNES (French National Spatial Agency) for the last example.

References

1. Anquez, J., Angelini, E., Bloch, I.: Automatic Segmentation of Head Structures on Fetal MRI. In: IEEE International Symposium on Biomedical Imaging (ISBI), Boston, USA, pp. 109–112 (2009)
2. Anquez, J., Bibin, L., Angelini, E.D., Bloch, I.: Segmentation of the fetal envelope on ante-natal MRI. In: IEEE International Symposium on Biomedical Imaging (ISBI), Rotterdam, The Netherlands, pp. 896–899 (2010)
3. Atif, J., Hudelot, C., Fouquier, G., Bloch, I., Angelini, E.: From Generic Knowledge to Specific Reasoning for Medical Image Interpretation using Graph-based Representations. In: International Joint Conference on Artificial Intelligence, IJCAI 2007, Hyderabad, India, pp. 224–229 (2007)
4. Bibin, L., Anquez, J., de la Plata Alcalde, J., Boubekeur, T., Angelini, E.D., Bloch, I.: Whole body pregnant woman modeling by digital geometry processing with detailed utero-fetal unit based on medical images. IEEE Transactions on Biomedical Engineering 57(10), 2346–2358 (2010)
5. Bloch, I.: Fuzzy Spatial Relationships for Image Processing and Interpretation: A Review. Image and Vision Computing 23(2), 89–110 (2005)
6. Bloch, I.: Spatial Reasoning under Imprecision using Fuzzy Set Theory, Formal Logics and Mathematical Morphology. International Journal of Approximate Reasoning 41, 77–95 (2006)
7. Bloch, I.: Duality vs. Adjunction for Fuzzy Mathematical Morphology and General Form of Fuzzy Erosions and Dilations. Fuzzy Sets and Systems 160, 1858–1867 (2009)
8. Bloch, I., Géraud, T., Maître, H.: Representation and Fusion of Heterogeneous Fuzzy Information in the 3D Space for Model-Based Structural Recognition - Application to 3D Brain Imaging. Artificial Intelligence 148, 141–175 (2003)
9. Bloch, I., Maître, H.: Fuzzy Mathematical Morphologies: A Comparative Study. Pattern Recognition 28(9), 1341–1387 (1995)
10. Cesar, R., Bengoetxea, E., Bloch, I., Larranaga, P.: Inexact Graph Matching for Model-Based Recognition: Evaluation and Comparison of Optimization Algorithms. Pattern Recognition 38, 2099–2113 (2005)
11. Chein, M., Mugnier, M.L.: Graph-based Knowledge Representation and Reasoning - Computational Foundations of Conceptual Graphs. In: Advanced Information and Knowledge Processing. Springer (2008)
12. Colliot, O., Camara, O., Bloch, I.: Integration of Fuzzy Spatial Relations in Deformable Models - Application to Brain MRI Segmentation. Pattern Recognition 39, 1401–1414 (2006)
13. Conte, D., Foggia, P., Sansone, C., Vento, M.: Thirty years of graph matching in pattern recognition. International Journal of Pattern Recognition and Artificial Intelligence 18(3), 265–298 (2004)

14. Cornelius, R., Mejino, J.L.V.: A reference ontology for bioinformatics: the Foundational Model of Anatomy. Journal of Biomedical Informatics 36, 478–500 (2003)
15. Deruyver, A., Hodé, Y.: Constraint satisfaction problem with bilevel constraint: application to interpretation of over-segmented images. Artificial Intelligence 93(1), 321–335 (1997)
16. Deruyver, A., Hodé, Y.: Qualitative spatial relationships for image interpretation by using a conceptual graph. Image and Vision Computing 27(7), 876–886 (2009)
17. Dubois, D., Fargier, H., Prade, H.: Possibility theory in constraint satisfaction problems: Handling priority, preference and uncertainty. Applied Intelligence 6(4), 287–309 (1996)
18. Fouquier, G., Atif, J., Bloch, I.: Sequential model-based segmentation and recognition of image structures driven by visual features and spatial relations. Computer Vision and Image Understanding 116(1), 146–165 (2012)
19. Ghorbel, I., Rossant, F., Bloch, I., Pâques, M.: Modeling a parallelism constraint in active contours. Application to the segmentation of eye vessels and retinal layers. In: ICIP 2011, Brussels, Belgium, pp. 453–456 (September 2011)
20. Ghorbel, I., Rossant, F., Bloch, I., Tick, S., Pâques, M.: Automated Segmentation of Macular Layers in Images and Quantitative Evaluation of Performances. Pattern Recognition 44(8), 1590–1603 (2011)
21. Hudelot, C., Atif, J., Bloch, I.: Fuzzy Spatial Relation Ontology for Image Interpretation. Fuzzy Sets and Systems 159, 1929–1951 (2008)
22. Itti, L., Koch, C., Niebur, E.: A model of saliency-based visual attention for rapid scene analysis. IEEE Transactions on Pattern Analysis and Machine Intelligence 20(11), 1254–1259 (1998)
23. Khotanlou, H., Colliot, O., Atif, J., Bloch, I.: 3D Brain Tumor Segmentation in MRI Using Fuzzy Classification, Symmetry Analysis and Spatially Constrained Deformable Models. Fuzzy Sets and Systems 160, 1457–1473 (2009)
24. Kitchen, L.: Discrete relaxation for matching relational structures. IEEE Transactions on Systems, Man, and Cybernetics 9(12), 869–874 (1978)
25. Mohr, R., Henderson, T.C.: Arc and path consistency revisited. Artificial Intelligence 28(2), 225–233 (1986)
26. Moreno, A., Takemura, C.M., Colliot, O., Camara, O., Bloch, I.: Using Anatomical Knowledge Expressed as Fuzzy Constraints to Segment the Heart in CT images. Pattern Recognition 41, 2525–2540 (2008)
27. Nempont, O., Atif, J., Bloch, I.: A constraint propagation approach to structural model based image segmentation and recognition. Information Sciences 246, 1–27 (2013)
28. Perchant, A., Bloch, I.: Fuzzy Morphisms between Graphs. Fuzzy Sets and Systems 128(2), 149–168 (2002)
29. Rosenfeld, A., Hummel, R.A., Zucker, S.W.: Scene labeling by relaxation operations. IEEE Transactions on Systems, Man and Cybernetics 6, 420–433 (1976)
30. Rossi, F., Van Beek, P., Walsh, T.: Handbook of constraint programming. Elsevier (2006)
31. Sowa, J.F.: Conceptual Structures: Information Processing in Mind and Machine. Addison-Wesley, Reading (1984)
32. Srihari, R.K., Zhang, Z.: Show&tell: A semi-automated image annotation system. IEEE Multimedia 7(3), 61–71 (2000)
33. Vanegas, C.: Spatial relations and spatial reasoning for the interpretation of earth observation images using a structural model. Ph.D. thesis, Telecom ParisTech 2011E003 (January 2011)

34. Vanegas, M.C., Bloch, I., Inglada, J.: Alignment and parallelism for the description of high resolution remote sensing images. IEEE Transactions on Geoscience and Remote Sensing 51(6), 3542–3557 (2013)
35. Vanegas, M., Bloch, I., Inglada, J.: A fuzzy definition of the spatial relation "surround" - Application to complex shapes. In: EUSFLAT, pp. 844–851 (2011)
36. Waltz, D.: Understanding line drawings of scenes with shadows. In: The Psychology of Computer Vision, pp. 19–91. McGraw-Hill (1975)
37. Wojak, J., Angelini, E.D., Bloch, I.: Introducing shape constraint via Legendre moments in a variational framework for cardiac segmentation on non-contrast CT images. In: VISAPP, Angers, France, pp. 209–214 (2010)

A Fuzzy System for Background Modeling in Video Sequences

Elisa Calvo-Gallego, Piedad Brox, and Santiago Sánchez-Solano*

Instituto de Microelectrónica de Sevilla (IMSE-CNM), CSIC-University of Seville,
Américo Vespucio s/n, 41092 Seville, Spain
{calvo,brox,santiago}@imse-cnm.csic.es
http://www.imse-cnm.csic.es

Abstract. Many applications in video processing require the background modeling as a first step to detect the moving objects in the scene. This paper presents an approach that calculates the updating weight of a recursive adaptive filter using a fuzzy logic system. Simulation results prove the advantages of the fuzzy approach versus conventional methods such as temporal filters.

Keywords: Background subtraction, moving object detection, video surveillance, fuzzy logic system.

1 Introduction

Background subtraction is a key task in computer vision. In fact, this is the first step to detect moving objects in video taken from a stationary camera. The detection of moving objects is required in many applications such as video surveillance, traffic monitoring, tracking humans, shadow detection or optical motion capture. The aim of background subtraction is to separate the moving objects (foreground) from the static image areas (background). This process is illustrated for a frame with one moving object in Figure 1(a).

Background subtraction is a topic that has been widely considered in the literature [1],[2]. The simplest way to model the background is to get a frame of the scene without moving objects. However, this is not always useful due to several factors. For instance, a frequent situation is a moving object that suddenly stops becoming a part of the next background. This situation is illustrated in Figure 1(b) where a car is incorporated to the background scene after parking. Ideally, a background representation model should be adaptive and robust enough to be insensitive to variations, such as for instance, changes of illumination, addition or removal of stationary objects, shadows of moving objects, or complex non-static backgrounds.

* This work was partially supported by TEC2011-24319 and IPT-2012-0695-390000 projects from the Spanish Government, and P08-TIC-03674 project from the Andalusian Regional Government (all with support from FEDER). E. Calvo-Gallego is supported under the FPU fellowship from the Spanish Government. P. Brox is supported under the program called Juan de la Cierva from the Spanish Government.

F. Masulli, G. Pasi, and R. Yager (Eds.): WILF 2013, LNAI 8256, pp. 184–192, 2013.

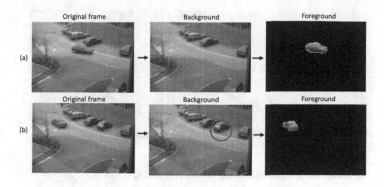

Fig. 1. An example of a modification in the background: (a) The moving object is the car before parking. (b) The car is incorporated to the background after parking.

In basic background modeling methods, background is generated using an average, a median [3]-[4], or a histogram analysis over time. For instance, if a mean filter is selected the background model is obtained as follows:

$$B(x,y,t) = \frac{1}{N} \sum_{i=1}^{N} I(x,y,t-i) \tag{1}$$

where $B(x,y,t)$ is the background model for a pixel with coordinates (x,y,t) in the frame t, N is the number of frames considered in the time domain, and $I(x,y,t-i)$ is the luminance value of the pixel with the same spatial coordinates (x,y) in the frame t-i.

Figure 2 shows the background obtained after applying a temporal mean (top) and a median filter (bottom) using different values of N. As it can be corroborated, the performance of both kinds of filtering is very dependent on the value of N. Usually, a large value of N is required to achieve acceptable results. Otherwise, a ghosting effect appears in areas of the frame where the moving objects were situated in the previous frames. The correct value of N, which provides a good background modeling, depends on the video sequence. For instance, N≥9 for the median filter is an adequate value for the sequence in Figure 2. From a hardware point of view, the use of a large value of N implies more memory resources in terms of frame buffers. This is a very important limitation for embedded platforms that include limited resources.

A well-known group of background subtraction techniques is based on statistical modeling [5],[6]. The background is represented using a single Gaussian probality density function on the last pixel values [7], a mixture of Gaussians [8], or a Kernel Density Estimation [9]. In practical cases, the model in [8] requires between 3 and 5 Gaussian distributions. In [9], the background distribution is given by a sum of Gaussian kernels centered in the most recent n background values, being n as high as 100. This high memory requirement makes its implementation unfeasible on embedded systems with low-memory resources. Other remarkable

Fig. 2. (a) Original frame. Filtering with: (b) N=3, (c) N=5, (d) N=7,(e) N=9.

background subtraction techniques use clustering[10], neural networks[11], or predictive filters [12] to model background.

The main difficulties in developing a background subtraction method are the presence of illumination changes and dynamic backgrounds. Both critical situations generate imprecise and uncertain situations that can be handled with fuzzy logic-based techniques. Some authors have proposed the use of fuzzy logic to provide background subtraction methods with a good model accuracy [13]. Type-2 Fuzzy Gaussian Mixture Models allow to model robustly dynamic backgrounds [14]. For foreground detection, the use of a linear saturation function avoids crisp decision in the classification [15]. Fuzzy integrals (Sugeno and Choquet integrals) consider the color and texture features to deal with illumination changes and shadows [16]. Fuzzy adaptive learning rates are able to deal with the critical situations providing an accuracy background model [17].

Background modelling techniques can be classified as recursive or non-recursive. Clearly, example of non-recursive techniques are temporal mean- and median-based algorithms. Recursive techniques recursively update a single background model based on each input frame [7]. In each frame, pixels are recursively updated using a simple adaptive filter:

$$B(x, y, t) = \alpha \cdot I(x, y, t) + (1 - \alpha) \cdot B(x, y, t - 1) \qquad (2)$$

where α is an empirical weight that allows to establish a trade-off between stability and quick update. The performance of this technique relies on the selection of a correct value of α. The updating process, with an accurate value of α allows the compensation for changes in illumination and object movement. Our approach aims to improve the recursive model in equation (2) by using a simple fuzzy logic system. The idea is to calculate a robust value of α using a fuzzy system that is able to model uncertainties in the scene. This paper is organized as follows. Section 2 describes the fuzzy logic-based approach and the tuning of parameters. Simulations of car traffic videos are included in Section 3. Finally, the conclusions of this work are expounded in Section 4.

2 Fuzzy Logic-Based System for Background Modeling

2.1 Description

The aim of this fuzzy system is to model the background dynamically. In order to detect the moving objects, each pixel of the current frame is evaluated to measure the difference with the previous frame:

$$d(x, y, t) = abs(I(x, y, t) - I(x, y, t - 1)) \tag{3}$$

where $I(x,y,t)$ is the luminance value at the current frame and $I(x,y,t-1)$ is the luminance of the pixel with the same spatial coordinates in the previous frame. This measurement is not robust enough since the presence of noise or illumination variations can introduce mistakes. For this reason, we have assumed that a moving object in the scene is composed of a set of pixels, that is, the movement should be detected in the current pixel as well as in its surroundings to be declared as a moving object. Our approach takes into account the above considerations by using a bi-dimensional convolution,

$$d\_conv(x, y, t) = \frac{\sum_{i=1}^{3}(\sum_{j=1}^{3} D_{i,j} \cdot C_{i,j})}{\sum_{i=1}^{3}\sum_{j=1}^{3} C_{i,j}} \tag{4}$$

where $D_{i,j}$ are the elements of the following frame difference matrix

$$D = \begin{pmatrix} d(x-1, y-1, t) & d(x, y-1, t) & d(x+1, y-1, t) \\ d(x-1, y, t) & d(x, y, t) & d(x+1, y, t) \\ d(x-1, y+1, t) & d(x, y+1, t) & d(x+1, y+1, t) \end{pmatrix} \tag{5}$$

and $C_{i,j}$ are the elements of the following weight matrix:

$$C = \begin{pmatrix} 1 & 2 & 1 \\ 2 & 3 & 2 \\ 1 & 2 & 1 \end{pmatrix} \tag{6}$$

whose values have been assigned giving more relevance to the current pixel and the nearest pixels to it.

The measure of frame difference in equation (4) is the input of a fuzzy logic-based system with one input and one output. In the fuzzification stage, the membership values of the (d_conv) signal to two fuzzy sets associated to the linguistic label SMALL and LARGE are calculated. The membership functions of these fuzzy sets are piece-wise linear, as shown in Figure 3(a). This shape is chosen since it is easily implemented in software and hardware implementations. Because of linguistic coherence, both membership functions, SMALL and LARGE, should be complementary. To model the background, the following knowledge base is applied (see Figure 3(b)):

1. When the d_conv signal at the current pixel is SMALL, the consequent asserts that a linear interpolation between the luminance of the current pixel

and the luminance of this pixel in the previous frame is the best way to model the background. A priori, there is no reason to give more importance to the luminance of the current pixel since d_conv is SMALL.

2. When the d_conv signal at the current pixel is LARGE, the consequent states that the previous background is the best solution.

The new value for the background model is calculated by applying the Fuzzy Mean defuzzification method (with corresponds to a weighted average), as follows:

$$B(x,y,t) = \alpha_1 \cdot (0.5 \cdot I(x,y,t) + 0.5 \cdot I(x,y,t-1)) + \alpha_2 \cdot B(x,y,t-1) \quad (7)$$

where α_1 and α_2 are the activation degrees of the first and the second rule, respectively. Since both membership functions are complementary, that is, their superposition is always the unitary value, only one of the rules has to be processed and the expression in (7) can be replaced as follows:

$$B(x,y,t) = \alpha_1 \cdot (0.5 \cdot I(x,y,t) + 0.5 \cdot I(x,y,t-1)) + (1-\alpha_1) \cdot B(x,y,t-1) \quad (8)$$

If the expression in (2) is compared with equation (8), we can conclude that the fuzzy approach implements a recursive adaptive filter but now with continuous values of α. This means that the output of the fuzzy system implements a recursive adaptive filter where the value of α is calculated as the activation degree of the second rule. Since the membership functions are piecewise-linear, the transition between the value '0' and '1' of α is linear with the frame difference.

2.2   Tuning of the Membership Function Parameters

Heuristic knowledge does not provide enough information to determine the values of the antecedents that describe the fuzzy sets in Figure 3(a). In order to obtain these values, we have employed a tuning process by using the well-Known supervised learning Marquardt-Levenberg algorithm within of the fuzzy system development environment Xfuzzy 3.3 [18],[19]. Several training files are generated for each video test sequence. These files are sets of inputs/output patterns where the desired output is obtained from the ideal background (a frame where

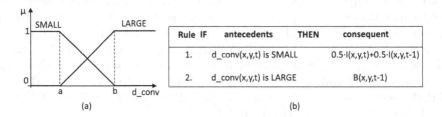

(a)   (b)

Fig. 3. (a) Membership functions for the SMALL and LARGE fuzzy concepts. (b) Fuzzy rule set.

Name of the sequence	Viptraffic	Video	Pets 2006	Highway1	Highway2	iRacing1	iRacing2
Number of used frames	90	90	90	90	90	90	74
Used frames resolution	161 x 120	321 x 176	352 x 238	596 x 190	596 x 190	1280 x 720	1280 x 720
Light	Shadowy	Shadowy	Shadowy - Illuminated	Illuminated	Illuminated	Illuminated	Illuminated
Shadows	Low	Low	Low	High	Medium	Low	Low
Speed of objects	Medium-High	Medium	Low	Low - Medium	High	Medium	Medium-High
Objects in movement	0-4	0-3	1	1-9	1-9	1	1
Dinamical Background	✗	✗	✓	✗	✗	✗	✗

Fig. 4. Characteristics of the video test sequences

appears the truly motionless elements of the scene). After the learning process, for each sequence, two values, a and b, have been obtained and a test, with all combinations in learned antecedents and sequences, has been carried out. Results prove that the best performace was achived, in all cases, with one of this two pairs (a,b): $(12,70)$ and $(1.3,14.4)$. The consequentes of the rules have been included in the learning process without obtaining sucessful results. This means that the tuned parameters for the consequents provide poor simulation results. Before learning, the values of the parameters were $(10,20)$. These initial values were approximately adjusted after a manual process.

3   Simulation Results

The performance of the fuzzy approach has been analyzed by modeling seven car traffic video sequences. The main characteristics of these video sequences are shown in Figure 4. Mean Squared Error (MSE) between the ideal and modeled background is used as figure of merit to measure the quality of the algorithm:

$$MSE(t) = \frac{1}{M \cdot N} \sum_{x,y} (B(x,y,t) - B_{ideal}(x,y,t))^2 \qquad (9)$$

where the frame has a resolution of $M \cdot N$ pixels, $B(x,y,t)$ is the value of the pixel in the background model, and $B_{ideal}(x,y,t)$ is the pixel value in an ideal background (it has been obtained directly from a frame of the sequence without moving objects or removing these objects manually). Strongly related to the MSE is the PSNR, which is:

$$PSNR(t) = 20 \cdot log \frac{255}{\sqrt{MSE(t)}} \qquad (10)$$

Actually a unique PSNR value is not meaningful, but the comparison between two values gives a measurement of quality. Generally, an improvement of 0.5dBs in PSNR is quite perceptible by the human visual system. Figure 5 shows the average PSNR values obtained after processing 90 frames of the sequences. The fuzzy approach clearly improves the results obtained by the crisp version. Furthermore, the tuning process outperforms the results achieved by the initial fuzzy approach. For PETS2006 and Highway1 sequences, the first pair of tuned

Method \ Name of the sequence	Viptraffic	Video	Pets2006	Highway1	Highway2	iRacing1	iRacing2
Crisp approach	24,67	26,65	28,80	18,11	21,43	38,42	29,85
Fuzzy approach before learning	24,91	26,86	28,89	18,39	21,80	38,70	30,16
Fuzzy approach after learning 1	23,56	27,05	29,28	19,03	21,05	36,92	28,70
Fuzzy approach after learning 2	25,96	27,84	28,93	18,51	23,79	40,12	32,04

Fig. 5. PSNR results (in dBs) for the crisp and fuzzy approaches

parameters gives a better performance. The second pair of tuned parameters provides better results in the rest of sequences. The selection of one pair of tuned parameters or the another one depends on the own features of the sequence.

Figure 6(a) illustrates the background model obtained for one frame in the 'viptraffic' sequence. In Figure 6(b), a comparative table with the background modeling based on the mean and median filtering is shown. The results prove that the fuzzy approach clearly outperforms all the temporal filters with less than nine frames in 'highway2' sequence.

4   Conclusions

A recursive background modeling approach, which uses a simple fuzzy logic system to calculate the value of the updating parameter, is presented in this paper. Simulation results prove the clear advantages of the fuzzy approach versus a crisp version. The performance of the fuzzy approach improves after a tuning stage of the parameters. In comparison with temporal techniques, the fuzzy approach outperforms these conventional techniques when eight frames or less are used

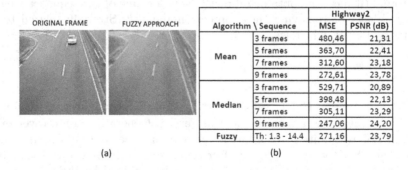

Algorithm \ Sequence		Highway2	
		MSE	PSNR (dB)
Mean	3 frames	480,46	21,31
	5 frames	363,70	22,41
	7 frames	312,60	23,18
	9 frames	272,61	23,78
Median	3 frames	529,71	20,89
	5 frames	398,48	22,13
	7 frames	305,11	23,29
	9 frames	247,06	24,20
Fuzzy	Th: 1.3 - 14.4	271,16	23,79

(a)   (b)

Fig. 6. (a) Resultant background for the frame 10 in the viptraffic sequence. (b) MSE and PSNR results (in dBs) for different background modeling algorithms.

in the temporal filtering. The proposed technique offers an accurate background modelling that is suitable for embedded platforms with limited resources since only two frame buffers are required for its implementation.

References

1. Piccardi, M.: Background Subtraction Techniques: a Review. In: IEEE International Conference Systems, Man, Cybernetics (SMC) 2004, pp. 3099–3104. IEEE Press, New York (2004)
2. Hassanpour, H.: Video Frame's Background Modeling: Reviewing the Techniques. Journal of Signal and Information 2(2), 72–78 (2011)
3. Lo, B.P.L., Velastin, S.A.: Automatic Congestion Detection System for Underground Platforms. In: International Symposium on Intelligent Multimedia, Video and Speech Processing (ISIMP) 2001, pp. 158–161. IEEE Press, New York (2001)
4. Cucchiara, R., Grana, C., Piccardi, M., Prati, A.: Detecting Moving Objects, Ghosts, Shadows in Video Streams. IEEE Transactions on Pattern Analysis and Machine Intelligence 25(10), 1337–1342 (2003)
5. Bouwmans, T., El Baf, F., Vachon, B.: Statistical Background Modeling for Foreground Detection: A Survey. In: Handbook of Pattern Recognition and Computer Vision, vol. 4, ch. 3, part 2, pp. 181–199. World Scientific Publishing (2010)
6. Bouwmans, T.: Recent advanced statistical background modeling for foreground detection: A systematic survey. Recent Patents on Computer Science 4(3) (September 2011)
7. Wren, C., Azarbayejani, A., Darrel, T., Pentland, A.P.: Pfinder: Real-time Tracking of the Human Body. IEEE Transactions on Pattern Analysis and Machine Intelligence 19(7), 780–785 (1997)
8. Stauffer, C., Grimson, W.E.L.: Adaptive Background Mixture Models for Real-time Tracking. In: Computer Society Conference on Computer Vision and Pattern Recognition (CVPR) 1999, pp. 246–252. IEEE Press, New York (1999)
9. Elgammal, A., Harwood, D., Davis, L.: Non-parametric Model for Background Subtraction. In: Vernon, D. (ed.) ECCV 2000, Part II. LNCS, vol. 1843, pp. 751–767. Springer, Heidelberg (2000)
10. Butler, D., Bove, V., Shridharan, S.: Real Time Adaptive Foreground/Background Segmentation. In: EURASIP, pp. 2292–2304 (2005)
11. Culbrik, D., Marques, O., Socek, D., Kalva, H., Furht, B.: Neural Network Approach to Background Modeling for Video Object Segmentation. IEEE Transaction on Neural Networks 18(6), 1614–1627 (2007)
12. Messelodi, S., Modena, C.M., Segata, N., Zanin, M.: A Kalman Filter Based Background Updating Algorithm Robust to Sharp Illumination Changes. In: Roli, F., Vitulano, S. (eds.) ICIAP 2005. LNCS, vol. 3617, pp. 163–170. Springer, Heidelberg (2005)
13. Bouwmans, T.: Background Subtraction For Visual Surveillance: A Fuzzy Approach. In: Handbook on Soft Computing for Video Surveillance, ch. 5, pp. 103–138. Taylor and Francis Group (2012)
14. Bouwmans, T., El Baf, E.F.: Modeling of Dynamic Backgrounds by Type-2 Fuzzy Gaussians Mixture Models. MASAUM Journal of Basics and Applied Sciences 1(2), 265–277 (2009)
15. Maddalena, L., Petrosino, A.: A Fuzzy Spatial Coherence-Based Approach to Bbackground/Foreground Separation for Moving Object Detection. In: Neural Computing and Applications, vol. 19, pp. 179–186. Springer, London (2010)

16. El Baf, F., Bouwmans, T., Vachon, B.: Fuzzy Integral for Moving Object Detection. In: International Conference on Fuzzy Systems (FUZZ-IEEE), pp. 1729–1736. IEEE Press, New York (2008)
17. Sigari, M., Mozayani, N., Pourreza, H.: Fuzzy Running Average and Fuzzy Background Subtraction: Concepts and Application. International Journal of Computer Science and Network Security 8(2), 138–143 (2008)
18. Baturone, I., Moreno-Velo, F.J., Sánchez-Solano, S., Barriga, A., Brox, P., Gersnoviez, A., Brox, M.: Using Xfuzzy Environment for the Whole Design of Fuzzy Systems. In: International Conference on Fuzzy Systems (FUZZ-IEEE), IEEE Press, New York (2007)
19. Fuzzy Logic Design Tools, http://www2.imse-cnm.csic.es/Xfuzzy/

Shape Annotation by Incremental Semi-supervised Fuzzy Clustering

Giovanna Castellano[1], Anna Maria Fanelli[1], and Maria Alessandra Torsello[2]

[1] Computer Science Department, University of Bari,
Via E. Orabona, 4 - 70126 Bari, Italy
{castellano,fanelli}@di.uniba.it

[2] Dep. of Informatics, Systems and Communication, University of Milano Bicocca
Viale Sarca, 336 - 20126 Milano, Italy
torsello@disco.unimib.it

Abstract. Automatic image annotation is an important and challenging task when managing large image collections. In this paper, we present an incremental approach for shape labeling, which is useful to image annotation when new sets of images are available during time. Every time new shape images are available, a semi-supervised fuzzy clustering algorithm is used to group shapes into a number of clusters by exploiting knowledge about classes expressed as a set of pre-labeled shapes. Each cluster is represented by a prototype that is manually labeled and used to annotate shapes. To capture the evolution of the image set, the previously discovered prototypes are added as pre-labeled shapes to the current shape set before clustering. The performance of the proposed incremental approach is evaluated on an image dataset from the fish domain, which is divided into chunks of data to simulate the progressive availability of shapes during time.

Keywords: image annotation, shape clustering, semi-supervised fuzzy clustering, incremental fuzzy clustering.

1 Introduction

With the advances of multimedia technologies and the availability of image capturing devices, the size of digital image collections has been increasing rapidly. In this scenario, the development of systems able to efficiently retrieve images in large collections is mandatory. Content-based image retrieval (CBIR) was proposed to allow users retrieve relevant images from large collections using visual features such as color, texture and shape [15], [12]. However, retrieval results of CBIR systems are not always satisfactory because humans recognize and describe images based on high-level concepts. This problem, known as "semantic gap" [15], can be addressed by image annotation, that is based on learning the correspondence between visual features and semantics of images.

The choice of visual features is a central tenet in image annotation. Several works have proved that visual features such as color, texture, and positioning,

F. Masulli, G. Pasi, and R. Yager (Eds.): WILF 2013, LNAI 8256, pp. 193–200, 2013.

though important, are insufficient to convey the information that could be obtained through shape analysis of objects contained into images [3], [16]. Shape plays a critical role for the representation of objects contained into images becoming a key feature exploited for indexing and retrieval purposes.

Annotation of images on the basis of shapes can be essentially viewed as a classification process. For each shape, its membership to a semantic category is derived according to certain similarity measures. Then the shape is classified into one of the considered categories. This process can be performed by means of supervised or unsupervised learning algorithms. Supervised techniques require labeled training data to perform classification, but providing these data is a very tedious and error-prone task, especially for large image database. Unsupervised learning techniques overcome these limitations. Specifically, clustering algorithms are applied to group unlabeled shapes so that shapes that are visually similar are supposed to have similar semantic content and thus they are arranged into the same cluster. A textual label descriptive of a semantic category can be associated to each cluster. Thus, a new unlabeled shape can be labeled by associating it to the cluster that best matches the considered shape. In [5] we proposed a shape annotation approach that uses unsupervised fuzzy clustering to derive prototypes that are manually annotated by textual labels corresponding to semantic categories. Thus, a new shape is automatically labeled by associating a fuzzy set that provides membership degrees of the shape to all semantic classes. However, unsupervised clustering methods often generate inconsistent clusters including shapes that, although visually similar, actually belong to different categories.

Generally, a large number of unlabeled images are available, whereas only a limited number of labeled reference shapes can be obtained since it is usually expensive and time consuming to collect them. This has recently motivated an increasing number of research interests in the semi-supervised learning (SSL) paradigm [7], which aims to improve the classifier performance by learning from a combination of both labeled samples and unlabeled data. Along with this idea, in [6] we proposed a shape annotation approach that employs a fuzzy clustering algorithm equipped with a partial supervision mechanism to derive consistent clusters of shapes. The adopted clustering technique, hereafter called SSFCM (Semi-Supervised FCM) is a modified version of the FCM algorithm originally proposed in [13]. SSFCM exploits domain knowledge about classes expressed as a set of pre-labeled data. Using SSFCM, in [6] we grouped all the available shapes into clusters according to their similarity as well as to a-priori knowledge about categories of some shapes. Then, a label was associated to each derived cluster. In this way an entire database of shapes was annotated in a single clustering step. However the single step approach is not always usable in the context of image annotation, as it assumes that the entire collection is available before clustering, while all images may not be available at the beginning of the analysis. Therefore, when new shapes are added to the collection, the static annotation scheme developed in [6] rebuilds the clusters starting from scratch by reprocessing the whole collection, i.e. it does not take advantage of the previously built clusters. According to such a scheme, the SSFCM algorithm is applied to chunks of shapes rather than to the entire dataset. This enables annotation of shapes when new images are continuously available over time.

The paper is organized as follows. Section 2 describes the incremental scheme for shape annotation. In sections 3 we provide some preliminary simulation results. Finally, section 4 concludes the paper.

2   Incremental Scheme for Shape Annotation

We assume that object shapes have already been extracted from the images and the shapes are available in form of contours. Of course, in many applications extraction of contours itself is a difficult problem but our focus here is on annotating shapes once the contours are extracted. Therefore we consider object shapes that are described by boundary coordinates. To represent shape boundaries, we use Fourier descriptors that are well-recognized to provide robustness and invariance, obtaining good effectiveness in shape-based indexing and retrieval [2]. Thus each shape is described by means of M Fourier descriptors and denoted by $\mathbf{x} = (x_1, x_2, ..., x_M)$.

The proposed scheme for incremental shape annotation is based on the assumption that sets of shapes belonging to C categories are available during time and processed as chunks, that is, N_1 shapes are available at time t_1, N_2 at t_2 and so on. We denote by X_t the set of shapes available at time t.

The shape chunks are processed as they are made available, by applying the SSFCM algorithm adopted in [6] to each chunk, as described in section 2.1.

As with any c-means approach, we need to fix the number of clusters each time the SSFCM algorithm is applied to a chunk. We established to set the number of clusters K to be always equal to the number of classes C. This does not cause any information loss. Indeed, if shapes in a chunk come from less than C classes, then we are overclustering the data, but overclustering does not cause any information loss. Information loss only occurs when we undercluster the data. If data in a chunk belong exactly to C classes, then we are partitioning the data correctly, that is, neither overclustering nor underclustering.

Each time a chunk is clustered, the output partition is condensed into K labeled prototypes. To capture the evolution of the image set, the prototypes discovered on one shape chunk are added as pre-labeled shapes to the next data chunk. Precisely, when the first chunk of shapes is available, the algorithm will cluster the chunk into K clusters and it will derive a set of K shape prototypes that are manually labeled. When a second or later chunk of shapes is available, it will be clustered with the labeled prototypes derived from the previous clustered chunks[1]. After each clustering process, the discovered prototypes are used to annotate all the available shapes. Specifically, each shape is annotated with the label of the best matching prototype, where matching is based on computing Euclidean distance between the shape descriptors and the prototype descriptors.

---

[1] How many chunks of history to use for clustering with a new chunk is predefined by the user.

Algorithm 1. Incremental shape annotation

Require: X: dataset;
Ensure: P: set of labeled prototypes;
 1: $H \leftarrow \emptyset$ /* Initialization of history */
 2: $t \leftarrow 1$ /* Initialization of time step */
 3: **while** $\exists$ non empty data chunk X_t **do**
 4: $X_t \leftarrow X_t \cup H$ /* Add the history to the current data chunk; */
 5: Cluster X_t with SSFCM;
 6: Derive the set P of labeled prototypes;
 7: Annotate shapes in $\bigcup_{\tau=1}^{t} X_\tau$ using P;
 8: Update H with P;
 9: $t := t + 1$
10: **end while**
11: **return** P

The overall scheme of the proposed incremental approach is summarized in algorithm 1.

2.1 Shape Clustering by SSFCM

The SSFCM algorithm works in the same manner as FCM [4], i.e. it iteratively derives K clusters by minimizing an objective function. To embed partial supervision in the clustering process, the objective function of SSFCM includes a supervised learning component, as follows:

$$J = \sum_{k=1}^{K} \sum_{j=1}^{N_t} u_{jk}^m d_{jk}^2 + \alpha \sum_{k=1}^{K} \sum_{j=1}^{N_t} (u_{jk} - b_j f_{jk})^m d_{jk}^2 \qquad (1)$$

where

$$b_j = \begin{cases} 1 & \text{if shape } \mathbf{x}_j \text{ is labeled} \\ 0 & \text{otherwise} \end{cases} \qquad (2)$$

f_{jk} denote the true membership values of the labeled shapes to the categories, d_{jk} represents the Euclidean distance between the shape $\mathbf{x}_j$ and the center of the k-th cluster, m is the fuzzification coefficient ($m \geq 2$) and α is a parameter that serves as a weight to balance the supervised and unsupervised components of the objective function. The higher the value of α, the higher the impact coming from the supervised component is. The second term of J captures the difference among the true membership of shapes f_{jk} and the membership u_{jk} computed by the algorithm. The aim to be reached is that, for the labeled shapes, these values should coincide.

As described in [13], the problem of optimizing the objective function J is converted into the form of unconstrained minimization using the standard technique of Lagrange multipliers. More specifically, by setting the fuzzification coefficient m to 2, the objective function is minimized by updating membership values u_{jk}

according to:

$$u_{jk} = \frac{1}{1+\alpha} \left[\frac{1 + \alpha(1 - b_j \sum_{l=1}^{K} f_{lk})}{\sum_{l=1}^{K} d_{jk}^2 / d_{lk}^2} \right] + \alpha b_j f_{jk} \tag{3}$$

and the centers of clusters according to:

$$c_k = \frac{\sum_{j=1}^{N_t} u_{jk}^m x_j}{\sum_{j=1}^{N} u_{jk}^m} \tag{4}$$

The clustering process ends when the difference between the values of J in two consecutive iterations drops below a prefixed threshold or when the established maximum iteration number is reached.

Once the clustering process is completed, a prototype is identified for each cluster. We define the prototypes as medoids (i.e. shapes that belong to the dataset) rather than means to allow a better interpretation of annotation results. Specifically we consider the shape with the highest membership to a cluster as prototype for that cluster. Then, each prototype is manually associated to a label corresponding to a specific shape category.

Summarizing, the result of SSFCM applied to each chunk is a set $P = \{p_1, p_2, ..., p_K\}$ of K labeled prototypes that are used to annotate shapes. Namely, all shapes belonging to cluster k are labeled by using the text label associated to prototype p_k.

3   Simulation Results

To assess the suitability of the proposed approach, we applied it to the Surrey Fish dataset [1]. consisting of 1,100 shape images, each image expressing the coordinates of boundary points of a marine animal silouette. In these preliminary experiments we employed a portion of the dataset composed of 265 shapes that have been manually classified into 10 different semantic categories, as follows: "Seamoths" (11), "Sharks" (58), "Soles" (52), "Tonguefishes" (19), "Crustaceans" (11), "Eels" (26), "U-Eels" (20), "Pipefishes" (16), "Seahorses" (11) and "Rays" (41). Figure 1 shows some images in the considered data set portion, along with their respective classes.

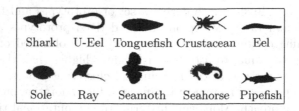

Fig. 1. Sample images from the Surrey Fish dataset

Similarly to [10], to evaluate our clustering algorithms, we used the average purity of the obtained clusters, a measure that evaluates the clustering quality. Precisely, the average purity error is defined as follows:

$$pur = 1 - \frac{1}{K} \times \sum_{k=1}^{K} \frac{|C_k^d|}{|C_k|}$$

where K denotes the number of clusters, $|C_k^d|$ denotes the number of points with the dominant class label in cluster k and $|C_k|$ denotes the number of shapes in cluster k.

In all the experiments reported hereafter, the algorithm was parameterized as follows: the number of cluster K was always set to the number of classes in the dataset (i.e. $K = 10$), the fuzzification coefficient m was set to 2, the data chunk size was set to 53 shapes (5 chunks were built starting from the considered data set), the history is set to 1, meaning that only the prototypes from the previous data chunks are taken into account. As the SSFCM is not deterministic (because of the random initialization of the centers), the results presented were averaged over 10 runs.

At the first time t_1, we applied the SSFCM to the union of the first two chunks ($N_1 = 106$) in order to obtain more stable and significant initial prototypes that can be exploited in the next steps of the incremental clustering process. In this way, our experiments concerned 4 different time steps. After clustering a chunk, 10 prototypes were derived and manually annotated by associating to each of them a label related to the corresponding semantic class. Prototypes derived at each time were used to annotate all shapes included in the chunks employed in the previous time step. Specifically, the Euclidean distance between descriptors of each shape and each prototype was computed and the shape was added to the cluster corresponding to the prototype with the minimum distance value and annotated with the respective label. Hence, the quality of the new shape partition was evaluated by computing the average purity error. In Fig. 2 we show the values of the average purity error obtained in each time after clustering each chunk and annotating all shapes contained in the chunks considered in the previous times.

To evaluate the effectiveness of the proposed incremental approach, we compared the average purity error obtained by the incremental clustering process in correspondence of the last time step with the average purity error obtained by applying the SSFCM algorithm in a one-shot way following the experimental procedure described in [6]. Specifically, SSFCM was applied to a portion of the data set including 240 shapes to derive a set of prototypes and the remaining 25 shapes were annotated by exploiting the derived prototypes and added to the corresponding clusters. The average purity error obtained on the derived shape partition was equal to 0.16 that is slightly higher than the purity error (0.14) obtained at the end of the incremental clustering process. This demonstrates that the proposed incremental approach for annotation outperforms the static one-shot approach. Moreover, in terms of computational time, the one-shot approach is faster than the incremental clustering scheme. However, the

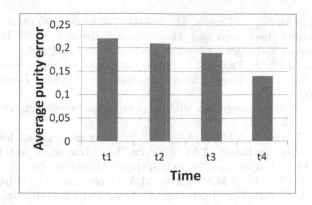

Fig. 2. Average purity errors obtained at each time instant

incremental approach has the advantage to be able to update prototypes when new chunks of data are available. Finally, the incremental approach can take advantage of the previously built clusters and prototypes when new shapes are added to the collection while the static annotation scheme needs to rebuild the clusters starting from scratch by reprocessing the whole collection.

4   Conclusions

In this paper, an incremental scheme for shape annotation has been proposed. The approach exploits a semi-supervised fuzzy clustering algorithm to derive a set of prototypes representative of a number of semantic categories. The derived prototypes are manually annotated by attaching labels related to semantic categories. The use of shape prototypes, which represent an intermediate level of visual signatures, facilitates the annotation process, since only a reduced number of shapes need to be manually annotated. Secondly, the use of prototypes simplifies the search process in a retrieval system. Indeed, since any single user query is likely to match with high degree only a small number of objects, a large number of unnecessary comparisons is avoided during search by performing matching with shape prototypes rather than with specific shapes.

Results on a benchmark dataset containing shapes of marine animals show that the incremental approach produces partitions which are very close to partitions obtained by one-shot approach that clusters all the data at one time. These preliminary results encourage the application of the proposed approach to wider contexts.

References

1. Abbasi, S., Mokhtarian, F., Kittler, J.: SQUID Demo Dataset 1,500 (1997), http://www.ee.surrey.ac.uk/Research/VSSP/imagedb/demo.html

2. Bartolini, I., Ciaccia, P., Patella, M.: WARP: Accurate retrieval of shapes using phase of Fourier descriptors and Time warping distance. IEEE Transaction on Pattern Analysis and Machine Intelligence 27(1), 142–147 (2005)
3. Belongie, S., Malik, J., Puzicha, J.: Shape matching and object recognition using shape contexts. IEEE Trans. Pattern Analysis and Machine Intelligence 24(4), 509–522 (2002)
4. Bezdek, J.C.: Pattern recognition with fuzzy objective function algorithms. Plenum Press, New York (1981)
5. Castellano, G., Fanelli, A.M., Torsello, M.A.: A fuzzy set approach for shape-based image annotation. In: Fanelli, A.M., Pedrycz, W., Petrosino, A. (eds.) WILF 2011. LNCS (LNAI), vol. 6857, pp. 236–243. Springer, Heidelberg (2011)
6. Castellano, G., Fanelli, A.M., Torsello, M.A.: Fuzzy image labeling by partially supervised shape clustering. In: König, A., Dengel, A., Hinkelmann, K., Kise, K., Howlett, R.J., Jain, L.C. (eds.) KES 2011, Part II. LNCS, vol. 6882, pp. 84–93. Springer, Heidelberg (2011)
7. Chapelle, O., Schoelkopf, B., Zien, A.: Semi-Supervised Learning. MIT Press, Cambridge (2006)
8. Guha, S., Meyerson, A., Mishra, N., Motwani, R., O'Callaghan, L.: Clustering data streams: Theory and practice. IEEE Trans. on Knowledge and Data Engineering 15(3), 515–528 (2003)
9. Hore, P., Hall, L., Goldgof, D., Cheng, W.: Online fuzzy c means. In: Fuzzy Information Processing Society, NAFIPS 2008, pp. 1–5 (2008)
10. Cao, F., Ester, M., Qian, W., Zhou, A.: Density-based clustering over an evolving data stream with noise. In: 2006 SIAM Conference on Data Mining, pp. 328–339 (2006)
11. Yixin, C., Tu, L.: Density-based clustering for real-time stream data. In: Proceedings of the 13th ACM SIGKDD International Conference on Knowledge Discovery and Data Mining, pp. 133–142. ACM (2007)
12. Lew, M., Sebe, N., Djeraba, C., Lifl, F., Ramesh, J.: Content-based Multimedia Information Retrieval: State of the Art and Challenges. ACM Transactions on Multimedia Computing, Communications, and Applications, 1–19 (2006)
13. Pedrycz, W., Waletzky, J.: Fuzzy clustering with partial supervision. IEEE Transaction System Man Cybernetics 27(5), 787–795 (1997)
14. Ruiz, C., Menasalvas, E., Spiliopoulou, M.: C-denStream: Using domain knowledge on a data stream. In: Gama, J., Costa, V.S., Jorge, A.M., Brazdil, P.B. (eds.) DS 2009. LNCS, vol. 5808, pp. 287–301. Springer, Heidelberg (2009)
15. Smeulders, A.W.M., Worring, M., Santini, S., Gupta, A., Jain, R.: Content-based image retrieval at the end of the early years. IEEE Trans. Pattern Analisys and Machine Intelligence 22(12), 1349–1380 (2000)
16. Veltkamp, R., Tanase, M.: Content-based image retrieval systems: a survey. Technical Report (2001)
17. Wu, J., Xiong, H., Chen, J.: Adapting the right measures for k-means clustering. In: Proceedings of the KDD 2009 Conference, pp. 877–885. ACM (2009)

Proficiency of Fuzzy Logic Controller for Stabilization of Rotary Inverted Pendulum based on LQR Mapping

Moez Ul Hassan[1,2], Muhammad B. Kadri[1], and Imran Amin[2]

[1] Electronics and Power Engineering Department
PN Engineering College, National University of Sciences and Technology, Islamabad, Pakistan
{moezulhassan,bilal.kadri}@gmail.com
[2] Centre of Renewable Energy Research, SZABIST Karachi, Pakistan
amin.imran@gmail.com

Abstract. Stabilization of an inverted pendulum is one of the most appealing and conventional problem for control engineering. This system has extremely nonlinear representation and entirely unstable dynamics. The main idea of this research was to design control algorithms for the balancing of rotary inverted pendulum.

Research gives an idea about a convenient approach to implement a real-time control which harmonizes the pendulum in vertical-upright position. Two stabilization controllers, LQR (Linear Quadratic Regulator) and Fuzzy Logic were designed to deal with the non-linear characteristics of the system.

Outcome of both control methods commencing computer simulation are specified to illustrate the efficiency of these controllers. The projected intelligent hybrid controller is evaluated by means of the conventional controller and reliability is demonstrated. The results showed that fuzzy controller exhibit improved performance than LQR near the linearized region.

The paper widened the dynamical representation and initiates the implementation of the considered schemes comparatively.

Keywords: rotary inverted pendulum, stabilization, LQR, fuzzy logic controller, simulink.

1   Introduction

The control of under actuated system is currently a dynamic field of research which is appropriate to the broad application in electromechanical systems like aerospace, robotics and marine vehicles. Pattern of under actuated systems comprised of flexible-link robots, walking robots, acrobatic robots, space robots, helicopters, satellites, under actuated marine vehicles, the pendubot, spacecraft's etc[1]. Under actuated systems comprised into eight classes [2]. The paper demonstrates the control of the rotary inverted pendulum, which belongs to class IIa, as it addresses the tracking problem [3-5]. The rotational configuration is on the whole an amendment of the well-known cart-on-rail pendulum structure.

Compensations of the rotary inverted pendulum system with unhinged poles and non-lowest phase dynamics, nonlinear equations with an uncomplicated arrangement

F. Masulli, G. Pasi, and R. Yager (Eds.): WILF 2013, LNAI 8256, pp. 201–211, 2013.

direct to choose RIP for testing new control procedure on as a benchmark. As a result engineers like to utilize it for authenticating and estimating the efficiency, robustness, and precision of their recommended control techniques[6].

This is an extremely typical and intellectual nonlinear control dilemma, and numerous techniques previously exist for its explanation [7], for instance, model-based control, fuzzy control, neural network(NN) control, pulse step control, genetic algorithms (GAs)-based control, and so on. On the other hand, the controller was complicated to wholly stabilize a pendulum system within a short period of time[8, 9].

In this paper, distinction of LQR and fuzzy logic control for a rotary-type inverted pendulum system has been identified.

Initially, an LQR was utilized to steady the rotary inverted pendulum in such a way that the pendulum is at all times to retain it upright position and to uphold the arm position in horizontal level surface by making use of a state feedback control to move about unhinged poles of a linear system to steady ones. Accordingly, a Mamdani FIS is deliberated which alleviates the pendulum in the linear region, imitating LQR control just about the stability position. The linear state feedback law is mapped to the system of the fuzzy presumption engine.

2   Mathematical Modeling of Rotary Inverted Pendulum

In this section, the model of the rotary inverted pendulum is established. Rotational inverted pendulum is a nonlinear system of fourth order with a single input variable. The variables relating internal states are as follows: a rotation angle of a base (θ_0), a rotational velocity of a base ($\dot{\theta}_0$), an angle of rotation of the pendulum (θ_1) and its corresponding rotational velocity ($\dot{\theta}_1$).

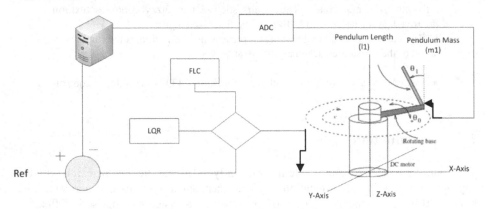

Fig. 1. Orientation and parameters of rotaryinverted pendulum

The input variable for the system is the torque delivered by the motor. The scheme is characterized by two equilibrium points. The steady equilibrium point is attained when the pendulum is leaning upright and pointing downwards. The second equilibrium point is also defined for the vertical orientation, but works for the pendulum pointing upwards[10].

The experimental bed comprised of three prime mechanisms: the plant, digital and analog edge and the digital regulator. The overall scheme is revealed in Fig. 1. The plant embraces of a pendulum and a revolving base type of aluminum rods, an undeviating DC motor to progress the base and two optical encoders as the angular point sensors. While the base swivels all the way through the angle θ_o, the pendulum is liberated to turn around through its angle $\theta_1$prepared with the vertical. Crossing point flanked by the digital controller and the plant comprised of two information possession cards and numerous signal conditioning circuitry[11].

The ordinary differential equations that approximately illustrate the dynamics of the plant are given by:

$$\theta = ap\theta o + Kp\vartheta a \tag{1}$$

$$\ddot{\theta}_1 = -\frac{C_1}{J_1}\dot{\theta}_1 + \frac{m_1 g l_1}{J_1}\sin\dot{\theta}_1 + K_1\ddot{\theta}_o \tag{2}$$

Where:

θ_o = angular displacement of the rotating base
$\dot{\theta}_o$ = angular speed of the rotating base
θ_1 = angular displacement of the pendulum
$\dot{\theta}_1$ = angular speed of the pendulum
ϑ_a = motor armature voltage

Equation (1) and (2) describing the dynamics of the model are extremely nonlinear. Table 1 represents the parameters involved in (1) and (2) of the RIP system:

Table 1. Parameter of Rotary Inverted Pendulum System

Parameter	Description	Value	Unit
K_p	Parameter of DC Motor	74.8903	rad-s^{-2}-v^{-1}
a_p	Parameter of DC Motor	33.0408	s^{-2}
K_1	Torque constant	1.03001×10^{-3}	Kg-m/rad
g	Acceleration due to gravity	9.8006	m/sec^2
m_1	Pendulum mass	0.086184	kg
l_1	Pendulum length	0.113	m
J_1	Pendulum inertia	1.3001×10^{-3}	N-m-s^2
C_1	Friction constant	2.9794×10^{-3}	N-m-s/rad

For the controller synthesis state variable description of pendulum system is required.

This is easily done by defining state variables as:$x_1 = \theta_o$, $x_2 = \dot{\theta}_o$, $x_3 = \theta_1$, $x_4 = \dot{\theta}_1$ and control signal $u = \vartheta_a$ to get:

$$\dot{x}_1 = x_2 \tag{3}$$

$$\dot{x}_2 = -a_p x_2 + K_p u \tag{4}$$

$$\dot{x}_3 = x_4 \tag{5}$$

$$\dot{x}_4 = -\frac{K_1 a_p}{J_1} a_p + \frac{m_1 g l_1}{J_1} \sin x_3 - \frac{C_1}{J_1} x_4 + \frac{K_1 K_p}{J_1} u \tag{6}$$

Linearization of (3), (4), (5) and (6) about vertical unstable equilibrium position (i.e., $[\theta_1, \theta_2, \dot{\theta}_1, \dot{\theta}_2] = [0, 0, 0, 0]$), results in the linear, time invariant state variable model. By using data in Table 1, linearized model of the rotary inverted pendulum results in:

$$\begin{bmatrix} \dot{x}_1 \\ \dot{x}_2 \\ \dot{x}_3 \\ \dot{x}_4 \end{bmatrix} = \begin{bmatrix} 0 & 1 & 0 & 0 \\ 0 & -33.04 & 0 & 0 \\ 0 & 0 & 0 & 1 \\ 0 & 49.30 & 73.41 & -2.29 \end{bmatrix} \begin{bmatrix} x_1 \\ x_2 \\ x_3 \\ x_4 \end{bmatrix} + \begin{bmatrix} 0 \\ 74.89 \\ 0 \\ -111.74 \end{bmatrix} u \tag{7}$$

$$\begin{bmatrix} y_1 \\ y_2 \\ y_3 \\ y_4 \end{bmatrix} = \begin{bmatrix} 1 & 0 & 0 & 0 \\ 0 & 0 & 1 & 0 \end{bmatrix} \begin{bmatrix} x_1 \\ x_2 \\ x_3 \\ x_4 \end{bmatrix} + \begin{bmatrix} 0 \\ 0 \end{bmatrix} u \tag{8}$$

Equation (7) and (8) is defined by the following equations:

$$\dot{x}(t) = Ax(t) + Bu(t) \tag{9}$$

$$y(t) = Cx(t) + Du(t \tag{10}$$

The linearized model in (7) and (8) are not truly represents the physical system, as during the linearization process some of the nonlinearities like motor dynamics, friction , dead-zone and other characteristics are neglected.

3   Full State Feedback (LQR) Design

Linearized model of RIP is completely controllable and observable, therefore linear state-feedback strategies, such as the LQR, are applicable.

In this optimal control technique we try to minimize the defined error as a cost function and the Linear Quadratic Regulator (LQR) method minimizes the cost function (J).

The performance index for the LQR is

$$J = \int_0^\infty (x(t)^\top Q x(t) + u(t)^\top R u(t)) dt \tag{11}$$

subject to

$$\dot{x}(t) = Ax(t) + Bu(t) \tag{12}$$

Q and R in Cost Function represent the weighting matrices of suitable dimension corresponding to the state x and input u, respectively.

The minimization of J results in moving suitable minimum phase poles to stabilize the RIP system immediately with as little controlling force and state deviations as reachable[12]. The control law has the state feedback form

$$u(t) = -\Sigma K_i x_i \tag{13}$$

Given fixed Q and R, the feedback gains K in (13) that optimize the function J in (11) can be uniquely determined by solving an algebraic Riccati equation given below:

$$0 = G + A^T S + SA - SBR^{-1}B^T S + Q \tag{14}$$

$$K = R^{-1}B^T S \tag{15}$$

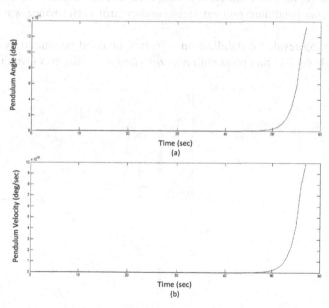

Fig. 2. Open system response with non zero initial condition. (a): simulation result of pendulum angle (θ_1); (b): simulation result of pendulum velocity($\dot{\theta}_1$).

By means of the linearized representation of the system, the subsequent constraints are allocated to devise most favorable gain by LQR technique. Unbolt sphere poles are initiate as 7.4991, -9.7891, 0 and 33.0400. In view of the fact that single pole is lying on the right half of s-plane the system is unbalanced. The unstable response of system with non-zero initial condition is shown in Fig. 2.

By giving the highest priority on controlling θ_1 than regulating the base position, choose the weighting matrices as

$$Q = diag(1,0,5,0) \text{ And } R = 1$$

The optimal feedback gains for the controller in (13) corresponding to the weighting matrices Q and R are:

$$K = (-1, -1.191, -9.699, -0.961)$$

On substituting (13) in (12) yields

$$\dot{x}(t) = [A - BK]x(t) \tag{16}$$

The closed loop system poles are -31.84, -14.02, -5.22 and -2.35. They all lie in the left half of s-plane and show the closed loop system is stable.

Applying the control law above, it is observed that the unstable equilibrium point of rotary inverted pendulum remains stable and control performance was found adequate.

The simulation result for stabilization of rotary inverted pendulum by using LQR around unstable equilibrium point with non-zero initial condition is given in Fig. 3.

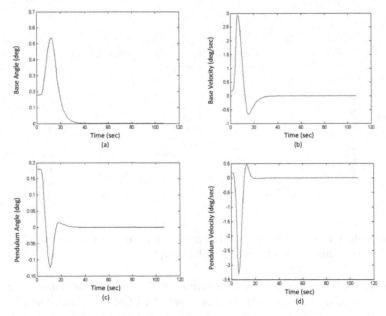

Fig. 3. Rotary inverted pendulum stabilization response by using LQR with non-zero initial condition. (a): simulation result of base angle (θ_o); (b): simulation result of base velocity ($\dot{\theta}_o$); (c): simulation result of pendulum angle (θ_1); (d): simulation result of pendulum velocity($\dot{\theta}_1$).

4   Fuzzy Logic Controller Design

Commencing the realistic point of observation, real-time control necessitates a number of simplifications of the investigational model, and human intrusion is for all time essential for this category of control. In common, a controller based on the understanding of the human machinist is preferred for the realistic function. Fuzzy controllers utilize heuristic information in mounting plan methodologies intended for control of non-linear vibrant systems. This loom eradicates the necessitate for widespread facts and statistical modeling of the system[8]. Within this segment the alleviation of the RIP system by means of FLC through a primary stipulation is presented. Simulink model of fuzzy control system is shown in Fig. 4(a).

The entire numeral of rules is an exponential purpose of the number of contribution and number of association functions. For example for an input system with N membership purpose for each input N^n rules are derived.

A four input system through seven connection functions is measured by[13]by means of 2401 rules. Encompassing such a huge amount of rules possibly will grounds difficulties owing to memory restrictions to accumulate the FIS for actual time action using Matlab/Simulink [14]. The instigators of this manuscript originate that for n =2, N =7 and originating 49 rules formulate the assemblage progression too fluctuating but later than additional alteration to the gain these vacillation can be condensed notably.

The two inputs to the fuzzy controller are the position error of the pendulum e_3 and the difference of error e_4. Seven connection functions for every input and output which are uniformly distributed across the universe of discourse are revealed inFig. 4(b), Fig. 4(c) and Fig. 4(d).A Mamdani FIS is deliberated which alleviates the pendulum in the linear zone, imitating LQR control just about the equilibrium position. The linear state feedback law is recorded to the policy of the fuzzy presumption engine. In common, designed for a fuzzy controller by means of n inputs and single output, the center of the controller output fuzzy set Y^smembership function would be situated at:

$$(j + k + \cdots l) \times \frac{2}{(N-1)n} \tag{17}$$

Where$s = j + k + \cdots l$ is the index of the output fuzzy set Y^s, $\{j, k, \ldots l\}$ are the linguistic-numeric indices of the input fuzzy sets, N is the number of connection functions on every input universe of dissertation, and n is the number of inputs.

We decide triangular membership functions for these, by means of centers specified by (17) and base widths equal to $\frac{1}{2.5}$.

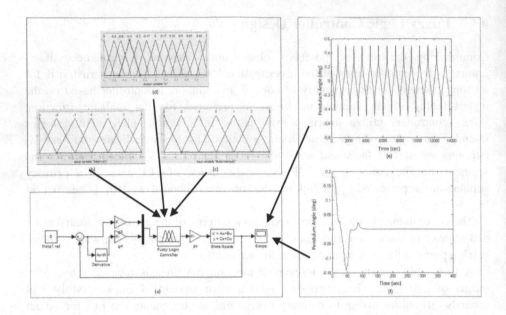

Fig. 4. (a) Simulink model of rotary inverted pendulum with fuzzy logic controller. (b): membership function of input variable (θ_1); (c): membership function of input variable ($\dot{\theta}_1$); (d): Normalized output variable membership function (ϑ_a); (e): simulation response of pendulum angle (θ_1) with derived gain; (f): simulation response of pendulum angle (θ_1) with tuned gains.

The rule-base of RIP system is shown in Table II, where -3, -2, -1, 0, 1, 2 and 3 denote fuzzy linguistic values of negative large, negative medium, negative small, zero, positive large, positive medium and positive small respectively.

Transformation of LQR gains into the scaling gains of fuzzy system is achieved by using following formula

$$g_o g_i = k_i \qquad (18)$$

Where k_i are the LQR gains? For $g_o = -4.6$ the fuzzy systems input gains g_1, g_2, g_3 and g_4 are 0.1975, 0.2391, 2 and 0.1957 respectively. Simulation results of RIP system by using FLC with derived and tuned gains are shown in Fig. 8.

5   Results

The simulation results of proposed control system for the rotary inverted pendulum with the SIMULINK in MATLAB 7.0 are shown in Fig. 2, Fig. 3, Fig. 4

and Fig. 5, respectively for conventional Hybrid controller and Intelligent Hybrid Controller.

Fig. 2 shows that rotary inverted pendulum is highly nonlinear model for consideration. To stabilize the system state feedback control technique was used. Fig. 3 shows an adequate stabilization controller response through LQR.

In Fig.4 angle of the pendulum are shown by using FLC. The pendulum shows fluctuating response with calculated gains but after adding tuned gains the response becomes more condensed.

The LQR method for non-zero initial condition couldn't set the pendulum to zero, but fuzzy controller doesn't have this problem[6]. The comparison results of both the controller with non-zero initial condition are shown in Fig.5. It was observed that both FLC and LQR have different steady-state error, settling time and overshoots. Through LQR, pendulum never attained its steady state value to zero. Analysis of obtained results shows that LQR controller relatively gives the fast response and attained its settling state quickly in comparison to FLC, but the pendulum keeps oscillating about its reference position. The proposed fuzzy controller is able to stabilize the pendulum system by tracking the reference signal remarkably, which indicates the disturbance rejection capability of FLC controller

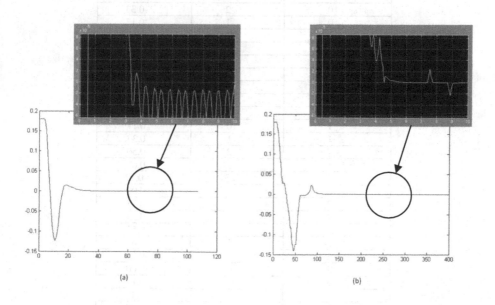

Fig. 5. Comparision results of FLC with LQR for the stabilization of rotary inverted pendulum. (a): simulation result of pendulum angle (θ_1) with LQR; (c): simulation result of pendulum angle (θ_1) with FLC.

Table 2. Inference Rules For Fuzzy Balance Controller

j	k	Y
-3	-3	-1.00
-3	-2	-0.83
-3	-1	-0.67
-3	0	-0.50
-3	1	-0.33
-3	2	-0.17
-3	3	0.00
-2	-3	-0.83
-2	-2	-0.67
-2	-1	-0.50
-2	0	-0.33
-2	1	-0.17
-2	2	0.00
-2	3	0.17
-1	-3	-0.67
-1	-2	-0.50
-1	-1	-0.33
-1	0	-0.17
-1	1	0.00
-1	2	0.17
-1	3	0.33
0	-3	-0.50
0	-2	-0.33
0	-1	-0.17
0	0	0.00
0	1	0.17
0	2	0.33
0	3	0.50
1	-3	-0.33
1	-2	-0.17
1	-1	0.00
1	0	0.17
1	1	0.33
1	2	0.50
1	3	0.67
2	-3	-0.17
2	-2	0.00
2	-1	0.17
2	0	0.33
2	1	0.50
2	2	0.67
2	3	0.83
3	-3	0.00
3	-2	0.17
3	-1	0.33
3	0	0.50
3	1	0.67
3	2	0.83
3	3	1.00

6   Conclusion

The aim of this research was to design a stabilizing controller meant for inverted pendulum and this has been fruitfully attained.

We subsequently compared the performance of the LQR and FLC for a rotary-type inverted pendulum system.

The robustness of both control techniques is verified by running simulation with different initial conditions, which confirms the control efficiency of the method. The results showed that fuzzy controller reveal enhanced performance than LQR near the linearized region.

On the whole, the manuscript presents a relative guide to individuals eager to learn the control laws on such a typical nonlinear and under actuated system.

References

1. Krishen, J., Becerra, V.M.: Efficient Fuzzy Control of a Rotary Inverted Pendulum Based on LQR Mapping. In: International Symposium on Intelligent Control, Germany (2006)
2. Saber, R.O.: Nonlinear control of underactuated mechanical systems with application to robotics and aerospace vehicles. MIT (2001)
3. Olfati-Saber, R.: Normal Forms for Underactuated Mechanical Systems with Symmetry. IEEE Transactions on Automatic Control 47(2) (2002)
4. Melin, P., Astudillo, L., Castillo, O.: Optimal design of type-2 and type-1 fuzzy tracking controllers for autonomous mobile robots under perturbed torques using a new chemical optimization paradigm. Expert Systems with Applications 40(8), 3185–3195 (2013)
5. Castro, N.R.C., Bustos, L.T.A., López, O.C.: Designing Type-1 Fuzzy Logic Controllers via Fuzzy Lyapunov Synthesis for Nonsmooth Mechanical Systems: The Perturbed Case. Computación y Sistemas 14(3), 283–293 (2011)
6. Khashayar, A., Nekoui, M.A., Ahangar-Asr, H.: Stabilization of Rotary Inverted Pendulum Using Fuzzy Logic. International Journal of Intelligent Information Processing (IJIIP) 2(4), 23–31 (2011)
7. Brock, S.: Practical approach to fuzzy control of inverter pendulum (for inverter read inverted). In: IEEE Intl. Conf. Industrial Technology (2003)
8. Liu, Y., Chen, Z., Xue, D., Xu, X.: Real-Time Controlling of Inverted Pendulum by Fuzzy Logic. In: International Conference on Automation and Logistics, Shenyang (2009)
9. Melba Mary, P., Marimuthu, N.S.: Minimum Time Swing Up and Stabilization of Rotary Inverted Pendulum Using Pulse Step Control. Iranian Journal of Fuzzy Systems 6(3), 1–15 (2009)
10. Dominik, I.: Fuzzy logic control of rotational inverted pendulum. Solid State Phenomena 177, 84–92 (2011)
11. Passino, K.M., Yurkovich, S.: Fuzzy Control. Addison-Wesley Longman, Inc., California (1998), Cheu, L. (ed.)
12. Akhtaruzzaman, M., Shafie, A.A.: Modeling and Control of a Rotary Inverted Pendulum Using Various Methods, Comparative Assessment and Result Analysis. In: IEEE International Conference on Mechatronics and Automation, China (2010)
13. Yurkovich, S., Widjaja, M.: Fuzzy controller synthesis for an inverted pendulum system. Control Engineering Practice 4, 455–469 (1996)
14. Fantoni, I., Lozano, R.: Non-linear Control For Underactuated Mechanical Systems. Springer, London (2002)

A Fuzzy Approach to Cloud Admission Control for Safe Overbooking

Carlos Vázquez[1], Luis Tomás[2], Ginés Moreno[1], and Johan Tordsson[2]

[1] Dept. of Computing Systems,
University of Castilla–La Mancha, Spain
{Carlos.Vazquez,Gines.Moreno}@uclm.es
[2] Dept. of Computing Science,
Umeå University, Sweden
{luis,tordsson}@cs.umu.se

Abstract. Cloud computing enables elasticity - rapid provisioning and deprovisioning of computational resources. Elasticity allows cloud users to quickly adapt resource allocation to meet changes in their workloads. For cloud providers, elasticity complicates capacity management as the amount of resources that can be requested by users is unknown and can vary significantly over time. Overbooking techniques allow providers to increase utilization of their data centers. For safe overbooking, cloud providers need admission control mechanisms to handle the tradeoff between increased utilization (and revenue), and risk of exhausting resources, potentially resulting in penalty fees and/or lost customers. We propose a flexible approach (implemented with fuzzy logic programming) to admission control and the associated risk estimation. Our measures exploit different fuzzy logic operators in order to model optimistic, realistic, and pessimistic behaviour under uncertainty. The application has been coded with the MALP language by using the FLOPER system developed in our research group. An experimental evaluation confirm that our fuzzy admission control approach can significantly increase resource utilization while minimizing the risk of exceeding the total available capacity.

Keywords: Cloud Computing, Admission Control, Fuzzy Logic Programming, Resource Utilization, Risk Assessment.

1 Introduction

Cloud computing is a recently emerged paradigm where computational resources are leased over the Internet in a self-service manner under a pay-per use pricing scheme. Organizations and individuals, the cloud users, can thus continuously adjust their cloud resource allocations to their current needs, so called elasticity [21]. The core of cloud infrastructure are data centers, large store-house like facilities hosting hundreds of thousands of servers, along with storage and networking equipment, as well as advanced systems for cooling and power distribution [24]. Through virtualization technologies, these data centers (cloud providers) can provision applications from multiple users on the same physical servers and thus make efficient use of their hardware. In cloud data centers, user applications are packaged as Virtual Machines (VMs) [7], which in essence

F. Masulli, G. Pasi, and R. Yager (Eds.): WILF 2013, LNAI 8256, pp. 212–225, 2013.

are software implementations of servers that are time-shared on the physical hardware. Users can thus at any time, themselves or through automatic elasticity management software, increase or decrease the number of VMs allocated. Consequently, it is common for cloud providers to require users to specify upper and lower limits to the number of VMs to be used in a *service request* [19], or to simply have predefined rules for all users, e.g., 1-20 VMs per data center for the largest cloud provider, Amazon [6].

For data centers, elasticity results in a long-term capacity allocation problem, as the exact number of VMs to be used at any time by each user is unknown. Running too few VMs in total results in poor data center hardware utilization and lowered incomes from users, whereas having too many VMs may lead to low performance and/or crashes, poor user experience, and may also have financial consequences if Service Level Agreements (SLAs) regarding user performance expectations are violated. To handle this trade off, *admission control* mechanisms [9] can be used by cloud providers to determine whether a new user service request should be admitted into the data center or not. In our previous work [22], we demonstrate how *resource overbooking*, a technique well-known from airline revenue management and network bandwidth multiplexing, can be used to increase provider utilization and revenue, with acceptable risks of running out of hardware capacity. Further examples of previous work in this area includes an algorithmic framework [9] that uses cloud effective demand to estimate the total physical capacity required for performing the overbooking, including probability of launching additional VMs in the future.

However, evaluating risk during admission control with respect to performing resource overbooking actions is far from trivial. Overbooking and the associated scheduling problems are multi-dimensional packing problems, commonly solved using heuristics. It is also not clear in the general case how to balance the short and long term impact when deciding whether to accept a new service. Furthermore, admission control is associated with several uncertainties, include limited knowledge of future workloads, potential side effects from co-locating particular VMs, and exact impact on applications of potential resource shortage. Based on these properties of the admission control problem, we propose a fuzzy approach to admission control. Since its initial development by L. A. Zadeh in the sixties [23], fuzzy logic has become a powerful theoretic tool for reaching elegant solutions to problems in various fields of software, industry, etc. More recently, there exist fuzzy extensions of the classical logic language Prolog, which can be used in a very natural way to solve problems where fuzzy logic plays an important role. A conceptual overview of how our cloud overbooking framework use fuzzy logic during admission control is shown in Figure 1. In must be noted that the risks are calculated for the three capacity dimensions that we consider for each VM: *CPU*, *memory* and *I/O*. For each one of these, the risk is calculated based on predicted information about future available capacity (referred to as *Free* in the rest of the paper), future amount of unrequested capacity (denoted *Unreq*) and the capacity requested by the incoming service (denoted *Req*). *Unreq* is the inverse difference between what users requested and what they really used (*Free*). All these future expected values are predicted by using exponential smoothing functions [22].

The structure of this paper is as follows. In Section 2, a brief introduction to the MALP (*Multi-Adjoint Logic Programming*) language and the FLOPER system is given.

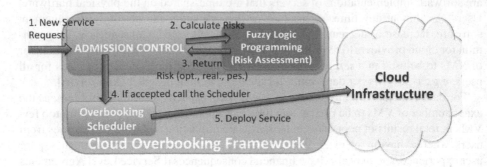

Fig. 1. Conceptual picture of the system

In Section 3 we explain the main features of our implementation based on fuzzy logic programming using MALP and FLOPER. Next, in Section 4, we present our experimental results. Finally, Section 5 concludes the paper and outlines directions for further research.

2   The Multi-adjoint Logic Language and FLOPER

Multi-Adjoint Logic Programming (see [14,11] for a complete formulation of this framework), MALP in brief, can be thought as a fuzzy extension of Prolog and it is based on a first order language, $\mathcal{L}$, containing variables, function/constant symbols, predicate symbols, and several connectives such as implications ($\leftarrow_1, \leftarrow_2, \dots, \leftarrow_m$), conjunctions ($\&_1, \&_2, \dots, \&_k$), disjunctions ($\vee_1, \vee_2, \dots, \vee_l$), and general hybrid operators ("aggregators" $@_1, @_2, \dots, @_n$), used for combining/propagating truth values through the rules, and thus increasing the language expressiveness. Additionally, our language $\mathcal{L}$ contains the values of a *multi-adjoint lattice* in the form $\langle L, \preceq, \leftarrow_1, \&_1, \dots, \leftarrow_n, \&_n \rangle$, equipped with a collection of *adjoint pairs* $\langle \leftarrow_i, \&_i \rangle$ where each $\&_i$ is a conjunctor intended to the evaluation of *modus ponens* [20,12,14]. A *rule* is a formula "$A \leftarrow_i \mathcal{B}$ with α", where A is an atomic formula (usually called the *head*), $\mathcal{B}$ (which is called the *body*) is a formula built from atomic formulas $B_1, \dots, B_n$ ($n \geq 0$), truth values of L and conjunctions, disjunctions and general aggregations, and finally $\alpha \in L$ is the "weight" or *truth degree* of the rule. The set of truth values L may be the carrier of any complete bounded lattice, as for instance occurs with the set of real numbers in the interval $[0, 1]$ with their corresponding ordering $\preceq_R$. Consider, for instance, the following program, $\mathcal{P}$, with associated multi-adjoint lattice $\langle [0, 1], \preceq_R, \leftarrow_P, \&_P \rangle$ (where label P means for *Product logic* with the following connective definitions for implication and conjunction symbols, respectively: "$\leftarrow_P(x, y) = \min(1, x/y)$", "$\&_P(x, y) = x * y$", as well as "$@_{\mathtt{aver}}(x, y) = (x + y)/2$"):

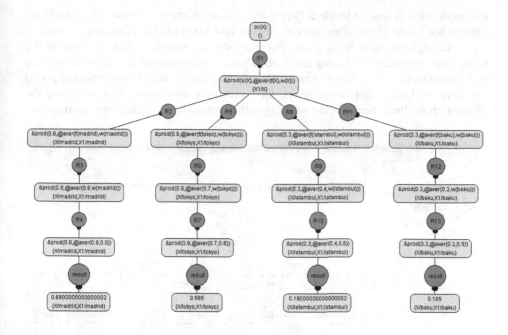

Fig. 2. Execution tree for program $\mathcal{P}$ and goal oc(X)

$$\mathcal{R}_1 : \quad oc(X) \qquad <\text{-} \; s(X) \, \&prod \; (f(X) \; @aver \; w(X)) \; with \; 1.$$

$\mathcal{R}_2 :$ $s(madrid)$ $with \; 0.8.$	$\mathcal{R}_5 :$ $s(tokyo)$ $with \; 0.9.$
$\mathcal{R}_3 :$ $f(madrid)$ $with \; 0.8.$	$\mathcal{R}_6 :$ $f(tokyo)$ $with \; 0.7.$
$\mathcal{R}_4 :$ $w(madrid)$ $with \; 0.9.$	$\mathcal{R}_7 :$ $w(tokyo)$ $with \; 0.6.$
$\mathcal{R}_8 :$ $s(istambul)$ $with \; 0.3.$	$\mathcal{R}_{11} :$ $s(baku)$ $with \; 0.3.$
$\mathcal{R}_9 :$ $f(istambul)$ $with \; 0.4.$	$\mathcal{R}_{12} :$ $f(baku)$ $with \; 0.2.$
$\mathcal{R}_{10} :$ $w(istambul)$ $with \; 0.8.$	$\mathcal{R}_{13} :$ $w(baku)$ $with \; 0.5.$

This program models, through predicate "oc", the chances of a city for being an "olympic city" (i.e., for hosting olympic games). Predicate "oc" is defined in rule $\mathcal{R}_1$, whose body collects the information from three other predicates, "s", "f" and "w", modeling, respectively, the *security* level, the *facilities* and the good *weather* of a certain city. These predicates are defined in rules $\mathcal{R}_2$ to $\mathcal{R}_{13}$ for four cities (*Madrid*, *Istambul*, *Tokyo* and *Baku*), in such a way that, for each city, the feature modeled by each predicate is better the greater the truth value of the rule.

In order to run and manage MALP programs, during the last years we have designed the FLOPER (*Fuzzy LOgic Programming Environment for Research*) system [16,15,17,18], which is freely accessible online [10]. The parser of our tool has been implemented by using the classical DCG's (*Definite Clause Grammars*) resource of the Prolog language, since it is a convenient notation for expressing grammar rules. Once the application is loaded inside a Prolog interpreter, it shows a menu which includes options for loading/compiling, parsing, listing and saving fuzzy programs, as well as for executing/debugging fuzzy goals. These actions are based on the *translation* of the fuzzy code into standard Prolog code: all internal computations (including compiling and executing) are pure Prolog derivations, whereas inputs (fuzzy programs and goals) and outputs (fuzzy computed answers) have always a fuzzy taste, thus producing the illusion on the final user of being working with a purely fuzzy logic programming tool.

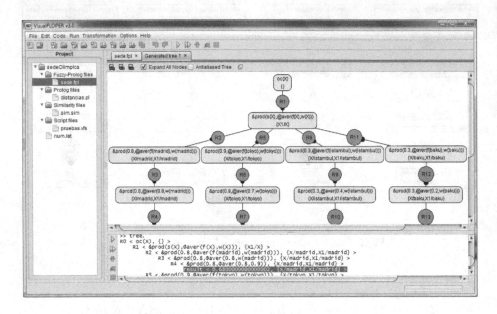

Fig. 3. The FLOPER System showing the execution tree for goal "`oc(X)`"

The FLOPER system is able to manage programs with very different lattices. By using option "`lat`" (and "`show`"), we can associate (and display) a new lattice to a given program. Such lattice must be loaded into the tool as a pure Prolog program. As an example, the following clauses show the program modeling the lattice of the real interval $[0, 1]$ with the usual ordering relation and connectives (conjunction and disjunction of the *Product logic*, as well as the average aggregator) where the meaning of the mandatory predicates "`member`", "`top`", "`bot`" and "`leq`" is obvious:

```
member(X):- number(X), 0=<X, X=<1.                    bot(0).
leq(X,Y):- X=<Y.                                       top(1).
and_prod(X,Y,Z)  :- Z is X*Y.
or_prod(X,Y,Z)   :- U1 is X*Y, U2 is X+Y, Z is U2-U1.
agr_aver(X,Y,Z)  :- U1 is X+Y, Z is U1/2.
```

FLOPER includes two main ways for evaluating a goal, given a MALP program and its corresponding lattice. Option "`run`" translates the whole program into a pure Prolog program and evaluates the (also translated) goal, thus obtaining a list of fuzzy computed answers, each one containing the truth-degree and the corresponding variable substitution for each concrete solution. For instance, in our example we can run goal "oc(X)" to obtain the following result indicating that the different chances of *Baku*, *Istambul*, *Tokyo* and *Madrid* for being "Olympic cities" are respectively 10.5%, 18%, 58.5% and 68%:

```
>> run.
    [Truth_degree=0.105,X=baku]
    [Truth_degree=0.180,X=istambul]
    [Truth_degree=0.585,X=tokyo]
    [Truth_degree=0.680,X=madrid]
```

On the other hand, option "tree" computes and displays the whole execution (or derivation) tree for the intended goal. Moreover, it is possible to select the deepest level to be built (which is obviously mandatory when trees are infinite) via option "depth" or even to indicate that only the set of leaves be displayed via option "leaves". Coming back again to our example, we can use option "tree" to obtain the execution tree for goal "oc(X)", which is generated by FLOPER in three different formats. Firstly the tree is displayed in graphical mode, as a PNG file, as shown in Figures 2 and 3. The tree is composed by two kinds of nodes. Yellow nodes represent states reached by FLOPER following the state transition system that describes the operational semantics of MALP [14]. The root node represents the first state (composed by the original goal together with the identity substitution), and subsequent lower nodes are its children states (that is, states reached from the root). A state contains a formula in the upper side and a substitution (obtained after composing all substitutions applied from the original goal to the current state) at the bottom. A final state, if reached, is a fuzzy computed answer whose associated formula is just an element (truth-degree) of the lattice. Blue rounded nodes appearing between a pair of yellow nodes (states) represent program rules; specifically, the program rule that is exploited in order to go from one state (the upper one) to another (the lower state). These rules are named with letter "R" plus its position in the program. For example, observe that from the initial state to the next one, the first rule of the program has been exploited, as shown in the blue intermediate node. As an exception, when all atoms have been exploited in (the formula of) a certain state, the following blue node is labeled with word "result", informing that the next state contains a fuzzy computed answer.

FLOPER can also generate the execution tree in two textual formats. The first one contains a plain description of the tree, while the second one provides an XML structure to that description. In this XML format, tag "node" is used to include all the information of a node, such as the rule performed to reach that state (tag "rule"), the formula of the state (tag "goal"), the accumulated substitution (tag "substitution") and the children nodes in a nested way (tag "children"). These XML files can be accurately explored with the *Fuzzy XPath* application we have recently developed in our research group with FLOPER [1,2,4,5], in order to perform some interesting debugging tasks with the same tool, as documented in [3].

$$\&_P(x,y) \triangleq x * y \qquad\qquad |_P(x,y) \triangleq x + y - x * y \qquad \leftarrow_P (x,y) \triangleq \min(1, x/y)$$

$$\&_G(x,y) \triangleq \min(x,y) \qquad\qquad |_G(x,y) \triangleq \max\{x,y\} \qquad \leftarrow_G (x,y) \triangleq \begin{cases} 1 & \text{if } y \le x \\ x & \text{otherwise} \end{cases}$$

$$\&_L(x,y) \triangleq \max(0, x+y-1) \quad |_L(x,y) \triangleq \min\{x+y, 1\} \quad \leftarrow_L (x,y) \triangleq \min\{x - y + 1, 1\}$$

Fig. 4. Fuzzy conjunction, disjunction, and implication connectives from *Łukasiewicz* (pessimistic), *Gödel* (optimistic), and *Product* (realistic) logics, resp., defined in the real unit interval

3   Implementation Based on Fuzzy Logic Programming

On towards fuzzy formulations of the admission control problem, in this section we present a flexible method that has been implemented in MALP using FLOPER. As we have just detailed in the previous section, the MALP language represents a fuzzy extension of the popular Prolog language in the field of pure (crisp) logic programming [13]. In this fuzzy declarative framework, each program is accompanied with a lattice for modeling truth-degrees beyond the simpler case of the (crisp) *Boolean* pair $\{true, false\}$. Hence, fuzzy program rules can utilize fuzzy connectives defined on such richer lattices for improving the expressive power of classical Prolog clauses. For instance, some standard connective definitions for conjunctions, disjunctions, and implications in the lattice of real numbers in the unit interval $[0, 1]$ are presented in Figure 4, where labels L, G, and P mean respectively *Łukasiewicz logic*, *Gödel logic*, and *Product logic*, with different capabilities for modeling *pessimistic*, *optimistic*, and *realistic scenarios*, respectively.

In our application we use a refined version of such a lattice, as we try to identify the notion of truth-degree with the one for "*overbooking risk along a time period*". This means that instead of single values, our program manipulates lists of real numbers as truth-degrees[1] after analyzing the behaviour's curves representing "*free, unrequested, and requested (CPU/memory/net) resources*" also expressed as input lists to the tool. For instance, if expression "$\&_P(x,y) \triangleq x * y$" refers to the conjunction of *Product logic* for pairs of values, its extended version coping with pairs of lists of values should look like "$\&_P([x_1, \ldots, x_n], [y_1, \ldots, y_n]) \triangleq [x_1 * y_1, \ldots, x_n * y_n]$". In our application this connective can be recursively defined with the following code:

```
and_prod([],[],[]).
and_prod([X|LX],[Y|LY],[Z|LZ]):- Z is X*Y, and_prod(LX,LY,LZ).
```

In the lattice we have also implemented extended versions managing lists of the remaining connectives seen in Figure 4, as well as other connectives like @*append* (for concatenating two lists of numbers), @*show* (which is described afterwards) and the two connectives @*very* and @*approx* (where @$very(x) = x^2$ and @$approx(x) = \sqrt{x}$) known as *linguistic modifiers*. These are useful for fine-tuning the more pessimistic or optimistic shape of the answers produced by our application under this uncertain scenario.

---

[1] Sometimes accompanied with annotations like max, avg, $peak$ and so on, for readability reasons.

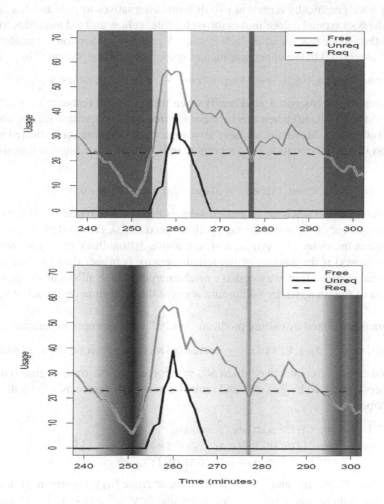

Fig. 5. Graphics showing different choices for estimating risk

Thanks to the high expressive power of the previous lattice, it is possible now to easily design a MALP program composed by a few rules starting with the following one, which receives as input parameters three lists representing the curves associated to free, unrequested and requested values, as well as a fourth argument indicating which resource, or `Field`, (CPU, network or memory) is considered:

```
risk([F|Free],[U|Unreq],[R|Req],Field)<-
        @append(combine(F,U,R), risk(Free,Unreq,Req,Field))
```

This definition of predicate "`risk`" produces a truth degree that is a list of numbers obtained after contrasting the input curves "`Free`", "`Unreq`" and "`Req`". This evaluation is recursively performed by calling predicate "`combine`" with three concrete values each time in order to compare the requested resources with the free and unrequested values.

In Figure 5 we graphically represent two different alternatives to perform this contrast where the background colour moves through white, yellow and red tonalities from the lower to the higher risk found in each instant. A preliminary version for predicate "combine" associated to the upper graphic in Figure 5 could be represented by:

```
combine(Free,Unreq,Req) <- (Req>=Free & [1])|(Req>Unreq & [0.5])
```

which, in essence, assigns risk 1 (red band) when the requested resource is over the free value, 0.5 (yellow band) when it is between the free and unrequested values, and 0 (white band) otherwise. Moreover, we have also implemented a more sophisticated version based on linear interpolation (down graphic in Figure 5) according the following formula:

$$inter(Req,Free,Unreq) = (Req-Unreq)/(Free-Unreq)$$

Thus, it can return risk 0 when the requested value is below the unrequested one, a risk in [0,1] (tonalities vary from white through yellow to red as risk grows) if the requested point is between the other two values, and risk above 1 (tonalities vary from red to black as risk grows) if the amount of requested capacity is higher than the free one. When requested is above free, we say that a *peak* emerges, which allows us to improve the evaluation of the final risk by taking into account the performance impact of each peak.

The program is invoked by calling predicate "main" with appropriate parameters:

```
main(Free,Unreq,Req,Field) <- @show(risk(Free,Unreq,Req,Field))
```

This rule makes use of connective "@show", which receives the truth degree (i.e., a list of numbers) produced by "risk" and returns a new truth degree as a list with the following shape:

$$
\begin{array}{l}
[\quad avg(n_1), \ min(n_2), \ max(n_3), \\
\quad over([peak(h_1,l_1,a_1),\ldots,peak(h_i,l_i,a_i)]), \\
\quad opt(n_4), \ real(n_5), \ pes(n_6) \qquad\qquad]
\end{array}
$$

Here, labels "avg", "min", and "max" contain the average (n_1), minimum (n_2), and maximum (n_3) values, respectively, of the input list; "over" gives the list of peaks (each one is represented by its maximum height (h_j), length (l_j), and area (a_j)) and finally, "opt", "real", and "pes" labels provide an optimistic (n_4), realistic (n_5), and pessimistic (n_6) estimation -based on the previous elements- about the risk of accepting the requested task. These estimations are produced by combining the average measure (appropriately modulated with the @approx and @very connectives, for referring to the pessimistic and optimistic cases, respectively) together with the disjunctions of all the peaks by using different versions of the disjunction operators. This is modeled according to Łukasiewicz, Product, and Gödel fuzzy logics, as shown in the table of Figure 4, where it is easy to see that $\forall x,y \in [0,1], x|_{\text{L}}y \geq x|_{\text{P}}y \geq x|_{\text{G}}z$. This justifies once again the power of fuzzy logic and the strong expressive resources of MALP for managing pessimistic, realistic and optimistic scenarios. For instance, when we introduce the following goal into FLOPER:

```
main([50,20,40,73,99],[25,10,2,51,40],[20,23,45,60,49],cpu)
```

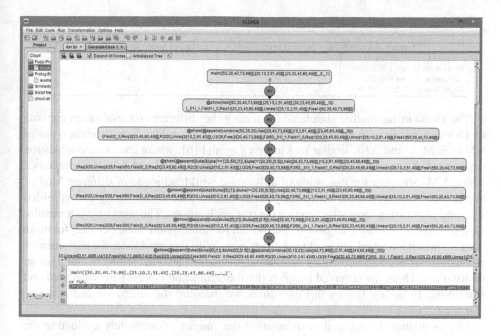

Fig. 6. FLOPER executing our application

The system solves it by generating a list representing the final truth degree associated to the query, with the following shape:

```
[  avg(0.9300780175180026), min(0), max(1.3),
   over([peak(2,1.3,0.27078683857231306)]),
   opt(0.8045594490364215), real(0.9015891243354114), pes(1)]
```

In Figure 6 we show a screen-shot of FLOPER when executing the previous goal. In the main window, we can observe (the initial portion of) the derivation tree for this goal which, in essence, consists in a transition system where each state is coloured in yellow and transitions appear as blue circles, so the initial state is just the original goal appearing in the root of the tree, and the final state (not explicitly displayed in the figure) contains the final truth degree associated to the query. In our case, this solution corresponds to the text darkened in blue in the box at the bottom of the screen.

4   Experiments

To evaluate our proposal, the fuzzy risk assessment is included into the framework presented in [22], which only included a simple admission control technique. This way, the admission control now uses this information to take the decisions about service acceptance or rejection when performing resource overbooking. In that previous work, a simulator to test the development was implemented which is reused here to simulate the cloud infrastructure and emulate the workload.

Table 1. Performance Summary (Figure 7)

	Average utilization	Node capacity overpassed (%)	Aggregated node capacity overpassed (%)
No Risk	38.9 % (1)	0	0
Pessimistic	69.1 % (1.78)	0	0
Realistic	84.6 % (2.17)	6.99	0.43
Optimistic	92.5 % (2.38)	11.88	0.84

The cloud infrastructure simulated for testing the different risk evaluators consists of 16 nodes where each one of them has 32 cores. We consider four different types of VMs (S, M, L and XL), similar to Amazon's model [6], where each one doubles the capacity of the previous one, starting from the S VM (1 CPU and 1.7GB of memory). Those VMs simulate the execution of a dynamic workload made of different kind of applications (some of them with steady behavior and others with bursty one), profiled by using monitoring tools after running the real applications. The workload is a mixture of applications, following a Poisson distribution for submission rates. See [22] for more details about the testbed and workload generation. With that workload, the performance evaluation has been carried out by generating service requests according to that Poisson distribution. Then, the accepted requests (by the admission control) are scheduled and run on the 16 nodes. During this execution, we measure the *utilization* and *resource shortage*.

Our evaluation is centered on measuring the impact of accurately evaluating the risks taken by the admission control when performing resource overbooking within data centers. The different risk values provided by the fuzzy logic engine are compared against each other and also against a base case where no overbooking is performed – no risks being taken. Those risk assessments from least risky to most are labeled as *"Pessimistic"*, *"Realistic"*, and *"Optimistic"* – mapping them to the respective values calculated by the fuzzy logic engine with those names. The base case is labeled *"No Risk"*.

Figure 7 (a) shows the resource utilization achieved by using the different risk values at the admission control. Clearly, the more risks we take, the higher utilization is achieved. However, this may have a negative impact regarding running out of resources if total capacity is overpassed, not only regarding the whole data center utilization but also regarding every single node into the system. Owing to that fact, Figure 7 (b) shows a histograms over how many times one of the nodes has overpassed its total capacity, and how large the impact on the performance is – performance degradation that may end up in resource SLA violations. The x-axis represents the performance degradation experienced when total capacity in (at least) one of the nodes is overpassed. So, the smaller the bars are, the better (less frequent risk situations) and it is desired that they remain as close to 0 as possible - fewer performance degradation and greater possibilities of resolving these. Notably, as shown in Figure 7 (a), the total infrastructure capacity is not overpassed. This means that *VM migration* can be used to decrease the risks by moving VMs from the overloaded nodes to the ones that still have enough available capacity. This way certain overload situations can be avoided, as has been proposed by Beloglazov et al. [8].

Finally, Table 1 highlights the improvement obtained thanks to performing resource overbooking (up to 2.38 times) and the cost that this entails. Pessimistic has the lowest improvement but without any performance degradation, while the other two techniques

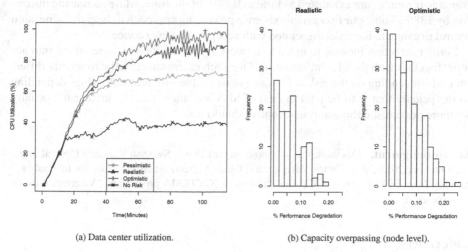

(a) Data center utilization.   (b) Capacity overpassing (node level).

Fig. 7. Resource utilization and risk assessment comparison

present higher utilization rates but at expense of higher performance degradation that may result in running out of resources. For the realistic and optimistic cases, the total capacity of a single node has been overpassed around 6 % and 12 % of the time, respectively. Despite this, the total impact on the final performance is not remarkable (below 1%) – calculated as the percent of time the capacity is overpassed at a node, weighted by the amount of overpassed capacity.

5   Conclusions

In this paper we have used the FLOPER programming environment developed in our research group for implementing with the fuzzy logic language MALP a real-world application in the field of cloud computing.

Admission control techniques that apply overbooking actions are a promising solution for low data center resource utilization, a problem that arises from the elastic nature of cloud applications. However, overbooking actions may lead to performance degradation if not planned carefully.

We propose an admission control that bases its acceptance or rejection decisions on the information about the risks being taken. A fuzzy logic engine provides the information that allows the admission control to estimate the long-term risks of accepting the incoming request. That risk assessment is a combination of several parameter regarding the relationship between available capacity and requested one, such as the difference between these and the information about the peaks when insufficient capacity is expected, providing different degrees of risk that leads to more (or less) aggressive decisions regarding job acceptance.

The evaluation shows significant increases in resource utilization obtained by our risk-aware fuzzy admission control methods. Even for the most optimistic estimates, available resources are exhausted as little as 0.84% of the time, while increasing utilization by 138%. Thus, our fuzzy methods are a promising approach to help the admission control to evaluate the risks associated with accepting a new service.

Further direction include to extend our work by taking the risk assessment into account together with the SLA information. One such extension could be to specify different costs depending on the risk to be taken or using the different risk values depending on the penalty that is to be paid in case of SLA violation, i.e., the greater the penalty the more pessimistic the admission control should be.

Acknowledgment. This work was supported in part by the Swedish Research Council under grant number 2012-5908. Carlos Vázquez and Ginés Moreno received grants for International mobility from the University of Castilla-La Mancha (CYTEMA project and "Vicerrectorado de Profesorado").

References

1. Almendros-Jiménez, J.M., Luna, A., Moreno, G.: Fuzzy logic programming for implementing a flexible xpath-based query language. Electronic Notes in Theoretical Computer Science 282, 3–18 (2012)
2. Almendros-Jiménez, J.M., Luna, A., Moreno, G.: A xpath debugger based on fuzzy chance degrees. In: Herrero, P., Panetto, H., Meersman, R., Dillon, T. (eds.) OTM-WS 2012. LNCS, vol. 7567, pp. 669–672. Springer, Heidelberg (2012)
3. Almendros-Jiménez, J.M., Luna, A., Moreno, G., Vázquez, C.: Analyzing fuzzy logic computations with fuzzy xpath. In: Fredlund, A. (ed.) Proc. of XIII Spanish Conference on Programming and Languages, PROLE 2013, Madrid, Spain, September 18-20, p. 15. ECEASST (to appear, 2013)
4. Almendros-Jiménez, J.M., Luna, A., Moreno, G.: A Flexible XPath-based Query Language Implemented with Fuzzy Logic Programming. In: Bassiliades, N., Governatori, G., Paschke, A. (eds.) RuleML 2011 - Europe. LNCS, vol. 6826, pp. 186–193. Springer, Heidelberg (2011)
5. Almendros-Jiménez, J.M., Luna, A., Moreno, G.: Annotating Fuzzy Chance Degrees when Debugging Xpath Queries. In: Rojas, I., Joya, G., Cabestany, J. (eds.) IWANN 2013, Part II. LNCS, vol. 7903, pp. 300–311. Springer, Heidelberg (2013)
6. Amazon Elastic Compute Cloud (Amazon EC2), http://aws.amazon.com/ec2/ (visited July 30, 2013)
7. Barham, P., Dragovic, B., et al.: Xen and the art of virtualization. SIGOPS Oper. Syst. Rev. 37(5), 164–177 (2003)
8. Beloglazov, A., Buyya, R.: Managing overloaded hosts for dynamic consolidation of virtual machines in cloud data centers under quality of service constraints. IEEE Transactions on Parallel and Distributed Systems 24(7), 1366–1379 (2013)
9. Breitgand, D., Dubitzky, Z., Epstein, A., Glikson, A., Shapira, I.: SLA-aware resource overcommit in an IaaS cloud. In: Proc. of the 8th Intl. Conference on Network and Service Management (CNSM), pp. 73–81 (2012)
10. FLOPER - A Fuzzy LOgic Programming Environment for Research, http://dectau.uclm.es/floper/ (Visited June 7, 2013)
11. Julián, P., Moreno, G., Penabad, J.: Operational/Interpretive Unfolding of Multi-adjoint Logic Programs. Journal of Universal Computer Science 12(11), 1679–1699 (2006)

12. Klement, E.P., Mesiar, R., Pap, E.: Triangular Norms. Trends in logic, Studia logica library. Springer (2000)
13. Lloyd, J.W.: Foundations of Logic Programming, 2nd edn. Springer, Berlin (1987)
14. Medina, J., Ojeda-Aciego, M., Vojtáš, P.: Similarity-based Unification: A multi-adjoint approach. Fuzzy Sets and Systems 146, 43–62 (2004)
15. Morcillo, P.J., Moreno, G.: Programming with fuzzy logic rules by using the FLOPER tool. In: Bassiliades, N., Governatori, G., Paschke, A. (eds.) RuleML 2008. LNCS, vol. 5321, pp. 119–126. Springer, Heidelberg (2008)
16. Morcillo, P.J., Moreno, G.: Modeling interpretive steps in fuzzy logic computations. In: Di Gesù, V., Pal, S.K., Petrosino, A. (eds.) WILF 2009. LNCS (LNAI), vol. 5571, pp. 44–51. Springer, Heidelberg (2009)
17. Morcillo, P.J., Moreno, G., Penabad, J., Vázquez, C.: A Practical Management of Fuzzy Truth Degrees using FLOPER. In: Dean, M., Hall, J., Rotolo, A., Tabet, S. (eds.) RuleML 2010. LNCS, vol. 6403, pp. 20–34. Springer, Heidelberg (2010)
18. Morcillo, P.J., Moreno, G., Penabad, J., Vázquez, C.: Fuzzy Computed Answers Collecting Proof Information. In: Cabestany, J., Rojas, I., Joya, G. (eds.) IWANN 2011, Part II. LNCS, vol. 6692, pp. 445–452. Springer, Heidelberg (2011)
19. Rochwerger, B., Breitgand, D., et al.: The Reservoir model and architecture for open federated cloud computing. IBM J. Res. Dev. 53(4), 535–545 (2009)
20. Schweizer, B., Sklar, A.: Probabilistic Metric Spaces. Courier Dover Publ. (1983)
21. The NIST Definition of Cloud Computing, http://csrc.nist.gov/publications/nistpubs/800-145/SP800-145.pdf (visited July 30, 2013)
22. Tomás, L., Tordsson, J.: Improving Cloud Infrastructure Utilization through Overbooking. In: Proc. of the ACM Cloud and Autonomic Computing Conference, CAC (to appear, 2013)
23. Zadeh, L.A.: Fuzzy Sets. Information and Control 8(3), 338–353 (1965)
24. Zaharia, M., Hindman, B., et al.: The datacenter needs an operating system. In: Proc. of the 3rd USENIX Conference on Hot Topics in Cloud Computing, p. 17 (2011)

Rule Learning in a Fuzzy Decision Support System for the Environmental Risk Assessment of GMOs

Francesco Camastra[1,*], Angelo Ciaramella[1], Valeria Giovannelli[2],
Matteo Lener[2], Valentina Rastelli[2], Salvatore Sposato[1], Antonino Staiano[1],
Giovanni Staiano[2], and Alfredo Starace[1]

[1] Dept. of Science and Technology, University of Naples "Parthenope", Isola C4,
Centro Direzionale, I-80143, Napoli (NA), Italy
{camastra,angelo.ciaramella,staiano}@ieee.org,
{alfredo.starace,salvatoresposato2010}@gmail.com
[2] Nature Protection Dept., Institute for Environmental Protection and Research
(ISPRA), via v. Brancati 48, 00144 Roma,
{valeria.giovannelli,matteo.lener,
valentina.rastelli,giovanni.staiano}@isprambiente.it

Abstract. Aim of the paper is the application of a Learning Classifier System (LCS) to learn the inference rules in a Fuzzy Decision Support System (FDSS). The FDSS is used for the Environmental Risk Assessment (ERA) of the deliberate release of genetically modified plants. The evaluation process permits identifying potential impacts that can achieve one or more receptors through a set of migration paths. The risk assessment in the FDSS is obtained by using a Fuzzy Inference System performed using jFuzzyLogic library. For the human experts might be hard developing complex FISs. We propose to use a LCS for automatically learning the appropriate fuzzy rules from the questionnaires produced by notifiers, named Fuzzy Rule Learning System (FRLS). FRLS is based on a special kind of LCS, namely the eXtended Classifier System (XCS). The derived rules have been validated on real world cases by the human experts that are in charge of ERA.

Keywords: Learning Classifier System, eXtended Classifier System, Fuzzy Decision Support System, Risk Assessment, Genetically Modified Organisms, jFuzzyLogic library.

1 Introduction

The development of genetic engineering in the last years produced a very high number of genetically modified organisms (GMOs). Whereas in USA the use of GMOs is widely spread in agriculture, in Europe there are discordant policies w.r.t. GMO usage. For instance, commercialization of food and feed containing

---

* Corresponding Author.

F. Masulli, G. Pasi, and R. Yager (Eds.): WILF 2013, LNAI 8256, pp. 226–233, 2013.

or consisting of GMOs is duly approved in European Community (EC), while cultivation of new genetically modified crops are not adopted. The maize MON 810, approved by the old EC legislation framework, is currently the unique GMO cultivated in the EC (e.g., Czech Republic, Poland, Spain, Portugal, Romania and Slovakia). According to EC, the environmental release of GMOs is ruled by Directive 200118EC and Regulation 18292003EC. The Directive refers to the deliberate release into the environment of GMOs and sets out two regulatory regimes: Part C for the placing on the market and Part B for the deliberate release for any other purpose, i.e., field trials [14]. In both legislations the notifier, i.e., the person who requests the release into the environment of GMO, must perform an Environmental Risk Assessment (ERA) on the issue. The ERA is formally defined as "the evaluation of risks to human health and the environment, whether direct or indirect, immediate or delayed, which the deliberate release or the placing on the market of GMOs may pose". ERA should be carried out case by case, meaning that its conclusion may depends on the GM plants and trait concerned, their intended uses, and the potential receiving environments. The ERA process should lead to the identification and evaluation of potential adverse effects of the GMO, and, at the same time, it should be conducted with a view for identifying if there is a need for risk management and it should provides the basis for the monitoring plans. The aim of this work is the development of a decision system that should advise and help the notifier in performing the ERA about the cultivation of a specific genetically modified plant (GMP). ERA process is often performed in presence of incomplete and imprecise data. Moreover, it is generally yielded using the personal experience and knowledge of the notifier. Therefore the usage of fuzzy reasoning in the ERA decision support system is particularly appropriate as witnessed by the extensive application of fuzzy reasoning to the risk assessment in disparate fields [1,2,6,9,10,17]. However, for the human experts might be hard developing complex Fuzzy Inference System (FIS)s. In this paper we propose to use a LCS, and in particular the eXtended Classifier System, to learn the appropriate fuzzy rules from the questionnaires produced by notifiers. The Fuzzy Decision Support System (FDSS) is inspired by the methodological proposal of performing ERA on GMP field trials [14]. The methodology would allow to describe the relationships between potential receptors and the harmful characteristics of a GMP field trial, leading to the identification of potential impacts. The paper is organized as follows: In Section 2 the methodological proposal that has inspired the system is described; The FDSS structure of the Fuzzy System is discussed in Section 3 and the proposed Fuzzy Rule Learning System is presented in 4; Section 5 describes how experimental results has been performed; finally some conclusions are drawn in Section 6.

2   The Methodological Approach

The methodological proposal, that has inspired the system object of the paper, is based on a conceptual model [14]. The schema, shown in Figure 1, illustrates the

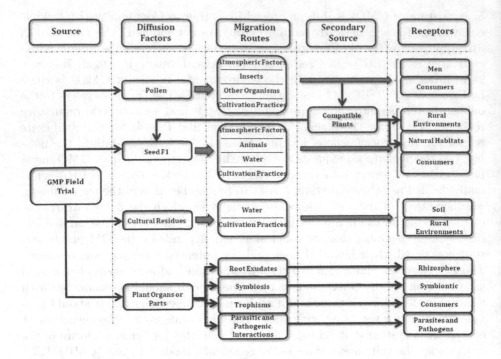

Fig. 1. Conceptual model of the impact source-receptors paths through diverse diffusion factors and migration routes

possible paths of the impact from a specific source to a given receptor through disparate diffusion factors and migration routes. The model implies that the notifier fills an electronic questionnaire. The notifier answers are collected in a relational database management system and, in a second time, become input of a fuzzy decision support engine that is the system core and provides to the notifier the overall evaluation of risk assessment related to a specific GM plant. The questionnaire can be grouped in specific sets of questions where each set corresponds to a specific box of the diagram of the conceptual model. For each block the potential effects are calculated by using fuzzy concepts and a fuzzy reasoning system. The questions can be of two different types, e.g., qualitative and quantitative. The former is typically descriptive and it is not used by fuzzy decision support system in the reasoning process. On the contrary, the latter is used by the fuzzy engine and can be an item chosen within a limited number of possible replies or a numeric or a boolean value.

3   The Fuzzy Decision Support System

The FDSS has the same architecture of a Fuzzy Logic Control System. Moreover, the FIS of FDSS has been implemented using the *jFuzzyLogic* library [4]. A Fuzzy

Logic Control (FLC) system incorporates the knowledge and experience of a human operator, the so-called *expert*, in the design of a system that controls a process whose input-output relationships are described by a set of fuzzy control rules, e.g., IF-THEN rules. We recall that the *antecedent* is the part of rule delimited by the keywords IF and THEN. Whereas the *consequent* is the part of the rule that follows the keyword THEN. The rules involve *linguistic variables* (*LV*s) that express qualitative high level concepts. A typical FLC architecture is composed of four principal components: a *fuzzifier*, a *fuzzy rule base*, an *inference engine* and a *defuzzifier* [12]. In particular, the fuzzy rule base stores the process knowledge of the domain experts. In most general cases, the fuzzy rule bases has the form of a *Multi-Input-Multi-Output (MIMO)* system. In this case the inference rules are combined by using the connectives AND and ELSE that can be interpreted as the intersection and the union for different definitions of fuzzy implications, respectively [3]. For instance, if we consider the LV *cultural cycle duration*, the fuzzy inference system of the LVs *cultural cycle duration* and *vegetative cycle duration* could be represented by:

> IF vegetative cycle duration is *Low* AND cultural cycle duration is *Low*
> THEN phenological risk is *High*
> ELSE
> IF vegetative cycle duration is *High* AND cultural cycle duration is *Low*
> THEN phenological risk is *Low* ELSE
> IF vegetative cycle duration is *High* AND cultural cycle duration is *High*
> THEN phenological risk is *High*

On the other hand, jFuzzyLogic is an open source software library for fuzzy systems which allows to design Fuzzy Logic Controllers supporting the standard *Fuzzy Control Programming* [11], published by the *International Electrotechnical Commission*(IEC). The library is written in Java and permits Fuzzy Control Language (FCL) design and implementation, fulfilling IEC standard. The standard defines a common language to exchange portable fuzzy control programs among different platforms. Moreover, jFuzzyLogic allows to implement a *Fuzzy Inference System* (FIS). A FIS is usually composed of one or more *Function Blocks* (FBs). Each FB has variables (input, output or instances) and one or more *Rule Blocks* (RBs). Each RB is composed of a set of rules, as well as Aggregation (i.e, *t-norms* and *t-conorms*), Activation (i.e., Minimum and Product) and Accumulation methods (e.g., Maximum, Bounded sum)[11]. Moreover, several implementations of membership functions and defuzzifcators are provided.

4   Learning Classifier Systems

Learning Classifier Systems (LCS) are rule-based, multifaceted, machine learning algorithms originated and have evolved in the cradle of evolutionary biology and artificial intelligence [7,8,18,19,15,16]. At the heart of this algorithm is the idea that, when dealing with complex systems, seeking a single best-fit model is less desirable than evolving a population of rules which collectively model that system. LCSs represent the merge of different fields of research encapsulated with a single algorithm. The core of a LCS is a set of rules (called the population of classifiers). Rules are typically represented in the form of "IF *condition* THEN *action*". The desired outcome of running the LCS algorithm is for those classifiers to collectively model an intelligent decision maker. To obtain that end, LCSs employ two biological metaphors, evolution and learning, where learning guides the evolutionary component to move toward a better set of rules. These concepts are respectively embodied by two mechanisms: the genetic algorithm and a learning mechanism appropriate of the given problem. While many different implementations of LCS algorithms exists, four practically universal components could be considered: (1) a finite population of classifiers that represents the current knowledge of the system, (2) a performance component, which regulates interaction between the environment and the classifier population, (3) a reinforcement component (also called credit assignment component), which distributes the reward received form the environment to the classifiers, and (4) a discovery component which use uses different operators to discover better rules and improve existing ones. The *eXtended Classifier System* (*XCS*) is a kind of LCS that differs from the traditional one primarily in its definition of classifier fitness and its relation to a robust reinforcement learning [19]. XCS noted for being able to reach optimal performance while evolving accurate and maximally general classifiers. XCS can be distinguished by the following key features: an accuracy based fitness, a niche Genetic Algorithm (GA) and an adaption of standard Q-Learning as credit assignment. Probably the most important innovation in XCS was the separation of the credit assignment component from the GA component, based on accuracy.

4.1   Fuzzy Rule Learning System (FRLS)

The FDSS has a knowledge base organized in 123 FBs and it consists of 6215 rules of the type described in Section 3. FDSS was tested producing about 150 ERAs related to GM plants (e.g., Bt-maize[1] and Brassica napus). The ERAs, yielded by FDSS, were submitted to a pool of ISPRA [2] experts, not involved in the FDSS knowledge base definition, in order to assess the consistency and completeness of FDSS evaluations. A great problem in a such FDSS is the presence of a high number of rules. To automatically extract an appropriate subset of rules we propose to use an XCS. Firstly the inference rules are coded in the XCS framework. In particular, in a "IF *condition* THEN *action*" schema each state of the classifier is a sequence of bits (language $0, 1, \#$). The *action* is coded by $0, 1, 2$ for *Low*, *Medium* and *High*, respectively. For example, the rule

IF vegetative cycle duration is *High* AND cultural cycle duration is *High*
THEN phenological risk is *High*

---

[1] Maize modified by using a Bt toxin (Bacillus thuringensis) [14].
[2] ISPRA is the institute governed by the Italian Ministery of the Environment that is in charge of GMO risk estimation.

is coded by the classifier in the following way:

$$Condition\ 111111\ Action\ 2 \qquad (1)$$

5   Experimental Results

We present two experimental results obtained by using the FRLS on a subset of the fuzzy rules of the FDSS. We concentrate on the extraction of the fuzzy rules adopted in the last step of the ERAs (i.e., potential impacts identification). The XCS requires some parameters that are initialized as described in [19]. Moreover the credit assignment can be 100 or 0 for exact or erroneous outputs, respectively. We use a training set composed by 80 rules and a test set of 16 obtained considering the ERAs, yielded by FDSS, that were submitted to the pool of ISPRA experts. The performance are considered as the percentage of the rules individuated in the test set. The prediction error is the difference between the predict and the real credit and the population has been normalized [19]. We observed that after 1000 iterations the performance is 100%, the prediction error decreases with a similar velocity and the population dimension has not an anomalous behaviour. However, some classifiers have worst performance than others and this is due by GA. For this reason a *condensation* mechanism [19] has been applied in the second experiment. In this case the *condensation* does not influence the performance and it improves the accuracy and the computational complexity. The final result that can be highlighted is that XCS is able to individuate the condition attributes (i.e., membership functions) that permit discriminating a determined class of the action part. For instance, we consider the rule generate by XCS as in Figure 2 that discriminate the class 2. As can be evidenced, the attributes that permit discriminating the class are the attributes 1, 2, 3 and 5. The other attributes are not fundamental to discriminate the class. This information is fundamental to identify the appropriate rules, and, in particular for this example, the one in the test set to have action 2.

6   Conclusions

In this paper the application of a Learning Classifier System for an automatic learning of the inference rules in a Fuzzy Decision Support System has been proposed. The FDSS is used for the ERA of the deliberate release of genetically modified plants. The risk assessment in the FDSS is obtained by using a FIS, performed using jFuzzyLogic library and a Fuzzy Rule Learning System. The Fuzzy Rule Learning System is based on a particular LCS that is the eXtended Classifier System. The learned rules have been validated on real world cases by the human experts that are in charge of ERA. In the next future we plan to develop a more general Fuzzy Rule Learning System that automatically learns the knowledge base of FDSS considering all the set of migration paths.

		Class
Generate rule (XCS)	1 1 1 # 1 1 # #	2
	1 1 1 1 1 1 0 0	2
	1 1 1 1 1 1 1 1	2
Training set	1 1 1 0 1 1 1 1	2
	1 1 1 0 1 1 0 1	2
	1 1 1 0 1 1 1 0	2
	1 1 1 0 1 1 0 0	2
	. . .	
Test set	1 1 1 1 1 1 0 0	2

Fig. 2. Experimental results

Acknowledgements. This research has been partially funded by the LIFE project MAN-GMP-ITA (Agreement n. LIFE08 NAT/IT/000334). Part of the work was developed by Salvatore Sposato as final dissertation project for B. Sc. in Computer Science at University of Naples Parthenope.

References

1. Chen, Y.-L., Weng, C.-H.: Mining fuzzy association rules from questionnaire data. Knowledge-Based Systems 22, 46–56 (2009)
2. Chen, Z., Zhao, L., Lee, K.: Environmental risk assessment of offshore produced water discharges using a hybrid fuzzy-stochastic modeling approach. Environmental Modelling & Software 25, 782–792 (2010)
3. Ciaramella, A., Tagliaferri, R., Pedrycz, W.: The genetic development of ordinal sums. Fuzzy Sets and Systems 151(2), 303–325 (2005)
4. Cingolani, P., Alcala-Fdez, J.: jFuzzyLogic: A Robust and Flexible Fuzzy-Logic Inference System Language Implementation. In: Proceedings of IEEE World Congress on Computational Intelligence 2012, June 10-15 (2012)
5. Cormen, T.H., Leiserson, C.E., Rivest, R.L., Stein, C.: Introduction to Algorithms, 3rd edn. The MIT Press (2009)
6. Davidson, V.J., Ryks, J., Fazil, A.: Fuzzy risk assessment tool for microbial hazards in food systems. Fuzzy Sets and Systems 157, 1201–1210 (2006)
7. Holland, J., Reitman, J.: Cognitive systems based on adaptive agents. In: Waterman, D.A., Inand, F., Hayes-Roth (eds.) Pattern-Directed Inference Systems (1978)

8. Holland, J.: Hidden Order: How Adaptation Builds Complexity. Addison-Wesley, Reading (1996)
9. Kahraman, C., Kaya, I.: Fuzzy Process Accuracy Index to Evaluate Risk Assessment of Drought Effects in Turkey. Human and Ecological Risk Assessment 15, 789–810 (2009)
10. Karimi, I., Hullermeier, E.: Risk assessment system of natural hazards: A new approach based on fuzzy probability. Fuzzy Sets and Systems 158, 987–999 (2007)
11. International Electrotechnical Commission technical committee industrial process measurement and control2. IEC 61131 - Programmable Controllers. Part 7: Fuzzy Control Programming. IEC 2000 (2000)
12. Lin, C.-T., Lee, C.S.: Neural Fuzzy Systems: A Neuro-Fuzzy Synergism to Intelligent Systems. Prentice Hall (1996)
13. Parr, T.J., Quong, R.W.: Software: Practice and Experience 25(7), 789–810 (1995)
14. Sorlini, C., Buiatti, M., Burgio, G., Cellini, F., Giovannelli, V., Lener, M., Massari, G., Perrino, P., Selva, E., Spagnoletti, A., Staiano, G.: La valutazione del rischio ambientale dell' immissione deliberata nell' ambiente di organismi geneticamente modificati. Tech. Report (2003) (in Italian),
http://bch.minambiente.it/EN/Biosafety/propmet.asp
15. Stolzmann, W.: Anticipatory classifier systems. In: Proceedings of the 3rd Annual Genetic Programming Conference, pp. 658–664 (1998)
16. Urbanowicz, R.J., Moore, J.H.: Learning Classifier Systems: A Complete Introduction, Review, and Roadmap. Journal of Artificial Evolution and Applications 2009, Article ID 736398, 25 pages (2009)
17. Wang, Y.-M., Elhag, T.M.S.: An adaptive neuro-fuzzy inference system for bridge risk assessment. Expert Systems with Applications 34, 3099–3106 (2008)
18. Wilson, S.W.: ZCS: A zeroth level classifier system. Evolutionary Computation 2(1), 1–18 (1994)
19. Wilson, S.W.: Classifier fitness based on accuracy. Evolutionary Computation 3(2), 149–175 (1995)

A Fuzzy Cellular Automata for SIR Compartmental Models

Walley da Costa[1], Líliam Medeiros[2], and Sandra Sandri[1]

[1] Instituto Nacional de Pesquisas Espaciais - INPE
12201-970, São José dos Campos, SP
walleycosta@gmail.com, sandra.sandri@inpe.br
[2] Universidade Estadual Paulista - Unesp
12245-000, São José dos Campos, SP
liliam.castro@gmail.com

Abstract. We propose a representation of the dynamics of epidemics through a compartmental SIR (Susceptible - Infected - Recovered) model, with the combined use of geo-referenced cellular automata and fuzzy systems. In this model, each cell does not correspond to an individual, but to groups of individuals inhabiting the physical space corresponding to the cell. The temporal evolution of the transmission consider is modeled by changes in the size of groups of individuals in each category (susceptible, infected and recovered). We applied our model on the spread of dengue in a region in Southeast Brazil. The application shows that the proposed model, using only a small set of simple fuzzy rules, is able to represent qualitatively the behavior of an epidemiological SIR mode, a rather complex problem.

Keywords: SIR, Infectious Diseases, Cellular Automata, Fuzzy Systems, Dengue.

1 Introduction

Epidemiology math [21] is a an area of science that proposes mathematical models to be used by policy-makers in infectious diseases control. Compartmental modeling, in particular, has been widely used to study diseases epidemiology [8], with *SIR* (Susceptible-Infected-Recovered) being the mostly used model to deal with the transmission dynamics of infectious diseases [10]. The study of spatial-temporal disease distribution can provide a wealth of information for the understanding, prediction, etiologic search, and prevention of diseases as well as assessing the impact of health interventions.

Cellular Automata are able to describe the spatial-temporal evolution of complex systems, such as the spread of epidemics [15]. A set of transition rules alters the attributes of each cell, according to the attributes of neighboring cells. Transition rules for cellular automata simulating real systems are sometimes ill-known.

Fuzzy Sets Theory extends classical set theory, allowing intermediate degrees of membership. It is a significant and powerful representation of uncertainty, valuable representation of vague concepts expressed in natural language [11]. This theory allows the creation of transition rules for cellular automata, ie, the behavior of a cell, by modeling the knowledge of an expert on the behavior of the real system. Some applications

F. Masulli, G. Pasi, and R. Yager (Eds.): WILF 2013, LNAI 8256, pp. 234–247, 2013.

using fuzzy systems to model transition rules in cellular automata in epidemiological problems can be found in [17] and [14].

Here we propose a representation of the dynamics of epidemics through a SIR model, using a combination of cellular automata and fuzzy systems. We also present an application of the proposed model on the spread of dengue in a region of Southeast Brazil.

2 General Concepts

This section presents the main concepts and definitions used in this work, with a brief description of SIR models, cellular automata and fuzzy systems.

2.1 SIR Model

SIR models divide the population into three compartments (or classes) of individuals:

- S: individuals who can contract the disease (Susceptible),
- I: individuals who can transmit the disease (Infected),
- R: individuals who have recovered from the disease (Recovered).

The classic way to present a compartmental model of SIR type is via a set of differential equations.

Figure 1 illustrates standard SIR models temporal evolution, without renewal of humans (constant population, no deaths or births and emigration and immigration) and with renewal, for a disease in which the recovered individuals obtain immunity against the disease. In Figure 1.b), regarding a SIR model without renewal of humans, the entire population is initially susceptible to disease, over time this ratio begins to fall, with the percentage of infected individuals simultaneously increasing, until, finally, the entire population is recovered and immunized. The exact form and inflection of the curves depend on the details of the infectious agent. Once the derivative of the infection rate becomes negative, more people will be recovered from the disease and these two trend lines will intersect.

2.2 Cellular Automata

Cellular automata were proposed in the 1960s, aiming at modeling biological phenomena such as self-reproductive systems [19]. Cellular automata are self-reproductive dynamic systems, with time and space described in discrete scales, consisting of a grid made up of cells. At each point of time, each cell has a state, taken from a predetermined finite set of states. The change of state in each time step depends on a set of transition rules (or bridging function), which are constructed based on the possible states of the cell itself and its neighboring cells [20].

A cellular automaton can be defined as a 4-tuple (L, E, N, f), in which:

- L is a regular d - dimensional grid, formed by cells,
- E is a finite set of states,

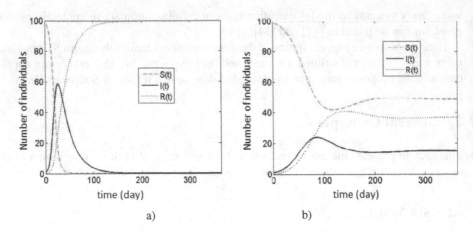

Fig. 1. Examples of SIR models: a) without and b) with renewal of humans (Source: [1])

- N is a finite set of neighborhoods, of size $|N| = n$ and dimension d, such that for any cell c in L, its neighborhood $N(c)$ is a subset of L,
- $f : E^{n+1} \to E$ is a state transition function (transition rule).

Once the transition rules and an initial state to all cells of the grid have been established, the system dynamics can be developed. To ensure a well-defined dynamics of cellular automata, it is important to obey some boundary conditions. These conditions indicate how the automaton is characterized beyond its limit and are necessary in order to complete the set of neighboring cells that lie on the edges of the automaton and influence the result of the application of the transition rules.

2.3 Fuzzy Inference Systems

A fuzzy set can be mathematically defined by assigning to each element of the universe of discourse a value on a limited scale. This degree represents how much each element is compatible with (or similar to) the concept represented by fuzzy set [11]. Formally, a fuzzy set A in the universe of discourse Ω is defined by a membership function $A : \Omega \to [0, 1]$.

In a Fuzzy Inference System (FIS), knowledge about a problem is encoded by a set of rules of thumb, having fuzzy sets in the premise and/or conclusion. Given the values of a set of input variables (measurements or observations), a value for the output variable is computed using the rules. In the so-called classical fuzzy systems, whose main representative is the Mamdani model, knowledge is modeled using rules of the type

$$R_j : \text{If } x_1 \text{ is } A_{1,j} \text{ and } ... \text{ and } x_n \text{ is } A_{n,j} \text{ Then } y \text{ is } C_j.$$

Variables x_i and y, called linguistic variables, take values in domains X_i and Y, respectively, and A_{ij} and C_j are normalized fuzzy sets associated to them, called fuzzy terms. A fuzzy set A in X is said to be normalized when $\exists x \in X, A(x) = 1$.

In classical fuzzy models, the inference process is described as follows. Let $x_i^* \in X_i$ be the realization value of x_i in a given application.

1. The compatibility of the i-th premise of j-th rule with x_i^* is computed as:

$$\alpha_{i,j} = A_{i,j}(x_i^*), 1 \leq i \leq n, 1 \leq j \leq m.$$

2. The overall compatibility of a rule with the input values is calculated as

$$\alpha_j = \top(\alpha_{1,j}, ..., \alpha_{n,j}), 1 \leq j \leq m.$$

3. Fuzzy set C_j in the consequent of the rule R_j is combined with α_j, yielding a fuzzy set

$$C_j'(y) = I(\alpha_j, C_j(y)), \forall y \in Y.$$

4. Fuzzy sets C_j' are aggregated into a single fuzzy set

$$C'(y) = \phi(C_{1'}(y), ..., C_{m'}(y)), \forall y \in Y.$$

5. A crisp value is obtained from C' as

$$y^* = Def(C').$$

Conjunctive operator $\top : [0,1]^2 \rightarrow [0,1]$ is a T-norm, a commutative, associative, mononotonic operator with neutral element 1. In most applications, the implication operator $I : [0,1]^2 \rightarrow [0,1]$ in fact a T-norm, but there exist models that use a residuated implication operator for I instead [6]. Operator ϕ is a T-norm when I is a residuated implication operator and a T-conorm (a commutative, associative, mononotonic operator with neutral element 0) when I is a T-norm. For example, in Mamdani model, we have $\top = min$ and $\phi = max$. Operator Def is a mapping $\mathcal{F}(Y) \rightarrow Y$, where $\mathcal{F}(Y)$ is the set of all fuzzy sets in Y; in most applications the center of gravity is used for Def.

3   A SIR Framework Using Fuzzy Cellular Automata

In the following, we propose to model the dynamics of a disease in a given community as a fuzzy cellular automaton, consisting of a two-dimensional geo-referenced grid of rectangular cells. Our dynamical model is based on the infection transmission rate of a cell (ρ_{tr}), calculated from the rate of infected individuals (ρ_I), and the rate of recovered ones (ρ_R) in that cell. We consider various levels of geographical vicinity influence and propose the use of a fuzzy system that has ρ_I and ρ_R as input variables and ρ_{tr} as output variable, at each influence level. In a nutshell, in each time step, the transmission rate calculated for one level of influence modifies the SIR composition of cell for the next level of influence.

3.1 Basic Elements of the Proposed SIR Framework

The model is based on a cellular automaton (L, E, V, f) as described in the previous section. We list below the main elements of our framework:

- Each cell c in the cellular automaton is defined by a vector that represents the population inhabiting the physical space corresponding to that cell.
- In the simplest model, the data stored on cell c includes the amount of susceptible, infected and recovered individuals in c, respectively denoted by I, R and S. The total number of humans is denoted by T and is given by $T = I + R + S$.
- In some problems, it is also necessary to divide the total infected humans I into m stages of infection $I^1, I^2, ..., I^m$.

Here we list some of the particularities of the basic model:

- The number of agents that transmit the disease is not explicit; it is taken implicitly into account in the number of infected humans.
- The population size of humans (and implicitly of vectors) are considered to be constant. The number of humans in each cell may vary, but we do not consider renewal, i.e., birth, death, immigration and emigration are not taken into consideration explicitly.
- We consider that a certain percentage of the population is asymptomatic and that individuals move to neighboring areas.
- We consider that diseases can have different infections stages.
- Climate variations are not considered, as well as the composition of the population is terms of age.
- Moore vicinity is assumed, with zero boundary condition [20].

Infection stages can last different lengths of time. However, in our simplified model, we considered the duration for all stages as the same length of the time step adopted in the implemented simulation environment.

3.2 Proposed Dynamic Model

Infectious diseases caused by viruses can have one or more hosts. In the case of flu in humans, the transmission is done from one individual to the other. In dengue, the transmission cycle is done with two hosts: humans and mosquitoes. In the case of more than one type of host, the dynamics of the disease can be modeled by addressing the dynamics of each host. For example in the case of dengue, we could use the SIR model for humans and SI for the mosquitoes. One can also model the dynamics of this kind of diseases, considering only the dynamics of a single host explicitly, and leaving the dynamics of other hosts implicit.

The dynamic model proposed here is the simple one, where transmitting agents (vectors) are not dealt with explicitly. It is thus as if a host infected another individual of the same type directly. The rules proposed above still apply, in the sense that the larger is the group of of infected individuals of the first type of hosts, the larger becomes the group of infected individuals of the second type of hosts, which in turn further enlarges the group of infected hosts of the first type.

Here we consider that the closer are infected neighbors to an individual, the larger their influence in getting that individual also infected. We propose to use the concept of *local influence*, considering the individuals inside a cell, and *non local influence* considering those from neighboring cells. We consider here that several levels of influence are possible, and number them; level 0 corresponds to the local influence. Using Moore vicinity, for instance, we would consider for instance 8 neighbors at the first level of non local influence, then 33 at the second level, etc. Figure 2 illustrates the cells involved in different influence levels.

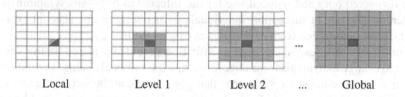

| Local | Level 1 | Level 2 | ... | Global |

Fig. 2. Different areas of influence of infection that may be present in a model, from local to global, with intermediary levels.

When we consider the influence of neighboring cells on the health of individuals inside a cell, we have to consider the mobility of the infected humans of the cell itself, as they can move to other cells and favor the infection of individuals on those cells. Moreover, we have to consider that infected individuals have reduced mobility, due to their physical condition, except for the asymptomatic ones.

We propose to use the following input parameters to model asymptomatic humans and human mobility:

- ρ_{asy} is the percentage of individuals with asymptomatic infections (no symptoms), which is related to environmental factors, individual agent and transmitter of the virus itself;
- ρ_{mob} is the human mobility rate to neighboring cells.

For each level of influence, we calculate parameters ρ_I, ρ_R and ρ_{tr}. The transmission rate ρ_{tr} is used to calculate a new SIR composition for the cell inhabitants; ρ_{tr} itself is derived using a fuzzy system (see below). The levels of influence are considered sequentially: the composition of a cell is changed after the local influence is treated, with some susceptible individuals becoming infected, and others recovered, the new composition is the basis for processing in the next influence level, and so on, until the influence of all relevant levels are addressed.

Let c be a cell of interest, with its corresponding SIR parameters I, R and S, with $T = S + I + R$. Let N_c denote the neighboring cells of c, considering a given level of influence. Let I_α and R_α denote the number of infected and recovered individuals in a cell α in N_c. We calculate ρ_I and ρ_R, in relation to a cell c, as:

1. Local influence (level 0):
   (a) $\rho_I = I/T$;
   (b) $\rho_R = R/T$.

2. Non local influence (levels greater than 0):

(a) $t_I = I \times \rho_{mob} \times \rho_{asy} + \sum_{\alpha \in N_c} I_\alpha$;

(b) $t_R = R \times \rho_{mob} + \sum_{\alpha \in N_c} R_\alpha$;

(c) $t_T = (S + R) \times \rho_{mob} + I \times \rho_{mob} \times \rho_{asy} + \sum_{\alpha \in N_c} T_\alpha$;

(d) $\rho_I = t_I / t_T$;

(e) $\rho_R = t_R / t_T$,

Values t_T, t_I and t_R respectively quantify the total number of individuals, the number of infected individuals and the number of recovered individuals in the neighborhood of a cell, taking into account the individuals from the cell that have mobility (full mobility for the recovered ones and reduced one for the infected as only the asymptomatic are considered). The rate of susceptible individuals ρ_S is not taken into account explicitly, since it can be determined from ρ_I and ρ_R, as $\rho_S = 1 - \rho_I - \rho_R$.

In some problems, several stages of an infection should considered. In this case, we propose to change individuals from stage k to stage $k+1$ after Δ_k steps. The individuals in the first stage are the susceptible ones that got infected at the step being processed. At the end of each time step, individuals in stage I^1 move to I^2, those in I^2 move to I^3 and so on, until people in the last stage move to R. Table 1 illustrates the behavior of a cell c of the automaton in an iteration, with three infection stages and m levels of influence (0 to $m - 1$); level m denotes the final results.

Table 1. Behavior of a cell of the automaton in an iteration, for m levels of influence

$$\boxed{T(0)} \boxed{S(0)} \boxed{R(0)} \boxed{I(0)} \boxed{I^1(0)} \boxed{I^2(0)} \boxed{I^3(0)} \Rightarrow$$
$$\Rightarrow \boxed{\rho_R(0)} \boxed{\rho_R(0)} \Rightarrow \boxed{\rho_{tr}(0)} \Rightarrow$$
$$\Rightarrow \boxed{T(1)} \boxed{S(1)} \boxed{R(1)} \boxed{I(1)} \boxed{I^1(1)} \boxed{I^2(1)} \boxed{I^3(1)} \& \boxed{t_T(1)} \boxed{t_I(1)} \boxed{t_R(1)} \Rightarrow$$
$$\Rightarrow \boxed{\rho_R(1)} \boxed{\rho_R(1)} \Rightarrow \boxed{\rho_{tr}(1)} \Rightarrow \ldots$$
$$\ldots \Rightarrow \boxed{\rho_R(m-1)} \boxed{\rho_R(m-1)} \Rightarrow \boxed{\rho_{tr}(m-1)} \Rightarrow$$
$$\boxed{T(m)} \boxed{S(m)} \boxed{R(m)} \boxed{I(m)} \boxed{I^1(m)} \boxed{I^2(m)} \boxed{I^3(m)}$$

3.3 Fuzzy Inference System

Some applications using fuzzy systems to model transition rules in cellular automata in epidemiological problems can be found in [17] and [14]. These works both extend the approach proposed by [5] to study the temporal evolution of a disease of type SIR using cellular automata, taking into account a spacial structure. In [5], the authors consider that each cell in the automata is occupied by an individual. The disease transmission takes into account two types of proximity: a local one, considering the cell immediate neighbours (8) and individuals in a distance of radius L from that cell. In the second type of proximity, the interaction between individuals is made considering random values for L. In [17] and [14], the cells still correspond to individuals but instead of aleatory values for L, a fuzzy system is used. In both works, a Mamdani fuzzy inference system is used, having the length L as the output variable in the conclusion of the rules.

Here we propose to create a fuzzy inference system that takes the percentages of infected and recuperated individuals in a cell to determine the percentage of individuals in that cell who are expected to become infected (in the first stage) in the next time step. More formally, the infection transmission rate determines, for each cell in the grid, the amount of people in set S that will pass to set I^1, after Δ_1. These values are then used to compute the state of each cell at the next time step.

The variables used in the fuzzy rule base are formally defined as:

- Input variables: $\rho_I \in [0,1]$ (rate of infected individuals in a cell) and $\rho_R \in [0,1]$ (rate of recuperated individuals in a cell).
- Output variable: $\rho_{tr} \in [0,1]$ (rate of susceptible individuals in a cell that will become infected).

The rate of susceptible individuals $\rho_S \in [0,1]$ is not taken into account since it can be determined from ρ_I and ρ_R, as $\rho_S = 1 - \rho_I - \rho_R$.

Here we present a simple general fuzzy cellular automaton, used in the remaining of this work. Each input and output variable is associated with the same set of linguistic terms: L (Low), M (Average), H (High) defined on domain [0,1]. The rule base was defined empirically and is described below:

1. If ρ_I is L, Then ρ_{tr} is L
2. If ρ_I is M, Then ρ_{tr} is M
3. If ρ_I is H, Then ρ_{tr} is H
4. If ρ_R is L, Then ρ_{tr} is H
5. If ρ_R is H, Then ρ_{tr} is L

The three first rules state that the highest the number of infected people, the higher the chances of susceptible individuals becoming infected. The two last rules state that the highest the number of recuperated individuals, the lower the chances of susceptible people becoming infected. Figure 3 illustrates the linguistic variables the dynamics of dengue (see Section 4).

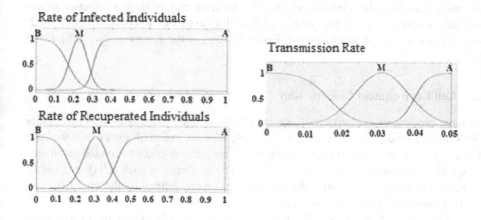

Fig. 3. Fuzzy terms of input and output used in dengue application

3.4 Implementation

This dynamical model was implemented using the programming environment for modeling spatial dynamics TerraME [3]. TerraME provides a connection to the geographic database TerraLib [2], and use Lua programming language [9] for creating models. TerraLib, a class library written in C++, provides functions to decode spatial data, spatiotemporal data structures and spatial analysis algorithms. It also providing a model for geographic databases. Lua combines simple procedural syntax with data description constructs based on associative arrays and extensible semantics. LuaFuzzy library[1], written entirely in Lua, was used to implement a Mamdani fuzzy system.

We have also used TerraView[2], a Geographic Information System (GIS), developed from TerraLib for acquisition of vector and matrix spatiotemporal data, as well as visualization and analysis. Using TerraView, one can construct a Geographical Data Base (GDB) for a given area. One of the layers of a with a layer may contains census tract maps, as well as static tables linked to the map, with identification data such as geocode and the district name for each census tract in an municipality. TerraView has an operator, called *majority class*, that determines, from all the polygons that intersect with a given cell (e.g. sectors tracts), the one that has the largest area of intersection with that cell. In this way, the attributes of each cell are the same attributes of the census tract that has the largest area of intersection with that cell.

4   An Application with Dengue Virus Infection

Dengue is an arthropod-borne disease and is caused by four different virus serotypes: DENV1, DENV2, DENV3 and DENV4. In Brazil, the main vector of transmission is the *Aedes aegypti* species. The spread of dengue virus infection in humans for each serotype can be modeled using compartmental SIR models.

Given the complexity of the epidemiology of dengue, due to interactions between humans, mosquitoes, infection stages and various serotypes, as well as effective strategies for mosquito survival, computational modeling approach to compartmental modeling can assist in understanding the diffusion process of the disease and its influencing factors.

4.1 Cell Environment Construction

We have created an application of our model for dengue, using Ilha do Governador (Governor's Island), located in the city of Rio de Janeiro, in Brazil. First of all, we have created a a GDB for Ilha do Governador using TerraView. A grid was created on an area map, with square cells of 134 x 116 resolution. The attributes of each cell (for example, the name of the district to which the cell belongs) were defined by the majority class function, described in the previous section.

By visual inspection on a satellite image, we have manually determined which cells could be consider as uninhabited (forests, parts of the airport, etc). Any cell whose

---

[1] http://luaforge.net/projects/luafuzzy/
[2] http://www.dpi.inpe.br/terraview/index.php

intersection area with the polygons of census tracts was less than 0.5 (50 %), was also considered uninhabited (e.g., small areas on the shoreline). Figure 4 depicts Ilha do Governador, by both census tracts and the obtained cellular space.

The data about the population in Ilha do Governador, as well as the number of registered dengue cases, were obtained from the Municipal Health and Civil Defense Agency of the City of Rio de Janeiro[3]. Both types of data are divided into districts. The dengue cases are relative to year 2001 and the population data wew obtained from the year 2000 census. We have used the hypothesis that only 40% of the total number of dengue cases were reported to SINAN (Information System for Notifiable Diseases), corresponding to the bedridden symptomatic infected individuals. The population was then distributed evenly in the inhabited areas, according to the district to which they belong. The total number of cases, calculated from the reported ones, was divided between recovered and infected individuals, and uniformly distributed in the cells. The number of susceptible individuals in each cell c have been calculated as the difference between the total number of humans and the sum of infected and recovered humans, i.e., $S = T - (I + R)$.

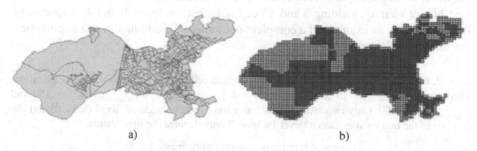

a)   b)

Fig. 4. Ilha do Governador represented by: a) census tracts b) cellular space (cells in yellow are considered uninhabited) [4]

4.2   Particularities of the Model

To simulate the spread of dengue virus infection on Ilha do Governador, the transmitting agent (which is implicit in the model) is the *Aedes aegypti* mosquito species; for simplicity, we considered that there was only one serotype circulating, DENV3, the predominant serotype since the 2001 dengue epidemic in Rio de Janeiro [16].

We considered two levels of influence: level 0 (local) and level 1 (non local), formed by neighboring cells of radius one in Moore vicinity, considering inhabited cells. In the real world types occur simultaneously influence, but for reasons of implementation and layout decided to apply the local influence and subsequently non-local (as described in subsection 3.2) to find the values of ρ_I and ρ_R. Using these values as input to the fuzzy system, we obtained the transmission rate as output. This rate was then used to calculate the new values of susceptible and individuals people in the 1st stage of infection.

This model has three stages of infection. The period in which people stay in any of the three stages of the infection is 2 days ($\Delta_1 = \Delta_2 = \Delta_3 = 2$), ie, a person infected

---

[3] http://www.rio.rj.gov.br/web/smsdc

remains a total of 6 days before recovering. At the end of an iteration, people in the last stage of infection moved to the recovered group. It is considered that at the time $t = 0$, all people infected in the cell environment (as constructed in Section 4.2), are in the first stage of infection.

The input variables of the Fuzzy Inference System and the range of numeric values defined for the output variable (0 to 0.05) were defined empirically. In the simulations were used sigmoidal and Gaussian functions.

In the simulation, the rate of human mobility to neighboring cells is 30 % ($\rho_{mob} = 0.3$) and In the simulations, as well as the construction of the cellular environment, it was considered that 40 % of cases of dengue are symptomatic, ie, $\rho_{asy} = 0.6$.

4.3 Results

Using the the GDB created for Ilha do Governador and the fuzzy rules presented previously, with the linguistic variables depicted in Figure 3, we have created the fuzzy system for the dengue dynamics described in the previous section. We ran a the simulation of the model, using this fuzzy system and the parameters described above. We have used Moore vicinity, yielding 9 and 33 cell neighbors in levels 0 and 1, respectively. Table 4.3 shows an example of a complete iteration of the automaton in a hypothetical cell using this simulation.

Table 2. Example of a partial iteration in a hypothetical cell c of the automaton in our application, with parameters $\rho_{asy} = .6$ and $\rho_{mob} = .3$ and $\sum_{\alpha \in N_c} I_\alpha = 80$, $\sum_{\alpha \in N_c} R_\alpha = 150$ and $\sum_{\alpha \in N_c} T_\alpha = 800$. Only two levels of influence have been considered, local (level 0) and the first one of the non local influence (level 1); level 2 only denotes the final results.

$T(0)$	$S(0)$	$R(0)$	$I(0)$	$I^1(0)$	$I^2(0)$	$I^3(0)$
100	68	22	10	3	5	2

$\Rightarrow$

$\rho_I(0)$	$\rho_R(0)$
0.1	0.22

$\Rightarrow$

$\rho_{tr}(0)$
0.0424

$\Rightarrow$

$T(1)$	$S(1)$	$R(1)$	$I(1)$	$I^1(1)$	$I^2(1)$	$I^3(1)$
100	65	22	13	6	5	2

&

$t_T(1)$	$t_I(1)$	$t_R(1)$
829	82	157

$\Rightarrow$

$\rho_I(1)$	$\rho_R(1)$
0.099	0.19

$\Rightarrow$

$\rho_{tr}(1)$
0.0437

$\Rightarrow$

$T(2)$	$S(2)$	$R(2)$	$I(2)$	$I^1(2)$	$I^2(2)$	$I^3(2)$
100	64	24	12	4	3	5

The result for a simulation in our application is shown in Figure 5. We see that the dynamical model has been able to represent qualitatively the behavior of a SIR epidemiological model. Changes in the various parameters result in different curves, but they should all follow the basic SIR graph, because we move the individuals from one state to the other following the SIR order.

It is important to note here that since the mosquito *Aedes aegypti* is not modeled directly, but implied by infected humans, this model only serves as an early example or illustration of the use of SIR model using fuzzy cellular automata, and is not meant to serve as a means of forecasting, planning, disease control or similar.

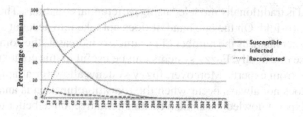

Fig. 5. Results of the proposed model in a simulation for dengue, without renewal of humans

5   Conclusions and Future Work

We have proposed a SIR model to represent the dynamics of an infectious disease in a given community. Our dynamical model is based on the infection transmission rate of a cell, calculated from the rate of infected individuals and the rate of recovered ones in that cell. We have also proposed to implement this model using a fuzzy cellular automaton, consisting of a two-dimensional geo-referenced cell grid. Our model considers various levels of geographical vicinity influence and uses a fuzzy system to calculate the infection transmission rate. Moreover, we have created an application of our model for dengue, a viral disease, using Ilha do Governador (Governor's Island), located in the city of Rio de Janeiro, in Brazil.

Our approach considers two important characteristics for transmission models of infectious disease type SIR: the percentage of recovered and the percentage of asymptomatic individuals. The larger the amount of people recovered from the disease (ie immunized), the slower the disease will be transmitted, since the number of contacts between the infected and susceptible individuals decreases. On the other hand, the asymptomatic individuals are directly responsible for the mass continuity of disease transmission, as they continue their daily mobility normally.

A variety of environmental factors influences the spatial and temporal dynamics of vector populations in the case of vector transmitted diseases [7]. Studying the factors influencing spatial patterns of mosquito transmitted diseases such as dengue is somewhat complicated, since it requires refined data about climate, vectors and their aquatic stages. Such studies and collection types still occur locally in some areas within municipalities in Brazil (see, for example, [18]), but are not done in a general basis. Thus, computational simulation becomes an important tool in the study of scenarios and spatial patterns of disease transmission, as well as to help decision making.

Our fuzzy cellular automaton creates an environment in which the spread of SIR diseases can be studied, allowing the observation of disease prevalence spatial patterns. The approach has yet to be validated by experts but they already indicate that the approach is very promising, since the dynamical model has been able to represent qualitatively the behavior of a SIR epidemiological model. It is important to note that, however, the model is not aimed at making forecasts about diseases, but rather to generate temporal, spatial or spatial-temporal scenarios that allow a better understanding of the complexity as well as the dynamics of disease transmission.

Disease spread is traditionally modeled using differential equations. The drawback of this approach is two-fold. On the one hand, it does not take into account spatial heterogeneity. On the other hand, as the number of parameters increases, the complexity of the equations increase drastically. Fuzzy systems can be useful in this context, by incorporating knowledge from experts. Moreover, fuzzy systems allow for a rapid prototyping process, which does not always occur when the transition function is analytical, given its complexity. Expert knowledge can also be an alternative to the better understanding of a given topic, in the lack of data. That is for instance the case of the study of disease dynamics, when spatially refined data is poor. The fuzzy approach allows dealing more easily with different levels of uncertainty and imprecision that occur, when using vague concepts and parameters of a subjective nature. Our dynamic model has shown that a small set of simple fuzzy rules is capable of dealing with a rather complex problem. Another advantage is that these rules are easily understood by disease scholars without deep mathematical training.

Our model differs from others in the literature for similar problems [17] and [14]. In those works, each cell corresponds to a single individual, whereas we consider that each cell is inhabited by a a population of individuals. In our case, the interactions between groups of susceptible, infected and recuperated humans are considered in a statistical basis and is thus less subject to individual mobility.

In the future, we intend to extend our model, by incorporating a human renewal rate, which will allow modeling the epidemic that occurs in cycles, since in this case there will always exist people susceptible to the disease. We also intend to extend the basic framework to more complex models of vector transmitted diseases, In this case, the population of vectors is taken into account explicitly, what requires the use of extra parameters. For example, in diseases such as dengue, the infection process of the vectors follows a SI (Susceptible-Infected) model and additional numbers would be needed to account for them. Also, in the particular case of the dengue model, other serotypes may be included. Last but not least, intervention measures may be considered, as the presence of Wolbachia bacteria in mosquitoes or vaccination strategies, considering that dengue vaccines are nowadays under development.

References

1. Biomat04, http://biomat04.wikispaces.com/conceitos
2. Câmara, G., Cartaxo, R., De Souza, M., Pedrosa, B.M., Vinhas, L., Monteiro, A.M.V., Paiva, J.A., De Carvalho, M.T., Gattass, M.: TerraLib: Technology in Support of GIS Innovation. In: II Brazilian Symposium on Geoinformatics, GeoInfo 2000, São Paulo (2000)
3. Carneiro, T.G.S.: Nested-CA: A Foundation for Multiscale Modeling of Land Use and Land Change. PhD Thesis. INPE, São José dos Campos, Brazil (2006)
4. da Costa, W., Medeiros, L., Sandri, S.: Um estudo de autômatos celulares com sistemas difusos para modelos compartimentais do tipo SIR. In: Proc. II CBSF, Natal, Brazil (2012)
5. Emmendorfer, L.R., Rodrigues, L.A.D.: Um modelo de Autômatos Celulares para o Espalhamento Geográfico de Epidemias. Tendências em Matemática Aplicada e Computacional 2(1), 73–80 (2001)
6. Godo, L., Sandri, S.: A similarity-based approach to deal with inconsistency in systems of fuzzy gradual rules. In: Proc. IPMU 2002 (2002)

7. Gubler, D.J., Reiter, P., Ebi, K.L., Yap, W., Nasci, R., et al.: Climate variability and change in the United States: potential impacts on vector and rodent-born diseases. Environmental Health Perspectives 109(2), 223–233 (2001)
8. Hethcote, H.W.: The Mathematics of Infectious Diseases. SIAM Review 42(4), 599–653 (2000)
9. Ierusalimschy, R.: Programming in Lua. 2nd edn. Lua.org (2006)
10. Kermack, W., Mckendrick, A.: A Contribution to the Mathematical Theory of Epidemics. Proc. of the Royal Society of London Series A: Mathematical and Physical Sciences 115, 700–721 (1927)
11. Klir, G.J., Yuan, B.: Fuzzy sets and fuzzy logic: theory and applications. Prentice Hall (1995)
12. Medeiros, L.C.C., Castilho, C.A.R., Braga, C., de Souza, W.V., Regis, L., Monteiro, A.M.V.: Modeling the dynamic transmission of dengue fever: investigating disease persistence. PLOS Neglected Tropical Diseases 5(1) (2011)
13. Ministério da Saúde. Guia de vigilância epidemiológica, 6th edn. Ministério da Saúde, Brasília (2005)
14. Missio, M.: Um Estudo de Autômatos Celulares com Parâmetros Fuzzy para a Disperão da Febre Aftosa em Bovinos no Mato Grosso do Sul. Biomatemática 16, 31–42 (2006)
15. Oliveira, E., Lacerda, M.J., Barbosa, A.M., Nepomuceno, E.G.: Desenvolvimento de estratégia de controle epidemiológico: Análise espacial e vacinação a partir do foco da doença. In: Proc XVII CBA, Juiz de Fora, Brazil, pp. 1–6 (2008)
16. Passos, M.N.P., Santos, L.M.J.G., Pereira, M.R.R., Casali, C.G., Fortes, B.P.M.D., Valencia, L.I.O., Alexandre, A.J., Medronho, R.A.: Diferenças clínicas observadas em pacientes com dengue causadas por diferentes sorotipos na epidemia de 2001/2002, ocorrida no município do Rio de Janeiro. Rev. Soc. Bras. Med. Trop. 37(4) (2004)
17. Peixoto, M.S., Barros, L.C.: Um Estudo de Autômatos Celulares para o Espalhamento Geográfico de Epidemias com Parâmetro Fuzzy. TEMA. Tendências em Matemática Aplicada e Computacional, São Paulo 5, 125–133 (2004)
18. Regis, L., Monteiro, A.M., Melo Santos, M.A.V., Silveira, J.C., Furtado, A.F.: Developing new approaches for detecting and preventing Aedes aegypti population outbreaks: basis for surveillance, alert and control system. Mem. I. Oswaldo Cruz 103(1), 50–59 (2008)
19. Von Neumann, J.: Theory of Self-Reproducing Automata. A.W. Burks (1966)
20. Wolfram, S.: Theory and Application of Cellular Automata. World Scientific (1986)
21. Yang, H.M.: Epidemiologia matemática: Estudos dos Efeitos da Vacinação em Doenças de Transmissão Direta. Ed. da Unicamp (2001)

Author Index